Winterthur Portfolio 6

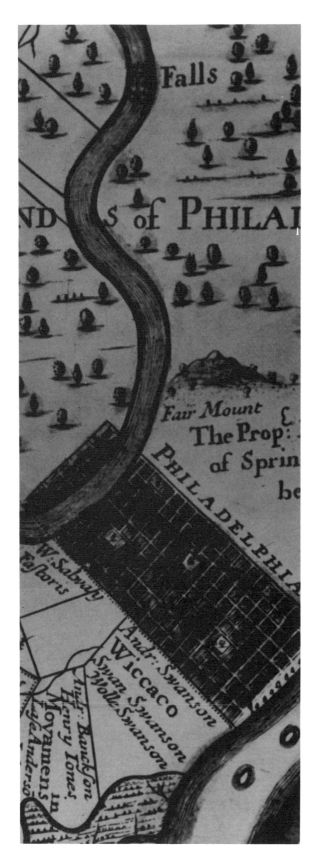

Winterthur Portfolio 6

Edited by Richard K. Doud and Ian M. G. Quimby

Published for

The Henry Francis du Pont Winterthur Museum

by the University Press of Virginia

Charlottesville

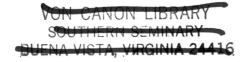

Statement of Editorial Policy

The objective of The Henry Francis du Pont
Winterthur Museum in publishing *Winterthur
Portfolio* is to make available to the serious student an
authoritative reference for the investigation and
documentation of early American culture.

The publication will present articles about many
aspects of American life. Included will be studies that
will extend current information about objects used
in America in the seventeenth, eighteenth, and
nineteenth centuries; or about the makers, the
manufacture, the distribution, the use, and the settings
of such objects. Scholarly articles contributing to
the knowledge of America's social, cultural, political,
military, and religious heritage, as well as those
offering new approaches or interpretations concerning
research and conservation of art objects, are
welcome.

Richard K. Doud and Ian M. G. Quimby, *Editors*
Carole J. Bower, *Assistant Editor*
Helen S. Shields, *Editorial Assistant*

Editorial Committee
John A. H. Sweeney, *Chairman*
Charles F. Hummel
Dorothy W. Greer

Contents

The Severed Head of Charles I of England
Its Use as a Political Stimulus

Paula Sampson Preston

THE medieval man's interest in the severed head of his fellow men goes back to biblical times when, for example, Herod gave the head of John the Baptist to the daughter of Herodias as a reward for her dancing. This he did, not from choice, but to keep his promise to give her whatever she desired. In the Middle Ages, the heads of executed political and social offenders were made public not only as evidence of the person's demise but also as a warning to others to exercise care lest their own heads be struck off.

In London, also, the heads of political prisoners and enemies of the Crown were exhibited to the populace. An encouraging instance of defiance of this gruesome custom occurred in 1535, when Sir Thomas More was executed and his head set up on the London Bridge. One night his head was stolen; according to tradition, his beloved daughter, Meg, took it down and carried it off to her house. She kept her father's head until her death in 1544, and it was buried with her.

With such a tradition behind it, the decapitation of Charles I of England, judged an offender and a traitor, was not in itself unique, nor can the display of his head after death be considered unusual. Yet, this tragic occurrence had an enduring effect that changed the course of history, for it was unprecedented that a King of England, anointed and crowned under the divine right of kings, be seized by representatives of his own people and duly executed by them in his own land. Charles I was decapitated on January 30, 1649, on a scaffold outside the Banqueting Hall of Whitehall, London. It was a public execution, and the populace came in droves to see it. A 1649 Dutch engraving shows the immense crowd, many of whom are perched on the roof for a better view (Fig. 1). The beheading has just taken place, and the head of the unfortunate king is being shown to the apparently composed crowd. In the foreground a spectator has fainted, while to the right a lone man weeps. The engraving depicts the execution as a somewhat ordinary occurrence; yet it is known that the crowd cried out and wept. Philip Henry, a lad of seventeen, was present and noted that "The blow I saw given, and can truly say, with a sad heart, at the instant whereof I remember well, there was such a grone by the thousands then present as I never heard before and desire I may never hear again."[1]

Another contemporary painted the event, an artist named Weesop, who is said to have witnessed the execution (Fig. 2). In this depiction, also, the decapitation has just taken place, and the head of Charles I is being held up for all to see (Fig. 3). In this rendition the crowd is more agitated: in the center a woman has fainted, and throughout the picture the spectators appear shocked and stunned. There are two vignettes on each side of the painting. The one in the upper left is a portrait of the king, and that below shows the king walking to his execution. On the right Halifax (?) is holding the severed head of the king. The scaffold was actually separated from the people by large ranks of soldiers, and in the description of Philip Henry, "There was according to order one troop immediately marching

---

[1] Matthew Henry Lee (ed.), *Diaries and Letters of Philip Henry, 1631–1696* (London, 1882), p. 12.

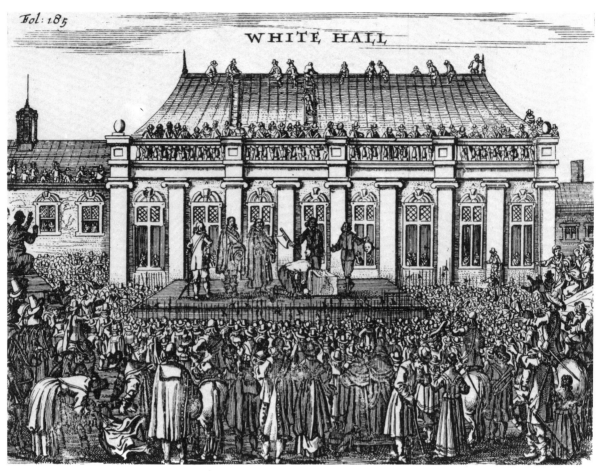

FIG. 1. *The Execution of Charles I of England*. Amsterdam, 1649. Engraving; H. 4⅛″, W. 5⅜″. (Spencer Collection, The New York Public Library.)

FIG. 2. (?) Weesop, *Execution of Charles I*. London, ca. 1649. Oil on canvas; H. 64″, W. 116½″. (Courtesy of Lord Primrose, West Lothian, Scotland: photo, Annan.)

fromwards Charing Cross to Westminster and another fromwards Westminster to Charing Cross, purposely to masker [overpower] the people and to disperse and scatter them, so that I had much adoe amongst the rest to escape home without hurt."[2]

The result of the execution of Charles I was an extraordinary revulsion of the people to the act. He soon came to be regarded as a martyr and a saint; his alleged crimes were completely forgotten; and from the Restoration onward, the anniversary of his death was observed as a day of fasting and humiliation. It is interesting to note that relatively soon after his death, the severed head of Charles I was used as a political instrument in an attempt to intimidate, or at least to give pause to, the opposition. The long-lasting effect of the troubled years in England, which culminated in the violent death of the king in 1649, is evident today in the numerous English political cartoons of the eighteenth century that include either his image or a reference to him.

As early as 1680 a print entitled *The Committee; or Popery in Masquerade* was published in

[2] *Ibid.*

FIG. 3. Detail of Fig. 2.

London (Fig. 4). This cartoon serves as the heading for a verse which states, in part, "You'll say this Print's a Satyr [satire], Against Whom? Those that Crowned Holy Charles with Martyrdom, By the same rule the Scripture you'l Traduce."[3] In a conspicuous place in the left foreground of the picture lies the head of Charles I with his symbols of office. The head is depicted as a sculptured bust, apparently thrown on the floor and forgotten, while the gathering, heedless of its presence, stands with backs turned away from it.

During the formative years leading toward rebellion of the American colonies against the mother country, the severed head of Charles I became a theme that occurred again and again. It was used in the colonies and in England in speeches, sermons, and pamphlets and was enjoyed in political satire, particularly in the English cartoons so popular at the time on both sides of the Atlantic. In Boston, in 1750, Rev. Jonathan Mayhew, in his important *Discourse Concerning Unlimited Submission and Non-resistance to the Higher Powers,* denounced that "unhappy Prince, King Charles I," in his position "as a great Saint and Martyr." He calls him, further on, "a lawless tyrant . . . laden with iniquity" and, in conclusion, urges all to "learn to be free and to be loyal. . . . It is our happiness to live under the government of a Prince who is satisfied with ruling according to law. . . . For which reason, I would exhort you to pay all due regards to the government over us, to the King and all in authority."[4] Thus, Charles I of England lost his sainthood. It should be understood, however, that although this is probably the earliest occurrence in America in which Charles's name and fate are linked together with a reigning monarch, the comparison is favorable to the present king. Here the reference is to George II, who is the "good Prince" ruling lawfully, as opposed to Charles I, the "lawless tyrant."

It was the destiny of Patrick Henry to link Charles I and George III together unfavorably. When he delivered his famous address against the Stamp Act before the House of Burgesses in Vir-

[3] The verse was written by Roger L'Estrange in 1680 and cited in Mary D. George, *English Political Caricatures, A Study of Opinion and Propaganda* (Oxford: Clarendon Press, 1959), Pl. 14.

[4] Bernard Bailyn (ed.), *Pamphlets of the American Revolution (1750–1776)* (Cambridge, Mass.: Belknap Press of Harvard University Press, 1965), I, 247.

FIG. 4. *The Committee; or Popery in Masquerade.* London, 1680. Engraving; H. 15¾″, W. 11⅛″. (Trustees of the British Museum.)

ginia, in 1765, he made dramatic use of the severed head theme in his warning to George III: "Caesar had his Brutus—Charles the First, his Cromwell —and George III—may profit by their example!" As a result of the storm of protest against the Stamp Act, it was summarily repealed in 1766, and soon thereafter an amusing print entitled *The Repeal. or the Funeral Procession, of Miss Americ-Stamp* was published (Fig. 5). To the left is an open tomb surmounted by two skulls on poles. In front of them is a tablet that reads:

The Englishmen referred to are the American colonists. The two skulls are called, further on, "Skeleton Heads," and "their elevation on Poles and the dates [referring to two former rebellion years] sufficiently show what party they espoused, and in what cause they suffered an ignominious exit." A leader in support of the Stamp Act heads the funeral procession, and the "Honorable Mr. George Stamp, full of grief and dispair, carries his favorite child's coffin, Miss Americ Stamp, who was born in 1765 and died hard in 1766." The

FIG. 5. *The Repeal. or the Funeral Procession, of Miss Americ-Stamp.* London, ca. 1766. Engraving; H. 7⅞", W. 13⅜". (American Antiquarian Society.)

Within this Family Vault,
Lie Interred,
it is to be hoped never to rise again,
The Star Chamber Court
Ship Money—Excise Money
& all Imposts without Parliament . . .
which tended to alienate the Affections of
Englishmen to their Country.

dog at the head of the procession adds the final touch to the whole affair.[5]

In 1769, another political satire was published in which Charles I was involved. It is interesting that Cromwell also enters into this print. The car-

[5] George, *English Political Caricatures*, Pl. 39 and pp. 135–36.

FIG. 6. *The Funeral of Freedom.* London, 1769. Engraving; H. 6½", W. 11½". (Trustees of the British Museum.)

toon, entitled *The Funeral of Freedom* (Fig. 6), again shows an open grave, this time in the center foreground, and the gravedigger has unearthed the skulls of Charles I and his antagonist, Oliver Cromwell, which have been tossed to each side of the grave. The label on the coffin inside the open grave reads "Right of Election."

Another print, *Political Electricity,* was published in 1770 (Fig. 7). This intricately detailed cartoon seems to have a bit of everything in it. At the top, the figure of George III is represented as a button maker. Of special interest is the book that lies beside him: it bears the title, *History of Charles, A Dissolution Dangerous to the Crown* (Fig. 8). Again, the subtle reminder appears. This is a pro–John Wilkes print—and therefore pro-American, since he was a staunch friend of the colonists—and may very well have been the earliest English attempt to needle George III by recalling Charles I's reign.

In Boston, on December 3, 1772, Rev. John Allen delivered a sermon entitled *An Oration Upon the Beauties of Liberty,* in which the following statement appeared:

For violating the people's rights, Charles Stewar[t]

lost his head, and if another King, who is more solemnly bound than ever Charles Stewar[t] was, should tread in the same steps, what can he expect? I reverence and love my King, but I rever the rights of an Englishman before the authority of any King upon the Earth.[6]

In a lighter vein is the print entitled *The Patriotick Barber of New York, or the Captain in the Suds* published in 1775 (Fig. 9). Decidedly pro-American, the implication here is more subtle, as well as wider in scope, for the severed heads are already on poles, while the barber with open razor in hand appears to threaten the English captain with much worse than the half-shave he has already been given. The verse reads:

Then Patriot grand, maintain thy Stand,
And whilst thou sav'st Americ's Land,
Preserve the Golden Rule;
Forbid the Captains there to roam,
Half shave them first, then send 'em home,
Objects of ridicule.

From this time forward there are many literary

[6] Published as a pamphlet by Kneeland and Davis (Boston, 1773), p. viii.

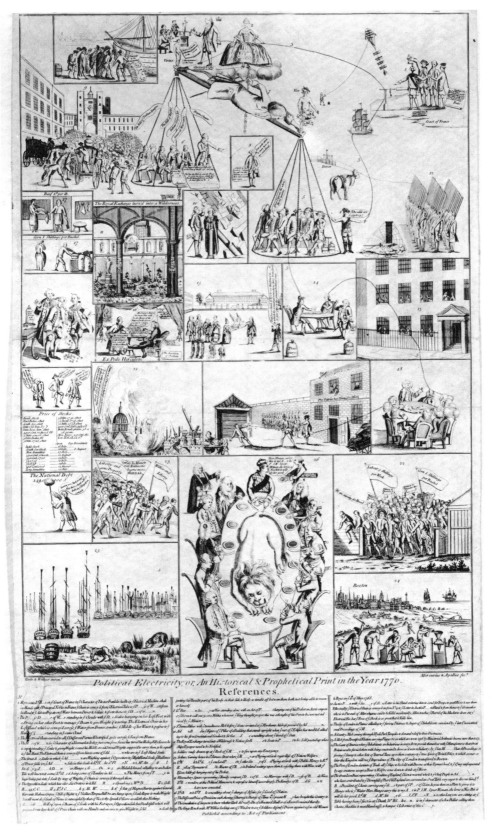

FIG. 7. *Political Electricity. or, An Historical & Prophetical Print in the Year 1770.* London, 1770. Engraving; H. 22¾″, W. 15¾″. (Winterthur, 60.58.)

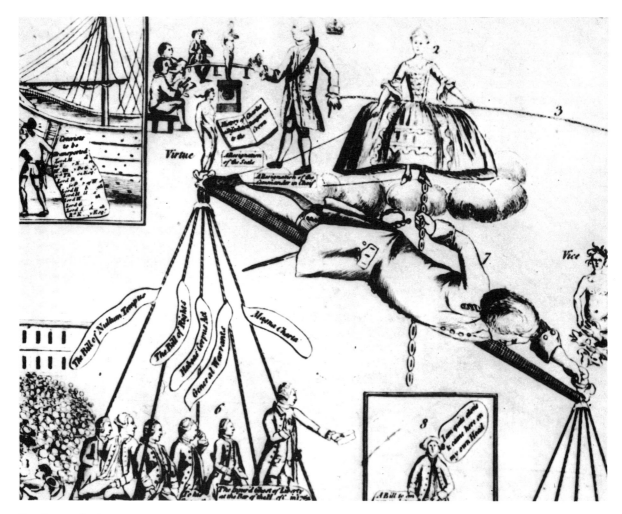

FIG. 8. Detail of Fig. 7.

and pictorial references to Charles I, who was recalled to the minds of the people again and again. For instance, the *London Magazine* of November, 1775, by way of introduction to a biographical sketch remarked: "When persecution in the reign of *Charles the First,* thirst of exploration, adventure or despair, winged away from these kingdoms a variety of emigrants, mechanics and artists of all denominations, mited in the ships that sailed for America; amongst these were the progenitors of Mrs. Wright."[7]

Thomas Paine continued in the same manner, when his rousing pamphlet *Common Sense* was published in 1776:

Individuals are undoubtedly safer in England than in some other countries; but the will of the king is as much the law of the land in Britain as in France, with this difference, that instead of proceeding directly from his mouth, it is handed to the people under the formidable shape of an act of Parliament. For the fate of *Charles the First* has only made Kings more subtle—not more just.[8]

Again, in 1778, when Paine wrote the *American Crisis (VII)*, he warned, "Take heed! Remember the times of *Charles the First!* For Laud and St[r]afford fell by trusting to a hope like yours."[9] Archbishop Laud and Sir Thomas Wentworth, the Earl of Strafford, ministers to Charles I, were

[7] "A Sketch of the Character of Mrs. Wright," *The London Magazine,* Nov., 1775, pp. 555–56.

[8] Original pamphlet, *Common Sense (on the Origin and Design of Government in General, with Concise Remarks on the English Constitution)*, published in Philadelphia, Feb. 14, 1776.

[9] Original pamphlet, *The American Crisis Number VII. To the People of England,* published in Philadelphia, Nov. 21, 1778.

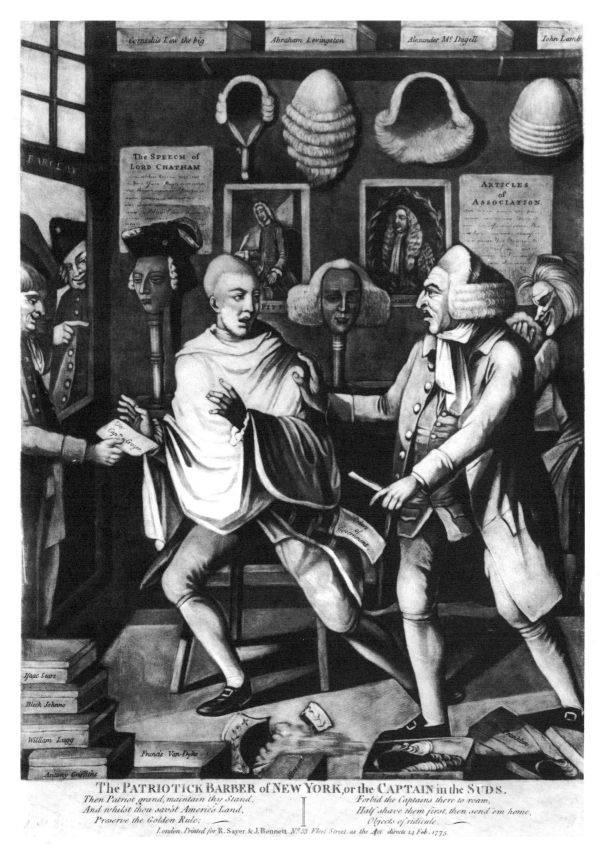

FIG. 9. Philip Dawe (?), *The Patriotick Barber of New York, or the Captain in the Suds*. London, 1775. Mezzotint; H. 13″, W. 9⅞″. (I. N. Phelps Stokes Collection, The New York Public Library.)

in 1640 arrested by order of Parliament and later tried for treason and executed.

In 1780, Joseph Wright, an American artist who was living in London during the Revolutionary years, exhibited a painting at the Royal Academy which caused a sensation. The painting, a depiction of his mother, was entitled *Portrait of Patience Wright Modeling a Head of Charles I*, and the reason for its sensational reception was the inclusion of the heads of King George III and Queen Charlotte, mounted on stands in the background. The reaction, of course, was immediate; all who saw the portrait grasped its meaning. The relationship between the head of Charles I and the head of George III, also severed, was obvious to the Revolution-conscious city of London. Furthermore, the subject, Patience Lovell Wright, an ardent American patriot, was outspoken in her praise of the American cause and was thought by many to be a spy for Benjamin Franklin. The *Gazetteer* published in London at the time, in one of its "Exhibition Epigrams," a most cogent

rhyme: "Wright in her lap sustains a trunkless head, And looks a wish—the King's was in its stead." Horace Walpole, who managed to get himself involved in everything that occurred in London, did not withhold his comment in this instance. In a letter written in May, 1780, he spoke of the opening at the Royal Academy: "By what lethargy of loyalty it happened I do not know, but *there* is a picture of Mrs Wright modelling the head of Charles I, and their Majesties contemplating it."[10] It is unfortunate that this intriguing portrait has since been lost. There is, at present writing, no knowledge of what happened to the picture after the exhibition, nor is it known whether or not the offending portrait was allowed to remain on exhibition.

Britania's Assassination. or the Republicans

[10] *Letters of Horace Walpole, 4th Earl of Oxford,* arranged and edited with notes and indices by Mrs. Page Toynbee (Oxford: Oxford University Press, 1903–1905), XI, 167–72, Letter No. 2047. The writer wishes to acknowledge the help of Mrs. Elisha Keeler of the Darien, Conn., Library, for finding the details of this reference.

Fig. 10. James Gillray, *Britania's Assassination. or The Republicans Amusement*. London, 1782. Engraving; H. 8½″, W. 13½″. (Prints Division, The New York Public Library.)

FIG. 11. Detail of Fig. 10.

Amusement was published in 1782 (Fig. 10). In this, Britannia has lost her head and is about to be pulled off her pedestal by the new Ministry, while a fox (Charles James Fox, liberal statesman) bites her leg. Within the ropes held by the Ministry is a group of statesmen: John Wilkes, nearest the statue, is about to strike it; the Duke of Richmond is about to strike Britannia with a musket; and behind is Edmund Burke (?) with arm raised. To the left, Britannia's foreign enemies run off with the spoil. On the extreme left is America, an Indian, who is running away with Britannia's head (Fig. 11). He also carries her arm (the hand of which clasps an olive branch), which he holds over his right shoulder. Behind America are figures of empty-handed France and Spain, while in the foreground Holland carries Britannia's shield.[11]

In 1784, *The Historical Painter* presented an interesting interpretation (Fig. 12). In this print Charles James Fox, dressed as Cromwell, is paint-

[11] British Museum, Department of Prints and Drawings, *Catalog of Political and Personal Satires* (London: British Museum, 1870–19—), Vol. V (by Mary D. George), No. 5987.

FIG. 12. *The Historical Painter.* London, 1784. Engraving; H. 9¼″, W. 9¼″. (Colonial Williamsburg Collection.)

THE HISTORICAL PAINTER.

FIG. 13. Detail of Fig. 12.

FIG. 14. *Smelling out a Rat; or The Atheistical-Revolutionist disturbed in his Midnight "Calculations."* London, 1790. Engraving; H. 9¾", W. 13¾". (American Antiquarian Society.)

ing a picture of Charles I's execution, putting his brush (actually a sceptre) against the king's head (Fig. 13). On the wall hangs a picture of a fox (again Charles James Fox) holding a liberty cap and presenting independence to America, an Indian warrior.[12]

A print entitled *Smelling out a Rat; or The Atheistical-Revolutionist disturbed in his Midnight "Calculations"* appeared in 1790 (Fig. 14). This print concerns itself with the French Revolution and shows Dr. Richard Price, clergyman and author, seated at his desk with a sermon before him. He is startled by a vision of his political enemy Edmund Burke, seen in a cloud. Of significance is the fact that once again Charles I is recalled, for in full view, not to be missed, is the painting on the wall (Fig. 15). It shows the execution of Charles I and is labeled "Death of Charles I, or the Glory of Great Britain."[13]

Addendum: On March 21, 1968, United Press International reported the following news item from London:

Britain's Law Commission came up with a list of recommendations Monday for repeal of all laws "that cannot positively be shown to perform a useful function." Heading the list was "An act for the attainder of several persons guilty of the horrid murder of his late sacred Majesty King Charles the First."

[12] *Ibid.,* VI (by Mary D. George), No. 6408.
[13] George, *English Political Caricatures,* I, 211.

Fig. 15. Detail of Fig. 14.

Caleb Buglass, Binder of the Proposed Book of Common Prayer, Philadelphia, 1786

Hannah D. French

A DEFINITIVE history of early American bookbinding comes a little closer to realization with each revelation of the work and tools of individual binders. A preliminary essay on the subject listed the names of more than five hundred craftsmen working in America from 1636 through 1820.[1] The names of binders, however, exceeded by several times the number of American bindings, discovered by that study, executed within the period covered. In the last twenty-five years many more early American books have been found in their original covers, and the pace has quickened as collectors, dealers, and librarians have been joined by conservators of books and manuscripts and by catalogers of manuscripts that have long lain unlisted and unknown.[2] Tooling, technique, style, and manuscript records have led to the identification of the work of a few binders of the seventeenth and eighteenth centuries: four in Boston; one in Newport, Rhode Island; two in Virginia; and now a third

in Philadelphia.[3] The discovery of Caleb Buglass as one of the distinguished binders of eighteenth-century Philadelphia resulted from a search for copies of a very significant book that was printed in that city in the spring of 1786—the Prayer Book proposed for the use of the Protestant Episcopal Church in the United States, then in the making. Two copies illustrated in *Bookbinding in America,* in gold-tooled morocco bindings, indicated the skill and taste of the then unknown binder.[4] These distinguished bindings prompted a long search for other comparable copies of this rare book, and the search has now been rewarded by the discovery of twenty-one additional copies in fine bindings.

The purpose of this paper is to establish Caleb

[1] Hannah D. French, "Early American Bookbinding by Hand," *Bookbinding in America,* ed. Hellmut Lehmann-Haupt (Portland, Maine: Southworth-Anthoensen Press, 1941), pp. 3–127.

[2] Willman Spawn, restorer of manuscripts at the American Philosophical Society has extended his work to make an invaluable record in the form of rubbings of thousands of early American bindings discovered in many scattered institutions and private collections. This collection, which provides a record of plain and elaborate bindings, is designed to serve the historian and make accessible in one place the record that may outlast some of the bindings themselves. It is especially rich in eighteenth-century Philadelphia specimens used in preparation for the detailed study Mr. and Mrs. Spawn have undertaken. I am deeply grateful to them for making this collection accessible and sharing their own identification of Buglass bindings made in connection with their study.

[3] See Thomas J. Holmes, "The Bookbindings of John Ratcliff and Edmund Ranger, Seventeenth Century Boston Bookbinders," *Proceedings of the American Antiquarian Society,* n.s., XXXVIII (April, 1928), 31–50, and XXXIX (Oct., 1928), 291–306; Hannah D. French, "The Amazing Career of Andrew Barclay, Scottish Bookbinder of Boston," *Studies in Bibliography* (Papers of the Bibliographical Society of the University of Virginia, Charlottesville, Va.), XIV (1961), 145–62, and "Bound in Boston by Henry B. Legg, *ibid.,* XVII (1964), 135–39; Willman and Carol M. Spawn, "Francis Skinner, Bookbinder of Newport, an Eighteenth-Century Craftsman Identified by His Tools," *Winterthur Portfolio II* (Philadelphia: The Museum, 1965), pp. 47–61, and "The Aitken Shop: Identification of an Eighteenth-Century Bindery and Its Tools," *Papers of the Bibliographical Society of America,* LVII (4th Quarter, 1963), 422–37; C. Clement Samford and John M. Hemphill, II, *Bookbinding in Colonial Virginia* (Williamsburg Research Studies; Williamsburg, Va.: Colonial Williamsburg, [1966]), pp. 2–13, 18–22 (William Parks), and pp. 24, 48–63, 90–92 (Thomas Brend); and Edwin Wolf, 2nd, "A Signed American Binding by John Lightbody on the First American Edition of Shakespeare," *Shakespeare Quarterly,* XII (Spring, 1961), 152–54.

[4] French, *Bookbinding in America,* Pls. 16 and 27.

Buglass of Philadelphia as the binder of the proposed Book of Common Prayer, but not to provide a record of all the tools owned and used by Buglass. An inventory of his tools such as that for other Philadelphia binders may have existed once, but it cannot now be found. In describing twenty-one copies of the proposed Prayer Book in decorative gilt morocco bindings by "the binder," a like number of volumes with other titles, three of them documented as the work of Caleb Buglass, have been used as evidence.

Devotional books have been associated with fine binding for centuries. The tradition may not have been very obvious in the American Colonies of the seventeenth century, but by the eighteenth the dark sheep- and calfskin and the black morocco of Puritan psalmbooks and Bibles had more than occasionally given way to red and olive green morocco lavishly ornamented in gold on covers and spines by a favorite binder. The Aitken Bible[5] and the proposed Book of Common Prayer were especially fine examples that invite comparison. Rev. William White of Philadelphia had a part in the production of both books. As one of two chaplains of the Continental Congress, he approved the Bible for authorization by Congress. As the young rector of Christ Church appointed chairman of the committee to oversee its printing, he played a far greater role in the proposed Prayer Book. What voice he had in selecting a binder, if any, it is not possible to say.

The Aitken Bible, or the "Bible of the Revolution," was printed in 1782, four years before the proposed Book of Common Prayer. It is important as the first Bible to bear an American imprint, but it cannot match the proposed Prayer Book in significance. The first was the work of a familiar text printed by a patriot who was also a Scotch Presbyterian. The latter was a new book for a new church. It was a text composed by committees and subcommitteees feeling their way toward a liturgy that would not be wholly unfamiliar but would serve a new "sister," rather than a "daughter," church in a way pleasing and comfortable to that remnant of churchmen who had cast their lot with the patriots. The book was intended to serve many purposes, not the least of which was to persuade the English bishops that the new church across the sea deserved their blessing and the consecration of its clergy to serve as American bishops. The alteration of the liturgy was "a nice and delicate affair," as Rev. Samuel Bass of Newburyport put it;[6] however, the book was never adopted because all the diplomacy that went into its making was insufficient—that the book was printed at all seemed miracle enough.

The Reverend Mr. White, as chairman of the printing committee and rector of the largest and most important church of the middle colonies, had anticipated problems and had managed to maintain a middle ground and to remain on negotiating terms with all factions. Against his better judgment he agreed to a prayer for civil liberty on the Fourth of July and saw a special committee formed for it. As the only Philadelphia resident on the committee of three, it was he who dealt with the printers, Hall and Sellers. Rev. William Smith, senior (but less diplomatic) member of the committee, was then residing in Maryland, and Rev. Charles Wharton, a converted Jesuit, was then in Delaware.

The Prayer Book was expected to appeal to the bishops of England as well as to the members of the newly formed Protestant Episcopal Church who were to use it in their worship, and to make money by its sale for the benefit of the widows and children of deceased clergymen. It failed on all counts. Looking back years later from his vantage point as bishop, the Right Reverend Mr. White saw the book doomed from the outset. Looking back even further, we find the failure of the book quite probably accounting for the large

[5] Comparison with Robert Aitken is inevitable as his work is the most thoroughly documented of that of any American binder of the eighteenth century. In Robert R. Dearden, Jr., and Douglas S. Watson's *An Original Leaf from the Bible of the Revolution, and an Essay Concerning It* (San Francisco: J. Howell, 1930), the Aitken Bible is described as a "national document, but the essay considers typography only, with brief reference to Aitken as a binder, and contains no description of bindings. "William McCulloch's Additions to Thomas's History of Printing," *Proceedings of the American Antiquarian Society*, n.s., XXXI (April, 1921), Pt. 1, 105, cites Robert Aitken as "a binder by trade, and a most excellent workman." McCulloch goes further in writing, "There was no better finished binding ever done than some of the books executed in his shop." It remained for the Spawns to establish Aitken as a master binder "of remarkable talent" by identification of some six hundred volumes from his shop, in their study in *Papers of the Bibliographical Society of America*, LVII (4th Quarter, 1963), 422–37.

[6] Letter of June 21, 1784, to Rev. Samuel Parker Autographs and Manuscripts of the Bishops of the Protestant Episcopal Church, Vol. II (Pierpont Morgan Library, New York).

number of copies which may still be traced, some rebound, some shabby, some in ordinary bindings, and twenty-three, at least, in fine specimens of the binder's art.

A careful comparison of these bindings, found in such distant places as England, Ireland, California, Connecticut, Rhode Island, New York, Pennsylvania, Delaware, Maryland, and Virginia, can be made only with the aid of rubbings.[7] With rubbings before one, it is possible to see that twenty-one of the twenty-three bindings are so similar in style, tools, and technique that they are unmistakably the work of one binder; that the twenty-second was produced with tools common to the other bindings but is unlike them in technique and taste (it is the only copy to be sewn on raised cords); and that the twenty-third copy, or-namented with completely different tools, is the work of a different binder. This last copy was, in fact, purchased in 1789 at the request of Martha Washington for her grandson George Washington Parke Custis and was doubtless bound then. That twenty-one of these bindings were done by one binder in Philadelphia close to the time of publication in the spring of 1786 can be deduced from a study of the rubbings and the history of the Prayer Book. Without further evidence, however, it is impossible to name the binder.

The history of the Prayer Book is replete with information about its content. It was prepared by committees, working against time, who submitted it to the printers, Hall and Sellers, in sections to be printed in half-sheets, thus enabling them to deal with other urgent matters without tying up their presses, for they were official printers for the state. They were also churchmen: William Sellers, the senior partner, held two pews at Christ Church from 1778 until his death in 1804; and

William Hall, a vestryman there from 1784 to 1790 and again later, and his brother David were members.[8] No records of the firm of Hall and Sellers covering the year 1786 have come to light. Details on the printing of the Prayer Book can be found only in the exchange of letters between members of the committee responsible for its preparation, chiefly the letters of White and Smith.[9] These letters disclose enough of the business arrangements to make it clear that Hall and Sellers were producing the book at a special price, doubtless because they were loyal church members and because any profit was to go to the widows and children of deceased clergymen. The committee advanced money to cover the cost of the paper, expecting repayment when the book was distributed and payment secured. Hall and Sellers were apparently pushed too much at one point, and Token G was let out to Robert Aitken for printing in December. The Aitken Waste Book records Hall and Sellers indebted, "To working off at Press 20 token Letter G of Prayer book, Dec. 15, 1785."[10] This seems to establish the edition as 5,000 copies, rather than the 4,000 previously recorded.[11] The first mention of the binder occurred in the Reverend Mr. Smith's letter of February 25, 1786, in which he asked the Reverend Mr. White "to direct the bookbinder to prepare half a dozen copies of the best and first binding in his power" for friends and patrons. Neither then nor in the four later references to the binder is his name given.[12]

In a letter to Samuel Parker of Trinity Church, Boston, early in December, 1785, White wrote that the printing of the Prayer Book "will be tedi-

[7] Of the copies of the proposed Book of Common Prayer used for this study, three are privately owned and nineteen are in the following institutions: John Carter Brown Library; Library of Congress; Pierpont Morgan Library; The New York Public Library; New-York Historical Society (2); General Theological Seminary, N.Y.; Maryland Diocesan Library; Virginia State Library; The Henry Francis du Pont Winterthur Museum; Watkinson Library, Hartford, Conn.; Yale University Library; Christ Church, Philadelphia; Philadelphia Divinity School; Historical Society of Pennsylvania; Cambridge University Library; and Henry E. Huntington Library (3, plus 2 plainer copies, for a total of 5). The three Prayer Books privately owned belong to Mr. Michael Papantonio, Yonkers, N.Y.; the estate of Mr. Stuart Jackson, Gloucester, Va. (whereabouts of this copy unknown); and Mr. Herbert A. V. Wilson, Dublin, Ireland.

[8] William W. Montgomery (comp.), "Pew Renters of Christ Church, St. Peters and St. James, from 1776 to 1815, compiled from existing records," Haverford, Pa., 1948 (typescript in the Boston Public Library).

[9] Francis L. Hawks and General Convention Collection of Early Episcopal Church Manuscripts (at one time in the custody of the New-York Historical Society, entitled "Archives of the General Convention"), I, 101 (The Church Historical Society, Austin, Texas).

[10] Robert Aitken MS Waste Book (The Library Company of Philadelphia). A token is defined as 250 pulls of a hand press in E. J. Labarre, *Dictionary of Papermaking and Papermaking Terms* (Amsterdam, Neth.: N. V. Swets & Zeitlinger, 1937), p. 299.

[11] See Rev. John Wright, *Early Prayer Books of America* (St. Paul, Minn.: Privately printed, 1896), p. 102; and John W. Suter, *The American Book of Common Prayer* (New York: Oxford University Press, 1949), p. 53.

[12] William Smith, *Life and Correspondence of the Rev. William Smith* (Philadelphia: Ferguson, 1880), II, 182.

ous." Obtaining sufficient paper for the edition, and other activities of Hall and Sellers, caused a delay.[13] Even before that date Dr. Smith had been prematurely formulating plans for advertising the finished book, suggesting "the gazettes of Sellers and Bradford, whose are the only papers that circulate."[14] The finished book was not advertised in the *Pennsylvania Gazette* (printed by Hall and Sellers) until May 10, 1786, as "Just published and to be sold by Hall and Sellers, Printers in Market-street, and William Woodhouse, Bookbinder and Stationer, in Front-street." The advertisement was repeated through August 9, with price never mentioned, nor was its price given in William Bradford's *Pennsylvania Journal,* in which the notice ran from June 10 through September 30, 1786. Although there had been some uncertainty about the pricing of the book, White and Smith favored one dollar, or £0.7.6 Pennsylvania currency, and Smith firmly proposed a dollar to purchasers in Philadelphia and South Carolina, the transportation costs to be paid out of hoped-for profits.[15]

Not only is the binder nameless, but also there is no mention of his remuneration in the correspondence. On March 5, 1786, Smith expressed hope that the addition of engraved psalm tunes would not increase the cost of paper and binding and again pressed for the bookbinder to prepare "among the first Copies half a Dozen for me in the best Binding in his Power." A month later he advised that "the Printers need only work a few of the Titles and Prefaces. . . . A few will keep the bookbinder at work." On April 17 he wrote that he regretted "the misplacing a Psalm and the need for the Bookbinder to cut a leaf out in every Sheet (Gg) and paste it in the Book which is immense trouble and will occasion much delay," and the following week he noted, "the Book-binder should get all the help he can. If not sent in a Bound Book, a few complete copies should be sent in sheets to Boston." He was understandably concerned for the binder and suggested that the 300 copies to be sent to Rev. William West, St. Paul's Parish, Baltimore County, Maryland, be divided into two boxes of 150 each to lower the

risk involved and "to make it more convenient for the Binder."[16] Whether or not the binder regarded his work as a partially charitable enterprise as did the printers, he, too, obviously suffered inconveniences.

On May 4, 1786, West wrote to White saying that he had received a box of ten dozen copies of the new Prayer Book but had no directions about the distribution or the price. He added sadly,

It has been rumored that the Prayer Book has been held up with artful Design so that haste would be necessary to ratify it. The Charge, I am convinced is as false as it is unchristian. But I am sorry that the neglect of the Printer or Binder has given such a Handle to those who, perhaps, wish Evil to the Protestant Episcopal Church in these States.[17]

West's accounting to White in September, 1787, may provide a clue to the cost of binding. In referring to copies for which he had the responsibility of distribution, he referred to those selling for £0.7.6, "and bound in Morocco at 12/6."[18] Some of the copies were shipped in sheets, but there is no indication of the number. The bulk of the edition was put into plain covers, doubtless with the help Smith advised the binder to obtain. A sizable number of copies bound in gold-tooled morocco was in demand for domestic consumption, particularly in Maryland, and there was pressure to produce them at a cost of £0.12.6 (£0.5.0 per binding). Out of 934 copies accounted for in Virginia, seventy-eight were described as "Morocco" and/or "Red Bound."[19]

The copies for the bishops in England, presumably the best the binder could provide, were not sent until June 17, 1786, nine months after the printing was started. They arrived early in September when the archbishop and bishops were "all in the country" and were forwarded to them by the committee's intermediary, Alexander Murray, a loyalist who left his parish in Reading, Pennsylvania, during the Revolution and returned to England.[20]

There were ten bookbinders working in Philadelphia in 1786. Of these, there were two Scots,

[13] Autographs and MSS of the Bishops, Vol. I (Pierpont Morgan Library, New York) .

[14] Hawks and General Convention Coll., I, 75 (The Church Historical Society, Austin, Texas) .

[15] *Ibid.,* p. 112.

[16] *Ibid.,* pp. 106, 110, and 112.

[17] *Ibid.,* p. 115.

[18] *Ibid.,* II, 182.

[19] MS. Account Book of David Griffith (Virginia State Library, Richmond, Va.) .

[20] Hawks and General Convention Coll., II, 142 (The Church Historical Society, Austin, Texas) .

two Germans, one Irishman, two Englishmen, and three of unknown origin. The two English binders, Caleb Buglass and William Woodhouse, are possible candidates for the binder. Woodhouse at first seems more likely, because the Prayer Book was advertised in the newspapers for sale at his shop. Furthermore, he, like Hall and Sellers, was a churchman. He held a pew in St. Peters, a chapel of ease of Christ Church under the jurisdiction of Reverend White, and had held an account with Hall and Sellers for stationery supplies as early as 1767.[21] A Woodhouse label in an account book, adorned with numerous masonic emblems, describes Woodhouse as "Stationer and ·Book Binder, in Front Street, next Door to the Coffee House, Philadelphia," where he "Makes & Sells all sorts of Merchants Accou.ᵗ Books, Bound in the neatest & Best Manner." The only bindings that have been identified as his cover such account books. The inventory of Woodhouse's estate lists miscellaneous binding equipment and supplies valued at more than £84. The list of tools is modest: "9 Bookbinders rolls, 1 box stamps, pallet etc. (100), etcetera." Copies of the Prayer Book under consideration are ornamented by a dozen separate rolls. Although certain inconsistencies in Woodhouse's biography remain unexplained, he appears to have been trained at Berwick-upon-Tweed in Northumberland, where Buglass, the second English binder, also learned printing and binding.[22]

Caleb Buglass was born in Berwick-upon-Tweed in 1738 or 1740, depending upon which record you choose—the town record in Berwick or the tombstone record in Philadelphia. He was apprenticed to his father, Caleb, Sr., who became a free burgess of Berwick in 1732 after serving seven years as apprentice to his father, Stephen Buglass. The indenture of one of his apprentices, dated 1736, refers to Caleb, Sr., as a mason by trade. He died two years before Caleb, Jr., was admitted a free burgess of Berwick on April 17, 1759. Not quite three years later, the *Newcastle Courant* of February 20, 1762, announced the marriage of Caleb Buglass, "Bookseller in Berwick," aged twenty-three years, "to Miss Johnson, a sister of Weyn Johnson of Hutton-hall, Esq., an agreeable

lady with a fortune of 2,000 pounds." Buglass is first mentioned as a bookbinder in the indenture of John Richardson, dated March 12, 1765, in which Buglass is designated "Burgess, Bookseller, Bookbinder."[23] Within two years it was ordered that Richardson "late Apprentice to Caleb Buglass . . . who has declined Business be allowed . . . to travel . . . there being no other ffreeman Bookseller in town." At the same time, March 6, 1767, an apprentice to William Woodhouse, "Burgess and Merchant," was "attornied over" to another master because Woodhouse, too, declined business. Caleb Buglass had already been listed among the bankrupts in the January, 1767, issue of *The Gentleman's Magazine.*

Further evidence that all was not well in Berwick is indicated by a memorial recorded in the Guild Book on January 23, 1767, that complained that various strangers and foreigners who had come to town had failed to observe the ancient customs and order of the Guild and its by-laws "to the great Prejudice of the free Burgesses." The memorial requested that a report be made to the Guild by the "Memorialists Bailiffs and their Attorney" after they had made "strict Scrutiny and Search with the ancient Customs and Usages of this Corporation." Whether or not the report was ever submitted, conditions were bad, and Buglass and Woodhouse both decided to leave. There is no further mention of Woodhouse in England, and the last record concerning Buglass there is the newspaper advertisement of the sale of his binding tools in the *Newcastle Chronicle* of February 6, 1768:

To be Sold at Berwick upon Tweed, A complete Set of Bookbinders Tools, etc. in good condition, viz. A standing Press, two cutting Presses, Ploughs & Knives for ditto; a Pair of Pasteboard Shears, several Pairs of pressing and cutting Boards for Folios, 4tos, 8vos, & 12 mos. Also Letters for all the aforesaid Sizes: with sundry flower and fillet Rolls, Stamps, Polishers, etc. etc. etc.—Enquire of Mr. Buglass, Bookseller in Berwick aforesaid. Also a large Bible Sign, cut in Wood and gilt, which cost 1£ 10s.

Buglass seems not to have intended to continue in the binding trade.

Both Buglass and Woodhouse, who declined business more or less simultaneously, appear next

---

[21] MS. Shop Book of Hall and Sellers, 1767–1769 (American Philosophical Society, Philadelphia).

[22] "McCulloch's Additions," *Proceedings of the American Antiquarian Society,* n.s., XXXI, Pt. 1, 220.

[23] Apprentice Records, Guild Book (Borough of Berwick-upon-Tweed).

in Philadelphia, Woodhouse arriving much earlier than Buglass. Isaiah Thomas did not recall Buglass at all in his copious records of early booksellers, printers, and binders in America, but he established Woodhouse in Philadelphia in 1766.[24] William McCulloch corrected this date to 1765, not the only error he was to make in his "Additions." In the same letter of additions sent to Thomas he supplied the name of Caleb Buglass, writing that he was from Berwick where he served his apprenticeship as a printer and bookbinder, that he commenced bookbinding and bookselling at Philadelphia in 1774, and that he died about 1797. McCulloch noted that Buglass's widow "still continues bookbinding, and supports herself genteelly. She may also be said to continue the bookselling if her little shop would justify the title."[25] In a later communication McCulloch associated Buglass, Woodhouse, and Robert Bell from Glasgow as bookbinders for Samuel Taylor at Berwick-upon-Tweed and stated that Buglass was indented to learn printing, bookbinding, and bookselling with Taylor of Berwick "where he wrought at printing in the day, and binding in the evening."[26] Buglass may, indeed, have finished his indenture with one of the Taylors at Berwick, but it must have been with either R. or J. Taylor, whose names appear in Berwick imprints. McCulloch seems to have confused Samuel Taylor, binder in Philadelphia from 1764 to 1781, with another Taylor in Berwick. He learned from Buglass's widow that Caleb arrived in Philadelphia in 1774 but did not open his own shop until August, 1778, after having served as Robert Bell's foreman in the interval. He commenced the business of bookbinding and selling in partnership with William Green, of Boston, "at (now) No. 9 North Front Street" and continued the operation after Green's death until his own death, March 27, 1797, when he was fifty-seven years and six days old.[27]

The wills of Caleb Buglass and of his brother Ralph furnish strong clues to the whereabouts of Caleb between 1768, when he advertised his tools for sale in Berwick, and his arrival in Philadelphia in 1774.[28] In Caleb's will, dated November 12, 1794, the first bequests are to his son "in the Town of Berwick upon Tweed . . . where he is clock and watchmaker" and to his daughters there, Margaret and Grace. The son, to whom he left his lands and tenements "in the Wool market in the said town," was probably born there in 1765, as he was admitted a free Burgess in Berwick on July 24, 1786. The rest of the will is complicated, and it is interesting chiefly because it mentions "all my real estate or estates in the Island of Tobago formerly the estate of my deceased brother, Ralph Buglass, and also the estate called Mon Tranquille in the Island of Granada." Ralph Buglass, whose name appears on the Buglass monument in St. Peter's churchyard, Philadelphia, as "Dr. Ralph Buglass of the Island of Tobago who died October 4, 1787," was younger than Caleb although he died ten years earlier. His indenture in Berwick was made on November 30, 1759. He would have served his apprenticeship by the end of 1766, and it seems probable that both brothers went to the West Indies from Berwick.

The will of Ralph Buglass is even more interesting than that of Caleb. He is referred to as "Ralph Buglass late of the Island of Tobago but now of Philadelphia." It was dated October 2, 1787, two days before his death. In it he remembered first his brother Robert of Berwick with "my two Houses and Four Lots in the Town of Carenage in the Island of St. Lucea." He bequeathed his "German Flute and Musick proper therefore equal to one half to William Woodhouse of Philadelphia" and his violin and violoncello and music to Col. Michael Wentworth of Portsmouth, New Hampshire. Caleb received his Negro woman and Negro boy, "who are or lately were in the said Island of Tobago," and the sum of £200 and the remainder of his estate. Although no record of landholdings of Caleb's in the West Indies has yet been found, Ralph Buglass is recorded as the owner with A. Scott of 200 acres, lot 29 on Tobago, in the Parish of St. John, as of May 9, 1769. Earlier they had an estate of 300 acres in the parish of St. Paul.[29]

[24] Isaiah Thomas, *The History of Printing in America* (*Transactions of the American Antiquarian Society*, VI; 2nd ed.; Albany, N.Y.: The Society, 1874), II, 238.

[25] "McCulloch's Additions," *Proceedings of the American Antiquarian Society*, n.s., XXXI, Pt. 1, 106–7.

[26] *Ibid.*, pp. 219–20.

[27] *Ibid.*, p. 220.

[28] Philadelphia Wills, Book 2, 46, No. 7 (Caleb); and Book T, 556, No. 318 (Ralph) (Historical Society of Pennsylvania, Philadelphia).

[29] [John Fowler], *A Summary Account of the Present Flourishing State of the Respectable Colony of Tobago* (London: Printed for A. Grant, 1774), pp. 48 and 52.

It is not known when Caleb's first wife, Rachel Johnson, died in Berwick, but he married again in Philadelphia just before he set up in business for himself. On March 24, 1778, he and Mary Early were married in St. Paul's Church.[30] Caleb was then aged forty (although the Philadelphia record said thirty-eight), and Mary Early was twenty-one; therefore, it is not strange that Mary Buglass outlived her husband by twenty-six years. The Philadelphia directories through 1823 list the widow as bookbinder and bookseller in Coombes Alley. Her death on May 8, 1823, was recorded in the newspaper, followed by a special eulogy in a later issue.[31]

Both Caleb Buglass and his widow seem to have concentrated on bookbinding, the references to their bookselling being few and slight. Buglass was never a printer, and excellent craftsman that he was, he seems never to have used a ticket or label as did Woodhouse and several other Philadelphia binders.

To consider Buglass, rather than Woodhouse, the binder of the Prayer Book requires some documentation, which fortunately is at hand. The *Catalogue* of The Library Company of Philadelphia included Caleb Buglass as a member.[32] Among the books catalogued was John Parke's translation of the *Lyric Works of Horace,* listed as the gift of Caleb Buglass. This book still stands on the shelves of the Library Company and, more remarkable, in the calfskin covers with heavily gilt spine put on by Buglass (Fig. 1). It is inscribed "Library Company of Philadª, Presented by Caleb Buglass, Book-binder."

Among the manuscripts in this early library are records of books bound for the Library Company by several of Philadelphia's eighteenth-century binders, including parcels of books bound by Buglass between March 25, 1786, and April 24, 1791, with the titles in each parcel recorded individually.[33] If Caleb Buglass had given the copy of Parke's *Horace* as a specimen of his skill with the

thought of gaining work, he was rewarded. In the five years recorded, Buglass bound over five hundred volumes, for which he was paid a total of £142.11.7. One of his plain bindings, billed at three shillings, is to be found on the shelves, as well as one of his most elaborate, in morocco gilt, which cost £0.11.3. The former, Justamond's translation of Raynal's *History,* was bound in sheep with a red title label and a volume label in black. Both labels were bordered by a gold roll similar to one used by other binders at the time. The lower corners of the black volume label, however, were distinctly ornamented. By employing a unique tool, the binder achieved a figure that resembles a man sitting beneath a tree (see Fig. 1). This same tooling appears in all four corners of the panels on the spine of the manuscript Prayer Book (actually a Book of Hours) whose binding cost £0.11.3 (Fig. 2). On the three books in The Library Company of Philadelphia proved by documentary evidence to be the work of Buglass, there are five rolls that also appear on the copies of the proposed Book of Common Prayer. The board edges of all are decorated with the same gold roll, and all have flat backs, two of which are divided into panels by a gold bull's eye roll, which performs the same function on all the Prayer Books except the two that do not have spines divided into panels at all. The backs of these latter two are decorated with a continuous reticulated pattern made by crossed dotted rolls in the same fashion as the panels on Buglass's presentation copy of Parke's *Horace,* although there the panels are alternated with a diaper pattern formed by a roll that does not appear on the proposed Prayer Book. While the books in the Library Company carry labels on the spines, no copy of the proposed Prayer Book has a label.

Before a more detailed comparison and record of tools is made, one more document should be introduced—a record of edition binding done by Buglass between 1787 and 1792 for Mathew Carey.[34] Much of the work was putting volumes of the *American Museum* into covers of various sorts. In the year 1788 Buglass bound two volumes of the *Museum* in "morocco, gilt," for £0.11.3, and, at the same time, he stitched volumes in blue boards at 1 shilling each, binding second volumes

[30] Pennsylvania Marriages, II, 461 (Historical Society of Pennsylvania). See also Genealogical Chart (Sophia Selden Rogers Coll., Historical Society of Pennsylvania, Philadelphia).

[31] *Poulson's American Daily Advertiser,* May 10 to 19, 1823.

[32] *A Catalogue of the Books Belonging to The Library Company of Philadelphia* (Philadelphia: Zachariah Poulson, Jr., 1789), p. xxxii.

[33] MS. Accounts, City Library to Caleb Buglass (The Library Company of Philadelphia).

[34] MS. Accounts of Mathew Carey, 1787–1792 (American Antiquarian Society, Worcester, Mass.).

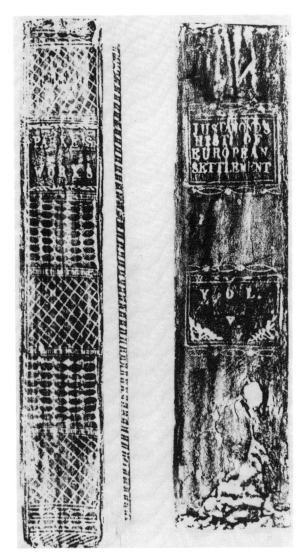

FIG. 2. Buglass, Rubbings from the binding on manuscript Book of Hours (15th century). Documented as billed for by Buglass in 1788. (The Library Company of Philadelphia.)

FIG. 1. Caleb Buglass, Rubbings (left) from the binding on *Lyric Works of Horace,* trans. John Parke (Philadelphia: Eleazer Oswald, 1786). Documented as a gift from Buglass to The Library Company of Philadelphia. (The Library Company of Philadelphia.) Rubbing (right) from the binding of Guillaume T. F. Raynal, *The Philosophical and Political History of the Settlements and Trade of the Europeans in the East and West Indies,* trans. John Justamond (3rd ed. in 5 vols.; London: Printed for T. Cadell, 1777). Documented as billed for by Buglass in 1786. (The Library Company of Philadelphia.)

"in sheep, lettered," at 3 shillings each (Fig. 3). On September 19 he bound four volumes in calf, gilt, at £0.7.6 each. The bulk of his work was routine, involving the ruling and binding of ledgers and journals and the binding of a number of periodicals, one hundred Vade mecums, one hundred Prayer Books, and some individual titles. The remuneration for the work came to less than £100. Only four items were designated "gilt," and of these the two volumes of the *Museum* in morocco are interesting, since the cost of binding was the same as that of the manuscript Prayer Book which Buglass bound for the Library Company in the same year. Although there is no proof that these were part of the set of the *Museum* that became the property of Richard Wood, Jr., Wood's nine-volume set exists in full morocco gilt with Buglass's unique corner tool of the man under the

[35] This set from the library of The Philadelphia Society for the Promotion of Agriculture, now in the Rare Book Collection of the University of Pennsylvania Library, was pointed out by Edwin Wolfe, 2nd, Librarian of The Library Company of Philadelphia.

FIG. 3. Buglass, Rubbings from the binding on *American Museum* (Philadelphia: Mathew Carey, 1787). Documented as billed to Mathew Carey in 1788. (The Library Company of Philadelphia.)

tree in all but the title panel of the spines.[35] Again the bull's-eye roll divides the six panels of each spine, although this time in a larger version, and the oblique-lined roll used on the presentation copy of Parke and on one of the proposed Prayer Books occupies the base and top of each volume. The leaf roll used on Parke is doubled across the bottom roll on one volume, and the broken scalloped fillet used on the proposed Prayer Book occurs on another. The board edges are decorated with the same roll used on all the other books described thus far. This roll of a broad gold line alternated with a narrow dotted line is very like one that almost every binder of the time used. The caps that Buglass stamped at the bottom and top of these *Museum* volumes, as he did on most of the Prayer Books, and on other books as well, differ from those of Robert Aitken in slanting from the left at the base to the right at the top. A large urn with teardrop handles, containing a portrait, adorns all panels except those bearing the title and the volume number. Urns of one kind or another were plentiful in the Federal Period, but there were distinguishing characteristics. For example, this urn of Buglass's was simpler than the portrait urn used by Aitken. It was also used on a copy of Fontaine's *History of the Old and New Testament,* translated from the French by Joseph Reeve and published in Philadelphia by M. Steiner in 1784 (Fig. 4). Buglass subscribed to twelve copies of this early Catholic book and covered one copy with more gilt than any other example of his work currently known. Handsome it is and costly it must have been; yet its owner never put his name or bookplate within. The five panels exclusive of the title panel are ornamented with the portrait urn and man-under-tree cornerpieces, and the top and bottom carry the familiar left-to-right tooling that adorns most of the Prayer Books. The leaf roll of the presentation Parke and the *American Museum* is doubled at the foot between double-line fillets, and the broken scallop of the Prayer Book is used at the top. A new roll, not used elsewhere, divides the panels. Bordering the covers, between double fillets, appears the daisy and loop roll used to border the labels of Raynal's *History*. Within this border five different fleurons are impressed, the pomegranates of the outer corners being of extra large size. The board edges are treated as usual. Perhaps the extra ornateness of this binding was too great a strain for

FIG. 4. Buglass, Rubbings from Nicolas Fontaine, le sieur de Royaumont, *The History of the Old and New Testament,* trans. Joseph Reeve (Philadelphia: M. Steiner, 1784). (Miss Julia Wightman, New York.)

Buglass, for he burned the leather in several places.

Although the original owner of Fontaine's *History of the Old and New Testament* is not known, no less a person than George Washington had two other volumes bound by Buglass in his library. Washington's copy of the *Catalogue of the . . . Library Company of Philadelphia* carries the large pomegranate of Fontaine's *History of the Old and New Testament* at its top and bottom panels flanked by four six-pointed stars, with man-under-tree cornerpieces. The diaper pattern of panels three and five is made by the same diamond-shaped roll used on the Parke presentation copy mentioned in the *Catalogue.* This tool was closer to one of Aitken's than the urn, but its diamond contains a center dot, which Aitken's does not. The bull's-eye roll again divides all the panels. The familiar left-to-right tool was used at the foot and top of the spine, and the broken scallop

used on the Prayer Book borders the title. In panel four, a new fillet of an oblong and bead divides the space with a St. Andrew's cross. In the upper and lower triangles are trefoil fleurons flanked by six-pointed stars, as are the large diamond-shaped ornaments containing bull's-eyes in the sides of the panel. A smaller version of the latter appears on one of the Prayer Books. Four of the rolls on the spine are to be found on various copies of the Prayer Book. Bordering the cover of the Library Company's *Catalogue* is a roll also found on the Prayer Books, an open loop connected by a diamond, half solid and half dotted or broken.

Washington's copy of the Constitutions of the Masons—*Ahiman Rezon,* as it was called—was probably bound by Buglass earlier than any of the books mentioned. It was published early in 1783 and is sewn on the traditional raised cords, unlike any of the others thus far described. On the spine are tulip ornaments in each panel, which are also found on two copies of the Prayer Book, and the same roll that is usually found on the Prayer Books appears vertically on its spine, as do the six-pointed stars found on a copy of the Prayer Book. The chevron roll used on the cords and board edges and the wide four-petaled roll at the foot and top of the spine do not appear on the books discussed thus far but can be found in other examples.

The chevron roll and the large four-petaled roll at the foot of the spine of *Ahiman Rezon* appeared much earlier on a book published in 1775 by Bell and Woodhouse when Buglass was working as Bell's foreman, namely, Burgh's *Political Disquisitions.* This copy, owned by Charles Willson Peale, also displays the large pomegranate in all panels save those giving title and volume number and is sewn on raised cords. The cornerpieces of the panels are a trefoil resembling, but not identical to, the one on Washington's Library Company *Catalogue.* A group of Benjamin Rush's books, all sewn on raised cords, display the smaller pomegranate used in 1786 on the Prayer Book and on a privately owned copy of Parke's *Horace,* a bird-in-bush, a large three-branch flower, and three of the rolls common to the Prayer Book.

Caleb Buglass handsomely bound more than one copy of the *Lyric Works of Horace* translated by the young Virginian John Parke and printed in Philadelphia by Eleazer Oswald, at the Coffee

House, the same year as the proposed Book of Common Prayer. Two privately owned examples resemble copies of the Prayer Book so closely in tools used, style, and technique as to leave no doubt that the same binder produced them. Both display the familiar pomegranate in a single panel of the flat back; one is divided into five panels and the other into six by the same bull's-eye roll used on all the Prayer Books; and each has two panels of the diaper pattern made by the diamond-shaped roll used by Buglass on his presentation copy, but not used on the Prayer Books. In each book these constitute the upper and lower panels. In one book there is one reticulated panel between the pomegranate and the title panel, and in the other the pomegranate is flanked by a similar panel above and below. This reticulation, it will be remembered, covered the entire spine of two copies of the Prayer Book. Rolled lengthwise on each side of the spine are a double-line fillet in one and the broken line bordered by double lines in another. The cornerpieces surrounding the

pomegranate in one are the loop and branches used in the majority of the Prayer Books. In the other is a large trefoil with dots, not found elsewhere, and a roll or pallet at the base of the spine peculiar to this volume—an oblong loop made by a floral line crossing a broken line terminating in an encircled fleuron. The other copy has the familiar left-to-right roll of the alternating broad line and broken fillet used on the Prayer Books. The label, in large letters on both the presentation copy of the Library Company and one of the privately owned copies, reads "Parke's / Works." It is bordered by a scalloped broken-fillet roll like that used on the Prayer Book and the three-leaf roll. The covers of both books are bordered by the leaf and circle roll used on a copy of the Prayer Book owned by the Philadelphia Divinity School.

Of the twenty-one copies of the Prayer Book that evidence suggests are the work of Caleb Buglass, six are especially distinguished by medallions in the center of their covers (Fig. 5) . This central ornament was made with two or more tools, one

FIG. 5. Buglass, Rubbings from bindings of The Protestant Episcopal Church in the U.S.A., *The Book of Common Prayer . . . Proposed to the Use of the Protestant Episcopal Church* (Philadelphia: Hall and Sellers, 1786) . Documented as having been owned by the bishops in England. (The Henry Francis du Pont Winterthur Museum; Cambridge University Library, Cambridge, England; John Carter Brown Library, Providence, Rhode Island.)

of branching acorns and another, more vertical, of leaves, dots, and a finial. Three of these have identical bindings, or as nearly alike as the craftsman can make them. The same medallion appears on three other copies of the book that have different cornerpieces on the cover and different spines. Three of these six books bear bookplates or inscriptions showing them to have been owned by English bishops. One of the three identical copies contains the bookplate of the Bishop of Durham; the other two contain no marks of ownership, but one was purchased in England. One of the two additional copies bearing the same medallion and identical spines contains an inscription reading, "Sent to the Bishop of Llandaff from Philadelphia" (Fig. 6). A copy with the same

medallion but a third variety of spine ornamentation carries the bookplate of Ely Episcopal Library and is inscribed, "From a collection made by the Right Rev. the Hon. James Yorke D.D. Bishop of Ely, 1781–1808 and bequeathed to his successors." From this evidence it seems likely that those books bearing the acorn medallion on their covers went to the bishops in England, some of whom were pleased to acknowledge ownership while others were not. The spines of all six books were divided into five panels and had flat backs. Three were ornamented with birds atop flowers in all panels, two with a stylized tulip and fleur-de-lis, and one with a bird-in-bush (see Fig. 5). All have the same cornerpieces and dividing fillet roll, the same vertical broken fillet between solid

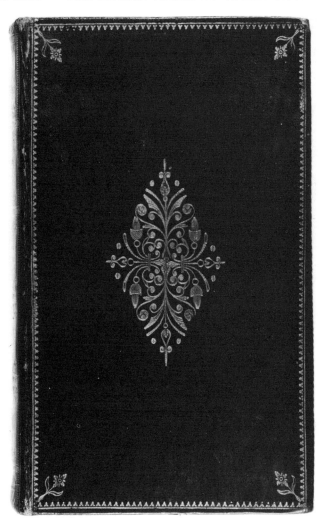

Fig. 6. Buglass, Binding on proposed Book of Common Prayer (1786). (The Henry Francis du Pont Winterthur Museum.)

lines bordering the spine lengthwise, and the same left-to-right solid line alternating with broken-line fillet at top and base of spine with a scalloped broken fillet over the same fillet as the vertical one dividing it from the base. The covers of all six books are bordered by a small cat-tooth roll, but the cornerpiecees of the covers differ. Five have a small flower with a circular center springing from branched leaves, and the Bishop of Ely's copy has a stylized fleur-de-lis. Presumably these were among the best bindings in the binder's power.

Buglass made one more binding, however, with a center medallion of an even more elaborate design, for which he used tools not utilized on the bishops' books. This central ornament was built from at least six different tools, prominent among them a crown, a tulip, a fleur-de-lis, another flower with the leaves of a thistle, six-pointed stars, and large and small dots. A copy was presented by James Abercrombie, teacher and clergyman, to Rev. Thomas Coombe (Fig. 7). Both men had been rectors of Christ Church, Philadelphia, but Coombe was charged with "having evinced a disposition inimical to the cause of America" and banished therefrom. He proceeded to England where he became chaplain to the Earl of Carlisle and eventually a prebendary of Canterbury and one of the forty-eight chaplains to the king. As a Tory he no doubt appreciated the crowns on his book, which were, perhaps, reminiscent of the crown that adorned the steeple of Christ Church before the Revolution. Coombe's book was further adorned on its covers by the narrow cat-tooth roll border and the same fleur-de-lis corners that graced the Bishop of Ely's copy. The flat spine was quite unlike any copy described thus far. It was divided into six smaller panels of equal size, each divided into a St. Andrew's cross by dotted fillet lines. A small diamond-shaped flower (possibly a stylized fleur-de-lis) was impressed in each segment of the cross, flanked by two dots. The familiar broken fillet between solid lines bordered the spine vertically and was impressed horizontally at the foot of the last panel, while the left-to-right tool was used at the top and foot of the book, as usual.

The eighth and the only other copy of the Prayer Book to be ornamented by a cover medallion was another presentation copy from Abercrombie, this time to his second wife, Mary (Fig.

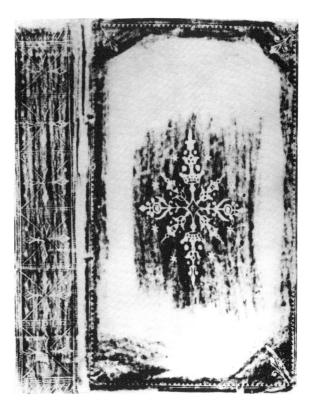

Fig. 7. Buglass, Rubbings from the binding on the proposed Prayer Book (1786). Documented as a gift from James Abercrombie to Rev. Thomas Coombe. (The Henry E. Huntington Library, San Marino, California.)

8). The date of the inscription, "Mary Abercrombie from her husband, James, 1817," makes it probable that it was a wedding present. It must have been bound by Buglass's widow, Mary. The medallion is simpler and stiffer in appearance, being made with three tools: a center circle enclosing a flower; another flower with the thistle-like leaves used by Buglass on the Coombe book impressed four times; and a smaller tulip also impressed four times. The cat-tooth roll bordering the cover is somewhat larger, and the three-branch fleuron in the corners much smaller, than the fleur-de-lis in the Coombe book. The most startling difference is in the spine, which is divided into six panels of unequal size by thick, raised cords. The four center panels of equal size are ornamented with the familiar bird-in-bush and the pomegranate. The loop cornerpiece common to most of the Prayer Books appears in the four panels. The larger upper and lower panels are reticulated in solid lines with larger spaces

Fɪɢ. 8. Mary Buglass, Rubbings from the binding on the proposed Prayer Book (1786). Documented as a gift from James Abercrombie to his wife, Mary. (New-York Historical Society.)

within the network than those of the 1786 books. A very oblique left-to-right tooling is at the top and base of the book. This tooling also appears atop the cords. A double solid fillet line borders the spine vertically and is impressed three times below the lower panel, bordering two rows of the scalloped broken fillet. The spine is wider than the other books, as other pamphlets are bound with the Prayer Book. Whether or not this is the reason for the raised cords, the book is a solid, substantial example of the binder's craft. One can scarcely generalize from a single example of the work of Mary Buglass, but in this instance, her work seems more admirable for its solid techniques than for its taste.

A dozen Prayer Books with covers decorated simply by a cat-tooth border and small corner fleurons are distinguished by four different styles of spine treatment: five identical panels (as on the bishops' copies); six identical panels; one continuous reticulated panel; and a combination of the reticulation in two panels and a single ornament

in three (Fig. 9). Only one copy of the Prayer Book has the name of its owner, Ann Watkin, tooled in large gold letters on the front cover in a variation of a style that was to become common some years later. Near the end of the eighteenth century, many prayer books were lettered with their owners' names lengthwise, but on this volume the name is lettered crosswise. The covers are far more elaborate than those copies bordered by the cat-tooth roll. Inside an outer bull's-eye roll is a wide border made of fleur-de-lis alternating in two different styles, with corner fleurons of thistles, tulips, and cockscomb, piled one above the other. The spine, identical with another Prayer Book (Fig. 9, third from left), has thistles in its six panels, within a St. Andrew's cross.

The technique used by Caleb Buglass in binding the 1786 Prayer Book and nine other books (presumably bound within their dates of publication, 1784–1789) was relatively new, with a flat spine resulting from sewn-in cords. The most elaborate of the lot, the 1784 *History of the Old and the New Testament,* carries double embroidered headbands in keeping with its elaborate gilding which, alas, shows an unsure hand in its execution. The Prayer Books were well capped and had silk headbands, which remain intact on only a few copies: one in crimson silk, one in red and gold, and a third in green and gold. The board edges were gold-tooled and the page edges gilt in most cases. However, Washington's copy of the Library Company's *Catalogue* had yellow page edges, and other books had sprinkled red, solid red, or plain edges. The end papers of the Prayer Books were combed Dutch marble or the larger feather pattern in the same red, blue, green, yellow, and white. Other books had ends of the familiar splash marble of the period or of plain paper.

The style of these later volumes was similar in that they all had gold tooling bordering the covers and gold-tooled board edges, and all but two had their spines broken up into five or six panels, depending on the binder's whim rather than on the height of the book. The cover borders ranged from a single decorative roll to a richly gilt border of three rolls with large fleurons at the outer and inner corners to a narrow roll with corner fleurons and a large central medallion. The panels of the spine were divided by the bull's-eye roll, and the caps were ornamented at the top and foot ei-

FIG. 9. Caleb Buglass, Rubbings from the bindings on Prayer Books for domestic use. (Henry E. Huntington Library, San Marino, California; General Theological Seminary, New York; New-York Historical Society; The New York Public Library; Historical Society of Pennsylvania, Philadelphia; Library of Congress.)

ther by the left-to-right tool of alternating solid and dotted lines or by the very oblique parallel lines of the Book of Hours done for the Library Company. Vertical rolls bordered the spines, and two decorative rolls appeared at the foot of the spine between the cap and the base of the lower panel.

Bindings in the traditional manner with raised cords appear to have been done prior to 1784. Gold tooling on six books from the library of Benjamin Rush is confined to the spines. With but one exception, the spines are divided into six panels; that one, because of its size, is sewn on four cords instead of five. All have morocco labels bordered with decorative rolls for titles and for volume when that is indicated. The volumes are substantial but lack the refinement of fine caps and headbands. The much more elaborate binding on Washington's *Ahiman Rezon,* also divided into six panels by raised cords, is capped but not as fully as the Prayer Books done three years later. It has red and natural silk headbands, dark blue

end papers sewn on, and board edges and caps decorated by a broad gold four-petaled roll.

In the forty-four bindings discussed in this paper, twenty-two rolls were used, twelve of them for the Prayer Books (Fig. 10), and some fifty stamps, twenty-eight of them on Prayer Books (Fig. 11). Two stamps and rolls appear to be unique with Buglass. The origin of most of the Buglass tools is unknown, but some were obtained from other Philadelphia binders, and others, used by several binders, were undoubtedly obtained from a common source. The cornerpiece of man-under-tree in left and right versions, the very oblique roll, and the wide flowered roll are not known to have been used by another binder. Two rolls were identical with Aitken's: the loop and diamond (Fig. 10:7), also used by Woodhouse, and the parallelogram (Fig. 10:18), also common to Craig and Lea and J. Wilson in Wilmington, Delaware. Two are very similar to Aitken rolls but not identical: the diamond (Fig. 10:13), which has a center dot where Aitken's and Benja-

Prayer Book Rolls   Rolls on Other Books

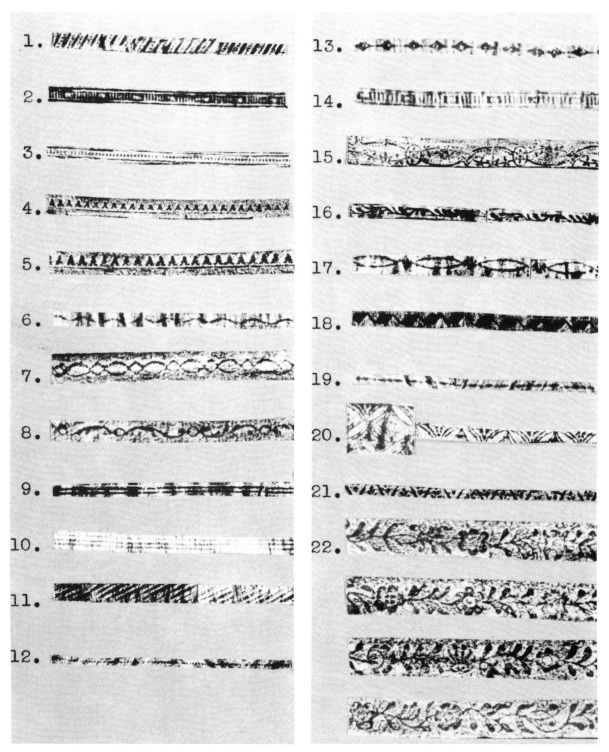

FIG. 10. Buglass, Rubbings of rolls from Prayer Books and other books.

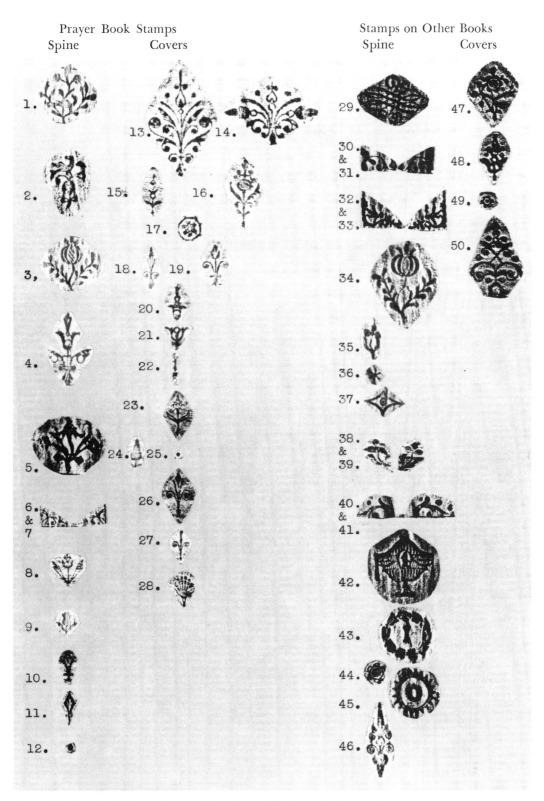

FIG. 11. Buglass, Rubbings of stamps from Prayer Books and other books.

min January's do not, and the familiar striated roll of solid alternating with dotted lines (Fig. 10:1), which is cut from left to right where Aitken's is from right to left. The daisy and chain (Fig. 10:17) was also used by January. The two cat-tooth rolls (Fig. 10: 4 and 5) had been used earlier by William Trickett, as had the narrow leaf roll (Fig. 10:16) and the chevron roll (Fig. 10:21). Trickett's tools may have been acquired, after his death, by Woodhouse when he moved to the Trickett property. The circle and leaf (Fig. 10:8) were used also by James Leishman and another unidentified Philadelphia binder. Among the stamps, the bird-in-bush (Fig. 11:1), the pomegranate (Fig. 11:3), the tulip (Fig. 11:4), and the urn (Fig. 11:42) were similar to tools of Aitken's, although not identical. In the absence of evidence to the contrary it seems most likely that all these tools came from London. These attributions, which have been made with the aid of Willman Spawn, show that a binder's work cannot be identified by tools alone; the way he uses them, the style of his work, and his technique must also be considered.

Documentation of the last eight years of Buglass's life in Philadelphia is almost as scarce as that for the seven between his bankruptcy in Berwick and his first appearance in the City of Brotherly Love. After 1789 his work for the Library Company and for Mathew Carey declined. In 1790 he did no work for the Library and none for Carey between March 19 and August 18. Like the Prayer Book purchased in 1789 by Martha Washington for her grandson, finely bound copies of the authorized Prayer Book of 1790 which have come to light are obviously the work of another hand than Buglass's.

The Buglass account with the Library Company ended on April 24, 1791. In the autumn of 1792 his bill to Mathew Carey for binding one hundred Prayer Books at £2.11.0 bore an apologetic note, "Mr. Carey, excuse me troubling you but my unhappy illness for three weeks renders it unavoidable." Two years later, on November 12, 1794, Caleb Buglass made his will. Although he died in December, 1797, the will was not proved until nine years later. By that time his widow and the one remaining daughter of four born in Philadelphia were his chief heirs. Mrs. Buglass, who died of "a lingering and powerful disease" on May 8, 1823, had continued to bind books in Coombes Alley as long as she was able. The property in the West Indies clearly had not brought a life of ease to the Buglass family.

Buglass was well trained at Berwick. Although he had "wrought at printing in the day and bookbinding in the evening," it was binding that he chose for his craft. Unlike Aitken he did not think of binding as a lesser career than printing. After various vicissitudes, he established himself in Philadelphia where he bound the proposed Book of Common Prayer at the height of his career. It is impossible to say how much help he may have had in forwarding and finishing plainer copies of the edition of five thousand. The Prayer Books that went to the bishops in England and the decorative copies in morocco gilt that remained in America have every appearance of the genius and taste of a master craftsman, Caleb Buglass.

John Hazlitt, Miniaturist and Portrait Painter in America, 1783–1787

Ernest J. Moyne

DURING the past fifty years sporadic interest in John Hazlitt as an artist in eighteenth-century America has been expressed by the compilers, editors, and authors of various reference works and listings of artists in this country[1] and by scholars who have come across his name in the course of their research on painting and sculpture in New England.[2] Whether in the form of summaries or longer accounts, all of these references to Hazlitt have been incomplete, inaccurate, or both. The purpose of this article is to give as full and accurate an account of Hazlitt and his career in America as possible.

John Hazlitt (Fig. 1), the son of the Rev. William Hazlitt (1737–1820) and Grace Loftus Hazlitt (1746–1837), was born in Marshfield, Glou-

cestershire, England, on May 13, 1767, and was baptized there on July 6.[3] In June, 1770, the Reverend Mr. Hazlitt, a Unitarian minister, moved his family from Marshfield to Maidstone, Kent, where he became pastor of a large and respectable society. Two Hazlitt children were born there: on December 10, 1770, Margaret, to whose autobiographical journal we are indebted for much of our knowledge of the Hazlitts' life in England, Ireland, and America; and on April 10, 1778, William, who was to achieve fame as an essayist and critic. In 1780 the Hazlitt family removed to Bandon, near Cork, Ireland, where they remained for three years. Then, the war between England and its American colony being happily ended and the independence of the United States settled on a firm basis, Mr. Hazlitt, an active advocate of the American cause during the Revolution, embarked for America with his family in the hope of beginning a new life in a land of civil and religious liberty. Sailing from Cove, Ireland, on April 3, 1783, the Hazlitt family arrived in New York on May 26 after a seven weeks' voyage.[4]

From New York the Hazlitts proceeded, by way of New Jersey, to Philadelphia, where they lived for fifteen months. Besides preaching occasionally in various Presbyterian churches there, Mr. Hazlitt also preached in New London and Carlisle, Pennsylvania, and in Centreville, Maryland. Because of his heterodox principles, however, he was

---

[1] See, for instance, William Dunlap, *A History of the Rise and Progress of the Arts of Design in the United States*, ed. with additions by Frank W. Bayley and Charles E. Goodspeed (new ed.; Boston: C. E. Goodspeed & Co., 1918), III, 307; Theodore Bolton, *Early American Portrait Painters in Miniature* (New York: F. F. Sherman, 1921), pp. 80–81, and *Early American Portrait Draughtsmen in Crayons* (New York: F. F. Sherman, 1923), p. 33; Mantle Fielding, *Dictionary of American Painters, Sculptors and Engravers* (Philadelphia: Printed for the subscribers, [1926]), p. 163; Henry Wyckoff Belknap, *Artists and Craftsmen of Essex County Massachusetts* (Salem, Mass.: Essex Institute, 1927), p. 10; and George C. Groce and David H. Wallace, *The New-York Historical Society's Dictionary of Artists in America, 1564–1860* (New Haven: Yale University Press, 1957), p. 303.

[2] Examples are Theodore Bolton, "John Hazlitt—Portrait Painter," *Essex Institute Historical Collections*, LVI (Oct., 1920), 293–96; Edward B. Allen, *Early American Wall Paintings, 1710–1850* (New Haven: Yale University Press, 1926), p. 18; Nina Fletcher Little, *American Decorative Wall Painting, 1700–1850* (Sturbridge, Mass.: Old Sturbridge Village, 1952), pp. 37, 39, 40, and 130, and "Carved Figures by Samuel McIntire and His Contemporaries," in "Samuel McIntire: A Bicentennial Symposium, 1757–1957," *Essex Institute Historical Collections*, XCIII (April–July, 1957), 195–96.

[3] W. Carew Hazlitt, "John Hazlitt the Miniaturist (1767–1837)," *The Antiquary*, XXXVI (Aug., 1900), 247.

[4] Ernest J. Moyne (ed.), *The Journal of Margaret Hazlitt: Recollections of England, Ireland, and America* (Lawrence, Kans.: University of Kansas Press, 1967), pp. 37, 39, and 45–47.

FIG. 1. John Hazlitt, *Self-Portrait*. London (?), *ca.* 1790. Painting on ivory; H. 3″, W. 2½″. (Maidstone Museums and Art Gallery, Maidstone, Kent.)

rejected everywhere. In May, 1784, he went to preach Unitarianism in Boston, where his family followed him in August. After staying in Boston and Lower Dorchester for a few months, the Hazlitt family moved to Weymouth, where they lived for a year and eight months, and then to Upper Dorchester, where they lived for one year.[5]

During the four years from May, 1783, to July, 1787, that the Hazlitts spent in America, John led an active and interesting life as he grew into manhood. On one occasion in Philadelphia he accompanied his father to St. Peter's Church to catch a glimpse of Gen. George Washington. At another time, when Mr. Hazlitt was ill with yellow fever in Centreville, Maryland, John went alone, on horseback, from Philadelphia to Centreville "over an unknown country and without a guide" to comfort his father and to bring him back home. On the journey from Philadelphia to Boston, he had an opportunity to explore New York, New-

[5] *Ibid.*, pp. 49, 50, *et passim.*

port, and Providence.[6] Everywhere that they lived, but especially in and near Boston, John assisted his father in caring for his mother and the rest of the family.

Apparently a self-taught artist, John Hazlitt began painting portraits before he was eighteen years old.[7] On February 17, 1785, Joseph Dunckerley,[8] a miniature painter in Boston, and Hazlitt inserted the following advertisement in the *Independent Chronicle:*

Drawing School. As it is generally and justly acknowledged, that Drawing form a necessary as well as polite part of education, the subscribers purposes opening a School for that purpose, as soon as a sufficient number . . . [of] scholars apply. For particulars, enquire of *J. Dunckerley*, at his house, North-Square.

J. Dunckerley.
J. Haslitt.

N. B. Miniature Pictures executed in the neatest manner.

Some weeks later, on March 7, 1785, they ran a more detailed advertisement for the first time in the *American Herald:*

DRAWING *in all its various Branches.*

It . . . [is] almost superfluous to mention the advantages of this art to young Ladies and Gentlemen in all the different situations of life. In the lowest estimation of it, it must be acknowledged to be an agreeable and pleasing accomplishment to employ their leisure hours. To the Naturalist, the Anatomist, the Geographer, to all Mechanicks, and especially to builders of every denomination, it is absolutely necessary, to enable them to form designs, to take plans, &c.

[6] *Ibid.*, pp. 51, 54–55, 59–61, 141, 144–45, and 147.

[7] In a letter written to W. Carew Hazlitt in 1897, the Rev. D. D. Jeremy of Dublin, Ireland, wondered whether a fine portrait of the Rev. Samuel Thomas in the vestry of Stephen's Green Unitarian Church in that city might have been painted by John Hazlitt. If John did paint this portrait of his father's old friend, who died in 1786, he must have done so between 1780 and 1783 when the Hazlitts lived in Ireland, and he must have had some training in art even before the Hazlitts left for America. Margaret Hazlitt, however, does not make any mention of John's painting in Ireland, and it seems rather unlikely that he started painting portraits before he was sixteen years old. For the Rev. Mr. Jeremy's letter, see W. Carew Hazlitt (ed.), *Lamb and Hazlitt: Further Letters and Records Hitherto Unpublished* (New York: Dodd, Mead & Co., 1899), pp. 8–9.

[8] For an account of Joseph Dunckerley, whose works have been confused with those of Copley, see Harry B. Wehle and Theodore Bolton, *American Miniatures, 1730–1850* (New York: Metropolitan Museum of Art, 1927), pp. 27 and 79.

Even those who are intended for trade, will find it an admirable assistant, where they wish to sketch out, or copy patterns, and young Ladies, it is obvious, cannot accurately delineate with their needles sprigs, flowers, birds, or landscapes, without a regular initiation into this art.

The subscribers, therefore, propose to open a Drawing School, as soon as a sufficient number of pupils apply, to instruct the rising generation in this most useful art. They will follow the lead of their parents, in particularly accomplishing them in that branch of Drawing to which they wish [them] to bend their attention, and they exert themselves to improve all that time to the utmost which they spend under their care.

The School will be open five days every week.

J. Dunkerly.

J. Hazlitt.

For particulars, inquire of J. Dunkerly, at his house in North-Square.

N. B. Portraits (in Miniature & Crayons) are executed in the best manner.

Apparently a sufficient number of pupils did not materialize to support the drawing school at Joseph Dunckerley's house in North Square (now known as the Paul Revere House), for three months later, on June 14, 1785, Hazlitt announced in the *Salem Gazette* that he intended to paint portraits, in all sizes, in Salem. It was probably at this time that he painted a miniature of his father's Salem friend, the Rev. William Bentley, who may have taken the young man under his wing since they were neighbors—Hazlitt stayed at Mrs. Elkin's, opposite the East Meeting-House in Salem, where Bentley boarded for almost eight years before he moved to the Crowninshield House in 1791.[9] William Bentley mentioned the miniature in his diary on November 20, 1818, saying, "My miniature was by Haslitt, now celebrated in London. The dress was changed by Verstille from Conn. It was known when taken at my ordination."[10] This seems to mean that Bentley had the dress in vogue at the time of his ordination in September, 1783, and still worn by him

two years later when Hazlitt painted his portrait, changed to bring his picture up to date, perhaps in 1802 when he recorded in his diary that a "Mr. Verstille has at present great fame & it is believed great success."[11]

William Bentley's diary also reveals that he dined with Mr. Winthrop on July 21, 1790, and the following day he noted that "Mr Winthrop favored me with a miniature of the first Governor Winthrop, which was with me a very high Compliment."[12] In 1797 and 1803 he again referred in his diary to this miniature, stating that it was from the original and that it had been taken from "the family picture."[13] On July 4, 1804, he described the decorations for the Independence Day celebration in his meetinghouse, noting that, "In the front below, in a Bust cut by Mr. Macintire, an ingenious artist of Salem, was Gov. Winthrop & a likeness taken by Haslitt."[14] This likeness painted by Hazlitt—which also served as the

FIG. 2. Hazlitt, *Governor John Winthrop.* Boston, Mass., 1785 (?). Painting on ivory; H. 1¹¹⁄₁₆″, W. 1⅝₁₆″. (American Antiquarian Society.)

model for Samuel McIntire's bust—was the same miniature of Governor Winthrop that James Winthrop had presented to Mr. Bentley in 1790 (Fig. 2).[15] Apparently James Winthrop had com-

[9] Abbott Lowell Cummings, "The House and Its People," in "Crowninshield-Bentley House, Special Issue, *Essex Institute Historical Collections,* XCVII (April, 1961), 85.

[10] *The Diary of William Bentley, D.D.: Pastor of the East Church, Salem, Massachusetts* (Salem, Mass.: Essex Institute, 1905–1914), IV, 561. William Verstille (*ca.* 1755–1803), miniaturist and portrait painter, worked in Philadelphia in 1782 and 1783, in New York City in 1784, and in Salem in 1802. Sometime during the 1790's he also worked in Connecticut.

[11] *Ibid.,* II, 452.

[12] *Ibid.,* I, 187. Mr. Winthrop has been identified by Lawrence S. Mayo as James Winthrop, son of Professor John Winthrop of Harvard College.

[13] *Ibid.,* May 19, 1797, II, 223, and Oct. 7, 1803, III, 52.

[14] *Ibid.,* III, 96.

[15] *Ibid.,* II, 269, and Lawrence S. Mayo, *The Winthrop Family in America* (Boston: Massachusetts Historical Society, 1948), pp. 32, 233.

missioned Hazlitt, who was then working in Boston, to reproduce a likeness of his ancestor from the original family portrait.

On October 7, 1802, after dining at the home of Mr. B. Ward, Bentley wrote in his diary: "We had several portraits before us & several interesting anecdotes. Mr. Hazlett's executions in miniature were excellent. Mr. Corné as a painter of ships has great excellence. Some of his paintings of portraits are good."[16] Bentley may have been referring only to the Hazlitt miniatures that belonged to him personally; however, it is possible to infer from this diary entry that there were others. Surely, John Hazlitt must have painted many miniatures in Salem, and perhaps some of them are still extant but with the identity of the artist unspecified. Bentley, in his will, dated May 3, 1819, bequeathed his "cabinet with all it contains" to the American Antiquarian Society.[17] The miniature of Governor Winthrop is now a part of the Society's collection, but Hazlitt's miniature of Bentley has disappeared. In his "Checklist of the Portraits in the Library of the American Antiquarian Society," published in 1947, Frederick L. Weis lists the Hazlitt portrait of John Winthrop as a "miniature on ivory . . . in a silver locket" with "date and artist unknown."[18]

During the Hazlitt family's residence in Weymouth, John painted not only there but also in Boston, Salem, and Hingham. His sister's journal supplies the information that the young artist at this time was becoming an ardent admirer of feminine beauty, for she wrote that John spent much of his time at Milton visiting a Blake family, whose several sons were fond of his company but whose daughter, "elegance personified, was his greatest attraction."[19] John also was smitten with Lucy Jones, the beautiful niece of the Hazlitts' neighbor in Weymouth, Dr. Cotton Tufts, and Margaret Hazlitt's close friend. In a letter of July 19–August 7, 1785, to her sister Abigail Adams, Mrs. Mary Cranch gave the following description of the youthful romance between Lucy and John,

who had already attained some prominence as an artist:

I once mention'd to you a clergemans Family Who were in our House at Weymouth. He has a Son almost eighteen Who tho he is a portrait Painter has not Sacrificed much to the Graces. He made several attempts to take the Face of our Cousin Lucy Jones, but could never acquire Stediness enough in his hands to do it. In Short her fine form had made Such an impression upon his mind and Lucy *all-together* had taken Such possestion of his Soul, that when he endeavoured to describe a Single feature he found it impossible. The tremor Was communicated to his Tongue and his Speech also fail'd him. Poor youth What Would he have done if it had not been for the bless'd invention of Letters, by Which he could pour out all his Soul and Save his Blushes—but alass this was only to insure his dispair, for She treated them with Such neglect and contempt that it almost depriv'd him of his reason.

In reaching the climax of her account, Mary Cranch really waxes romantically eloquent:

In the Silent Watches of the night—When the Moon in full orb'd Majesty had reach'd her nocturnal height He left his Bed and upon the cold ground told her his tale of Woe, in accents loud and Wild as Wind. Forgive the Stile my dear Sister. No common one Would do to relate this extraordinary affair in. It has caused us much amusement. They are both so young they did not know how to manage the matter. He all Passion. She full of coquettry and at present without any kind of attachment to him is playing round the Flame Without any aprehension of danger. There are Some Symptoms however of either Vanity or Love that make their appearance. She dresses more than usual and parades before the windows opposite to those he Sets at. The other day She dress'd herself in White and Walked into Capn. Whitmans [Capt. Abiah Whitman's] Poppes [Copse] Set herself upon a rock under a fine Spreading oak and Was excited by the melody of a variety of Birds that were perch'd upon almost every bough, to add her note to theirs. The Sighing Swain was raking Hay at a little distance. The pleasing Sound Soon reach'd his ears. He left his Rake and pursu'd it and (She Says) Was close by her before She perciev'd him but She like a nimble-footed Dauphne was out of his Sight in a moment and Was as pale aunt [Mrs. Cotton Tufts] Says When She enter'd the House as if She had been pursu'd by a Snake.[20]

---

[16] *Diary of William Bentley*, II, 452. Michel Felice Corné (*ca.* 1752–1845), marine and portrait painter, worked in Salem from 1799 to 1806, in Boston from 1807 to 1822, and in Newport, Rhode Island, from 1822 to 1845.

[17] Little, *Essex Institute Historical Collections*, XCIII, 196.

[18] *Proceedings of the American Antiquarian Society*, LVI (1947), 118.

[19] Moyne, *Journal of Margaret Hazlitt*, p. 69.

[20] Quotation from the Adams Papers is from the microfilm edition, by permission of the Massachusetts Historical Society. See *Microfilms of the Adams Papers*, Pt. IV, "Letters Received and Other Loose Papers," Reel 365.

In addition to attempting to portray Lucy Jones, whom Margaret likened to Fielding's heroine Sophia Western, John probably painted miniatures of many of the Hazlitts' friends and neighbors in Weymouth, as well as of members of his own family.[21] Like his father, who frequently visited Hingham and preached more than forty times there for the venerable Rev. Dr. Ebenezer Gay, John "spent a great part of his time in Hing[h]am with Dr. Barker and some others, where he painted many portraits, and perhaps some of his first pictures are to be seen there even at this present time."[22] In Hingham he executed likenesses of Dr. Gay, Gen. Benjamin Lincoln, Col. Nathan Rice, Dr. Joshua Barker, and many others of his father's friends.[23] The portrait of Gay, according to W. Carew Hazlitt, was painted for a parishioner who had asked the aged minister to grant him a favor without saying what it was. Gay, who had a strong aversion to having his likeness taken, granted the favor and then was obliged to keep his promise (Fig. 3). According to W. Carew Hazlitt's American correspondent, a great-nephew of General Lincoln, John's portrait of Gay, representing the head and shoulders only, seemed "to be rather hard and stiff in execution, and to betray the hand of a novice."[24] This portrait, done in pastel, is still owned in Hingham by Gay's descendants, but the other portraits known to have been painted during Hazlitt's stay there have disappeared. Of special interest is a miniature of the Reverend Mr. Hazlitt, by John Hazlitt

FIG. 3. Hazlitt, *The Reverend Ebenezer Gay.* Hingham, Mass., 1785 (?). Pastel on paper; H. 20″, W. 16″. (Courtesy of Ebenezer Gay: photo, Stephen Grohe.)

(no doubt painted during the Hazlitt family's residence in Weymouth), which was presented in 1901 by Miss Susan Barker Willard to the Wompatuck Club in Hingham. Presumably this miniature was originally given to the Hazlitts' close family friend Dr. Joshua Barker and then handed down in his family until it was bequeathed to the Wompatuck Club.[25]

Although Hazlitt was mainly a miniaturist and portrait painter, he may have ornamented some panels in two houses in Hingham owned by the Thaxter family. The fireplace wall of the principal room in each house—one was torn down in 1865 and the other, purchased by the Wompatuck Club in 1900, still stands on its original site— "consisted of multiple raised panels, upon the surface of each of which was painted a landscape

---

21 Moyne, *Journal of Margaret Hazlitt*, p. 76.

22 *Ibid.*, p. 72.

23 Henry T. Tuckerman, *Book of the Artists: American Artist Life* (New York: G. P. Putnam & Sons, 1867), p. 54. Among other friends of Mr. Hazlitt whose portraits may have been painted by John Hazlitt is Madam Derby, of Hingham, an original portrait of whom has been reported as lost. See *History of the Town of Hingham, Massachusetts* ([Hingham]: Published by the town, 1893), p. 138.

24 [William Carew Hazlitt], *The Hazlitts: An Account of Their Origin and Descent* (Edinburgh: Ballantyne, Hanson & Co., 1911), p. 46. In a letter of Feb. 6, 1864, Solomon Lincoln of Hingham, Mass., wrote to William B. Sprague concerning the Rev. Ebenezer Gay: "He was of about the middle size, of dignified and patriarchal appearance, and, if we can judge of his features as delineated by the pencil of Hazlitt, they were not particularly handsome. He had, however, in the recollection of those who knew him, a grave, yet benignant expression of countenance. Those who loved him held him in such affection and reverence that they would not admit that Hazlitt's portrait was not a beautiful picture." See William B. Sprague, *Annals of the American Unitarian Pulpit* (New York: R. Carter & Brothers, 1865), p. 5.

25 See Francis H. Lincoln, "The Thaxter, Now the Wompatuck Club, House," in *Hingham: A Story of Its Early Settlement and Life, Its Ancient Landmarks, Its Historic Sites and Buildings* ([Hingham]: Old Colony Chapter, Daughters of the American Revolution, 1911), pp. 112–14.

scene."[26] In her account of these painted panels, Nina Fletcher Little wrote:

When the Thaxter-Lincoln house was taken down a number of the panels were saved. One of these hangs in the Hingham Historical Society, several are locally owned. . . . In the Wampatuck [sic] Club the entire chimney wall incorporates seventeen panels, each decorated with a different view. . . . They are well painted in a style more competent than that of the usual travelling decorator. The subjects bear no resemblance to American scenery but might be either English or Continental. However, the British Jack flies over the turretted castle which surmounts the fireplace.

She then commented on the attribution of these painted panels to John Hazlitt:

Probably because of the foreign character of these subjects their authorship was many years ago credited to John Hazlitt, a portrait and miniature painter who lived in nearby Weymouth during the 1780's. . . . John was only eighteen years of age at this time, but he was already proficient in the media of miniature, pastel, and oil. . . . Were the Hingham panels done by Hazlitt? There appears to be no evidence to support this attribution except the facts that he was painting portraits in the town between 1784 and 1787, that he was a competent artist, that the panels are unusually well executed, and that the subject matter appears to be European rather than American. If Hazlitt did indulge in a bit of architectural painting it must have been as a sideline from his regular occupation of portrait painter.[27]

That John was concerned primarily with portrait painting is shown by his lack of interest in "a large and very old picture in oil of the meeting of Esau and Jacob" which hung in the small square entry to the house the Hazlitts occupied in Weymouth, the former home of the Rev. William and Elizabeth Quincy Smith.[28] On this picture, re-

puted to be one of the first attempts of John Singleton Copley, Margaret Hazlitt "used to gaze with delight" and wonder "at the skill of the artist who had made so natural and lively a representation of the scene," the effect of which she described as follows: "The embracing of the two brothers, the meeting of their followers on either side, with the groups of camels and other cattle, and the background winding up between the hills and seeming to vanish in the air completed the enchantment." However, "as John never copied or said much about it," Margaret decided that he was not interested in it, and she suspected at last that it was not so fine a painting as she had imagined.[29]

In the fall of 1786, after the Hazlitt family had moved from Weymouth to Upper Dorchester and Mr. Hazlitt had departed for England (his wife and children would follow him the next summer), John was improving himself in painting. For Samuel Vaughan, a friend of the Hazlitt family then in Boston, he painted a picture of two wild turkeys, which, according to Margaret's journal, was sent to Germany.[30] While in Dorchester, Hazlitt also did a crayon portrait of his sister that Susan Butt, a friend of Margaret, persuaded him to give to her.[31] It must have been about this time, too, when he was teaching Latin grammar to his brother William, that he painted a charming brooch-size ivory miniature of William, which has been reproduced in various works a number of times since then (Fig. 4). Either at this time or earlier Hazlitt may have painted portraits of some of his father's many friends in Boston, among whom were such well-known ministers as Charles Chauncy, John Clarke, John Eliot, Oliver Everett, James Freeman, Simeon Howard, and John Lathrop, as well as such important merchants as Kirk Boott, William Pratt, and John Gregory, not to speak of Elias Hasket Derby, of Salem. If any of these men, like many of Mr. Hazlitt's other friends here and in England, gave their patronage to John Hazlitt, portraits of them by "an unknown artist" may still exist somewhere in New England.

In a letter of March 15, 1786, the Rev. John Palmer, of Islington, wrote to Mr. Hazlitt in America:

---

[26] Little, *American Decorative Wall Painting*, p. 37.

[27] *Ibid.*, p. 37. Since finding painted panels resembling those at Hingham in Middletown and East Hartford, Conn., Mrs. Little is more skeptical than ever about the attribution of the painted panels in Hingham to John Hazlitt. See Nina Fletcher Little, "Engraved Sources for American Ornamental Panels," *Antiques*, LXXXVIII (Oct., 1965), 500–501. Margaret's journal does not give any evidence that John ever painted in Connecticut.

For the attribution of the painted panels in Hingham to John Hazlitt, see, for instance, Benjamin F. Stevens, "A Reminiscence of the Past," *Hingham Magazine*, 1898, pp. 43–44, and Allen, *Early American Wall Paintings*, p. 18.

[28] The Smiths' daughter Mary married Judge Richard Cranch; Abigail married President John Adams; and Elizabeth married the Rev. John Shaw, and after his death, the Rev. Stephen Peabody.

[29] Moyne, *Journal of Margaret Hazlitt*, p. 63.

[30] *Ibid.*, p. 89.

[31] *Ibid.*, p. 90.

The account of your son's proficiency and success in portrait-painting affords me a peculiar pleasure, both for his sake and yours; and though the assistance of some of our masters here in that line could not but greatly forward his improvement, I cannot yet but promise myself that he will do very well without it; nor can I suppose you would be willing to part with him to such a distance, even for a year, for many reasons which your own mind will readily suggest, unless such a proposal was to come from some friend who was both able and willing to take him under his patronage and care.[32]

After the Hazlitts' return to England in 1787, which came about partly because "John's profession was not wanted in the woods [of Maine: the Reverend Mr. Hazlitt had sought to settle as a minister in Hallowell], where good hunters and husbandmen were more needed," John was left in London in the care of David Lewis, a very close friend, while the rest of the family went to Wem in Shropshire.[33] Establishing himself in London, where he won praise from Sir Joshua Reynolds, John Hazlitt exhibited at the Royal Academy every year from 1788 to 1819 and, also, in various years, at the British Institute. In London he made the acquaintance not only of eminent artists but also of some of the leading literary men of the time, becoming a member of the circle that included Thelwall, Holcroft, Stoddart, Godwin, Coleridge, and Lamb.

Although a detailed account of Hazlitt's career as a "celebrated" painter in England is beyond the scope of this paper,[34] it may be in order to note that there he painted portraits of such well-known people as Mary Lamb, sister of Charles Lamb, the essayist; Samuel Taylor Coleridge, poet, critic, and philosopher; Joseph Priestley, theologian and natural philosopher; and Edward

Fig. 4. Hazlitt, *William Hazlitt.* Dorchester, Mass. (?), 1786 (?). Painting on ivory; H. 3¾″, W. 3⅛″ (Maidstone Museums and Art Gallery, Maidstone, Kent.)

[32] "The Hazlitt Papers," *Christian Reformer,* V (Nov., 1838), 759.

[33] Moyne, *Journal of Margaret Hazlitt,* p. 74. The main reason for the Hazlitts' departure from America was the Rev. William Hazlitt's inability to find a means of supporting his family here. Being a Socinian, Mr. Hazlitt discovered that his beliefs prevented his being permanently settled in any church in America immediately after the Revolution.

[34] According to the *Catalogue* of the sale of the Francis Wellesley Collection at Sotheby's in London, June 28–July 2, 1920, p. 136, a miniature of Margaret Hazlitt (Catalogue No. 425) by John Hazlitt and a "miniature in the Pierpont Morgan Collection prove Hazlitt to be a miniaturist of the highest rank."

Jenner, discoverer of vaccination. Today he is represented in the National Portrait Gallery by an oil portrait of Joseph Lancaster, the Quaker, who was the founder of the system of popular education known by his name. This portrait probably was painted by Hazlitt fairly late in life when, his eyesight becoming less trustworthy for minute work, he turned to large pictures in oil. Very little is known about him between 1819 and 1832, when he moved to Stockport. There he died on May 16, 1837, at the age of seventy.

One cannot help wondering about John Hazlitt's career if he had stayed in the United States. Would he have achieved fame in America, or would all traces of his work have disappeared? As it is, what little notice he receives is due largely to the fact that he was the elder brother of the far more distinguished William Hazlitt. Perhaps one may be permitted to suggest that this overshadowing of John by his better-known brother is not entirely fair. Certainly, from the American point of view at least, John Hazlitt deserves to be remembered as a competent miniaturist and portrait painter who began his career under anything but favorable circumstances early in the history of the newly created United States.

Surveyor General Thomas Holme's "Map of the Improved Part of the Province of Pennsilvania"

Walter Klinefelter

THE instrument signed by Charles II of England on March 4, 1681, investing William Penn with the sole proprietorship of a domain so vast that its extent, as eventually determined, fell only a little over 5,000 square miles short of equaling the area of England proper, must be conceded to have been one of the most significant documents executed during the early period of our colonial history. Its importance stems not so much from its terms and conditions as from the good intentions that motivated their implementation. Although the concept of a colony in America founded on the principle of religious freedom was not original with Penn, his plan for setting up what he once called his "Holy Experiment" was highly novel indeed. Having as its objective, in the cause of colonial development, the disposal of real estate on a scale never before undertaken, or perhaps even contemplated, the scheme was the most enterprising ever put into operation for peopling a wilderness. It probably was the most widely advertised, too, for over a period of three years no fewer than eight separate promotional pamphlets and broadsides appeared, three of which were translated into a foreign language, and one into three such tongues.

Among the earliest of these releases was one presenting *A Map of Some of the South and east bounds of Pennsylvania in America, being partly Inhabited,* which Penn commissioned to give prospective purchasers a visual image of the regions to which they were being invited to commit their destinies. It seems unlikely, however, that this delineation could have conveyed a clear impression of the surface aspects of the country, for the anonymous cartographer simply met the request by combining some detail from the upper parts of Augustine Herrman's map of Virginia and Maryland with a fair amount of none-too-accurate detail from other sources for a northward extension of the Delaware Bay and Delaware River regions to a distance of about forty miles.[1] That this cartographical creation would not long retain its dubious authority appeared well assured, for one year after Penn initiated the promotion of his colonial venture he had sold over a half-million acres in Pennsylvania, and purchasers, hopeful that tracts of their choice would be laid out quickly by the official surveyors, were arriving by the shiploads. In due course, then, the agents of the Land Office would acquire a knowledge of the physical features of the countryside, which, combined with the cultural detail of the sort that surveyors themselves create, would provide the materials from which a dependable map of the seated parts of the province could be composed.

No one looked forward to that eventuality with greater anticipation than the proprietor himself. It would be not only a tribute to his accomplishments but also a fitting climax to his promotional schemes. It is not known at what stage in the de-

[1] For a brief treatise on Penn's map, see Dr. Lawrence C. Wroth, *A Note on the William Penn Map of Pennsylvania (London, 1681)*, written "To accompany the Facsimile issued by The John Carter Brown Library, Providence, 1943." The Herrman map has been described by P. Lee Phillips in *The Rare Map of Virginia and Maryland* (Washington: W. H. Lowdermilk & Co., 1911) and by Edward B. Mathews in *The Maps and Map-Makers of Maryland* (Baltimore: Johns Hopkins Press, 1898).

velopment of the province he first requested Thomas Holme, his surveyor general, to produce a map, but apparently his eagerness for its preparation prompted him to do so before an adequate amount of material was available. In any case, there is evidence that he urged its composition prior to his return to England in August, 1684, and that he exacted a promise from Holme to complete it before the end of that year. With Holme's promise as surety, Penn advised his friends and intimate acquaintances in England that cartographical evidence of the progress being made in the planting of the province would appear shortly.

The evidence did not materialize according to the proprietor's expectations, however, largely for reasons that were attributable to acts of his own commission, beginning with his choice of the method to be employed for disposing of his land. In deciding to issue deeds of lease and re-lease for tracts without specifying metes and bounds and permitting purchasers to select their locations, he displayed a profound trust in the uprightness of his fellow sectarians that this subsequent behavior did not justify. In fact, of the several methods he might have chosen, his was the one that offered purchasers the widest opportunity to get the most for the least when they had the connivance of unscrupulous surveyors. Holme stands out among Penn's appointees for his faithful commitment to the best interests of his employer, but it was the surveyor general's misfortune to have several deputies of questionable honesty, the most unreliable being Charles Ashcombe, who contrived to breach nearly every regulation the proprietor had laid down for field work. His surveys, both authorized and unauthorized, almost invariably included greater acreages than the warrants specified. His unauthorized surveys, run in areas that had already been laid out and patented to others, were performed as an additional source of surveyor's fees, one third of which he was supposed to turn over to Holme but did not do so; and to avoid a full accounting on that score, he refused to make exact returns of his work to the surveyor general. Although, before departing for England, Penn had been fully informed of the deputy's misconduct, he let him off with a reprimand on receiving Ashcombe's pledge to mend his ways. The deputy had no intention of keeping the pledge, however, and the proprietor's failure to deal forcefully with

him only compounded Holme's difficulties, for, observing the leniency shown to this scoundrel, other deputies were emboldened to commit similar breaches of Land Office procedure.

Thus two years went by during which Holme found himself so involved in attempting to undo the mischief wrought by his unscrupulous deputies that he was not able to complete the map. By then the proprietor's appeals had become almost frantic, and he beseeched a correspondent to bring all possible suasion to bear on Holme to fulfill his obligation with the utmost dispatch, since "we want a map to the degree that I am ashamed here; . . . all cry out, where is your map, what, no map of your Settlements."[2]

Holme had not put aside his map making entirely, however, for in October, 1686, undoubtedly in response to appeal by Penn, he revealed that he intended "to send the Draughts for a Map by the first."[3] Whatever his intentions regarding the map may have been at the time of his writing, they were not immediately realized, for by the end of the following month he informed the proprietor that the map was not yet completed. In giving the reason why, he named the leading villain of the piece: "C[harles] A[shcombe] will neither give me his draughts and regular returns, nor account of the survey money."[4] Holme finally sent drafts for his map to London about the end of the following winter, or soon thereafter,[5] where they were engraved by F. Lamb and published by Robert Green and John Thornton as *A Map of the Improved Part of the Province of Pennsylvania in America,* with the subtitle, *A Map of the Province of Pennsilvania, Contaning the three Coun-*

[2] Letter from William Penn, Sept. 21, 1686, to Thomas Lloyd, quoted in Frederick B. Tolles, "William Penn on Public and Private Affairs, 1686," *Pennsylvania Magazine of History and Biography* (hereafter *PMHB*), LXXX (April, 1956), 246.

[3] "A Letter from Doctor More," *PMHB,* IV, No. 4 (1880), 453.

[4] Gary B. Nash (ed.), "The First Decade in Pennsylvania: Letters of William Markham and Thomas Holme to William Penn," *PMHB,* XC (July, 1966), 351.

[5] From a careful check of Land Office records, it appears that the last survey Holme included in the detail of his map was the one made in the upper parts of Philadelphia County in execution of the warrant that was issued to Jacob Pellison on Feb. 7, 1686/87. In writing to Penn on May 24, 1687, Holme used the words "as per mapp thou wilt see," which would seem to indicate that he then supposed that his drafts would shortly be received by the proprietor. See Nash, *PMHB,* XC (Oct., 1966), 491.

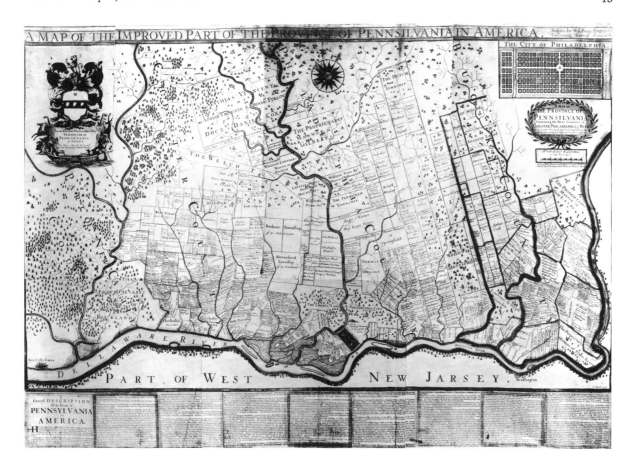

FIG. 1. F. Lamb, *A Map of the Improved Part of the Province of Pennsilvania in America*. London, 1687. Engraving; H. 33½", W. 55½" (to border, without "General Description"). 1st ed., from drafts by Thomas Holme; published by Robert Green and John Thornton. (British Museum: photostatic copy, Library of Congress.)

tyes of Chester, Philadelphia, & Bucks as far as yet Surveyed and Laid out, yᵉ Divisions or distinctions made by yᵉ different Coullers, respects the Settlements by way of Townships (Fig. 1). Publication may be assumed to have taken place about the time of the appearance of the second of the two issues of *The London Gazette,* dated Thursday, Janaury 5, to Monday, January 9, 1687/88, in which Green and Thornton advertised, "A New and Exact Map of the improved part of the Province of Pensilvania in America, being three Counties, viz. Bucks, Philadelphia, and Chester. Giving the Figure of every particular Persons piece or parcels of Land taken up there, it contains 7 sheets of Paper, and is Five Foot long, and three Foot six Inches deep. Surveighed by Captain Thomas Holmes, Surveyor General

of the said Province. Price rouled and coloured 10 s."[6]

The year of publication does not appear on the map itself but in "A General Description of the Province of Pennsylvania in America" printed on a bottom margin wide enough to accommodate the more than four thousand words to which it ran. The second paragraph of this account states that "The Business of this Map, is to shew the Im-

---

[6] *The London Gazette* was then dated according to the Julian calendar, in which the year ended with the month of February. Proof copies of the map may have been pulled from the plate as early as some time in Sept., 1687, when Penn, enroute from London to the Bristol Fair, exhibited a "mapp" of Pennsylvania at Marlborough in Wiltshire. See Albert Cook Myers (ed.), *Narratives of Early Pennsylvania, West New Jersey and Delaware, 1630–1707* (New York: C. Scribner's Sons, 1912), 292 n.

provements of the said Proprietary and Inhabitants of the said Providence: It being but six Years ago, when this Patent was granted in *Spring 1681*"; and at the end of the account is the imprint, *"London,* Printed by J. D. for *Robert Green* at the Rose and Crown in *Budg-Row,* and *John Thornton* at the Sign of *England, Scotland* and *Ireland,* in the *Minories, 1687."*[7]

The year of initial publication is now so definitely established as to require no further confirmation, but until a quarter-century ago no copy of the map containing the above extracts had been the subject of extensive notice.[8] Prior to that time, those who concerned themselves with Holme and his activities as a map maker based their studies on the later, slightly amended edition, from which "A General Description" was

omitted (Fig. 2), and on undated, reduced-scale issues of a delineation based on the first edition. Therefore, the exact year of the appearance of the first edition was for them a matter of conjecture. The dates they advanced ranged from shortly after 1681, the year given on the map itself as that of the founding of Pennsylvania, to 1688, with most writers inclined to fix the time of its publication toward the end of that period. They accepted the advertisement in *The London Gazette* of May 7–10, 1688, offering "a Map of Pensilvania, by William Pen Esq. made and sold by Mr. Robert Green,"[9] as referring to Holme's map, and for more substantial evidence, with greater leeway in dating, they cited the entry in the minutes of Provincial Council, March 25, 1689, that stated "that yᵉ mapp of The Province . . . the work of

[7] Copy in the British Museum, London, Add. MS 5414.23.
[8] The first edition does not appear to have been noticed at any length in print prior to the publication of Homer Rosenberger's "Early Maps of Pennsylvania" in *Pennsylvania History,* XI (1944), 103–17.

[9] Oliver Hough, "Captain Thomas Holme, Surveyor-General of Pennsylvania and Provincial Councillor," *PMHB,* XIX, No. 4 (1895), 424. The advertisement announced the death of Robert Green and the continuance of his business by his daughter.

Fɪɢ. 2. Lamb, Second edition of Fig. 1. London, probably between 1701 and 1705. Engraving; H. 32½″, W. 55″ (to border). (Winterthur, 63.853.)

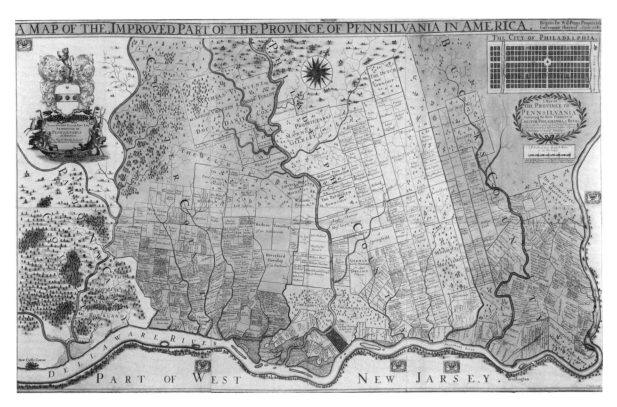

Thomas Holme, Surveyor Gene[11] . . . was dedicated to yᵉ Proprietor by yᵉ Publisher,"[10] which appears to be the earliest known reference to the map in official records. Unfortunately, they overlooked the advertisement of it in *The London Gazette* of January 5–9, 1687/88, which would have settled the matter once and for all.

At least one historian found it impossible to reconcile the above dating with the detail in the map as he knew it and concluded that "as respects dates the map is calculated to deceive, for although it may have been commenced near the close of 1681, yet there is positive evidence from the sale of the tracts that it was filled up even after 1730."[11] On the other hand, the first writer to discuss the map at any length was led to deduce, because he accepted resurveys of certain tracts as the earliest surveys made of them, that the same edition was the last of several and that each one after the first had been amended to record the progress made into the interior by the Land Office surveyors. Regrettably, apart from the faulty dates, this historian did not state his evidence.[12] It would be interesting to know on what other records he grounded his conclusions. Some of them, presumably, were deeds or patents of "the sale of the tracts," but their acceptance as proof of date of original survey could be very misleading. Patents were issued by the proprietor or his agents only after warrantees had satisfied the conditions stated in the warrants regarding fees and partial payments; when warrantees then disposed of part or all of their land, they usually held the deeds until full payment had been rendered in cash or goods. In numerous instances both original purchasers and those to whom they later sold their land did not meet these conditions until many years after the time of survey. Holme, of course, did not base his map on instruments of patent but worked from surveys that were made as the land was taken up and from various resurveys, copies of many of which are no longer available in Land Office records. Therefore, it is impossible to prove conclusively from that source that each and every tract laid down from the Delaware River to the outer limits of the map had actually been surveyed prior to the time Holme is supposed to have submitted his drafts to Penn. But, since evidence is available (in dated warrants, the minutes of the Commissioners of Property, and Penn's correspondence) that all the large outermost tracts—the Colonel Mildmay and Thomas Hudson grants, The Dutch Township, Gilberts Manor, the Vincent-Vrouzen-Furly-Coxe grant, the Welsh Tract, and the Charles Pickering and Company tract—and various smaller tracts on and near Brandywine Creek had been surveyed before Holme completed his drafts, it seems safe to assume that the intermediate ones had likewise been laid out.[13]

Thus, it is obvious that the map was never intended to be deceptive. True, it was not perfect, for perfection was not to be expected in a first attempt, nor were its shortcomings attributable to Holme alone. In fact, he appears to have done as well as he could in spite of failing eyesight, the proprietor's impatience, the unremitting press of his official duties, the recalcitrance and chicanery of some of his deputies, the numerous errors (intentional or otherwise) committed in surveying, and the resurveys that had to be run to correct them—all of which were conditions highly adverse to the achievement of a faultless map.

The area embraced in the map, extending from

---

[10] *Colonial Records of Pennsylvania* (hereafter *CRP*) (Philadelphia: [The state], 1852), I, 264.

[11] William J. Buck, in *History of Montgomery County*, ed. Theodore W. Bean (Philadelphia: Everts & Peck, 1884), 874.

[12] Hough, *PMHB*, XIX, No. 4, 424–25. "This first edition," says Hough, "could not have shown the bounds of lands that were surveyed at a later date, but copies preserved at the present time contain . . . tracts that were laid out later; for instance, Laetitia Penn's Manor of Mount Joy, and William Penn, Jr.'s Manor of Williamstadt, both taken up in 1704, Samuel Carpenter's great tract north of Moreland . . . laid out in 1706, and others in the more distant parts, some of which were not surveyed before 1725, or even a few years later." As a matter of fact, Holme laid out Mountjoy Manor in the summer of 1686, and Penn appears to have assigned the Manor of Williamstadt to his son after Holme's drafts came to hand. In any case, the survey run in 1704 is specifically denoted in Land Office records as a resurvey; see Old Rights, B-22, p. 142 (Bureau of Land Records, Harrisburg, Pa.; hereafter *BLR*).

Hough's statement that Carpenter's large tract on Pennypack Creek was first surveyed in 1706 is disproved by the following entry in the minutes of the Commissioners of Property under date of March 23, 1702: "Samuel Carpenter having Originally Purchased of the Prop'ry 5000 acres of Land in this Province . . . by Vertue of a Warrant from the Prop'ry dated 4th 6 mo. 1684, took up 4420 a's, his full Complement, (having taken up 580 a's before) adjoining to the . . . Tract of Joseph Fisher's and the Line of Bucks County, on which he Requests a Resurvey and a Confirmation." See *Pennsylvania Archives*, 2nd ser. (Harrisburg, Pa.: [The state], 1893 [hereafter *PA-2*]), XIX, 281.

[13] This evidence will be presented hereinafter in connection with accounts of the various tracts named.

New Castle, Delaware, to the longitude of the great bend in the Delaware River and from the Delaware River inland to the headwaters of Brandywine and Neshaminy creeks, is approximately fifty-five miles long by thirty-three miles wide, plotted to the scale of one mile to the inch. The result was a delineation of such imposingly ample proportions that it appears to include far more than the approximately 1,800 square miles of this area. Actually, less than two-thirds of the expanse included in the map contains any purely geographical detail, so the area mapped probably represents somewhat over 200,000 acres in addition to the half million or so subscribed for during the first year of Penn's promotion of his colony.

In the making of his map, Holme availed himself of a variety of the means employable for cartographic representation. He plotted the courses of the rivers and larger creeks in the area for groundwork, but once that was laid down (and not too accurately in all respects), he provided only scant delineative denotation of other physical detail beyond the islands and falls in the Schuylkill and Delaware rivers, the extensive tidal marshes along the western shore of the latter stream, and the hilly elevation of Fairmount. In his display of the major part of the cultural detail, consisting of the outlines of nearly 750 tracts with the names of their holders inscribed upon them, he made use of elements that figure predominantly in the plotting of cadastral surveys. Among the inscriptions were two that identified cultural landmarks, namely, the Old Swede's Mill on Mill (Cobbs) Creek and the Free School property in Chester Township. The towns of New Castle and Bridlington (Burlington) were presented pictorially as well as by name; and in such graphic lineament as he gave to the city of Philadelphia, both on small scale in the map proper and on larger scale in the inset, he had recourse to yet another way of recording cultural detail.

Holme adapted the plan of Philadelphia from the officially plotted record of the street surveys and the allocations of city lots that had been made up to the time he composed his map. This record probably was begun by surveyor Thomas Fairman under the direction of William Markham, Penn's deputy in the colony, shortly after the location of the city site had been determined and the titles of local occupants and landholders

had been extinguished.[14] In any case, the basic scheme for laying out the city already was under way when Holme arrived, in June, 1682, and began his duties as surveyor general. At the time Markham selected the place known to the natives as Coaquanock for the site of the capital, it was covered largely by forests and thickets, and the only habitations were the wigwams of some straggling bands of aborigines and the log cabins of a few whites who had settled there under previous colonial regimes. Within six months or so after Holme took over and began working from lists of purchasers furnished to him by Philip Ford, Penn's agent in Britain, the street plan of the area lying between the Delaware and the Schuylkill was laid out, and approximately 550 lots, in sizes proportionate to the acreages they had subscribed for in the countryside, had been surveyed as bonuses to purchasers. These particulars were set forth in *A Portraiture of the City of Philadelphia,* which was drawn by Holme and published in London in 1683 as part of *A Letter from William Penn . . . to the Committee of the Free Society of Traders.*[15]

This publication also contained the following description by Holme:

The City of Philadelphia, now extends in Length, from River to River, two Miles, and in Breadth near a Mile; And the Governour, as a further manifestation of his Kindness to the Purchasers, hath freely given them their respective Lots in the City, without defalcation of any of their Quantities of purchased Lands; and as it is now placed and modelled between

---

[14] Thomas Fairman was in the country when Markham arrived, having come there by way of a Quaker settlement in West Jersey. He had advanced his fortunes considerably through his marriage to Elizabeth Kinsey, who owned a tract in Shackamaxon upon which its former owner, Lasse Cock, had erected a fine residence.

[15] More completely, the title, containing mention of the *Portraiture,* runs thus: *A Letter from William Penn Proprietor and Governour of Pennsylvania In America, To the Committee of the Free Society of Traders of that Province, residing in London. Containing a General Description of the said Province, its Soil, Air, Water, Seasons, Produce, both Natural and Artificial, and the good Encrease thereof. To which is added An Account of the City of Philadelphia Newly laid out. . . . With a Portraiture of Plat-form thereof, Wherein the Purchasers Lots are distinguished by Certain Numbers inserted, directing to a Catalogue of the said Purchasers Names* (London: Printed and sold by Andrew Sowle, 1683) .

two Navigable Rivers upon a Neck of Land, and that Ships may ride in good Anchorage, in six or eight Fathom Water in both Rivers close to the City, and the Land of the City level, dry and wholsom: such a Scituation is scarce to be parallel'd.

The Model of the City appears by a small Draught now made, and may hereafter, when time permits, be augmented; and because there is not room to express the Purchasers Names in the Draught, I have therefore drawn Directions of Reference, by way of Numbers, whereby may be known each mans Lot and Place in the City.

The City is so ordered now, by the Governour's Care and Prudence, that it hath a Front to each River, one half at Delaware, the other at Schuylkill; and though all this cannot make way for small Purchasers to be in the Fronts, yet they are placed in the next Streets, contiguous to each Front, viz. all Purchasers of One Thousand Acres, and upwards, have the Fronts (and the High Street) and to every five Thousand Acres Purchase, in the Fronts about an Acre, and the smaller Purchasers about half an Acre in the backward Streets. . . .

The City, (as the Model shews) consists of a large Front-street to each River, and a High-street (near the middle) from Front (or River) to Front, of one hundred Foot broad, and a Broad-street in the middle of the City, from side to side, of the like breadth. In the Center of the City is a Square of ten Acres; at each Angle are to be Houses for publick Affairs, as a Meeting-House, Assembly or State-House, Market-House, School-House, and several other Buildings for Publick Concerns. There are also in each Quarter of the City a Square of eight Acres, to be for the like Uses, as Moore-fields in London; and eight Streets (besides the said High-street), that run from Front to Front, and twenty Streets (besides the Broad-street) that run cross the City from side to side; all these streets are fifty feet breadth.

Philip Ford wrote to Holme concerning the *Portraiture*, stating that "it was needful that it should be printed; it will do us a kindness, as we were at a loss for want of something to shew the people," and that he "would fain know how many houses are in Philadelphia; and if the city goes on apace."[16] Holme's reply is unknown, but it has been supposed that by the end of the year 1683 there were sixty some houses scattered here and there throughout the site, much of which still was

so overgrown with trees, underbrush, and weeds that Francis Pastorius, who colonized Germantown after arriving in October of the same year, declared that on several occasions he had become lost while trying to find his way from the water front to the intersection of Third and Chestnut streets. Nevertheless, the city grew, its unprepossessing aspect changed, and by 1687, when Holme's map was published, the author of the "General Description" asserted therein:

The City is advanced in Building and Planting to admiration, both in the Front and backward, there is about 800 Houses in it. In the Center there is a large Brick House for Worship, sixty foot long and about forty foot broad. On the front of the River there is also a large Meeting-House for the same Purpose. . . . There are many fair Brick Houses building, with good Cellars, three Stories, and most have Balconies.

There is also a fair Key of about three hundred foot square, to which a Ship of 500 Tuns may lay her broad side: and more are designed to be built. There is also a Rope-walk, where abundance of Cordage for Shipping is spun.

As Holme showed in this map, not only had the limits of the city been extended to some distance beyond the Schuylkill, but also the adjacent Liberty Lands had been reserved as additional space for plots when it became apparent that the area of the city site would prove inadequate for the fulfillment of the proprietor's original plan. Penn had envisioned a spacious metropolis covering an area of 10,000 acres, to be laid off in 100 lots of 100 acres each. He intended that each purchaser of a manorial tract be awarded one of these city lots by a drawing; furthermore, the purchaser would be required to build his house in the center of his lot and surround it with gardens and orchards, to the end that Philadelphia might be a "green country town." When this scheme proved impractical, Penn abandoned it and had the Liberty Lands set aside for assignment to purchasers who could not be accommodated with lots in the city.

The order for the survey of the Liberty Lands (Fig. 3), a large tract on the northern and western sides of Philadelphia, had gone out from the proprietor to Richard Noble sometime before February 28, 1682/83, and although its boundaries had not yet been run by that date, Holme re-

---

[16] *Pennsylvania Archives*, 3rd ser. (Harrisburg: [The state], 1896 [hereafter *PA-3*]), III, 306.

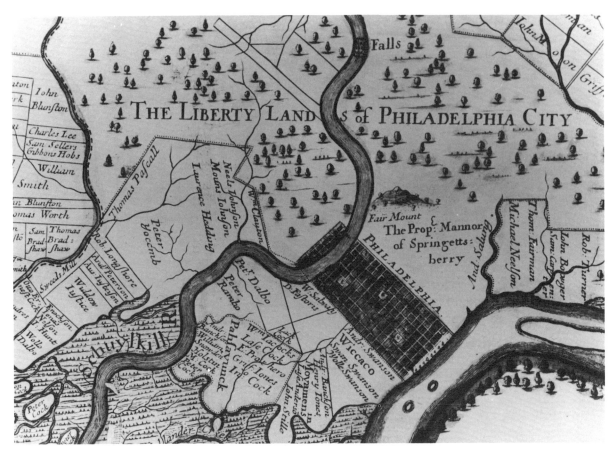

FIG. 3. Detail of Fig. 1; Liberty Lands.

quired Thomas Fairman to lay out plots therein for first purchasers.[17] Noble's return of his survey was mislaid or lost, but the original bounds of the Liberty Lands were redefined by virtue of a warrant issued for a resurvey in 1703, according to the return of which they ran as follows:

Beginning on Vine-Street, then up Delaware river to the mouth of Coach-que-naw-que; (which creek divides this from Jurian Hartfielder's land) then up the same, by the several courses, to a corner of the aforesaid land; then N. by W. by the same, 112 perches to a white oak; then N. by E. by the same, 184 perches, to a corner white oak standing by the S. W. side of Cohocksink; then down the same, on the several courses, till it intersects the line of Shackamexunk, in the fork of Cohocksink; then up the N. W. branch of said creek, to a corner white oak marked A, it being a corner of Shacamaxin and John Goodson's land; then E. N. E. by said land to B, a corner white oak, standing by a run; then down the run to C, a corner maple of the said land; then E. N. E. by the said land and Peter Cock's to D, a corner white oak, standing by Quissinomink; then up the same to E, standing by the mouth of Tackoney; then up Wiggohooking, on the several courses, to F, a white oak; it being a corner of Griffith Jones and John Moon's land; (note, this creek is the line that divides Griffith Jones's land in Bristol township, from the Philadelphia liberties) then W. by N. to G, a corner Spanish oak, it being a corner of Germantown and Bristol township; then N. E. by E. to H, a corner marked white oak, it being another corner of Germantown township; then N. W. by N. to I, a marked white oak, standing in Germantown line, and a corner of Robert Turner's land; then W. S. W. to K, a marked Spanish oak standing by the Schuylkill, another corner of Robert Turner's land; (these are the courses of the liberties on the east side of Schuylkill). Beginning now at L, a corner hickory, standing by the mouth of a small run, on the west side of Schuylkill; then W. S. W. to M, a corner of Mill Creek, alias Cobb's creek; then down the same, on the

[17] *Ibid.*, p. 311. Noble, who came over to West Jersey with John Fenwick in 1675, had served the government of the Duke of York as surveyor of Upland County, to which position he was appointed in December, 1679, succeeding Walter Wharton, deceased.

several courses to N, a Spanish oak, standing by a small run; then north to O, a marked white Oak; then east to P; then south to Q; then east to R; (note, the last five letters are courses of Thomas Paschall's land) then S. E. to S, a corner standing by Schuylkill; then up the same, on the several courses, to the city of Philadelphia; then N. 18 degrees E. to the corner of Vine-Street; then S. 72 degrees E. by Vine-Street to the place of beginning, containing 16,236 acres, 1 quarter, 20 perches.[18]

Holme laid down all these limits except the several courses extending from the mouth of Co-aquanock Creek to point *A*, along most of which the Liberty Lands bordered on Jurian Harts-felder's large tract lying between Coaquanock and Cohocsink creeks.[19] Thus, Hartsfelder's holdings were not recognized, nor were those of John Goodson and Peter Cock in Shackamaxon. The extent of Thomas Paschall's land, stated as form-ing a boundary on five courses, was indifferently defined, for the names of at least four Swedish settlers appear over parts of it. Although many tracts, both large and small, had been laid out in the Liberties prior to Holme's composition of his map (the records designated as the Old Rights, incomplete as they are, list the issuance of over 100 warrants by the end of 1686),[20] he limited his plotting of the large ones to four tracts near the falls of the Schuylkill without noting ownership,

and he titled areas "The Prop^r: Mannor of Springettsberry" and "Society [Land]" without in-dicating their extent. The scale of the map pre-vented him from delineating the small tracts. Thus his map did not constitute an adequate in-dex to the activities of the official surveyors in the Liberties during the preceding four and one-half years,[21] and it failed similarly with regard to his delineation of the tracts held or claimed by resi-dent settlers who had been granted titles thereto under previous colonial regimes.

In the province of Pennsylvania, the old settle-ments were located on a strip ranging up to three miles in width that extended along the Delaware River from Naaman's Creek, on the southern lim-its of Chester County, to Potquessin (Potques-sing) Creek, the boundary between the lower parts of Philadelphia and Bucks counties (Fig. 4). Holme's representation of the settlements within this extent of terrain affords little evidence that much of it had been peopled throughout some forty years. At first, the area was somewhat

---

[18] *Ibid.,* p. 312.

[19] The bounds of Hartsfelder's grant from Gov. Edmund Andros are given in *PA-2,* XIX, 444.

[20] The Old Rights are the records of those lands that were granted by "deeds of lease and release in the province at large, not specifying metes or bounds or situation." They are preserved in the Bureau of Land Records, Harrisburg, Pa. An index to them is to be found under "Old Rights" in *PA-3,* II and III.

[21] The Liberty Lands as ultimately allocated were plotted by John Reed in his *Map of the City and Liberties of Philadelphia, With the Catalogue of Purchasers* (Philadel-phia, 1774). From this work it can be ascertained that the four tracts of the area plotted by Holme were credited by Reed as follows: The upper one to Swan Lums (Swen Lom), the next two below to John Bowle (Bowles) and I. Scotsink (John Scotson) in one tract, and the lower one to Wood and Sharlow. Lom had his grant by action of the Upland Court, which gave him permission on Sept. 11, 1677, to take up 300 acres at a place called Wiessahitkonk (Wissahickon); see *Records of Upland Court (Memoirs of the Historical Society of Pennsylvania,* VII; Philadelphia: The Society, 1860 [hereafter *RUC*]), pp. 62–63. Bowles and Scotson's tract of 400 acres was confirmed to them by Penn on July 30, 1684 (see Patent Book A-1, p. 15, BLR). Wood and Sharlow were among the first purchasers.

FIG. 4. Detail of Fig. 1; Old Settlements.

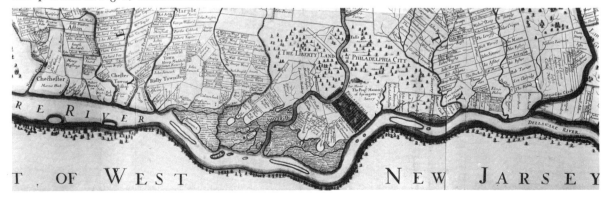

sparsely populated by the initial colonization of the Swedes, but the number of inhabitants increased during the later periods of Swedish, Dutch, and English occupancy until there were well over one hundred landholders in this area at the time Penn received his charter. The Marcus Hook region and the site of the town of Chester, two of the earliest points of colonization within the province, are altogether devoid of any indication of settlement. In the lower parts of Ridley Township, north of Crum Creek, there are only five names of old settlers, incompletely assigned to their respective holdings. All of Calcon Hook, also attributed to five men, is similarly delineated. More names appear in unnamed Kingseeing, and in Pahsavunck (Passayunk), Movamensin (Moyamensing), and Wiccaco (Wicaco), although here too there is a noticeable lack of demarcation. In Toaconinck (Tacony) Township, the northernmost place with any considerable concentration of old settlers, about half the area stands blank.

The fact of the matter is that the proprietor did not scrupulously honor the petition presented to him shortly after his arrival by the resident Swedish, Finnish, and Dutch settlers, pleading that their lands be entailed to them and their heirs forever. Consequently, although records of their titles from the Duke of York, supported by returns of surveys performed by his appointed officials, were then on file with the local court at Chester, and although Penn had issued a warrant to Holme on June 28, 1683, for surveying the holdings of the old settlers (as was stated in some of the returns of resurveys that were run for them), recognition of all such landed rights had not been forthcoming by the time Holme completed the drafts for his map. Not only were Swedes, Finns, and Dutch affected, but also some of the English landowners who had patents from the Duke of York received short shrift from Land Office officials. This seeming indifference on Penn's part is understandable: he was more concerned with seating new settlers than with adjusting claims based on old titles. In addition, it must be presumed that his Commissioners of Property, in whom he had vested the authority to approve or deny petitions, still were adhering to the policy he had set for extinguishing the titles to lands on the site they chose for laying out the provincial capital: "Herein be as sparing as ever you can," Penn then wrote Markham, "and urge the weak bottom

of their grant, the Duke of York never having had a grant from the King."[22]

Where titles had been confirmed to claimants to small tracts, their limited acreages precluded representation even on a map drawn on so large a scale as that employed by Holme. Thus, it is not difficult to see why he could not take cognizance of the density of settlement that obtained in places such as Marcus Hook, Chester, Calcon Hook, and Tacony.

Oddly, in several instances where the rights of old settlers had been recognized, the names of four or more owners are inscribed on a single tract, as in the area below Swede's Mill on Mill Creek, in Passayunk and Moyamensing, and in Shackamaxon. Multiple ownership of some tracts is supposed to have dated from the year 1677, when the Duke of York required all owners of, or claimants to, land in the Delaware regions to bring in their current titles and take out new ones, a procedure for which a rather exorbitant fee was charged. His actions seem to have had no purpose other than to increase his revenues at further expense to his subjects. Some of the claimants are presumed to have eased the burden of his exaction by pooling their interests in large tracts and paying one fee instead of the multiple fees they would have had to hand over under single ownership patents.

In marked contrast to the indifferent representation given by Holme to the plantations of the old settlers, a much more orderly and comprehensive arrangement was apparent in the tracts laid out for purchasers in the areas adjacent to those plantations and farther inland. In the lower parts of Chester County (Fig. 5), this arrangement assumed an oblique pattern that probably was imposed initially by the irregularity of the interior limits of the old settlements, and later by preferences expressed by purchasers as to the shape and situation of the tracts they desired, rather than by the nature of the terrain. This pattern extended for varying distances northward through the central valleys of the county before giving way to the strictly rectangular scheme of the compact surveys made prior to the time Holme completed his drafts.

22 J. Thomas Scharf and Thompson Westcott, *History of Philadelphia, 1609–1884* (Philadelphia: L. H. Everts & Co., 1884), I, 89 n.

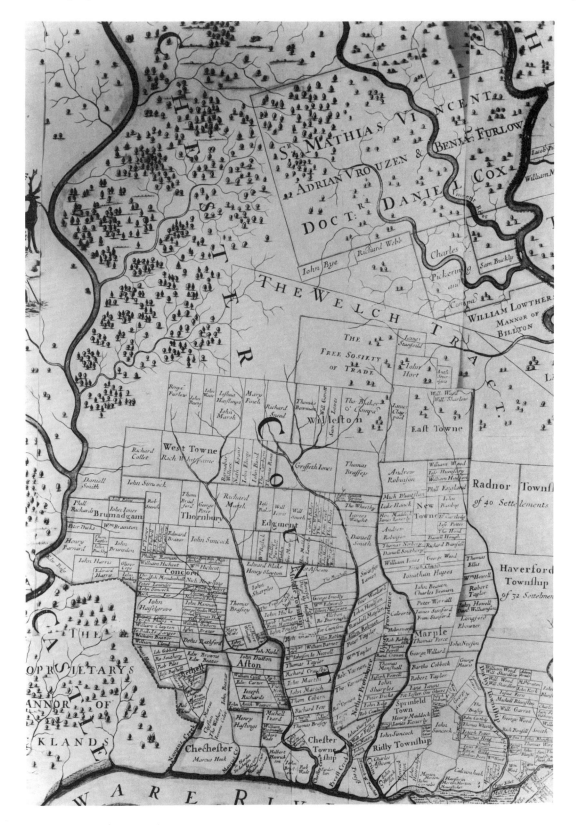

FIG. 5. Detail of Fig. 1; Chester County.

Holme's plotting of this field work indicates that the tracts generally were laid out in accordance with Penn's stipulations regarding the location of settlers by townships, as mentioned in his "Conditions and Concessions" and stated more specifically in "A Proclamation concerning Seating of Land" that was issued January 24, 1686/87:

Since there was no other thing in my Eye in the Settlement of this Province next to the advancement of Virtue, than the comfortable Situation of the Inhabitants therein and for that end, with the advice and consent of the most eminent of the first Purchasers, ordained that every Township consisting of 5000 acres should have tenn familys at the least, to the end that the Province might not lie like a Wilderness as some others yet do by vast vacant tracts of Land, but be regularly improved for the benefit of Society.[23]

But insofar as Chester County was concerned, the map failed to bear out the proprietor's statement in *A Further Account of the Province of Pennsylvania,* prepared in London in 1685, that "Our Townships lie square; generally the Village in the Center; the Houses either opposit, or else opposit to the middle, betwixt two houses over the way, for near neighbourhood." Of all townships of the county that were given delineation, only Newtown, with its townstead at the center, in which each landholder had his house lot, came close to a realization of the proprietor's conception of the ideal geographical structure of such units.[24]

How the townships of Radnor and Haverford fared in this respect cannot be ascertained from the map because of a lack of detail attributable almost entirely to the erratic behavior of deputy surveyor Charles Ashcombe. These two townships were subdivisions of the 40,000-acre Welsh Tract granted by Penn as a barony reserved for immigrants from Wales. By his warrant for its survey, dated March 13, 1684, Holme was required to locate the barony "upon yᵉ West side of Skoolkill river, running three miles upon yᵉ same & two miles backward, & then extend yᵉ parallell wᵗʰ yᵉ river six miles and to run westwardly so far till yᵉ sᵈ quantity of land be Compleatly surveyed."[25] He assigned the execution of the warrant to David

Powell, one of his deputies in Chester County, directing him "to survey and sett out unto the said purchasers the said quantity of land there, in manner as before expressed, and in method of townships lately appointed by the Governor att five thousand acres for a township and . . . make me a true return of the original field work and protracted figures, as well as the distinct quantity of each purchasor, &c."[26]

Holme made use of none of the details thus acquired for Radnor and Haverford townships beyond noting down their bounds and the number of settlements in each township, which totaled seventy-two. While it might appear that he could have inserted the lines of some of the more extensive tracts, the fact of the matter is that Ashcombe had so muddled the situation with his unauthorized surveys and refusals to make exact returns that it was impossible for Holme to supply correct detail. Although Ashcombe had given his word to Penn that he would mend his ways, the proprietor had been gone from the province less than three months when Ralph Fretwell informed the Provincial Council that the deputy had refused to run the limits of a tract whose lower line, as Holme defined it, began "halfe a mile above Concord and soe through New Towne, saveing Every man's right their already Surveyed to them in yᵉ said Towns Ship, and Soe up N.N.W. . . . to yᵉ full Extent on that side, and soe onwards untill the said Warrant be Accomplished, by a Square of ten or twelve miles, or any Quantity that may be conteined in the same."[27] Under compulsion from the Provincial Council, Ashcombe duly ran the line, and no more was heard of the matter in council discussions until September 16 of the following year, when representatives of the Welsh settlers entered a complaint stating that "their Lines runn out Regularly, according to yᵉ Govrˢ Warrᵗ, were notwithstanding, by Charles Ashcombe, Deputy Surveyor, his undue Execution of severall Later Warrants, prevented from yᵉ quiet Enjoymᵗ of yᵗ tract that was legally laid out for them." The council ordered Ashcombe to prepare and submit a draft "by a scale of 160 perches in an Inch, for all yᵉ Land Surveyed and Laid out by him Westwardly of yᵉ N. N. W. line run by Ralph ffretwell

---

[23] *PA-2,* XIX, 5–6.

[24] In Penn's terminology a township was not necessarily a municipality; that status was conferred by the courts when it became warranted for purposes of local government.

[25] George Smith, *History of Delaware County* (Philadelphia: H. B. Ashmead, 1862), p. 164.

[26] *Ibid.,* pp. 164–65.

[27] *CRP,* I, 124.

and himself, . . . & in the meantime to Survey no more Land until further Ordr."[28] Six days later Ashcombe brought in the desired draft, whereupon the council compared it with one of the Welsh Tract settlements drawn to the same scale by their principal surveyor, David Powell, found discrepancies, and recommended that an adjustment be made to the satisfaction of the Welsh settlers. The council also continued a suspension previously imposed upon Ashcombe until such time as he should make correct returns of his surveys and pay Holme his share of the surveyor's fees.

This decision came just a few days after the council had dealt with Ashcombe on charges of illegal operations in Chester Township. The plaintiffs in that instance were James Sanderland and Neels Lawson, who protested

of wrong & Injustice don to them, as being two of yᵉ six Claymers of their allotment in Chester, Alias Upland Township, by Charles Ashcome, yᵉ Deputy Survᵉyʳ, Surveying of Land Contrary to Warrᵗ, the first for Charles Pickerin[g], in Right of Eustas Anderson, near yᵉ supposed bounds of Upland & a second Warrant for Charles Pickerin[g], for part of his purchase, wᶜʰ being from yᵉ Survᵉyʳ Genᵃˡˡ, only to be Executed upon land as near as Could be to Upland, and not in yᵉ township of Upland.[29]

In this case the council had also held that the service of the warrants was irregular and declared the surveys invalid.

On February 1, 1686/87, Penn, who had the final say in these matters, directed his Commissioners of Property to rectify any wrongs that had been done the Welsh settlers by Ashcombe and to exact from him a promise to pay Holme one-third of the fees he had received. If Ashcombe complied with the order he was to be retained in his position, but if he proved to be "disorderly or Refractory you are hereby Impowered to Displace him."[30] It appears doubtful that full reparation was ever made to the Welsh settlers, for they eventually lost much of the original acreage surveyed to them through continuing encroachments on their tract by other warrantees whose rights were later confirmed by the Commissioners of Property. James Logan blamed this state of affairs on

Holme, saying that when the surveyor general was getting his map engraved in London he inserted the names of several persons in the Welsh Tract whom "he was willing to oblige there, without any manner of survey, either precedent or subsequent to that nomination, but suffered others afterwards to take it up, as all the land there is patented long ago."[31] Logan was trying to placate a disgruntled purchaser and needed a scapegoat, and in such situations it is always expedient to select one who cannot refute or deny the charges. Besides, it would not have sufficed to place the blame on Ashcombe, with whom the fault really lay, for he was merely a deputy.

As for that worthy, he was no longer in the province when the proprietor was penning his instructions to the Commissioners of Property. Having made no amends to Holme in the matter of fees, and having failed to provide him with "a mapp of his work don in Chester County" (as Holme again complained to Provincial Council on November 16, 1686),[32] Ashcombe was sued for the fees shortly thereafter by the surveyor general. The deputy thereupon put an end to his nefarious career in Pennsylvania by abandoning his estate and sailing for England. Holme completed his map as well as he could without the benefit of his former deputy's drafts. However, he had to wait nearly seven years before he obtained redress by law for the fees owed him.[33]

There appear to have been no allegations of misconduct against two of Ashcombe's fellow deputies in Chester County, David Powell and Henry Hollingsworth. The latter, reputed to have assisted Holme in laying out the ground plan of Philadelphia, is remembered in local history as a man with a wry sense of humor, which he displayed while laying out the highway from Chester

---

[28] *Ibid.*, p. 155.
[29] *Ibid.*, p. 154.
[30] *PA-2*, XIX, 6–7.

[31] *Correspondence between William Penn and James Logan, II* (Philadelphia: The Historical Society of Pennsylvania, 1872 [hereafter *WP-JL*]), 60.
[32] *CRP*, I, 193.
[33] "Tho. Holme (by his Attorney) for a debt due him from the said Cha. [Ashcombe] to the said Tho., obtained a Decree at the Provincial Court at Chester the 18ᵗʰ of the 2ᵈ month, 1692, for one Moiety of £201, 11s, and in pursuance thereof an Execution, which was levied by Caleb Pusey, Sheriff of the said County, Upon 280 Acres, part of the Premises [of the said Charles Ashcombe], and the said C. Pusey, as Sheriff of the said County, by Indenture dated 20ᵗʰ 2 mo. 1693, granted and Convey'd the said 280 Acres to the said Thos. Holme for payment of the said Debt." See *PA-2*, XIX, 297–98.

to Edgemont by planting an apple tree to mark the terminus of each mile of road except one that happened to fall on the land of one Richard Crosby in Middletown, with whom he was at odds. There he bent two saplings in such a manner as to form a cross, saying, "Richard Crosbie, thee crosses me, and I will cross thee." And it is further averred that in writing to friends in England about the incident he jokingly stated that he had planted an apple orchard nine miles long.[34]

At the time the Welsh settlers were disturbed by the Ashcombe affair they were also dissatisfied with the dividing line between Chester and Philadelphia counties. Although, soon after its establishment, the province had been declared to consist of three counties, the bounds that set these subdivisions apart were not well defined at the time. Therefore, on April 1, 1685, in response to a growing need for specific demarcation, the Provincial Council, following verbal instructions given by the proprietor just prior to his departure for England on August 6, 1684, directed that

The County of Chester . . . begin at y[e] mouth or Entrance of Bough [Bow] Creek, upon Delaware River, being the uper End of Tenecum Island, and soe up that Creek, deviding the said Island from y[e] Land of Andros Boone & Co; from thence along the severall courses thereof to a Large Creek called Mill Creek; from thence up the severall courses of the said Creek to a W. S. W. Line, which Line devided the liberty Lands of Philadelphia from severall Tracts of Land belonging to the Welch & Other Inhabitance; and from thence E. N. E. by a line of Marked trees, 120 perches more or less; from thence N. N. W. by the harford [Haverford] Township, 1000 perches more or less; from thence E. N. E. by y[e] Land belonging to Jno: Humphreis, 110 perches more or less; from thence N. N. W. by y[e] Land of Jno: Ekley, 880 perches more or less; from thence continueing y[e] said course to the Scoolkill River, w[ch] s[d] Scoolkill River afterwards to be the naturall bounds.[35]

The map reveals that the running of this line resulted in the division of the Welsh Tract in such manner that Merion Township, unnamed in the map, was placed under the jurisdiction of Philadelphia County officials. Since the Welsh purchasers had been promised autonomous government at the local level, they were much disaffected and for a time refused to recognize the validity of the

dividing line. This situation prevented Holme in some degree from supplying a more complete delineation of the areas lying athwart a portion of the boundary line between Chester and Philadelphia counties.

The broken line at the opposite side of the county, by which Holme separated it from the proprietor's Manor of Rocklands, might seem to fall rather wide of defining the arc of a circle of twelve miles' radius with New Castle as a center, which had been specified by Penn in his application for his patent as the boundary with New Castle County. This, however, was not a case of intentional default on Holme's part. The circular line constituted a factor of primary consideration in the determination of the dividing line between two provinces; and, since it had not yet been run, and could not be run legally except by surveyors acting by royal sanction, Holme doubtless felt that he could not very well presume to anticipate their findings even on a temporary basis. In the light of later developments it is apparent that he acted with discretion: a running of the circular line, made on the authority of a locally granted warrant fifteen years after he composed his map, awaited approval from the Provincial Assembly for fourteen years and then was disallowed four years later by the king. An officially authorized running of the circular line was made in 1753 — thirty-four years later — just before Charles Mason and Jeremiah Dixon undertook their survey of the boundary line between Pennsylvania and Maryland.

Although this constitutes substantial evidence of Holme's regard for cartographical veracity, the presence of the word "Improved" in the main title of his map might well raise doubts about his integrity were it not for the likelihood that the responsibility for its being there lay pre-eminently with the proprietor. Even so, the mere fact that the name of a purchaser stood inscribed on a tract did not necessarily denote improvement or occupancy. Well over half the earliest purchasers never took up the land for which they had subscribed,[36] and among those who did locate were some who let their titles lapse either by not keeping up their payments or by failing to meet the

---

[34] Smith, *Delaware County,* p. 401.
[35] *CRP,* I, 126–27.

[36] The first, second, and third "catalogues" of purchasers released by Philip Ford on July 11, 1681, Oct. 25, 1681, and April 30, 1682, respectively, listed 595 subscribers, of whom only 236 later had their names inscribed on Holme's map.

land improvement requirement within a stated period of time.

Whether or not the tracts delineated actually represented the province "as far as yet Surveyed and Laid out," as the subtitle of the map states, cannot be proved in all instances by the incomplete Land Office records. However, the surveying activities that took place in connection with a number of outlying tracts may be cited as pointing to the general dependability of Holme's map in this respect. The westernmost tract outlined in the county was the one over which he inscribed the names of "Sʳ Mathias Vincent," "Adrian Vrouzen," "Benja: Furlow [Furly]," and "Doct:ʳ Daniel Cox." Although there might seem to be a possibility that Vrouzen and Furly became associated with the tract initially on March 7, 1682, when "Benjohan Furly, of Rotterdam, in Holland, as agent for William Penn . . . conveyed five thousand acres in Pennsylvania to Burgomaster Adrian Vroesen, of the same place,"[37] the latter does not appear to have exercised his warrant for land within the tract. The first known Land Office record pertaining to the westernmost tract states that a warrant was issued to Sir Mathias Vincent for 10,000 acres on April 3, 1686.[38] This act evidently constituted part of a larger transaction completed when "William Penn by his Seperate Deeds of foeffment all bearing date the 20th April, 1686, did grant to Sʳ Mathew Vincent, Major Robert Thompson and Daniel Cox" 30,000 acres, part of which they intended as a refuge for persecuted Huguenots.[39] The minutes of the Commissioners of Property state that these 30,000 acres were laid out in one tract "Soon after the first Purchase," and this is confirmed by Holme's account submitted in 1686 for performing the survey.[40] Before he completed the drafts for his map, Holme presumably had information to the effect that Thompson's interest in the tract had been acquired by others, probably

Vrouzen and Furly; but received too late to be taken account of therein was an order from Doctor Cox that "his tract of 10,000 acres in Pennsylvania, lying between two rivers, now called Vincent river and Skulkill river, . . . be divided into two equal parts, on one of which, containing 5000 acres, several families are already planted."[41] Settlement was not permanently maintained, however, and in consequence of the failure of the grantees to fulfill this and other conditions imposed by the proprietor, Hannah Penn, in 1724, requested that James Logan take action to void the original grants of title and make the entire tract available for resale.[42]

There is more definite information regarding the circumstances connected with the survey of the adjacent Charles Pickering and Company tract, also known as the Mine Hole Tract, whose lines Holme ran personally in the summer of 1686 in order to thwart what may have been the first attempt at claim jumping in the history of mining in this country. The incident began with the disclosure by an Indian to Pickering that in a place beyond the Welsh Tract there were mineral deposits whose appearance seemed to indicate the presence of silver. Pickering went there to verify the information and came away satisfied of its truth, but he failed to keep the matter a secret. Shortly thereafter, a Bucks County resident named Robert Hall sought to obtain a warrant for a survey to be run if he should succeed in finding the site of the deposits. When the Commissioners of Property refused to issue the desired warrant, Hall found a ready ally in John Gray, alias Tatham, a chronically troublesome Bucks County landholder, who held Land Office warrants available for execution. With the help of an Indian, Gray succeeded in ascertaining the location of the mine and then induced Thomas Fairman, regularly assigned to Philadelphia County as a deputy, to go beyond the limits of former surveys and lay out 1,000 acres there.[43]

[37] J. Smith Futhey and Gilbert Cope, *History of Chester County* (Philadelphia: L. H. Everts, 1881), p. 209.

[38] "Old Rights," Chester County, *PA-3*, III, 175.

[39] Frederick Sheeder, "East Vincent Township, Chester County, Pennsylvania," *PMHB*, XXXIV, No. 1 (1910), 75.

[40] *PA-2*, XIX, 289; Phineas Bond, West New Jersey Society Papers, No. 30 (Cadwalader Collection, Historical Society of Pennsylvania; hereafter HSP). Holme's account, which is among the Bond documents, included a 10 shilling charge for executing "a large fair draught of the 30000 acres."

[41] Futhey and Cope, *Chester County*, p. 209.

[42] Sophie H. Drinker, *Hannah Penn and the Proprietorship of Pennsylvania* (Philadelphia: Privately printed, 1958), pp. 163–64. The widow Penn's intentions were thwarted by actions at law which were not resolved until years after Pennsylvania became a state.

[43] Letter from William Markham, Aug. 22, 1686, to William Penn, quoted in Nash, *PMHB*, XC (July, 1966), 330–31. For an account of John Gray and his activities in Pennsylvania, see Henry H. Bisbee, "John Tatham, Alias Gray," *PMHB*, LXXXIII (July, 1959), 253–64.

On learning of the breaches of Land Office procedure thus committed by his deputy, Holme advanced proposals to Thomas Lloyd, president of the Provincial Council, for countering Gray's action, and having obtained Lloyd's assent, he proceeded to carry them out by going up Schuylkill with an assistant to the northern limits of the John Pennington and Company grant. There he laid out contiguously, as the proprietor's instructions required all legal surveys to be made, the tract assigned in his map to William Penn, Jr., Letitia Penn's Manor of Mount Joy, and William Lowther's Manor of Billton. When these operations were completed, Holme was in a position to execute a warrant in Pickering's favor in the amount of 4,000 acres, among which he took care to include those embraced in the Fairman survey.[44] Penn was greatly incensed by Holme's actions, mainly because his proprietorial prerogative of granting mining rights had been violated. He ordered the Commissioners of Property to "put a stop to yᵉ Irregular grant that was made to Charles Pickering and John Gray, alias Jathan [Tatham]," declaring that his surveyor general "deserves to loose his office, if I am rightly informed."[45] Penn could never be quite sure, of course, that he was being "rightly informed" about what was going on in the province during his absence: there were so many talebearers, and all but a very few of them were motivated by self-interest. However, Holme succeeded in mollifying him temporarily with assurances that the survey had indeed been regularly made and that no patent had yet been issued to Pickering, nor would one be issued except at the proprietor's express order.

When Penn saw Holme's drafts for his map, however, he was displeased by the shape and size of the tract Holme had laid off for Letitia, and he made his displeasure known to his Commissioners of Property. They, in turn, in a directive dated May 11, 1688, advised Holme of it as follows:

And whereas by the advice of yᵉ Proprietary, we are given to understand that his daughter Letitia's land along the river side, is incroached upon or devoured quite, by Will. Lowthers, yᵉ which yᵉ Proprietary commands shall be rectified, and not such a slant as was sent over by yᵉ Mapp to be endured, yᵉ which thou

art hereby ordered to rectify and enlarge; and forasmuch as the Proprietary is given to understand yᵗ between Doctor Coxe's land and Samuel Buckley's land upon yᵉ Schoolekill, there is about eighteen hundred acres of land, yᵉ which land, together with yᵉ said Samuel Buckley's land and all yᵉ land thereunto contiguous, which was laid off for Charles Pickerin[g], in whose right so ever yᵉ Warrᵗ were granted, was a very irregular survey, and therefore not to be allowed of, whereupon he doth will and require, and in his name we will and require thee forthwith to survey or cause to be surveyed and laid out the said Samuel Buckley's and Charles Pickerin[g]'s land, together with yᵉ aforesaid eighteen hundred acres of land unto yᵉ Proprietary's manner of Pehkeoma [that is, Gilberts], of all which remisses thou art hereby required to make speedy execution.[46]

Other outlying grants in the same area whose boundaries had been determined were the Welsh Tract and that part of the 20,000 acres allotted by Penn to the Free Society of Traders on March 22/23, 1681, which the Society had chosen to take up in Chester County. The latter was bordered on two sides by the Welsh Tract, whose lines were run in 1684, and on a third side by the upper line of Willeston, part of which formed a boundary of the large tract inscribed "Tho: Baker [Barker] & Compa," of whose survey a return had been made on October 25, 1683.[47]

As for the situation that obtained in Brumadgam (Birmingham)[48] on the southern limits of Chester County, the Land Office records contain warrants issued for land to Richard Collet and Daniel Smith on February 10, 1684/85, and November 24, 1686, respectively, and returns of sur-

[44] Nash, *PMHB*, XC (Oct., 1966), 491–92.

[45] *PA-2*, XIX, 7.

[46] Quoted from an unidentified source by Charles Huston, *An Essay on the History and Nature of Original Titles to Land in the Province and State of Pennsylvania* (Philadelphia: T. & J. W. Johnson, 1849), pp. 71–72. Penn had originally intended that his daughter's manor should include 10,000 acres, for which amount he had issued a warrant to her on Sept. 13, 1683. See Original Purchases (BLR).

The former Pickering tract again came to the attention of the Commissioners of Property on Jan. 28, 1705/06, when "Griff Jones Producing the Pat. granted by the Prop'ry at his Departure to Edward Shippen and 15 Others for the Tract of Land lying above the Welsh Tract Called Pickering's Mines, Complains that there is an error in the Survey of it, for that upon the Resurvey to make a Partition of the Tract among the sev'l Claimers, it was found that the Lines in the Woods do not agree w'th those In the Pat." See *PA-2*, XIX, 469.

[47] Old Rights, D-62, p. 77 (BLR).

[48] "Brumadgam" is a corrupted form of "Brumwycheham," the ancient name of Birmingham.

veys made there for Thomas Taylor on December 9, 1682, Henry Barnard in June, 1684, John Binkley (Buckley) on November 8, 1684, and William Brinton in August, 1685. According to the draft that was made of Barnard's tract, it was bounded by the lands of John Harris, Edward Baly (Bailey), and Peter Dicks, just as shown on the map.[49]

Save for a few grants on its western limits, and for the manor lands set aside nearby for the proprietor's relatives, Holme's map showed Chester County as predominantly an area of small land-holdings, with a well-developed township system attestant to fairly widespread occupation and improvement. On the other hand, those areas of Philadelphia County (Fig. 6) not previously considered herein were largely taken up by grants ranging in size from 1,000 to 10,000 acres and by extensive manors reserved by the proprietor for himself and members of his family; except in the regions lying between German Township and Moreland Manor, the township system there lacked that fullness of detail indicative of extensive settlement.

Typical of the larger grants were the Manor of Moreland, patented to Dr. Nicholas More by the proprietor in November, 1682 (of which a return of survey was made on August 7, 1684); the 5,000 acres granted "to Jasper Farmer and his two Sons Rich'd and Jasper . . . On Skuylkill, On Part of the Lands Called by the Indians Umbilicamenca, without Any Other Location, Only that yᵉ Prop'ry himself marked the Place and Tree with his Own hands";[50] and a number of other tracts on and beyond the headwaters of Whitpaines (now Wissahickon) Creek. Soon after receiving his patent, Dr. More established a residence called Green Spring on the eastern side of Moreland Manor where he maintained a staff of over fifty servants for the care of his estate and the conduct of the business of the Free Society of Traders. Jasper Farmer, Sr., died at sea, en route to Pennsylvania, and his widow, arriving at Philadelphia in November, 1685, with her family and a large entourage of servants, located on the Farmer grant. By the following September she had "found as good Lime-Stone on the Schoolkill as any in the World" and was building there with it.[51] These

large tracts were otherwise mostly uninhabited; although it was not Penn's wish that they should long remain so, by his very act of granting them he had unwittingly contributed to keeping them in that state until it should please their owners to break them up into smaller units.

Similarly inconsistent with Penn's policy of requiring the Land Office to maintain contiguity of survey and settlement was his proclivity for setting aside large acreages for himself and his family as manors, most of which were reserved in Philadelphia County. His first personal pre-emption of land in the county took place in 1683 when he set up Springettsbury Manor in the Liberties adjacent to the city limits. In the course of the next three or four years, he assigned the Manor of Springfield to his wife, Gulielma Maria, the Manor of Williamstadt to his son William, Jr., and the Manor of Gilberts to himself. All three bordered on the eastern side of the main artery of inland transportation, and they, together with the previously mentioned Mount Joy Manor of Letitia Penn and the large grant made to her brother on the western side, represented a considerable extent of river frontage from which purchasers in any sizable number were excluded for a time.

It probably was on that account that the upper manors on the Schuylkill figured infrequently in the early Land Office records, which fail to substantiate a number of statements made about them that have long been accepted as factual. For example, the earliest survey of Williamstadt Manor was not run in 1704, as has been asserted on occasion; an old, extant draft of this manor shows that 1704 was the date of its resurvey by Thomas Fairman and not of its first survey.[52] Also, the story offered as an explanation for the long, narrow strip that connected Gulielma Maria's manor with the Schuylkill River has no basis in actual fact. It relates that Gulielma expressly requested that the manor be laid out with a corridor to the river so that she and her successors would always have a means of access to that stream by way of their own land. The truth of the matter is that when Fairman executed the warrants issued to the Farmers, he ran his surveys in such a way as to exceed by 2,000 acres the amount of land granted in their warrants. The result was

[49] Old Rights, D-66, p. 282 (BLR).

[50] *PA-2*, XIX, 433.

[51] "A Letter from Doctor More," *PMHB*, IV, No. 4 (1880), 451.

[52] Old Rights, B-22, p. 142 (BLR).

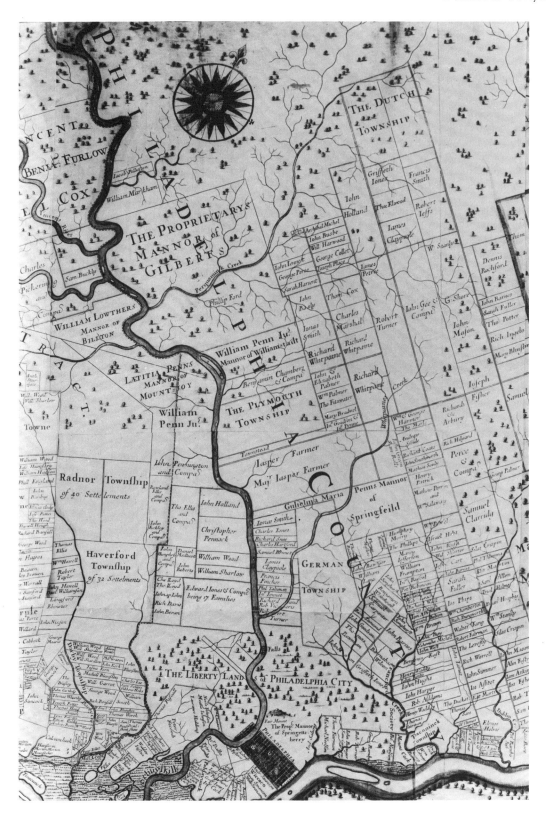

Fig. 6. Detail of Fig. 1; Philadelphia County.

the reduction of the intended size of Gulielma's manor to that extent, which explains the shape it took on the map.[53]

The assignment of the Manor of Williamstadt to the younger Penn, together with the insertion of its name, may have been a spur-of-the-moment act on the proprietor's part, for Holme seems to have left the tract blank in his drafts to await Penn's pleasure as to its disposition; he appears to have done the same with regard to the large tract he outlined above Perquamink (Perkiomen) Creek, where Penn had ordered a manor to be reserved for himself.[54] Since Penn is known to have named it after his mother's family, the Gilberts, he presumably caused its designation to be inserted in Holme's drafts after they came to hand.

As regards the newer townships of Philadelphia County, Holme left indication of their extent pretty much to "distinctions made by y[e] different Coullers," identifying only German Township, Plymouth Township, and The Dutch Township by name. He supplied no more interior detail for them than he did for Radnor and Haverford townships in Chester County. As a matter of fact, insofar as the Land Office records show, there was little material at hand for delineative purposes. These records supply no evidence of surveys run in The Dutch Township, but there is some indication from another source that the township had been at least partially subdivided.[55] In German Township only fourteen plots of very limited extent are known to have been surveyed. These had been laid off on October 24, 1683, twelve days after the proprietor had issued a warrant to Francis Pastorius for 6,000 acres in behalf of the German purchasers of Frankfort and the Dutch purchasers of Crefeld. In addition to this acreage for the use of the settlers Pastorius had brought with him, he received a warrant on February 14, 1683/84, for 200 acres in his own right. Jurian Hartsfelder (the old settler on Coaquanock

Creek), who had joined the immigrants, received a warrant on April 25, 1684, for 150 acres. When German Township was laid off shortly thereafter, no distinction was made with respect to these smaller grants, for all were included in the execution of the warrant to Pastorius and formed part of the 6,000 acres.[56]

The original surveyor was Fairman, who had not yet left known evidence of obstructiveness in public records, but who eventually acted out the same role in Philadelphia County that Ashcombe played in Chester County. Unlike Ashcombe, however, he appears to have been motivated by jealousy and resentment more than by a desire for pecuniary gain. Already a resident of Shacka-maxon in better than average circumstances when William Markham arrived, Fairman provided temporary accommodations in his home for the deputy governor, who then employed him in making examinations of the Delaware and Schuylkill river fronts preparatory to the selection of a site suitable for Penn's capital. According to a bill he later rendered to Penn, Fairman charged £10 for seven weeks' work spent in "taking the courses and soundings of the Delaware, etc.," and £6 for "taking the courses of the Schuylkill, etc., for sounding and placing Philadelphia on Delaware River, etc.," the last item seemingly for the services he rendered to Markham in laying out those parts of the city allotted to purchasers prior to Holme's arrival.[57] He also lodged Holme and his family for some months in his home and then gave the freedom of it to Penn during the first winter he spent in Pennsylvania. Having made himself of service in these and other ways, Fairman appears to have expected preferment beyond appointment to a deputyship under Holme. When that was not forthcoming, he became resentful; and, after witnessing the leniency shown toward Ashcombe's malfeasance, he took a leaf out of that deputy's book and thenceforth displayed indifference toward turning over the surveyor general's share of the fees and making returns of surveys. By the middle of July, 1686, when he laid out Plymouth Township for a group of Friends from Plymouth, England, he had be-

---

[53] Letter from Thomas Holme, March 24, 1688, to William Penn, quoted in Nash, *PMHB*, XC (Oct., 1966), 502-3.

[54] *Ibid.*, p. 503. Penn had issued a warrant in his own name on Oct. 18, 1683, for 10,000 acres "for a manor at Skoolkill on Perkioma Cr. on both sides said Creek." See Original Purchases (BLR).

[55] The source is the will of James Claypoole, dated Feb. 5, 1686/87, in which a devise of 500 acres of land "in the new Duch [Dutch] Township" was made to his son Nathaniel. See *Publications of the Genealogical Society of Pennsylvania* (hereafter *PGSP*), I (1895), 60.

[56] Lawrence Lewis, Jr., *An Essay on Original Land Titles in Philadelphia* (Philadelphia: Kay and Brother, 1880), pp. 84-87.

[57] Scharf and Westcott, *History of Philadelphia*, I, 94-95.

come a confirmed imitator of Ashcombe's tactics.[58]

The order given by the Commissioners of Property for the survey of Plymouth Township to James Fox, Francis Rawle, Richard Gove, Nicholas Pearce, John Chelson, and others required that the township be seated and improved within six months after the surveys were run. These conditions were met prior to Holme's completion of his map; but, since no details of individual surveys were provided therein, the likelihood is that Fairman failed to report them. In any case, he displayed his disregard for authority on this occasion by the manner in which he laid out the 600-acre townstead allotted to the township. Four miles long and only a quarter of a mile wide, its shape and location were both contrary to Penn's specifications regarding the structure of townships and wholly unsuitable for development as a townsite. No successful attempt was ever made to convert it to such use, and in 1690, on petition of James Fox and Francis Rawle (the principal purchasers in Plymouth Township), the tract was taken in as part of the original grant and so lost its identity.[59]

Holme instituted suit against Fairman to recover the fees due him, but he was dissuaded from continuing by influential persons in the province who may have felt that they had benefited from the deputy's practice of including acreages in excess of what the warrants specified. Ashcombe, when detected in the same practice, had also been able to rally support from some of the principal landholders of the county in which he functioned. These individuals vilified Holme in order to minimize the gravity of the charges he had preferred against that deputy to the proprietor, the Commissioners of Property, and the Provincial Council. In the end, however, the surveying practices employed by Ashcombe and Fairman produced little material gain to anyone but themselves.

Even before his map was published, Holme, furnished by the proprietor with a warrant which empowered him to run resurveys of any tracts whose original surveys he had reason to believe irregular, had begun to rectify such intentional errors. Thus, it came about that in the very process of righting the wrongs done the proprietor's interests, Holme made his map subject to correction, for all overpluses reverted to the proprietor and on resale were not always bought by the original warrantees of the tracts in which they were found.

Although little documentation is available concerning The Dutch Township, the likeliest supposition is that it was laid out for the most part in behalf of the Dutch-speaking Crefeld purchasers, who lived on the borders of Holland. Similarly, little contemporary information has come to light concerning the large tract below Perkiomen Creek on which Holme inscribed Philip Ford's name beside the fact that the surveyor general did not then know its extent or whether Penn actually wanted his London agent to have land there.[60] Apparently Penn did not, for he never patented the tract to Ford. In October, 1705, however, Ford's son produced a draft of 5,000 acres purportedly laid out there for his father and requested the Commissioners of Property to confirm the same to him. They refused to do so on the grounds that "the said 5000 acres were never Surveyed to Philip Ford as the Method of Locating Lands Indispensably Requires; But that the Draught was only Prickt off from One of the Printed Maps, w'ch Map is now in this town to be seen with Penholes Exactly Answering those in the Draught then Produced to us." Since it was "Insisted On that Philip Ford duely Paid the Charges of the Survey'r's Office as fully as if the Land had been Actually Surveyed and had an Expectation that he was fully Secured of it in that Place without further trouble," the commissioners referred the matter to the proprietor,[61] who was hardly in a position to give favorable consideration to the claim. Pursuant to Penn's order, a resurvey of his son's manor had been run in May, 1704, in the amount of 10,000 acres, which took in everything from the Plymouth Township line to Gilberts Manor, including a former grant to Ben-

[58] Nearly twenty years later, on an occasion when Fairman was in trouble with Penn, he did not hesitate to remind the proprietor of his services "at Governor Markham's first arrival" and of his "unprofitable travels with Thomas Holme, . . . who at last died my debtor as per account one hundred and forty-seven pounds, of which I never had a penny." The veracity of this last statement may perhaps be given proper assessment when it is considered in conjunction with James Logan's estimate of the man who gave it utterance: "Had he any truth in him he would show it to thee." See *WP-JL*, I, 49 and 103.

[59] *PA-2*, XIX, 35. Neither Fox nor Rawle, nor any of the other patentees named, have any surveys credited to them in the "Old Rights."

[60] Letter from Thomas Holme, March 24, 1688, to William Penn, quoted in Nash, *PMHB*, XC (Oct., 1966), 505.
[61] *PA-2*, XIX, 464.

jamin Chambers previously abrogated by Penn.[62] Almost immediately after the resurvey was completed, his somewhat wayward son, who was playing the prodigal in his father's province at the time, sold the manor to Isaac Norris and others.

An actual example of a tract that was regularly laid out and then forfeited by the warrantee for failure to meet the conditions regarding improvement is provided by the uppermost of the two tracts laid off above the Manor of Gilberts. The attendant circumstances are known from a directive that was issued by William Markham, acting as a Commissioner of Property, to Holme on May 9, 1689:

Whereas there was fformerly a tract of land of three thousand acres Lay'd out on yᵉ Skulkill ffor Wᵐ Markham Purchᵈ adjoyning to yᵉ Proprietary Mannour of Gilberts as it now stands in yᵉ printed Mapp of yᵉ Improved part of Pennsilvania ffor yᵉ Laying out of wᶜʰ there was no warrᵗ but only a verball dedᵉ to yᵉ Survey'ˢ Deputy; And whereas there is five hundred acres of Land Contiguous unto yᵉ aforesaid tract wᶜʰ was fformerly layd out unto Jacob Pollisson [Pellison] by vertue of a warrᵗ ffrom yᵉ Commissioners bearing date yᵉ 7ᵗʰ day of yᵉ 12ᵗʰ month [February 7] 1686/7 upon Rent and yᵉ said Jacob Pollisson being absent out of the Province and hath been about Two Years and no Improvement being made thereon according to the Regulations; These are therefore in yᵉ Proprietors name to will and There to Make return to yᵉ Secretarys office of both the aforesaid tracts of Land in one tract in yᵉ name and for yᵉ aforesaid Wᵐ Markham as part of his purchase with yᵉ Exact bounds and time they were lay'd out.[63]

As has already been stated (see n. 5 above), the return made of the survey of this Pellison tract appears to have furnished Holme with the last element of cultural detail that he inserted in his drafts prior to sending them to Penn.

Holme's delineation of Bucks County (Fig. 7) reveals that, in most areas, the tracts were laid out in such fashion that they readily resolved themselves into groups resembling patterns of surveys previously observed in Chester and Philadelphia counties. For the area between Neshaminy Creek and the Delaware River, his map has an aspect very much like that which it presents in the lower parts of Chester County; and on the other side of

Neshaminy Creek its display of the lower areas closely resembles the layout of the tracts across the line in Philadelphia County between Moreland Manor and German Township, while its plotting of the upper areas corresponds with the disposition of surveys made above Moreland Manor.

In Bucks County, as in Philadelphia County, the amount of land available for immediate purchase and settlement was reduced by the proprietor's manorial reservations. Pennsbury, the first manor to be set aside, was also chosen as his country seat. The construction of the manor house, begun in 1683, was incomplete at the time Holme forwarded his drafts to Penn, and perhaps did not figure in the detail on that account. According to Holme's delineation, by the end of the year 1686, two tracts had been granted to others within the confines of the manor: one to James Harrison, Penn's steward in charge of the erection of the manor house, and the other to George Heathcote. The Manor of Highlands appears to have been laid out at some time in the period of Penn's first visit to his province, for mention of its lower line as a boundary has been found in a deed issued for the adjacent tract taken up by Richard Huffe (Hough) prior to the end of the year 1683.[64]

The upper lines of Highlands Manor and the unnamed township beside it (Wrightstown) [65] were regarded by the Delaware Indians as above the limits of the land purchased by William Markham on July 15, 1682, which lay between the falls of the Delaware and Neshaminy Creek. Accordingly, in the summer of 1686 they protested that encroachments had been made by Israel Taylor, deputy surveyor of Bucks County, on lands to which they had not relinquished title, and they threatened to kill Taylor if they should detect him in the act of running any more surveys there.[66] The Delaware Indians actually had no tribal equity in the land in dispute. Those rights had been abrogated by the Iroquois six years be-

---

62 Old Rights, B-22, p. 142 (BLR).

63 In "Notes and Queries," *PMHB*, XXXIII, No. 3 (1909), 375.

64 Oliver Hough, "Richard Hough, Provincial Councillor," *PMHB*, XVIII, No. 1 (1894), 21; Patent Book A-2, p. 166 (BLR).

65 Wrightstown was so called prior to June 9, 1686, when Bucks County Court of Quarter Sessions ordered that a road be laid out thence to the ferryhouse on the Delaware opposite Burlington. See *Records of the Courts of . . . Bucks County, Pennsylvania* (Meadville, Pa.: Colonial Society of Pennsylvania, 1943 [hereafter *RCBC*]), p. 49.

66 Letter from William Markham, Aug. 22, 1686, to William Penn, quoted in Nash, *PMHB*, XC (July, 1966), 334.

Fig. 7. Detail of Fig. 1; Bucks County.

fore Penn received his charter, when they attained control over the Delawares as a result of their conquest of the Susquehannocks, who, prior to that time, had held the Delawares in subjection. Nevertheless, when the area in dispute was eventually acquired for settlement through the meanly contrived effectuation of the terms of the so-called "former agreement" of 1686 (that is, by the Indian Walk Purchase of September 19/20, 1737), provincial officials recognized the Delawares as rightful owners of the land and started the walk from a point near Wrightstown.

Israel Taylor was, like Ashcombe and Fairman, a source of trouble and vexation to Holme, and for the same reasons. The surveyor general brought suit against him for delinquency in the return of surveys and the remittance of fees. On October 8, 1686, Holme produced his commission from Penn in Bucks County court and showed that, by its terms, Taylor was accountable to him. The court accordingly found that the deputy should make returns of his surveys and pay Holme the monies due him. Taylor then promised that he would "p[er]fect al his Surveys & make returns thereof in three months time & that he will make Returns of wrights town in twoo weeks time: & that he will give an account in ten days time of all the lands he has surveyed or begun to Survey Since he Came into office & the time when it was surveyed."[67] He must have kept his promise to the extent of providing Holme with information of a sort that enabled him to amplify his map considerably in Bucks County, since the Old Rights records list only seventeen returns of surveys made before the end of the year 1686. Taylor, however, appears to have been remiss in furnishing complete information about the surveys he had run in Wrightstown, and he did not submit an account of his surveys and resurveys until sometime after March 17, 1687, the date of the last of a total of eighty-seven he reported as having made since April 5, 1683.[68] As for his performance in the matter of discharging his debt to Holme, the latter reported about eighteen months after the court had found in his favor that he entertained little hope of recovering what was due him.[69]

Although Holme suffered financially from his unfortunate experiences with his obstructive deputies, his disclosures of their machinations redounded to the public weal, for they resulted in the passage of a law by the General Assembly on May 10, 1688, for the regulation of the conduct of surveyors and the establishment of standard fees. The text of the law, although brief, takes note of the pecuniary advantages accruing to persons holding the position of surveyor and of the injustices that had been done by some of them to purchasers:

Whereas . . . The surveyor's Fees, (being the principal office of profitt in this government) hath not been hitherto by anie Law reduced to an establishment: And the generalitie of the freemen frequentlie complaining not onlie of their Neglect and Undue proceedures, but of the excess of the fees and sums demanded and Exacted for their Service therein, And to prevent farther uncertainties and to avoid as much as in us lyes any cause of Complaint therein for the time to come, and yet Continue a Competent encouragement to such an Officer, *Be it enacted . . .* That the Surveyor's Fees for any Survey which shall be made or Done within this Province and Territories for the future Shall be as follows, and such as shall be Convicted of taking more Shall Refund the Same and Shall be Dismissed their Imploy:

	Lb	S.	P.
Survey of a single one hundred acres and return thereof	00	6	00.
Survey of a lesser quantity to an acre and return	00	6	00.
Survey of each one hundred above a single one hundred	00	3	00.
Survey and return of any Lesser quantity to half a lott	00	6	00.
Survey and return of half a lott, back lott, or Lesser quantity, each	00	3	00.[70]

Save for a single exception, the townships of Bucks County were distinguished entirely by the "distinctions made by yᵉ different Coullers." That exception, Newtown, showed several features not found in any of the townships previously considered. One was its unusual layout, which exemplified the alternate form of township structure of which Penn wrote in *A Further Account of the Province of Pennsylvania:*

We have another Method, that tho the Village be in

---

[67] *RCBC*, pp. 69–70.

[68] "Isreall Taylors Account of Survey in yᵉ County of Buckes," in Old Rights, D-67, p. 167 (BLR).

[69] Letter from Thomas Holme, March 24, 1688, to William Penn, quoted in Nash, *PMHB*, XC (Oct., 1966), 505.

[70] *Charter to William Penn, and Laws of the Province of Pennsylvania* (Harrisburg, 1879), pp. 187–88.

the Center, yet after a different manner: Five hundred Acres are allotted for the Village, which among ten families, comes to fifty Acres each: This lies square, and on the outside of the square stand the Houses, with their fifty acres running back, where ends meeting make the Center of the 500 Acres as they are to the whole. Before the Doors of the Houses lies the high way, and cross it, every man's 450 of Land that makes up his Complement of 500, so that the Conveniency of Neighbourhood is made agreeable with that of the Land.

Newtown was an exact example of this arrangement in which, except for the intervening highway, each landholder had his town lot contiguous to his larger tract.

Another feature was the presence of the word "Governors," which denoted the retention of a town lot and 450 acres in the right of the proprietor, the only instance of such reservation to appear in the map. The proprietor had, from the outset, intended that he should be represented thus in each township. Holme, however, had not always provided for the proprietor's interests in this manner, as he admitted when he was called to account by Penn for the omissions: "As for the 500 acres in every Township reserved for thee, [it] was sometimes observed, but when purchasers came in and were hard to be pleased (as they are still more and more) I was fain to let them have such reservations, but for the future shall not, come what will."[71]

It is quite obvious from the map that adjacent, unnamed, and only partially mapped Wrightstown was begun on the same plan as Newtown. However, the square laid out in unnamed Southampton Township, with the names of Enoch Flower and John Swift inscribed across its lower parts and four rectangular lots outlined in one of its upper quarters, doubtless represented the partial application of an altogether different concept of township layout. At least one mention of the plot has been found in early Land Office records.[72] It underwent gradual development and appears in present-day maps as Southampton.

No further evidence of similar attempts to meet the proprietor's requirements for improving the province is present in Holme's mapping of Bucks County. In fact, little progress had yet been made

in settlement immediately above Southampton Township, and virtually none in the extreme upper areas of the county, where 5,000-acre tracts had been granted to Thomas Hudson and Colonel Mildmay (K. Mildmay & Company).[73] Hudson's right to his tract was then being contested by Dennis Rochford (Rotchford), whose name appears on an adjacent tract just across the line in Philadelphia County. In 1683 Hudson and Rotchford had received warrants almost simultaneously from Holme for 5,000 and 3,000 acres, respectively, which were directed for execution to Israel Taylor, the official deputy for Bucks County. But Rotchford took his warrant to Fairman, the Philadelphia County deputy, who went at once into Bucks County and executed it there. At a later date Taylor, unaware that Fairman had been in the same area before him, laid out the Hudson grant, taking in 2,000 of the 3,000 acres Fairman had measured off for Rotchford. The dispute was not resolved until shortly after May 28, 1692, when Hudson received confirmation of his grant of 5,000 acres from the Commissioners of Property. He retained possession until 1697, when he disposed of the tract to five purchasers from Long Island, who requested that it be surveyed according to their several interests therein.[74]

Approximately ten years earlier, either Hudson or his resident agent, Jacob Hall, appears to have been interested in acquiring the Mildmay tract. Hall, who was established on the 1,000-acre Hudson tract on Delaware River (which served as a base for trading with the Indians), evidently had inspected the tract and then decided not to take it up, "pretending the Lands not good."[75] This is the last reference to the Mildmay tract in known records of that period. It may have reverted to the proprietor or changed hands as the Hudson tract did.

Thus these large grants, like others of equal or greater extent on the outer perimeter of surveyed

---

[71] Letter from Thomas Holme, May 24, 1687, to William Penn, quoted in Nash, *PMHB,* XC (Oct., 1966), 493.

[72] *PA-2,* XIX, 456.

[73] Penn's order to Holme regarding the survey of the Mildmay tract, dated April 15, 1686, went as follows: "Whereas Col. Henry Mildmays daughter Katherine [and nine others] . . . have bought & payd me for five thousand acres of land . . . These are to order & command thee or thy Deputy to lay or cause to be layd out yᵉ said land as near as may be to the lands of tho [Thomas] Hudson in yᵉ County of Bucks." See Old Rights, D-69, p. 108 (BLR).

[74] *PA-2,* XIX, 87 and 434; *RCBC,* p. 309.

[75] Letter from Thomas Holme, March 24, 1688, to William Penn, quoted in Nash, *PMHB,* XC (Oct., 1966), 504.

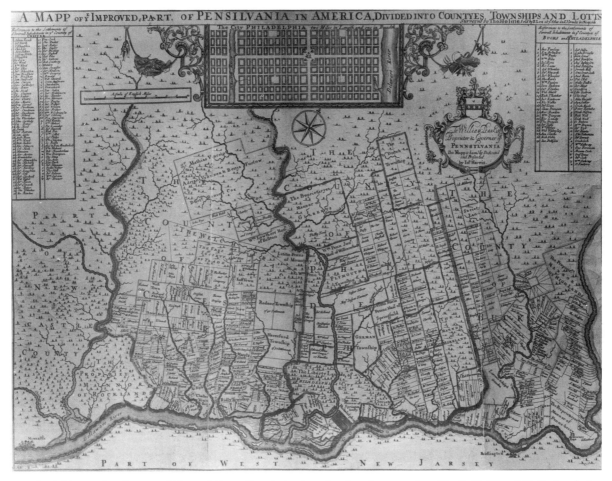

FIG. 8. *A Mapp of y^e Improved Part of Pennsilvania in America.* London, *ca.* 1697. H. 16¼", W. 20⅝" (to border). Smaller-scale revision of Green-Thornton map; published by John Harris. (Philip Lea issue; photostatic copy, Library of Congress.)

lands, were not improved as stated in the title of the map and obviously did not serve the best interests of the proprietor. But, in any case, Penn at long last had his map, and to him that undoubtedly compensated for a great deal that had gone contrary to his expectations. Holme had expended considerable time and effort on its composition and felt that he had done rather well in the process, but Penn apparently allowed him nothing for his work except a few copies of the map, and the surveyor general anticipated no demand for these in Pennsylvania.[76]

The John Harris edition of the Holme map, an amended, smaller-scale copy of the Green-Thorn-

ton edition (Fig. 8), was also issued without indication on its face of the time of publication; and, since it had no dated descriptive matter appended to it as the other had, the approximate date of its appearance must be deduced largely from internal evidence. The amendments were very few: the reassignment of the holdings of Joseph Steedman in Springfield Township, Chester County, in consequence of the division of his estate among his heirs after his death in 1688; the assignment of a tract—not previously recorded—to Luke Brinsto (Brindley?) in Moyamensing and of an additional one to Mouns Cock in Passayunk;[77] and the

---

[76] *Ibid.,* p. 502. In this connection Holme also mentioned Robert Longshore, his deputy surveyor general, from which it must be taken that the latter had assisted substantially in the preparation of the map.

[77] No mention of a Luke Brinsto has been found in any of the Land Office and Philadelphia County records consulted. He may have been the Luke Brindley who served in Bucks County as a deputy sheriff in 1684. Holme undoubtedly overlooked Mouns Cock's tract when he prepared the

denotation of the site of "the Governors House" in Pennsbury Manor. On the other hand, the deletions were quite numerous—fifty-two, in fact —some of which undoubtedly resulted from lack of space or because of oversight, and the rest from sales of tracts or the deaths of their original owners. While available records do not afford irrefutable evidence in every case, there is enough to warrant the conclusion that all the owners whose names were omitted from the detail of the Harris map were in possession of tracts before Holme completed the drafts for his map. Also, the more significant of these omissions came about as the result of circumstances that affected ownership status prior to the end of 1696; this evidence will presently be set forth *in extenso* for each of the three original counties. Although the supplier of the information on which the additions and major omissions were based is unknown, it was neither Holme nor his deputy Longshore, for both had died before the above-mentioned date, the former in 1695, the latter the previous year.

There were at least three issues of the Harris map. The first was denoted in the upper right-hand corner as having been "Sold by P. Lea at y° Atlas and Hercules in Cheapside." Harris is known to have been in business in London as a bookseller and dealer in maps from 1685 to 1698; Lea is supposed to have engaged in the same trade until sometime in 1699.[78] Consequently, the first issue of the map could not have appeared after 1698, nor could Lea's name have remained on the plate as its seller for any extended length of time. After Lea had passed from the London scene, the lettering pertaining to him was obliterated, and a rectangular box was inserted in the lower left-hand part, between the frame and the Delaware River, in which it was stated that the map was being "Sold by Geo. Willdey at the Great Toy, Spectacle, China-Ware and Print Shop at the corner of Ludgate Street near St. Paul's, London." Willdey, about whom virtually nothing is known, probably published his issue soon after 1699. His notice was, in turn, removed from the plate at an undetermined date when a third issue was printed

for an anonymous sponsor. Apart from these changes, no alterations were made in the plate.

The reduced scale of the Harris map obliged its engraver to list the owners of 175 tracts in two insets and to key them to their respective holdings by numerals and letters, an arrangement that undoubtedly widened the range of possibility for omissions through oversight. By referring to the Green-Thornton edition, it is found that the names of owners or part owners dropped from various tracts in the Chester County detail were John Blunston and William Smith, on the lower course of Mill Creek in Darby; Henry Sweeft (Swift), in Springfield; Lanchlet Loyd (Lancelot Lloyd), (Joseph) Allebon (Allibone), and (John) Boweter (Bowater), adjacent to David Ogden, in Middletown; James Kenerly (Kennerley), joint owner with Henry Maddock, in Newtown; (John and/or Andrew) Henreck (Hendricks), holding jointly with W. Pretchet (Pritchett), in Chester Township; Jaco(b) Chanler (Chandler) and James Brown, in Chichester; Edward Brown, joint owner with Edward Beazor (Bezer), in Bethel; Thomas Martin, John Sanger, and George Stroud (Strode), in Concord; and Edward Brazor (Bezer) and Edward Turner, in Thornbury. In addition, the Green-Thornton edition recorded the names of (James) Sandarlan (Sanderland) and (Richard) Townsend, the former on a sizable tract of undefined limits in Chester Township, the latter on a small plot in the same municipality.

As none of the known records pertaining to the tract on Mill Creek over which Holme inscribed the name of John Blunston confirms his ownership of it at any time, it has been assumed that its omission from the Harris map was intentional.[79] William Smith's tract on Mill Creek, for which a return containing a draft of the same was made on November 10, 1682, became the property of Anthony Morgan on October 15, 1692, after Smith's death.[80] In the case of

---

drafts of his map, for it was surveyed at least three years prior to their composition, as the patent Cock received for it in 1693 reveals. See Letter of Attorney, E-3, V, 26 (BLR).

[78] Henry R. Plomer, *A Dictionary of the Printers and Booksellers Who Were at Work in England, Scotland and Ireland from 1668 to 1725* (Oxford: Oxford University Press, 1922), pp. 147 and 185.

[79] Benjamin H. Smith, who made an intensive search of Land Office and Chester County records in preparation for the composition of his *Atlas of Delaware County, Pennsylvania* (Philadelphia, 1880), attributed the ownership of this tract to Peter Erickson on the basis of a patent issued to him by the Upland Court on Nov. 30, 1681. Smith notes that 120 acres of this tract were sold to Joseph Wood on May 29, 1695 (see Pl. 10 of the *Atlas*).

[80] Old Rights, D-82, p. 71 (BLR); *Records of the Courts of Chester County, Pennsylvania* (Philadelphia, 1910 [hereafter *RCCC*]), p. 274.

Henry Swift, no contemporary documents have been located that certify him as a landholder in Chester County before Holme completed his drafts. However, he is known to have come to the county about the year 1682, ostensibly indentured to Henry Maddock.[81] In payment of their passage, such bound persons were obliged to labor for a stated number of years, usually no more than five, and at the end of their terms of servitude were given outright ownership of a tract of up to 50 acres. Henry Maddock is known to have made a deed of gift to Swift for 32 acres in Springfield Township, and a survey presumably must have been run by a Land Office deputy, but neither deed nor return of survey is known to be among extant records. In view of the size of the tract given Swift by Maddock, it is likely that the former had discharged his obligation in less than the usual period for which servants were indentured and had received his gift of land in three years or so after coming to Chester County. The land embraced by the deed of gift eventually was confirmed to Swift by Mordecai Maddock, Henry's son and heir, and as the former indentured servant did not transfer title to his holdings in Springfield Township until 1716, his name could readily have been denoted in the keyed inset for Chester County.[82] The name of Lancelot Lloyd (whose tract of 100 acres bordering the property of William Johnson between Chester and Ridley creeks was surveyed on April 11, 1684) also appears to have been overlooked, for there is no known record of a property transfer involving his tract prior to 1696.[83] Joseph Allibone was designated on the draft of Oswin Musgrave's tract dated February 4, 1683/84, as holding the adjoining tract below, but as its outlines were not given on the Harris map, and as Allibone's name did not figure in a list of Chester County taxables for 1693, their omission may have been intentional.[84] John Bowater received a deed from David Ogden on November 24, 1685, for 50 acres in the tract that had been surveyed to the latter on June 27, 1684, and remained in possession there until August 9,

1704, when he sold to Joseph Baker.[85] Here, too, the engraver failed to insert the outlines of the tract as well as the name of its owner, not for lack of space, perhaps, but through oversight. The omission of James Kennerley's name in Newtown probably was owing to lack of space, for he and Henry Maddock were issued joint deeds of lease and release on March 21/22, 1681, for 1,500 acres in Chester County; and, according to an official 1689 record of landholders in that county, they had taken up 1,480 acres by Land Office calculation and were paying taxes on them.[86] The Hendricks-Pritchett property, title to which dated from before the time Holme completed his map, was listed in the same 1689 record as then being held jointly; but as the first surname did not appear in combination with Pritchett's in the 1693 tax list for Chester County, the partnership presumably had been dissolved in the meantime. There does not appear to be any record of the original survey of Jacob Chandler's tract in Chichester, but since it was mentioned in Chester County court proceedings held in June, 1686, as one of those through which the recently opened road from Bethel to Chichester passed and was resurveyed in his name in 1703, its failure to receive denotation of outline and ownership in the Harris map must be attributed to an oversight.[87] James Brown also was one of those named in the above Chester County court proceedings held in June, 1686, through whose land the Bethel-Chichester road passed; but, since no subsequent records pertaining to the history of the tract seem to be available, it is not known why Brown's name did not appear on the Harris map.[88] Edward Brown and Edward Bezer had been issued a warrant jointly for a 500-acre tract in Bethel for which a return of survey was made on July 28, 1684, and its area was not reduced in the Harris map, although they sold three-fifths of the land in 1695 and 1696. Brown's name, therefore, was not inserted because of lack of room.[89] Thomas Martin, who received a deed from John Mendenhall on No-

[81] *PA-2*, XIX, 600.

[82] Deed Book A, Pt. II, p. 226 (Recorder's Office, Chester County Court House, West Chester, Pa.); *PA-2*, XIX, 600.

[83] Old Rights, D-74, p. 92 (BLR).

[84] Old Rights, D-73, p. 81 (BLR); Futhey and Cope, *Chester County*, pp. 31–33.

[85] *RCCC*, p. 149; Old Rights, D-65, p. 43 (BLR); Smith, *Atlas*, Pl. 10.

[86] *PA-2*, XIX, 294; Futhey and Cope, *Chester County*, pp. 31–32. Smith, *Atlas*, Pl. 12 shows lots in Newtown townstead assigned jointly to Maddock and Kennerley.

[87] *RCCC*, p. 71; Smith, *Atlas*, Pl. 17.

[88] *RCCC*, p. 71.

[89] Original Purchases (BLR); Old Rights, D-62, p. 52 (BLR); Smith, *Atlas*, Pl. 2.

vember 27, 1686, for a parcel of his grant in Concord and who apparently did not sell any of it prior to 1696, was not given representation of his tract in the Harris map,[90] although room could have been found for its identification in the inset. In April, 1688, John Sanger (a landholder in Concord) signed a petition presented in Chester County court opposing the road that had been laid out through the township in October, 1687; but, since his tract was located among others known to have been surveyed several years prior to Holme's completion of his map, it would be safe to assume that his land also had been laid out.[91] Since he retained the property into the next century, denotation of his ownership may have been omitted from the Harris map through oversight. George Strode acquired a 300-acre tract in Concord by virtue of a warrant issued to him on February 6, 1682/83. On November 27, 1686, he transferred 100 acres each to Goddin (Godwin) Walter and Thomas Hale.[92] None of the remaining land changed ownership before 1701, from which it may be concluded that the engraver either passed over or disregarded Strode's name. No Land Office record of a survey to Edward Bezer made in Thornbury has been found. His ownership of the tract ascribed to him by Holme in the first edition is supported, however, by an entry in the Chester County court proceedings of March, 1688, in which he was mentioned as one of those whose land was traversed by the new road from Thornbury to Chichester.[93] Here, as in the case of Sanger, it seems reasonable to assume that the survey of his tract had been made before Holme completed his map. What reason the engraver had, if any, for omitting his name has not been determined. Edward Turner, whose tract in Thornbury had been surveyed on February 20, 1685/86, died prior to May 10, 1688.[94] The same sort of circumstance accounted for the absence from the smaller map of James Sanderland's name. On February 22, 1683/84, he received a warrant from the Commissioners of Property for a resurvey of his 600 acres, but by 1693 James Brown was designated in the Chester County tax list as being accountable for the taxes assessed against the "Ja. Sanderling Estate."[95] Because of damage to the original warrant issued to Richard Townsend for 50 acres in Chester Township, its date appears in Land Office records as April 9, 168–, but it is known that a survey of the tract was run before December 15, 1685, when Thomas Brasey entered a caveat against its return. On this basis Holme felt that representation of the tract in the Green-Thornton edition was warranted.[96] Why it was not included in the detail of the Harris map has not been ascertained.

The latter map presented other points of difference in Chester County, most of which were of a minor nature. Its engraver omitted the place names "Bethel" and "Tenecunck" (Tinicum), and as a result of a misconstruction which he placed upon the word "Calcoonhook" (Calcon Hook), it was converted from a place name into "Col. Hook," making of it a designation indicating the presence of an additional landholder.

The names of Philadelphia County owners presented in the detail of the Green-Thornton edition but not in the Harris map were: Peter Cock on Schuylkill Island and Aharommony Island; Andres Boon (Boone) and Ernest Cock on Minquas Island, in the marshes of the Schuylkill; Lase Anderson (Lasse Andreis), in Moyamensing; E(van) Prothero, in Passayunk; W(illiam) Jacocks, on part of the land credited in the latter delineation to Lasse Cock, also in Passayunk; Jonas Nelson, a little below the sizable tract of the Widow Justice; And(res) Salung .(Saling) on a tract of undefined limits in Springettsbury Manor next to Shackamaxon; Elinor Holme, on the lower reaches of Dublin (also known as Pennypack) Creek; John James, a short distance above the last-named; John Tibby, between the tracts of Thomas Cross and Giles Knight, on Poquessing Creek; John Goodson and John Denne (Denny?), on the tract lying at the southeastern corner of Plymouth Township; Robert Jeffs and Francis Smith, just below The

---

[90] *RCCC*, p. 83; Smith, *Atlas,* Pl. 5.

[91] *RCCC*, p. 132.

[92] Old Rights, D-82, p. 128 (BLR) ; *RCCC*, p. 85; Smith, *Atlas,* Pl. 5.

[93] *RCCC*, p. 146.

[94] Patent Book A-1, p. 269 (BLR) ; *PGSP*, I, 64. It should be noted, however, that the names of some owners who are known to have died before the supposed date of the publication of the Harris map were included in its detail.

[95] Old Rights, D-82, p. 99 (BLR) .

[96] Old Rights, D-69, p. 158, and D-66, p. 64 (BLR) ; *PA*-2, XIX, 41.

Dutch Township; and William Markham and Jacob Pelleston (Pellison), on the Schuylkill above Gilberts Manor.

Peter Cock, Andres Boone, and Ernest Cock (also known as Otto Ernest Cock) had obtained their island holdings through titles that were older than Penn's charter.[97] Peter Cock died before March 4, 1689, when, by the terms of his will, he left Schuylkill Island to his son Gabriel and Aharommony Island, on which he had lived, to his widow.[98] Andres Boone died before June 1, 1696, and left his part of Minquas Island to his widow.[99] Ernest Cock, by virtue of a conveyance that passed under the hand of Gov. Francis Lovelace on June 7, 1672, acquired that half of Minquas Island that Peter Stuyvesant had patented to Maes Hanson on May 10, 1663,[100] and he continued in possession there for some years into the next century. Since no notice was taken of the changes in ownership status mentioned above, it is quite likely that Ernest Cock's name was passed over for lack of room on the plate. Lasse Andreis's name over the tract "of marrish or meddow betweene the hollanders Kill & Rosemonds kill on the west syde of this River of delowar" that had been granted to him by the Upland Court on April 3, 1678, was rightfully omitted, for he had died in the fall of 1689, leaving this property to Mitchell Nielson and Andrew Wheeler.[101] Evan Prothero received a deed on July 8, 1684, for his 100 acres in Passayunk, which were bounded for the most part by the lands of Lasse and John Cock, and on July 8, 1689, he deeded them to Thomas Waite.[102] Because Jacocks failed to make improvements and pay quitrent on the tract between the Schuylkill and Delaware rivers adjoining Peter Rambo's land (which had been surveyed to him by Richard Noble under the authority of the Upland Court prior to the date of Penn's charter), he had long since forfeited his right to it.[103] Jonas Nelson, whose name appeared

in a list of early settlers made in 1684, died in 1693.[104] On June 24, 1687, the Commissioners of Property ordered a resurvey of Andres Saling's land "lying between ye North End of Philadelphia and ye Gover^rs Mill" because they had been "Credibly Informed yt ye And^w Salung hath or is about to Dispose of Severall peeces or parcells of yt Land to severall, before ye overpluss thereof be Divided from his true quantity."[105] Why his name did not appear there in the Harris map has not been ascertained, for no further mention of him in connection with this tract has been found in the Land Office records. Elinor Holme, whose name previously appeared on part of the 1,635-acre grant laid out for her father on Dublin Creek on September 11, 1683, entered into an agreement with him on January 14, 1694/95, whereby she surrendered to him all her rights there.[106] John James received a warrant on September 12, 1684, for a tract of 300 acres in Philadelphia County, which he requested to be laid out "as near to ye River as may be," and Holme was directed "forth^th to survey or cause to be survey'd unto him ye s^d Number of Acres,"[107] whose subsequent disposition has not been determined. John Tibby, a first purchaser, died not long before November 10, 1688, when his will was proved, and his tract had changed hands.[108] John Goodson (apparently a co-owner in this instance with John Denny [?], although not so indicated in any known warrant), Thomas Fitzwater, and Zachariah (?) Whitpaine were named in the draft of 200 acres surveyed to Mary Bradwell by virtue of a warrant dated February 4, 1685/86, as owning one of the adjoining tracts. Although the draft was not dated, it is known from another source that the survey was run on May 17, 1686, and that Richard, not Zachariah, Whitpaine was intended.[109] Whether the Goodson-Denny (?) tract was left blank in the Harris map because of a change in its ownership status is not known. In

---

[97] "Notes and Queries," *PMHB*, VII, No. 1 (1883), 106.

[98] *PGSP*, I, 73.

[99] *PGSP*, II, 29.

[100] Patent Book A-15, p. 445 (BLR).

[101] *RUC*, p. 100; *PGSP*, I, 77. Rosemond's Kill, which has disappeared, was a stream whose main branch rose in Wicaco and flowed for a short distance through the upper parts of Moyamensing and then through Passayunk to join Hollander's Creek below.

[102] Commission Book A-4, p. 40 (BLR); Deed Book I-11, pp. 481–82 (Recorder's Office, City Hall, Philadelphia).

[103] *PA*-2, XIX, 496–97.

[104] Lawrence Dalboe, "True Account of all ye male Inhabitants from Peter Coxs (Cock's) Island to Andros Boons and Carcors Hooks and a Long ye mile Crick (Mill Creek) to Peter Yocumbs & King Sas (Kingsessing) to Siamancen . . . ," *PMHB*, VII, No. 1 (1883), 106–7. See also *PGSP*, II, 13.

[105] Old Rights, D-78, p. 98 (BLR).

[106] Patent Book A-1, p. 93, and Record Book F-6, p. 90 (BLR).

[107] Old Rights, D-76, p. 227 (BLR).

[108] *PGSP*, I, 70.

[109] Old Rights, B-22, p. 128 (BLR); *PA*-2, XIX, 340.

the cases of Robert Jeffs and Jacob Pellison, action had been taken by the Commissioners of Property of which the person responsible for the detail of the Harris map must have had personal knowledge. The first instance of such action occurred on September 20, 1690, when "The Petition of Mary Jeffs was read to allow of her Surrendering up of 1500 Acres of Land her deceased Husband Had taken up in the County of Bucks in Expectation of several out of Ireland to Seat it."[110] As the map shows no land laid out to Jeffs in Bucks County, the warrant issued to him for 1,500 acres in Chester County on December 5, 1684, presumably was executed in Philadelphia County,[111] and this tract reverted to the proprietor on acceptance of the widow's petition. The land remained in Penn's possession until disposition of it was made by the Commissioners of Property on April 12/13, 1703, as the following entry in their minutes attests:

The Prop'ry, having Ord'd that there should be laid out to Jonathan Hayes 1100 Acres in Lieu of that laid out to Benja. Chambers in the Manor of Williamstadt, . . . Thomas Fairman having undertaken to find him Other Land he at Length fixed on a tract laid out formerly to Robert Jeffs, and Another tract above adjoyning, Bearing Fra. Smith's name in the Mapp, . the Survey of which Land, if Ever made, is Void, the said Smith having no right to Land in this Province.[112]

Although this action transpired about five or six years after the supposed time of publication of the Harris map, it would appear that the information on which its contents were based came from someone in the Land Office who was already aware of the invalidity of Francis Smith's right to the tract at the time the plate was engraved. The directive of William Markham of May 9, 1689, to Holme regarding Pellison's loss of his up-country tract through his failure to improve it and the action to be taken for its acquisition by Markham (see pp. 00–00 above) would account for the removal of Pellison's name, but why Markham was no longer denoted as the owner of the lower tract remains a matter for conjecture.

In Philadelphia County the smaller map differed further from the larger one in its omission of the four Liberty Land tracts and the names of Moyamensing, Passayunk, and Tacony townships and in its erroneous assignment of John Nickson's (Nixon's) up-country tract near Perkiomen Creek to Richard Wall. According to the draft of the resurvey of this tract, dated October 24, 1703, it still was in Nixon's possession at that time.[113]

The Bucks County tracts that had names inscribed upon them in the Green-Thornton edition but were left without identification of their owners in the Harris map were more numerous than similar Philadelphia County tracts. Those whose ownership can be ascertained from the Green-Thornton edition belonged to Joseph Jones, Thomas Groom, and Thomas Hould (Houle), just above the extensive Growdon tract; Joab Howle (Job Houle), adjoining Arthur Cook's large holding; Thomas Rowland, below the adjoining William Buckman tract; John Martin, and Robert Presmore (Presmall), to the left of the above; John Rowland, Abraham Wharley (Wherley), Jonathan Eldredg (Eldridge), and John Otter, in Newtown; James Ratliff (Radcliffe), in Wrightstown; Edward Luffe (Luff) and Henry Sidwell (Siddall), below Highlands Manor; Thomas Janny (Janney), adjacent to Newtown; Randal Blackshaw, above Pennsbury Manor; John Luffe (Luff), jointly with Daniel Gardner (Gardiner), above Pennsbury Manor; and James Harrison, in Pennsbury Manor.

Joseph Jones and Thomas Houle were named as holding tracts adjacent to the one for which a return of survey was made in the name of Peter Groom on November 16, 1683. The Groom tract was erroneously attributed in the original edition to Thomas Groom, but its true status is clarified by the fact that Peter gave power of attorney to his brother Thomas in March, 1692, to act in his person for the selling of the above tract to Hugh Marsh.[114] Jones sold his tract to Peter Chamberlain on October 4, 1696,[115] but the later history of the Thomas Houle tract has not been determined. Job Houle's 200 acres adjoining the Arthur Cook and William Buckman tracts were laid out on July 26, 1684, and sold to William

[110] *PA-2*, XIX, 44. Letters of administration on Jeffs's estate were granted on April 3, 1688. See *PGSP*, I, 218.
[111] "Old Rights," Philadelphia County, *PA-3*, III, 149.
[112] *PA-2*, XIX, 368–69.

[113] Old Rights, D-87, p. 3 (BLR).
[114] Old Rights, D-68, p. 179 (BLR); Power of Attorney Docket, I, 370 (Recorder's Office, Bucks County Court House, Doylestown, Pa.).
[115] *RCBC*, p. 394.

Rawles on January 17, 1690/91.[116] The warrant issued to Buckman on November 22, 1683, for 300 acres in Bucks County specified that his tract was to be laid out adjoining that of Thomas Rowland, who had died by September 9, 1690.[117] John Martin took up a tract of 500 acres in Southampton Township and disposed of half of it to Robert Presmall, for whom a return of survey was made on July 6, 1685; Presmall sold half of his tract on March 1, 1686.[118] These subdivisions probably accounted for the omission of the owners' names in the Harris map. John Rowland was named in the warrant issued to Elizabeth Barber on August 7, 1684, as the holder of the tract adjacent to which 300 acres were to be laid out for her in Newtown.[119] He sold much of his Bucks County land between 1685 and 1690, but in this instance his name may have been omitted from the Harris edition to make room for the *S* in "BUCKS." Abraham Wherley, Jonathan Eldridge, and John Otter were reported in "Isreall Taylors Account of Survey in y[e] County of Buckes" as having had surveys run for them on August 11, 12, and 14, 1685, respectively, which dating would indicate such adjacency or close proximity as existed among their tracts in Newtown. The explanation for the deviation here from Holme's correctly plotted disposition of their tracts is furnished by the map itself. An examination of it shows that the engraver erred initially by placing the name of Israel Taylor on William Sneed's tract, after which he moved up the names of Shadrach Walley and Benjamin Roberts, with the result that there was no room left for Wherley, Eldridge, and Otter. A resurvey of Eldridge's tract run in 1702 showed Wherley as still in possession of the adjacent tract.[120] Although James Radcliffe did not receive a deed for his 200 acres in Wrightstown until February 10, 1689/90, he is believed to have been settled there by 1686; on April 1, 1693, let-

ters of administration were granted on his estate.[121] Edward Luff received a warrant on November 9, 1683, for 300 acres, with the direction that they be laid out "above y[e] Falls," and the warrant was executed on November 18 following; he deeded the tract to Henry Marjorum on December 19, 1688.[122] Israel Taylor surveyed 100 acres on May 21, 1686, for Henry Siddall, on whose estate letters of administration were granted on November 24, 1694.[123] Thomas Janney was named in the return of the survey run by David Powell in April, 1683, for the Richard Vickeris tract on the Delaware River as the owner of both adjoining tracts ascribed to him in the Green-Thornton edition. He left this land to his sons at his death in 1695.[124] Randal Blackshaw, by deeds of lease and release dated August 13 and September 1, 1682, acquired 500 acres in Falls Township, upon which he established his homestead by 1685, and for which he passed a deed to Joseph Kirkbride on March 1, 1696.[125] The John Luff shown on David Powell's "Draft of Pennsbury Manor" made on March 13, 1700, as owning the adjacent tract jointly with Daniel Gardiner was the son of the original grantee of that name, who is known to have died shortly before February 17, 1686/87.[126] James Harrison already was the holder of the tract assigned to him in Pennsbury when the warrant to George Heathcot (Heathcote) was issued for land there on August 8, 1684. His tenancy came to an end while he was overseeing the construction of the Pennsbury manor house, and letters of administration on his estate were granted on February 10, 1687/88.[127]

In addition to the differences between the two maps already mentioned for Chester and Philadelphia counties, there were a number in Bucks County that resulted from omissions or faulty abbreviations of given names, or from

[116] Old Rights, D-68, p. 230, and D-67, p. 90 (BLR).

[117] Old Rights, D-72, p. 144 (BLR); Deed Book I, p. 323 (Recorder's Office, Bucks County Court House, Doylestown, Pa.).

[118] Old Rights, D-72, p. 1, and D-87, p. 50 (BLR); *PA-2*, XIX, 456; *RCBC*, p. 71.

[119] Old Rights, D-72, p. 108 (BLR).

[120] Old Rights, D-72, p. 78 (BLR). The locations of the Taylor, Sneed, Walley, and Roberts tracts as shown in the first edition are substantiated by a warrant for a resurvey issued to Shadrach Walley on Oct. 26, 1702. See Old Rights, D-67, p. 224 (BLR).

[121] *PA-2*, XIX, 525; *PGSP*, I, 224.

[122] Old Rights, D-68, p. 83, and Original Purchases (BLR); Deed Book I, p. 192 (Recorder's Office, Bucks County Court House, Doylestown, Pa.).

[123] Old Rights, D-67, p. 167 (BLR); Philadelphia Administration Book A, 1683–1702, p. 196 (Register of Wills Office, City Hall, Philadelphia).

[124] Warrants & Surveys of the Province of Pennsylvania, IV, 5 (Department of Records, City Hall, Philadelphia).

[125] Deed Book II, p. 127 (Recorder's Office, Bucks County Court House, Doylestown, Pa.); *RCBC*, p. 33.

[126] Old Rights, B.B. 2, p. 50 (BLR); *PGSP*, I, 52.

[127] Old Rights, D-68, p. 239 (BLR); *PGSP*, I, 217.

other minor errors made in transcription of detail. Particular notice of them would add nothing of substantial weight to the body of fact and conjecture assembled above to account for the deletion or omission of fifty-two landholders' names from the Harris edition. More fact and less conjecture would have been desirable, yet the cumulative effect of the circumstances adduced for the omission of the names of such original owners of large tracts as Edward Turner, William Smith, Jonas Nelson, James Sanderland, Jacob Pellison, Robert Jeffs, Francis Smith, Elinor Holme, Thomas Janney, Randal Blackshaw, and James Harrison is sufficient to warrant the conclusion that the Harris map was produced sometime between 1696 and the end of 1698. So considerable a reduction in the amount of important detail could hardly have come about through mere coincidence.

During the period of Penn's second visit to his province from 1699 to 1701, when he occupied his manor house at Pennsbury, two large maps hung on the walls of "the best parlor" there.[128] While no specific information seems to be available by which they may be identified, it is conceivable that one of them was a copy of the Green-Thornton edition and that the other was a copy of the Harris edition. Whether or not such was the case, by 1701 both the Green-Thornton edition and the Harris map were so much out of date that any effort to remedy that defect would have required the preparation of entirely new plates. Unfortunately, no such advancement in cartography was made. After undergoing about a dozen alterations and additions, the plate of the Green-Thornton map was again utilized, presumably sometime between 1701 and 1705, for the printing of another edition. The second edition was issued in six sheets rather than in the seven sheets of the original edition with its "General Description."

In Chester and Philadelphia counties the detail presented in the original edition was subjected to very few changes and additions. The former subdivision underwent revision only to the extent of the conversion of "Furlow" on the Vincent-Vrouzen-Furly-Coxe tract to "Furloy" and the deletion of the lettering "Charles Pickering and Compa" from the so-called Mine Hole Tract, the original survey of which Penn had disallowed in 1688. It had then remained in Penn's possession until his departure for England in 1701, when, as previously noted, he granted a patent for it to Edward Shippen and fifteen others.[129] Among its new owners were some of the most influential men of the province, to oblige whom it would have been characteristic of Penn to have Pickering's name removed from the original plate. That he actually caused this to be done cannot be stated with any degree of certainty, but it must be observed that the name of Samuel Buckley, whose adjoining grant the proprietor had also disallowed, was not deleted.

In Philadelphia County there were two amendments: the insertion of the lettering "Jacob Vandewall [Van de Walle] and Company" in German Township and the addition of the large tract adjoining Gilberts Manor identified as "Margaret, John and Anthony Lowthers Mannor of Lowther," the history of which is sketchy and vague. Penn issued a warrant to John, Anthony, and Margaret Lowther for 10,000 acres on September 13, 1683, the same day on which he had also issued a warrant to William Lowther and Company. Except that of the Manor of Billton, the first known record of a survey made to any of the Lowthers was on February 6, 1686/87, when Penn charged his Commissioners of Property as follows: "For my Brother Lowther's Children Advance backwards and add 2000 acres more, which makes 4 Mannors at 3000 acres to a Mannor for his 4 Children, Margaret, William, John and Anthony."[130] While this directive seems to signify that surveys had been run also for Margaret, John, and Anthony, known contemporary Land Office records contain no mention of them. As a matter of fact, the drafter of the resurvey made on October 24, 1703, of John Nixon's tract, now shown on the map as bordering on the Manor of Lowther, denoted the land above the Nixon tract as still being vacant at that time.[131] No record of a survey, as such, made thereafter of the Manor of Lowther has been located. It is possible, of course, that the tract was delineated in the plate

---

128 "A Catalogue of Goods left at Pennsbury, the 3ᵈ of the 10ᵗʰ mo. 1701," *WP-JL*, I, 63.

129 *PA-2*, XIX, 469.
130 *Ibid.*, p. 13.
131 Old Rights, D-87, p. 3 (BLR).

without the benefit of actual mensuration. This seems even more likely in view of the fact that the deeds by which the interests of the surviving heirs of the original grantees of the manor were conveyed to others in 1731 contain no mention whatsoever of specific metes, bounds, and locations.[132]

The greatest number of changes were made in Bucks County and involved both cultural and physical detail. There, John Gray (alias Tatham) appeared for the first time as owner of land on the lower course of Neshaminy Creek, where the tract formerly inscribed with the names of Francis Walker and Claus Johnson was considerably reduced and laid off in two separate tracts under their respective names. A number of tracts unidentified in the original edition were now labeled as belonging to (?) Giles and John Fettiplace, adjacent to John Cow's (Clow's) land below the Society Tract; to John Blayling and (?) Drawell, below the Giles-Fettiplace tract; to R(ichard) Sneed and R(ichard) Vickeris, between John Clows and Richard Ingelo; to Ch(arles) Jones, Jr., below Sneed and Vickeris; and to Ch(arles) Hartford, in Wrightstown.

John Gray's name appeared in the original edition on two up-country tracts that Israel Taylor had surveyed on April 3, 1686, and February 4, 1686/87, respectively.[133] Apparently, it also should have been recorded over a 1,000-acre tract on the lower reaches of Neshaminy Creek that Gray had purchased from Joseph Growdon late in the summer of 1685. The tract was surveyed; and, at Gray's request, Growdon gave him a deed for it before the conditions of the sale agreement were fulfilled. These called for partial payment in merchandise (Gray was in the mercantile business) and the balance in cash. Gray took possession and erected an imposing mansion on the tract before he had fully paid for it. But as the usual requirements had been met insofar as the Land Office was concerned, the tract was entitled to cartographic representation. That such display was not given it may have been owing to Gray's and Growdon's differences over settlement for the tract—differences

that eventually ended in a trial held in Bucks County court on October 20, 1699, when Gray, as plaintiff, submitted in evidence an account of goods delivered and cash paid by him to Growdon over the years. The latter questioned the correctness of this account and produced the original given him by Gray, which, when compared with the other, showed that the plaintiff had revised his prices upward on a number of items. The court accordingly found for Growdon and then cited Gray for making false attestation.[134]

About a year after Gray had purchased the 1,000 acres from Growdon, an adjoining 450-acre tract of overplus land was discovered through an official resurvey of the lands patented to Francis Walker, Claus Johnson, and Dunk Williams under previous colonial regimes. This overplus reverted to the proprietor, by whose order it was sold to Gray on December 4, 1687. Penn then required another survey to be made of the entire acreage involved. This was run by Israel Taylor, who submitted a draft, dated June 12, 1688, that delineated the area with the same outlines it had in the first edition under the names of Francis Walker and Claus Johnson.[135] In Taylor's draft, however, Walker's tract was much reduced in size and Johnson's name was not in evidence thereon. Between Walker's holding and the original Gray tract lay the overplus from the Walker and Johnson tracts, divided in the middle by Mill Creek, not shown on either of the former maps. Above Gray's original holding Taylor laid down a tract then belonging to Dunk Williams, beyond which there was a segment representing the overplus that had been found in his tract. Legally, all this overplus belonged to Gray, having been so confirmed to him by patent from Penn; but Growdon, who was a man of considerable influence in the province, somehow contrived to prevent him from taking possession.

Gray died in July, 1700, leaving his estate to his widow, Elizabeth, who died less than a year later; and on September 9, 1702, Thomas Revel, executor of the estate, delivered a deed in Bucks County court transferring the Gray holdings on the lower Neshaminy to Thomas Steven-

---

[132] Deed Book F-5, p. 557, and Deed Book G-2, pp. 113–14 (Recorder's Office, City Hall, Philadelphia).
[133] Old Rights, D-67, p. 167 (BLR).

[134] *RCBC*, pp. 402–13.
[135] Old Rights, D-68, pp. 148, 150, and 173–74 (BLR).

son, Jr.[136] Apparently, the first recorded notice of this transaction received by Penn from an official source was dated April 5, 1705, when James Logan reported to him that Revel had "sold the plantation on Neshamineh to Thomas Stevenson, and the 400 and odd acres sold by thee in England to the said Tatham having been so long in dispute, tho' he had a patent for it between him and Jos'h Growdon."[137] Thereafter, cartographical attribution of this land to John Gray or to any of his survivors would have been unwarranted.

As for the others named in the second edition to whom tracts were initially or additionally assigned in Bucks County, only in the case of Charles Jones, Jr., do the known collections of Land Office records contain any mention of purchase; and his acquisition, charged against the 2,000-acre grant made to him and his father by Penn on September 26/27, 1681, was not dated.[138] It is recorded, however, that by November 3/4, 1711, when the 2,000 acres were conveyed to Edward Shippen and his wife, Esther, it was the senior Jones alone who effected the sale, Charles, Jr., being then "for some time deceased."[139] The date of his death has not been determined; however, the phrase "for some time" might suggest that his death had occurred after Penn was informed by Logan of the sale of the Gray land on the lower course of the Neshaminy, and that the insertion of his name, like that of Gray's,

therefore had taken place before Penn's receipt of Logan's communication of April 5, 1705.

The two most notable additions in cultural detail reflected in the second edition would make it appear that the purpose of its issue was primarily to serve the interests of the Lowthers and the heirs of John Gray. If this was so, it would then follow that the insertion of the several other names, which were only a few of the many new ones that could have been inscribed on the map, must have been more or less incidental.

The improvements made in the map with regard to physical detail came about as a result of the Israel Taylor survey of Gray's lower Neshaminy holdings under date of June 12, 1688, and of resurveys made of his upper tracts prior to their sale to William and Thomas Stevenson on March 16, 1702.[140] In addition to the insertion of the course of Mill Creek, an emendatory relocation of the course of Neshaminy Creek was effected in the Society Land and up-country Gray tracts and along the James Claypoole tract.

The detail of the second edition, transcribed from the copy in The Library Company of Philadelphia, and reproduced by the anastatic process, was published in 1846 in an edition of two hundred copies by the Anastatic Printing Office of Philadelphia and Lloyd P. Smith, librarian of the Library Company. Some detail was omitted in the process of transcription: notably, the names of Randal Blackshaw, in the lower parts of Bucks County, and Gunnar Rambo, in Shackamaxon.

Another reproduction, also transcribed from the second edition, and more nearly approximating the original in appearance than does the anastatic copy, was published by Charles L. Warner in Philadelphia in 1870. Its maker also failed to include all the detail of the original. An edition of the Harris map, reproduced in facsimile, was published in Philadelphia in 1876 by Samuel L. Smedley, chief engineer and surveyor of that city.

[136] Deed Book III, pp. 72–75 (Recorder's Office, Bucks County Court House, Doylestown, Pa.).

[137] From Logan's statement it would appear that the sale was made in spite of the fact that ownership of the "400 and odd acres" still was in contention. Revel had tried to get possession by entering a declaration of ejectment against Growdon in Bucks County court in 1702, but trial was put off from time to time and finally denied (see *WP-JL*, II, 4–5). The executor then appealed to Provincial Council on Dec. 11, 1704, for a fair hearing and trial (*CRP*, II, 179–81). Nothing could have come of this attempt to gain possession, for in June, 1713, "John Tatham, Son of John Tatham, Esq'r, . . . against the Ensuing Court for the County of Bucks, renewed the Suit against Jos. Growdon for a Tract of Land on Neshamineh, of about 400 acres, which his father had about the year 1686 purchased of the Proprietor in England, but he and his Successors have to this Time been kept out of Possession" (see *PA-2*, XIX, 559).

[138] Original Purchases (BLR).

[139] *PA-2*, XIX, 728.

[140] Deed Book III, pp. 69–72 (Recorder's Office, Bucks Country Court House, Doylestown, Pa.).

Neoclassicism in Textile Designs by Jean-Baptiste Huet

Margaret A. Fikioris

PRINTED cottons produced at the Oberkampf factory at Jouy near Versailles accurately reflect the changing taste of the French public in the last decade of the eighteenth century. This change can be observed in the subject matter chosen by their chief textile designer, Jean-Baptiste Huet, who was associated with the firm from 1783 until his death in 1811. In his earlier work, Huet portrayed both historical anecdotes and refined political allegories in addition to lively genre and romantic pastoral scenes. After the mid-1790's, he turned to the stricter, more academic neoclassic form of decoration that was in vogue during this period.

Five examples of this later style are found on printed textiles designed by Huet and now in the collections of The Henry Francis du Pont Winterthur Museum. Their designs are generally organized within a dominant geometric framework, and the individual figures, scenes, and motifs are usually isolated and placed either in a void or set against a two-dimensionally patterned background. Depicting classical subjects in such a manner without specific spatial reference offers a clue to the sources from which Huet drew: antique coins, engraved gems, pieces of sculpture, and classical wall painting with similar organization of decorative elements. Because of the balanced composition, repetition of decorative units, and profusion of small details, the textiles make a striking display for window curtains, bed dressings, and slip covers. Pleasing to the eye, these textiles challenge the scholar to search for the sources used by the artist for his classical ornament.

Of the five examples at Winterthur, the figures in the print labeled "Scènes antiques" (Fig. 1), and dated *circa* 1800 by Henri Clouzot, are the most readily identifiable.[1] Another portion of this print, in the Winterthur textile study collection, shows the Oberkampf stamp which, if in a complete form, would read: "MANUFACTURE DE OBERKAMPF. A JOUY. PRÈS VERSAILLES. BON TEINT." (Fig. 2).[2] In this piece there is an obvious overlap of another print. From the details of the head of Minerva, the tympanum in the bottom of a larger medallion, and the leaf-and-floral pattern in the background, it can be identified as "Médaillons à l'antique, directoire" (Fig. 3).[3]

The repeat of "Scènes antiques" consists of four circular medallions, each with a different border design, framing an individual group of mythological figures. The medallions alternate with pointed elliptical forms containing representations of real and mythological animals. Filling the space between the ellipses and the medallions are small lozenges displaying either profiles of classical men and deities or objects with classical allusions. These design elements are set against a lined background with an over-all pattern of overlapping scallops or scales that change direction at each row of medallions.

The draped female figure in the top left me-

[1] Henri Clouzot, *Histoire de la manufacture de Jouy et de la toile imprimée en France* (Paris: G. van Oest, 1928), II, Pl. 28.

[2] *Ibid.,* I, 23.

[3] Armand Guérinet (ed.), *Nouvelles collections du Musée des Arts Décoratifs, série 9, dessins de J.-B. Huet pour la manufacture de Jouy (1745 à 1811)* (Paris: Librairie d'Art Décoratif, n.d.), Pl. 8. The plate for "Scènes antiques" can be found illustrated as No. 14 in this volume.

FIG. 1. Jean-Baptiste Huet, "Scènes antiques." Jouy, France, *ca.* 1800. Copperplate print on cotton; dimensions of repeat, H. 20″, W. 36½″. (Winterthur, 60.381.1.)

FIG. 2. Detail of Fig. 1 showing the Oberkampf stamp and an overlap of the print "Médallions à l'antique, directoire." Area shown, H. 7⅝″, W. 13½″. (Winterthur, 58.35.5.)

FIG. 3. Huet, "Médallions à l'antique, directoire." Jouy, France, *ca.* 1800. Engraving reproduced from *Nouvelles collections du Musée des Arts Décoratifs, série 9, dessins de J. -B. Huet pour la manufacture de Jouy (1745 à 1811)*, ed. Armand Guérinet (Paris: Librairie d'Art Décoratif, n.d.), Pl. 8. (Photo, Winterthur.)

FIG. 4. Huet, "Minerva." Detail of Fig. 1. Area shown, H. 11⅛", W. 18¼".

FIG. 5. "Venus and Cupid" and "Venus victorieuse." Engravings; H. 3⁵⁄₁₆", W. 2⅝" (each). Reproduced from Bernard de Montfaucon, *L'Antiquité expliquée et représentée en figures* (Paris: F. Delaulne *et al.*, 1722), I, Pt. 1, Pl. CV, Nos. 1 and 2. (Photo, Winterthur.)

dallion is Minerva (Fig. 4), recognized by her common attributes of the owl, helmet, lance, and shield decorated with the head of Medusa. From the abundant representations of the goddess of wisdom in classical art, Huet chose as the pictorial source for this figure the representation of "Venus victorieuse" on a classical gem found in Bernard de Montfaucon's *L'Antiquité expliquée et représentée en figures* (Fig. 5).[4] Montfaucon describes her as "standing alone, resting against a column, holding a lance and a helmet, with a shield at her feet."[5] Pierre Mariette shows a similar example of the "Venus victorieuse"; however, she is displayed leaning against a tree trunk rather than a column.[6]

Compared with Montfaucon's "Venus victorieuse," Huet's representation of Minerva is more

[4] Paris: F. Delaulne *et al.*, 1722, I, Pt. 1, Pl. CV, No. 2. See also Lionardo Agostini, *Le gemme antiche figurate* (Rome, 1657), p. 23, Pl. 117; and Paolo Alessandro Maffei, *Gemme antiche figurate*, III (Rome, 1708), 8–11 and Pl. 4.

[5] Montfaucon, *L'Antiquité expliquée*, I, Pt. 1, p. 169.

[6] Pierre Jean Mariette, *Traité des pierres gravées* (Paris: Mariette, 1750), I, 24, Pl. XXIV. See also Géraud de La Chau, *Dissertation sur les attributs de Vénus, qui a obtenu l'accessit, au jugement de l'Académie royale des inscriptions & belles-lettres, à la séance publique du mois de Novembre 1775* (Paris: Prault, Chez Pissot, librarie, 1776), p. 46.

FIG. 6. Huet, "Venus and Cupid." Detail from Fig. 1. Area shown, H. 11⅛", W. 17⅜".

elaborate. She is shown fully clothed wearing a chiton tied with a double girdle, and her left shoulder is draped with a long sash that flows out behind her, providing the scene with a feeling of movement. Huet also included her owl and added the head of Medusa to her shield. The staff, the column, and the lower drapery of the chiton remain essentially the same as in Montfaucon's version.

Beside the figure of "Venus victorieuse" in *L'Antiquité expliquée* is another representation of the goddess of love (Fig. 5).[7] She is shown holding a cluster of vine leaves and poppies which, according to Montfaucon, are the symbols of Bacchus and Ceres, two deities who are her inspiration.[8] The small figure of Cupid at her feet reaches up, trying to grasp the poppies. This grouping could be the source for the two figures in the second rhombus medallion encircled by a

wreath in "Scènes antiques" (Fig. 6). The figures are reversed in the textile, although in the design for the original copperplate they face in the same direction as they do in the gem.[9] The chiton of the figure in the textile, with the drapery of the skirt flowing gracefully behind, is almost identical to that of the gem. Huet showed the winged Cupid in flight and added a loose sash that billows around the small figure, giving a lively quality to the composition. The flying Cupid reaches up for a cluster of grapes held in the outstretched hands of his companion.

In addition to substituting grapes for poppies and rendering the leaves and stems in a natural manner, Huet changed the posture of the female figure: both arms extend forward, her back is not arched as in the gem, and the billowing sash is free instead of being held close to the body. The hair of the figure in the textile is uncovered and loosely tied.

Josiah Wedgwood also used the gem as the

[7] Montfaucon, *L'Antiquité expliquée,* I, Pt. 1, Pl. CV, No. 1; see also Agostini, *Le gemme,* p. 23, Pl. 116, and Maffei, *Gemme antiche,* pp. 6–7 and Pl. 3.

[8] Montfaucon, *L'Antiquité expliquée,* I, Pt. 1, p. 169.

[9] Guérinet, *Nouvelles collections,* Pl. 14.

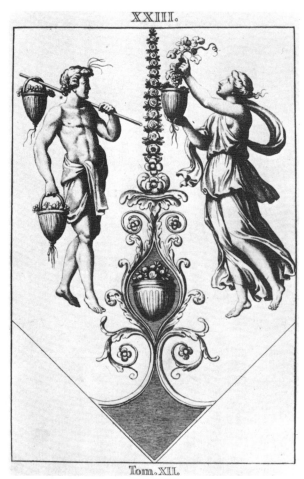

XXIII.

Tom. XII.

FIG. 7. F. A. David, "Season of Autumn." Paris, *ca.* 1803. Engraving; H. 5⅝″, W. 3¾″. Depiction of the Tomb of Nasons, from Pierre Sylvin Maréchal, *Antiquités ou les plus belles peintures antiques d'Herculanum* (Paris: F. A. David, 1803), XII, Pl. XXIII. (Photo, Winterthur.)

source for a medallion entitled "Aphrodite carrying flower of fertility, preceded by an eros," also called "Venus and Cupid," but did not greatly modify it.[10] Did Huet change it by whim, or could he have seen still another source that inspired him to make his innovations? There is an interesting example of a bacchante figure in the depiction of the season of autumn in the Tomb of Nasons illustrated in *Antiquités d'Herculanum* by Pierre Maréchal (Fig. 7).[11]

Here are a similar billowing sash, a naturalistically rendered cluster of grapes held by both hands (with the addition of a basket), and, again, loose wisps of hair at the back of the neck. Perhaps Huet used this example from Herculaneum to give richness and variety to this popular pictorial theme.

Opposite the medallion with Minerva in "Scènes antiques" is a roundel, encircled by a stylized olive wreath, that portrays a scene of Cybele, "the mother of the gods," riding upon a chariot drawn by two lions (Fig. 8). Among her common attributes are the turreted crown, the tympanum, and the cornucopia, all seen in the enigmatic monument of the Empress Otacilla illustrated in Montfaucon (Fig. 9).[12] Huet incorporated the details of the turreted crown and the cornucopia into his design; instead of showing Cybele holding a cornucopia in her arms as customary, however, he used this motif to decorate the front of her chariot.

Another example of Cybele in Montfaucon appears in the illustration of the altar of L. Cornelius Scipio (Fig. 10).[13] Here she is sounding her tympanum while seated in her chariot drawn by a pair of lions. Across from her Attis leans against a pine tree, playing a similar instrument, with his staff planted in the ground next to him. Vicenzo Cartari, doubtless borrowing from this scene, modified it by including two extra soldiers and a half figure with a cornucopia and by changing the pine tree to a grapevine with a heavy trunk (Fig. 11).[14] Huet placed a cluster of grapes beneath the path of Cybele in his textile design. He may have known this particular source or tradition or, once again, may have spontaneously decided to include this particular decorative element in his design.

Represented in the other roundel, framed by a stylized wreath of bellflowers, is an unusual group composed of Venus playing on a harp and Cupid hovering above her holding before him two laurel wreaths, which appear to be attached to two long braids (Fig. 12). In the design for the copperplate from the collection of the Musée

[10] Carol Macht, *Classical Wedgwood Designs* (New York: M. Barrows and Co., 1957), p. 58, Pl. 31.

[11] Pierre Sylvain Maréchal, *Antiquités ou les plus belles peintures antiques d'Herculanum* (Paris: F. A. David, 1803), XII, 37, Pl. XXIII.

[12] Montfaucon, *L'Antiquité expliquée,* I, Pt. 1, p. 8, Pl. II, No. 10.

[13] *Ibid.,* p. 9, Pl. III, No. 2.

[14] Vicenzo Cartari, *Imagini Delli Dei de Gl'Antichi* (Venice, 1647; reprinted, Graz, Austria Akademische Druck-u. Verlagsanstalt, 1963), p. 111.

Fig. 8. Huet, "Cybele." Detail of Fig. 1. Area shown, H. 11⅛", W. 17¼".

Fig. 9. Monument of the Empress Otacilla. Engraving; H. 4⁹⁄₁₆", W. 3⁵⁄₁₆". Reproduced from Bernard de Montfaucon, *L'Antiquité expliquée et représentée en figures* (Paris: F. Delaulne *et al.*, 1722), I, Pt. 1, Pl. II, No. 10. (Photo, Winterthur.)

Fig. 10. Altar of L. Cornelius Scipio. Engraving; H. 4⅞", W. 3¹⁵⁄₁₆". Reproduced from Bernard de Montfaucon, *L'Antiquité expliquée et représentée en figures* (Paris: F. Delaulne *et al.*, 1722), I, Pt. 1, Pl. III, No. 2. (Photo, Winterthur.)

Fig. 11. "Cybele and Attis." Engraving; H. 3³⁄₁₆". W. 4⅜". Reproduced from Vicenzo Cartari, *Imagini Delli Dei de Gl'Antichi* (Venice, 1647; reprinted, Graz, Austria: Akademische Druck-u. Verlagsanstalt, 1963), p. 111. (Photo, Winterthur.)

de l'Union Centrale des Arts Décoratifs, and in another version printed on cotton at Winterthur, there is another design for this roundel (Fig. 13).[15] In both pieces, the figure of Venus playing on the harp is identical, but in the latter Cupid holds the mask of Jocus supported by the two braids. The number of birds in the background has been changed from three to two because of Jocus's scarf. Montfaucon shows a similar grouping by Petrus Appianus (Fig. 14) that identifies the figures.[16] Montfaucon traces the pictorial source to verses in Horace, in which the winged celestial Venus is described as sitting and playing her harp, while above her flutters Cupid, who holds up the mask of Jocus.[17] Comparing the two roundels, the proportions of Cupid and Jocus are essentially the same, although their positions vary. Perhaps Huet was inspired by the first example of "Cupid enchained" illustrated on the same page in Montfaucon, for in the textile design Cupid is shown raised in flight.[18] Huet's

[15] Guérinet, *Nouvelles collections*, Pl. 14.
[16] Montfaucon, *L'Antiquité expliquée*, I, Pt. 1, Pl. CXVI, No. 3.
[17] *Ibid.*, p. 182.
[18] *Ibid.*, Pl. CXVI, No. 1.

Fig. 12. Huet, "Venus and Cupid." Detail from Fig. 1. Area shown, H. 11³⁄₁₆", W. 18⅛".

FIG. 13. Huet, "Venus, Jocus, and Cupid." Detail of another version of "Scènes antiques." Area shown, H. 10⅞", W. 11⅝". (Winterthur, 57.1310.)

FIG. 14. Representations of Cupid. Engravings; No. 1, H. 3¾", W. 2¹⁵⁄₁₆". No. 2, H. 2¾", W. 1¾". No. 3, H. 4¼", W. 4¼". Reproduced from Bernard de Montfaucon, *L'Antiquité expliquée et représentée en figures* (Paris: F. Delaulne *et al.,* 1722), I, Pt. 1, Pl. CXVI, Nos. 1, 2, and 3. (Photo, Winterthur.)

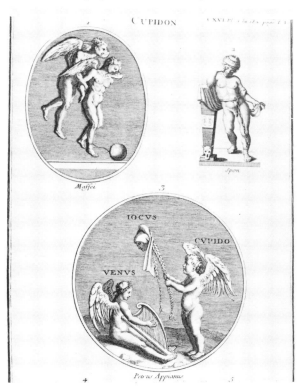

portrayal of Venus, however, is quite different from that of Appianus. She is more ethereal and is shown fully robed with a billowing sash instead of wings.

An earlier edition of Cartari (1624) portrays a manneristic nude figure of Venus, winged, with loose, flowing hair, seated with her legs bent to support the harp in a position somewhat similar to that in Huet's drawing (Fig. 15).[19] The folds

[19] Vincent Cartari, *Les images des dieux contenant leurs pourtraits, coustumes & ceremonies de la religion des payens* (Lyons: Paul Frellon, 1624), p. 657. I am indebted to Dr. Frank H. Sommer, III, for bringing this illustration to my attention. Another grouping influenced by the 1624 edition of Cartari is the emblem illustrating "Charme de l'amour," in *Le trésor des artistes et des amateurs des arts* (Paris: Amable Costes, 1810), III, 14.

FIG. 15. "Venus, Cupid and Jocus." Engraving; H. 5³⁄₁₆", W. 3¾". Reproduced from Vincent Cartari, *Les images des dieux contenant leurs pourtraits, coustomes & ceremonies de la religion des payens* (Lyons: Paul Frellon, 1624), p. 657. (Courtesy of Frank H. Sommer, III: photo, Winterthur.)

FIG. 16. Raphael Sanzio, Detail from wall decoration of Loggia in the Vatican. Engraving reproduced from Raffaele Sanzio, *Loggie di Rafaele nel Vaticano* [proof before letters; Rome, 1772], Pl. XI. (Photo, Winterthur.)

of the scarf of Jocus and the arrested motion of Cupid (although on the ground) are also comparable in design. Nevertheless, the variation of the construction of the harp, the grotesqueness of the mask, and the outward gazes of Venus and Cupid are not carried over into the neoclassic textile design.

Another interesting facet of this particular roundel is the reason for Huet's, or the factory's, substitution of two wreaths for the mask of Jocus that appears in the design for the copperplate. It is possible that this head supported on the braids would have brought back memories of recent bloody events in France during the Revolution, and so the laurel wreaths, symbols of victory, were substituted as a more genteel and equally suitable attribute to be carried by Cupid.

The sources for the animals in the subsidiary medallions of the textile can be traced to classical, Renaissance, and contemporary ornament. The naturalistic rendering of the birds and the other small creatures seated upon branches of a stylized plant or flower stalk seen in the pointed ovals (see Figs. 6 and 12) was used previously by Raphael in the Loggia of the Vatican (Fig. 16) to organize one section of a wall panel.[20] Although Huet never traveled to Rome, books on these frescoes, such as *Loggie di Rafaele nel Vaticano* (1772), must have been accessible to the artists employed at Jouy. In fact, the toile selected by Oberkampf, the owner-director of the Manufactory, for his own bedchamber contains numerous decorative motifs that appear to have been taken directly from Raphael.[21] By linking the design for this toile in Oberkampf's personal possession to Raphael, it seems permissible to suggest that Huet had access to the same design sources.

The frontal figure of a winged sphinx in the second oval (see Fig. 4) was also a popular motif in grotesque design. An exact source for Huet's partially draped sphinx with outstretched wings and without front paws has not been discovered in either classical or Renaissance decoration. Charles Normand, a contemporary of Huet,

[20] Raffaele Sanzio, *Loggie di Rafaele nel Vaticano* [proof before letters; Rome, 1772], Pl. XI.

[21] Egon Hessling, *Le style directoire étoffes & papiers de tenture* (Paris: Librairie E. Hessling, n.d.), p. 8, Pl. XXXIX. See also Raffaele, *Loggie di Rafaele* (Proof), Pls. III, VI, X, and XIII.

FIG. 17. Charles Normand, Detail from an arabesque. Reproduced from Charles Normand, *Nouveau recueil en divers genres d'arabesques de plafonds, meubles, vases & du décor en général* (Paris: Joubert, 18–?), Pl. 4-G. (Photo, Winterthur.)

used a related sphinx with flowers incorporated in one of his designs (Fig. 17).[22] There must be a common source for both figures.

Each medallion of "Scènes antiques" is accented by small rhombus motifs filled with either classical objects or profiles of mythological or historical figures. The four beneath Minerva and Cybele show Diana with her crescent, quiver, and bow; a shepherd's profile (perhaps Apollo, god of the shepherds and brother of Diana); an altar with a burning sacrifice, flanked by a knife and a tympanum (possibly referring to Bacchus); and an unidentifiable urn. In the alternating row of rhombus motifs are the caduceus and purses of Mercury, the lyre of Apollo or Orpheus, the Panpipes of Bacchus and a horn, the profile of Mercury, and the profile of a god or sage.

[22] Charles Normand, *Nouveau recueil en divers genres d'arabesques de plafonds, meubles, vases & du décor en général* (Paris: Joubert, [180–]), Pl. 4-G.

Huet's figure of Mercury could have been derived from an engraved gem such as the one portrayed by Mariette, in which the head of Mercury is seen in profile with a winged hat, a caduceus, a head of a ram, joined hands, and poppies (Fig. 18).[23] Huet varied his representation, however, in the detail of Mercury's hat and hair, and by the addition of a collar. He excluded the majority of the attributes but presented the staff around which a single serpent was wound. A similar staff is found in the image of Aesculapius, the god of healing, who is portrayed as a wise old man—bearded and

[23] For the meaning and illustration of Mercury's attributes, see George Ogle, *Antiquities Explained* (London: C. L. Du Bosc, 1737), I, 22–23; and Cartari, *Imagini Delli Dei*, p. 165. See also Mariette, *Traité des pierres gravées*, I, 30, Pl. XXX.

FIG. 18. Pierre Jean Mariette, Head of Mercury. Engraving; H. 3½", W. 3 1/16". Reproduced from Pierre Jean Mariette, *Traité des pierres gravées* (Paris: Mariette, 1750), I, Pl. XXX. (Photo, Winterthur.)

FIG. 19. "Aesculapius." Engraving; H. 2½″, W. 2⁵⁄₁₆″. Reproduced from Bernard de Montfaucon, *L'Antiquité expliquée et représentée en figures* (Paris: F. Delaulne et al., 1722), I, Pt. 2, Pl. CLXXXVI, No. 4. (Photo, Winterthur.)

crowned with laurel—in Montfaucon (Fig. 19).[24] At first, this appeared to be the exact source and identity of the profile in the final rhombus of "Scènes antiques." However, closer still is the physiognomy of Homer, seen in profile and crowned with laurel, on coins from the Greek island of Ios illustrated by Huet in 1778 for Choiseul-Gouffier's *Voyage pittoresque de la Grèce* (Fig. 20).[25]

From this discussion of "Scènes antiques," it becomes apparent that artists in the late eighteenth century, such as Huet, borrowed freely from classical works of art. It is equally apparent that they had a variety of sources from which to draw: actual examples in Parisian collections, accounts of archaeological discoveries, and books of design illustrated by Renaissance and contemporary artists inspired by the classics.

The textile print "Emblems of Harvest" (Fig. 21) is similar to "Scènes antiques" in that the design is organized within a strict geometric frame-

FIG. 20. Huet, Profile of Homer on coins from Ios. Paris (?), 1778. Engraving reproduced from Marie Gabriel Auguste Florent de Choiseul-Gouffier, *Voyage pittoresque de la Grèce* (Paris, 1782), I, 38. (Library Company, Philadelphia: photo, Winterthur.)

FIG. 21. Huet, "Emblems of Harvest." Jouy, France, *ca.* 1800. Copperplate print on cotton; dimensions of repeat, H. 20⅜″, W. 37¼″. (Winterthur, 69.591.1.)

[24] Montfaucon *L'Antiquité expliquée*, I, Pt. 2, 285, Pl. CLXXXVI, No. 4; see also Maffei, *Gemme antiche*, pp. 115–18 and Pl. 54.

[25] Marie Gabriel Auguste Florent de Choiseul-Gouffier, *Voyage pittoresque de la Grèce* (Paris, 1782), I, 38.

Fɪɢ. 22. Huet, "The Offering of Ceres." Detail of Fig. 21. Area shown H. 11⅛″, W. 16⅞″.

work.[26] The major scenes in this pattern are portrayed in isolated frames set against a network of oblique quadrangles filled with trophies and symbols of the gods and seasons. One author described it as follows:

A Huet pattern from Jouy, made about 1800, illustrates the tendency toward a compact, rigidly controlled design that came in with the nineteenth century. . . . In the large oval medallion is an altar to Demeter, the corn goddess, attended by two priestesses. Demeter holding a serpent is probably intended by the figure in the rectangular motif. Between is a sacrificial ram with a stalk of corn, symbolical of the harvest. The altar attended by Cupid and doves is probably that of Venus.[27]

The scene in the medallion (Fig. 22) probably concerns the worship of Demeter, or Ceres (the Roman counterpart of the Greek goddess of agriculture and fertility). Two of her attributes—

the shaft of grain and the snake—are present in this medallion.[28] The presence of the goddess at the sacrifice is witnessed by a visage encircled by a delicate garland of bellflowers, above the altar. The meaning of the owl shown in relief on the altar, however, is still not clear.

The composition of two women flanking an altar and presented in a gesture of sacrifice was a popular motif in classical art and in periods of its revival. Related examples can be found on coins such as the one from the island of Chios used as an illustration by Huet (Fig. 23); on gems (Fig. 24); and on wall and ceiling decorations, such as that in Hadrian's Villa (Fig. 25).[29]

---

[26] From notes of Florence Waterman, "Classical Designs on French Cottons," *Antiques*, LXIV (Sept., 1953), 206–7.

[27] *Ibid.*, p. 207.

[28] For another example of two women on either side of an altar holding fruit and grain, see Michael Angelo Pergolesi, [*Designs*], (London: 1792), Pl. 64, No. 415.

[29] Choiseul-Gouffier, *Voyage pittoresque*, p. 96; Anne-Claude-Philippe, comte de Caylus, *Recueil d'antiquités Egyptiennes, Etrusques, Grecques, et Romaines* (Paris: Desaint & Saillant, 1761), I, 164, Pl. LIX, No. IV; and Nicolas Ponce, *Arabesques antiques des bains de Livie, et de la ville Adrienne, avec les plafonds de la ville-Madame, peints d'après les dessins de Raphael, et gravés par les soins de M. Ponce* (Paris: M. Ponce, 1789), Pl. 11.

Fig. 23. Huet, Coins from the islands of Chios and Mytilene. Paris (?), 1779. Engraving, reproduced from Marie Gabriel Auguste Florent de Choiseul-Gouffier, *Voyage pitioresque de la Grèce* (Paris, 1782), I, 96. (Library Company, Philadelphia: photo, Winterthur.)

Fig. 25. Detail of ceiling decoration from Hadrian's Villa. Engraving after depiction by Raphael. Reproduced from Nicolas Ponce, *Arabesques antiques des bains de Livie, et de la ville Adrienne, avec les plafonds de la ville-Madame* (Paris: M. Ponce, 1789), Pl. 11. (Photo, Winterthur.)

Fig. 24. "Sacrifices to Vesta." Engraving of cameo; H. 2¹⁵⁄₁₆″, W. 3¼″. Reproduced from Anne-Claude-Philippe, comte de Caylus, *Recueil d'antiquités Egyptiennes, Etrusques, Grecques, et Romaines* (Paris: Desaint & Saillant, 1761), I, Pl. LIX, No. IV. (Photo, Winterthur.)

Fig. 26. "Two Priestesses of Vesta." Engraving; H. 5¼″, W. 3¹³⁄₁₆″. Reproduced from Vincent Cartari, *Les images des dieux contenant leurs pourtraits, coustumes & ceremonies de la religion des payens* (Lyons: Paul Frellon, 1624), p. 288. (Courtesy of Frank H. Sommer, III: photo, Winterthur.)

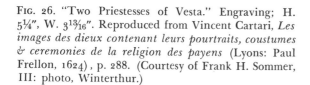

FIG. 27. Normand, Detail from an arabesque. Reproduced from Charles Normand, *Nouveau recueil en divers genres d'arabesques de plafonds, meubles, vases & du décor en général* (Paris: Joubert, 18–?), Pl. 3-G. (Photo, Winterthur.)

Normand's *Nouveau recueil* (Fig. 27).[31] In Normand's example, the figure is turned slightly toward the altar holding the sacrifice directly over the flame with her left hand, while her right hand grasps her cloak and holds it to her side. The left figure in Huet's textile roundel closely resembles this figure in gesture, *contrapposto*, and placement upon a base line against a plain background (see Fig. 22). As with the figure of the winged sphinx (see Fig. 17), Huet could have used Normand's design for the inspiration of this female figure, or there could have been a common source for both, as yet not discovered.

The second focal point of this textile design is the figure with billowing drapery, holding a coiled snake and a mirror, which appears to be suspended in flight within a rhombus frame (Fig. 28). A similar figure in classical sources is

FIG. 28. Huet, Detail of Fig. 21. Area shown, H. 11¾", W. 17⅛".

Hygia, daughter of Aesculapius and goddess of health, who was often portrayed with a sacrificial vessel and a snake (Fig. 29).[32] Huet's subject, however, holds a mirror instead of a dish and possibly represents Prudence, one of the seven allegorical virtues. In Cesare Ripa's *Nova iconologia*, Prudence is shown gazing into a mirror (symbolic of the reflection of the mind upon itself) while she holds a serpent twisted around

In the 1624 edition of Cartari, two priestesses of Vesta are shown inside a domed temple with a winged head placed in the metope above the pediment (Fig. 26).[30] Huet possibly saw this source or a similar one, wanted to show the head of Ceres without an architectural framework, and merely enclosed it within a thin floral swag.

In the decorations of the late eighteenth and early nineteenth centuries, the theme of this ancient rite reappears in books on ornament such as Huet's own *Premier cahier des arabesques* and

[30] Cartari, *Les images des dieux*, p. 288.

[31] Jean-Baptiste Huet, *Premier cahier des arabesques dessinés par J. B. Huet, peintre du roi* (Paris: Bonnet, n.d.), No. 684. See, specifically, Normand, *Nouveau recueil*, Pl. 3-G.

[32] Pietro Santi Bartoli, *Le antiche Lucerne sepolcrali figurate raccolte dalle cave sotterranee, e Grotte di Roma, . . . divise in tre parti* [*Le Lucerne antiche sepolcrali figurate parte seconda*] (Rome, 1729), Pt. 2, p. 15, Pl. 45.

FIG. 29. Pietro Santi Bartoli, Roman lamp with figure of Hygia. Engraving; H. 5¾″, W. 4½″. Reproduced from Pietro Santi Bartoli, *Le antiche Lucerne sepolcrali figurate . . .* (Rome, 1729), Pt. 2, Pl. 45. (Photo, Winterthur.)

FIG. 30. "Prudence." Engraving; H. 3¾″, W. 3¹⁄₁₆″. Reproduced from Cesare Ripa, *Nova iconologia di Cesare Ripa Perugino* (Padua: Pietro Paolo Tossi, 1618), p. 428. (Photo, Winterthur.)

an arrow (Fig. 30).[33] The figure of Prudence was used in a later printed textile from Jouy, "Monuments of Paris," also in the Winterthur collection (Fig. 31). Designed by Hippolyte Lebas and dated 1816 by Clouzot, the work shows Prudence as a part of a decorative frame for an architectural scene.[34] Her attributes are again the mirror and the coiled snake. Opposite her is a female figure representing Fortitude wearing the Nemean lion skin and holding the club of Hercules. It was quite common for artists to combine these two allegorical figures, but why should Huet include one of the Christian virtues amid

all the references to the ancient rite of sacrifice in this textile design? Why, too, did he add what appear to be symbols of Venus in the spandrels? The goddess of love was frequently represented gazing into a mirror, as seen in the statue of the Venus from Arles (Fig. 32), but why should Huet represent her with a snake, which is not one of her usual attributes?[35] The precise identification of this figure and her relationship to the meaning of the whole design is uncertain.

On either side of the "Offering to Ceres" in two small roundels are representations of a ram and a goat (see Fig. 21). Huet's inspiration for these animals came directly from Greek coins

[33] Cesare Ripa, *Nova iconologia di Cesare Ripa Perugino* (Padua: Pietro Paolo Tossi, 1618), p. 428. See also George Richardson, *Iconology* (London: G. Scott, 1779), II, p. 23, Pl. LXI, Fig. 231. Huet knew the virtues and their attributes because he included a statue of Hope with her anchor in his "Offrande a l'Espérence," in La Chau, *Dissertation,* opp. p. 38.

[34] Clouzot, *Histoire,* I, 42 and II, Pl. 47.

[35] Bernard de Montfaucon, *Supplement au livre de l'antiquité expliquée et représentée en figures* (Paris: La veuve Delaulne *et al.,* 1724), I, 125–26, Pl. XLVI, No. 3; for other examples of Venus with a looking glass, see Ogle, *Antiquities Explained,* pp. 64–72, and La Chau, *Dissertation,* pp. 87–88.

FIG. 31. Hippolyte Lebas, Detail from "Monuments of Paris" showing Prudence and Fortitude. Jouy, France, 1816. Copperplate print on cotton; H. 6", W. 13¼". (Winterthur, 58.118.1.)

FIG. 33. Huet, Detail of Greek coin with goat. Paris (?), 1779. Engraving reproduced from Marie Gabriel Auguste Florent de Choiseul-Gouffier, *Voyage pittoresque de la Grèce* (Paris, 1782), I, 82. (Library Company, Philadelphia: photo, Winterthur.)

FIG. 32. "Venus." Engraving; H. 3½", W. 1⅞". Reproduced from Bernard de Montfaucon, *Supplement au livre de l'antiquité expliquée et représentée en figures* (Paris: La veuve Delaulne *et al.*, 1724), I, Pl. XLVI, No. 3. (Photo, Winterthur.)

from the islands of Skyros and Paros, which he illustrated earlier in Choiseul-Gouffier's *Voyage pittoresque* (Figs. 33 and 34).[36] He retained the original scale of the animals and their placement on an abstract base line. Fruits of the harvest decorate the background of these roundels, and behind the ram is the thyrsus or staff carried in Bacchanalian festivals.

The other small roundels on the same vertical axis with the main medallions (see Fig. 21) contain a large vase, similar to one illustrated in Lalonde, and the head of Mercury (Fig. 35) wearing a winged hat and framed by what appear to be apples, with the caduceus behind the roundel.[37] The fruit may represent poppies, however,

[36] Choiseul-Gouffier, *Voyage pittoresque*, pp. 64 and 82; see also Maffei, *Gemme antiche*, II (1707), 176–78 and Pl. 83.
[37] Richard de Lalonde, *Oeuvres diverses de Lalonde* (Paris: Chereau, [17–]), I, Pt. 9, Pl. 5.

FIG. 34. Huet, Detail of Greek coin with ram. Paris
(?), 1779. Engraving reproduced from Marie Gabriel
Auguste Florent de Choiseul-Gouffier *Voyage pittoresque de la Grèce* (Paris, 1782), I, 82. (Library Company,
Phildelphia: photo, Winterthur.)

symbols of abundance and an attribute of the
god illustrated in Mariette (see Fig. 18).[38]

In the textile repeat, pairs of cupids are depicted within the two large rhombus motifs (see
Fig. 21), and their clarity is accentuated because
they are not framed by an elaborate border design. In the rhombus on the right the cupids with
billowing drapery lift their torches to the flame
of the central candelabrum, while on the left the
cupids carry over their shoulders a heavy swag
that is draped about an elaborate urn. A similar
use of the rhythmic movement of *putti* and swag
to decorate a flat surface can be found on a sar-
cophagus illustrated by Piranesi (Fig. 36).[39]

The intervals between the network of crossing
diagonal bands in "Emblems of Harvest" (see
Fig. 21) are filled with symbolic trophies reminiscent of those found in contemporary design
books.[40] Inspiration for some of these trophies
and their details can also be traced to Huet's il-

FIG. 35. Huet, "Mercury." Detail of Fig. 21. Area
shown, H. 6½″, W. 4¼″.

lustrations of coins in *Voyage pittoresque* and in
his studies in draftmanship that appeared in
1778.[41] The cithara used with the owl and horn
on the diagonal above the ram might have been
derived from a coin from Mytilene (see Fig.
23).[42] The pair of doves next to the cithara and
the owl are almost identical to ones shown in his
designs for students (Fig. 37),[43] although here

---

[38] Mariette, *Traité des pierres gravées,* p. 30, Pl. XXX.

[39] Jean Baptiste Piranesi, *Coupes, vases, candélabres, sarcophages, trépieds, lampes & ornéments divers, dessinés et
gravés par J.-B. Piranesi,* ed. Auguste Vincent (reprinted,
Paris: The editor, 1905), Pl. 19.

[40] Lalonde, *Oeuvres diverses,* I, Pt. 9, Pls. 1–6; and Jean
Charles Delafosse, *Receuil des portes, cheminées, pyramides,
cartouches, monumens, bordures, vases, tables, pendules, girandoles, chandeliers, trophées & c.* (Amsterdam: C. S. Roos,

n.d.), II, Pls. 92–103, published in *Algemeen Kunstenaars
Hanboek; of, Schatkamer* (Amsterdam: Jan Willem Smit,
[1787]).

[41] Choiseul-Gouffier, *Voyage pittoresque,* p. 96. See also
Jean-Baptiste Huet, *Premier [–18ᵉ] cahier de fragmens et de
principes de desseins de tous les genres, dessinés d'une
manière nouvelle et facile pour les éleves* (Paris: L. Bonnet,
1778), Pt. 13, p. 3.

[42] Choiseul-Gouffier, *Voyage pittoresque,* p. 96.

[43] Huet, *Premier cahier de fragmens,* Pt. 13, p. 3.

FIG. 36. Jean Baptiste Piranesi, Detail of *putti* and swag. Reproduced from Jean Baptiste Piranesi, *Coupes, vases, candélabres, sarcophages, trépieds lampes & ornéments divers dessinés et gravés par J. B. Piranesi,* ed. Auguste Vincent (reprinted; Paris: The editor, 1905), Pl. 19. (Photo, Winterthur.)

FIG. 37. Huet, Detail of trophy. Reproduced from Jean-Baptiste Huet, *Premier [–18ᵉ] cahier de fragmens et de principes de desseins de tous les genres, dessinés d'une manière nouvelle et facile pour les éleves* (Paris: L. Bonnet, 1778), Pt. 13, p. 3. (Photo, Free Library of Philadelphia.)

Huet removed the chain linking the birds and placed them against a background of roses.

There can be little doubt of Huet's interest in archaeology. In his book for students he included detailed drawings of neoclassic vases and urns, and he devoted a section to the study of classical human proportions illustrated by drawings of specific pieces of sculpture.[44] He had easy access to Greek and Roman works of art because his father was a court painter and the

family lived in one of the apartments in the palace of the Louvre. Even after Huet was married he kept his residence there and lived on the premises until 1801.[45]

The toile "Diane chasseresse" was named by Clouzot and dates between 1800 and 1805 (Fig. 38).[46] Although the central figure (Fig. 39) is similar to the statue of Diana in the Louvre (Fig. 40),[47] there are obvious differences: the substitution of a dog for the hind, a single arrow for a quiver, and a long, billowing chiton for a shorter one. The figure of Diana in Huet's design for "Le loup et l'agneau," titled by Clouzot and illustrated by Guérinet (Fig. 41), more closely resembles the Louvre's statue in movement, dress, and gesture.[48] Nevertheless, Huet again substituted a dog for the hind and placed the missing bow in her left hand.

Other sources were available that could have served as an inspiration for the figure of Diana in Winterthur's textile. Montfaucon shows different representations of the goddess of the hunt holding a bow with a running hound at her feet. In one example with these attributes, she wears a double girdled chiton with a loose flowing scarf over her shoulder (Fig. 42).[49] Somewhat similar in costume is a representation that shares with Huet's Diana the running hound and the pose of holding in either hand a bow and what appears to be a part of an arrow (Fig. 43).[50] The positions

[44] *Ibid.,* Pt. 16, p. 2; Pt. 17, p. 2; Pt. 11, p. 3; and No. 407.

[45] Agnes J. Holden, "Jean-Baptiste Huet Master Designer of Toiles de Jouy," *The Bulletin of the Needle and Bobbin Club,* XXIII, No. 2 (1939), 9–10.

[46] Clouzot, *Histoire,* I, 36, and II, Pl. 32. See also Henri Clouzot and Frances Morris, *Painted and Printed Fabrics: The History of the Manufactory at Jouy and Other Ateliers in France, 1760–1815* (New York: The Metropolitan Museum of Art, 1927), p. 34, Pl. XXVIII.

[47] Joseph Lavallée, *Galerie du musée Napoléon* (Paris: Filhol, 1809), VI, 7–8, Pl. 6, No. 366.

[48] Clouzot, *Histoire,* I, 36 and II, Pl. 30. Guérinet, *Nouvelles collections,* Pl. 1. The inspiration for the figure of Venus holding the golden apple with Cupid at her feet in Fig. 41 is also derived from a classical statue (see Fig. 32). She is the Venus of Versailles illustrated by Montfaucon in his *Supplement* (see n. 35 above) and described as recently unearthed in Arles and presented to the king. Huet has added additional drapery over her arms and the kneeling figure of Cupid. She no longer gazes into a mirror but looks down at the little figure at her feet. The figure of Venus is reversed in the design for the copperplate but not in the textile print.

[49] Montfaucon, *L'Antiquité expliquée,* I, Pt. 1, 148, Pl. LXXXVII, No. 5.

[50] Montfaucon, *Supplement,* I, 108, Pl. XLII, No. 4.

FIG. 38. Huet, "Diane chasseresse." Jouy, France, *ca.* 1800. Copperplate print on cotton; dimensions of repeat, H. 20⅜″, W. 36½″. (Winterthur, 69.592.1.)

FIG. 39. Huet, "Diana." Detail of Fig. 38. Area shown, H. 12⅜″, W. 7⅜″.

FIG. 40. "Diana." Engraving after marble statue; H. 7⅜″, W. 4¾″. Reproduced from Joseph Lavallée, *Galerie du musée Napoléon* (Paris: Filhol, 1809), VI, Pl. 366. (Photo, Winterthur.)

FIG. 41. Huet, "Diana and Venus." Detail from the design for "Le loup et l'agneau." Engraving reproduced from *Nouvelles collections du Musée des Arts Décoratifs, série 9, dessins de J.-B. Huet pour la manufacture de Jouy (1745 à 1811)*, ed. Armand Guérinet (Paris: Librairie d'Art Décoratif, n.d.), Pl. 1. (Photo, Winterthur.)

FIG. 42. "Diana." Engraving; H. 2³⁄₁₆″, W. 1½″. Reproduced from Bernard de Montfaucon, *L'Antiquité expliquée et représentée en figures* (Paris: F. Delaulne *et al.*, 1722), I, Pt. 1, Pl. LXXXVII, No. 5. (Photo, Winterthur.)

FIG. 43. "Diana." Engraving; H. 5¼″, W. 3¼″. Reproduced from Bernard de Montfaucon, *Supplement au livre de l'antiquité expliquée et représentée en figures* (Paris: La veuve Delaulne *et al.*, 1724), I, Pl. XLII, No. 4. (Photo, Winterthur.)

of their arms, however, are reversed. Probably Huet made a synthesis of these different figures and put forward his own concept of the goddess.

Above the figure of Diana in the textile is a rhombus showing a wild boar with two rabbits perched on the frame; both boars and rabbits were favorite game animals. The meaning of the five-pointed star directly above Diana, near the base of the rhombus, is, however, not known. Perhaps it is a reference to Diana as the goddess of the moon and night. Huet portrayed the goddess in this role in a design for another copperplate print illustrated in Guérinet (Fig. 44).[51] Montfaucon was the source for this representation (Fig. 45), for Huet's depiction of Jupiter in the form of an eagle with Ganymedes (Fig. 46), and for Cybele, flanked by two lions, seated on a throne holding a branch and resting her arm on a tympanum (Fig. 47).[52]

The pointed elliptical medallion opposite Diana contains a second female figure shown running, with a billowing sash flowing behind her and a wreath of roses in either hand (Fig. 48). A comparable figure with two wreaths is included in Raphael's design for the Loggia in the Vatican, and its position in a grotesque composed of geometric and natural forms is similar (Fig. 49).[53] The identity of this figure is difficult to discern; possibly it represents Venus, with her wreaths of roses and a pair of doves above her.[54] The star in the medallion might have been included for mere decorative purposes, or as a reference to the planet bearing her name. Another instance of a figure carrying two wreaths is the muse Calliope, although her wreaths are made of laurel branches instead of roses.[55]

Huet perhaps used another detail from Raphael's wall decoration in the Vatican for the figure of the lion attached as a pendant to the medallion (see Fig. 48). Among the Loggia grotesques is a lion with drapery over its back, shown three-dimensionally on a decorative base line (Fig. 50).[56] The lion appears in earlier classi-

FIG. 44. Huet, Detail of design for copperplate, "Figures mythologiques, antiques, médaillons d'animaux." Reproduced from *Nouvelles collections du Musée des Arts Décoratifs, série 9, dessins de J. -B. Huet pour la manufacture de Jouy (1745 à 1811)*, ed. Armand Guérinet (Paris: Librairie d'Art Décoratif, n.d.), Pl. 11. (Photo, Winterthur.)

FIG. 45. "Diana." Engraving; H. 4⅜", W. 3¹¹⁄₁₆". Reproduced from Bernard de Montfaucon, *L'Antiquité expliquée et représentée en figures* (Paris: F. Delaulne et al., 1722), I, Pt. 1, Pl. XCI, No. 4. (Photo, Winterthur.)

[51] Guérinet, *Nouvelles collections*, Pl. 11.

[52] Montfaucon, *L'Antiquité expliquée*, I, Pt. 1, Pl. XCI, No. 4; Pl. XIX, Nos. 1, 2, and 3; Pl. II, No. 6.

[53] Raffaele, *Loggie di Rafaele* (Proof), Pl. VII.

[54] See La Chau, *Dissertation*, p. 82.

[55] Richardson, *Iconology*, I, 46, Pl. XXIII, No. 85.

[56] Raffaele, *Loggie di Rafaele* (Proof), Pl. VI.

FIG. 46. "Jupiter and Ganymedes." Engravings; Nos. 1 and 2, H. 3⅞″, W. 3¼″; No. 3, H. 3¹³⁄₁₆″, W. 3¹⁄₁₆″. Reproduced from Bernard de Montfaucon, *L'Antiquité expliquée et représentée en figures* (Paris: F. Delaulne et al., 1722), I, Pt. 1, Pl. XIX, Nos. 1, 2, and 3. (Photo, Winterthur.)

FIG. 47. "Cybele." Engraving; H. 1⅜″, W. 1⅜″. Reproduced from Bernard de Montfaucon, *L'Antiquité expliquée et représentée en figures* (Paris: F. Delaulne et al., 1722), I, Pt. 1, Pl. II, No. 6. (Photo, Winterthur.)

FIG. 48. Huet, Detail of Fig. 38. Area shown, H. 14⅜″, W. 6¾″.

FIG. 49. Raphael, Detail from wall decoration of Loggia in the Vatican. Engraving reproduced from Raffaele Sanzio, *Loggie di Rafaele nel Vaticano* [proof before letters; Rome, 1772], Pl. VII. (Photo, Winterthur.)

FIG. 50. Raphael, Detail from wall decoration of Loggia in the Vatican. Engraving reproduced from Raffaele Sanzio, *Loggie di Rafaele nel Vaticano* [proof before letters; Rome, 1772], Pl. VI. (Photo, Winterthur.)

cal wall and ceiling decorations, such as those in Hadrian's Villa (Fig. 51).[57] The position of the lion's tail between its legs can be seen in a statue in the Barberini Palace; in a cameo design with Cupid astride a lion, which was later translated into the textile design "La marchande d'amour," produced at Jouy in the early nineteenth century (Fig. 52); and in an arabesque design illustrated by Le Noir, whose inspiration came from Raphael.[58] Huet's reason for placing

the lion in this spot in the design scheme is perplexing. It may have been so placed to complement the elephant and rider in the roundel beneath Diana, or to illustrate the concept of the strong tamed by love implied in the cameo mentioned above showing Cupid riding the lion (see Fig. 52).[59] This second possibility would reinforce the identification of the figure with the two wreaths as being that of Venus, the goddess of love.

As enigmatic as the meaning of the lion is the

[57] Ponce, *Arabesques antiques*, Pl. 4. See also Jean-Nicolas-Louis Durand, *Recueil et parallèle des édifices de tout genre, anciens et modernes; remarquables par leur beauté, par leur grandeur ou par leur singularité, et dessinés sur un même échelle* (Paris: The author, [1800]), Pl. 81.

[58] Charles Percier and P. F. L. Fontaine, *Palais, maisons, et autres édifices modernes dessinés à Rome* (Paris: The authors, 1798), Pl. 80. See also Hessling, *Le style directoire*, Pl. XXXVII; Clouzot and Morris, *Painted and Printed Fabrics*, Pl. XXXVIII; Montfaucon, *L'Antiquité expliquée*, I, Pt. 1, Pl. CXV, No. 2; Sir William Hamilton, *Collection of Etruscan, Greek, and Roman Antiquities from the Cabinet of the Hon.ᵇˡᵉ W.ᵐ Hamilton* (Naples: [Imprimé par F. Morelli], 1767), III, 211. See also M. Alexander Le Noir, *Nouvelle collection d'arabesques propres à la décoration des appartemens; dessinées à Rome par Lavallée, Poussin, et autres célèbres artistes modernes, et gravées par Guyot* (Paris: Treuttel et Würtz, [1810]), Pt. 1, Pl. 4.

[59] Jean-Baptiste Huet, *Oeuvres de J. B. Huet, peintre français gravé à l'eau forte par lui, d'après ses dessins et tableaux* (Paris: Huet, fils, n.d.), Nos. 21 and 27; see also Nos. 3, 9, and 20.

FIG. 53. Huet, "Elephant and Rider." Detail of Fig. 38. Area shown, H. 11¾″, W. 18¾″.

FIG. 51. Ceiling decoration from Hadrian's Villa. Engraving after drawing by Raphael; H. 8⅞″, W. 8¹³⁄₁₆″. Reproduced from Nicolas Ponce, *Arabesques antiques des bains de Livie, et de la ville Adrienne, avec les plafonds de la ville-Madame* (Paris: M. Ponce, 1789), Pl. 4. (Photo, Winterthur.)

FIG. 54. Huet, Detail of "Africa" from "Les quatre parties du monde." Copperplate print on cotton; area shown, H. 13¼″, W. 12″. (Winterthur 69.594.1.)

FIG. 52. Detail of Cupid on lion from copperplate print, "La marchande d'amour," France, early nineteenth century. Reproduced from Egon Hessling, *Le style directoire étoffes & papiers de tenture* (Paris: Librairie E. Hessling, n.d.), Pl. XXXVII. (Photo, Winterthur.)

female figure with the unusual headdress riding an elephant (Fig. 53). One is reminded of the "Four Continents" with Africa accompanied by an elephant or wearing an elephant headdress.[60] Huet illustrates this theme in the toile "Les quatre parties du monde," dated *circa* 1788 (Fig. 54).[61] There is, however, no reason why Af-

[60] Montfaucon, *L'Antiquité expliquée*, III, Pt. 1, 184, Pl. CVI.

[61] Clouzot and Morris, *Painted and Printed Fabrics*, Pl. XXVI.

rica should appear among classical ruins and
bucolic scenes, for the three parallel allegorical figures of Europe, Asia, and America are absent.
This roundel, moreover, does not illustrate La
Fontaine's "Le rat et l'éléphant" because of the
absence of the rat.[62]

Because the elephant is said to consume the
same amount of nourishment at each feeding, it
has been associated with the Christian virtue of
temperance. It would be strange, however, to
find but a single reference to Christian symbol-
ism in the design.[63] The Comte de Caylus in *Receuil d'antiquités* discusses the ancient idea that
the elephant represented eternity because of its
alleged longevity.[64] This concept is compatible
with the two landscape scenes in the textile design depicting romantic ruins of the past (see
Fig. 38). The design source for the elephant and
rider may stem from a detail of Raphael's Vatican decoration (Fig. 55).[65]

The first plate of *Loggie di Rafaele nel Vaticano* includes a small decorative unit composed
of a woman's head flanked by two swans with
arched necks and extended wings (Fig. 56).[66]
Huet used a similar grouping on either side of
his elephant roundel. The probable classical
source for this motif is a funerary monument
(Fig. 57), illustrated by Montfaucon, which
shows two flanking swans holding up the head
of Medusa.[67] Her head has been simplified by
Huet in the textile in comparison with others illustrated in Montfaucon (Fig. 58), although the
snake knot beneath her chin has been retained.[68]
As in Raphael's design, the swans face outward
and three drapery swags hang beneath, although
somewhat separated from this decorative motif.

On the row with the elephant and Medusa
heads is an octagonal medallion framed by an

FIG. 55. Raphael, Detail from wall decoration of Loggia in the Vatican. Engraving reproduced from Raffaele
Sanzio, *Loggie di Rafaele nel Vaticano* [proof before
letters; Rome, 1772], Pl. XI. (Photo, Winterthur.)

FIG. 56. Raphael, Detail from wall decoration of Loggia in the Vatican. Engraving reproduced from Raffaele
Sanzio, *Loggie di Rafaele nel Vaticano* [proof before
letters; Rome, 1772], Pl. I. (Photo, Winterthur.)

elaborate rectangular border; two female figures
are portrayed dancing around a large urn surmounted by an owl (Fig. 59). Their movement
is frozen within a two-dimensional space, and
the urn appears to be a creation for a grotesque
design. Within the four spandrels are tympa-
nums and chalices possibly referring to bacchanalian rites.

Identical figures with festoons and ribbons
placed on either side of a central object provide
a balanced composition to any design. Raphael
used them on either side of Artemis of Ephesus

[62] Jean de La Fontaine, *Oeuvres complètes de La Fontaine, ornées de cent vingt gravures, d'après les dessins de
Desenne, Chaudet, Huet, etc., et d'un portrait inédit d'après
Lebrun* (Paris: A. Nepveu, 1820), III, 37–38. See also Jean
de La Fontaine, *Fables choisies, mises en vers par J. de La
Fontaine* (new ed.; Paris: Des Lauriers, 1773), IV, 97. Huet
had illustrations in both these editions.

[63] Richardson, *Iconology*, II, 24–25.

[64] Caylus, *Recueil d'antiquités*, VI, 171, Pl. L, No. II.

[65] Raffaele, *Loggie di Rafaele* (Proof), Pl. XI. Huet
includes studies of elephants from nature in *Oeuvres de
J. B. Huet*, Nos. 32–34.

[66] Raffaele, *Loggie di Rafaele*, Pl. 1.

[67] Montfaucon, *L'Antiquité expliquée*, V, Pl. LXXV.

[68] *Ibid.*, I, Pt. 1, Pl. LXXXV.

FIG. 57. Funerary monument. Engraving; H. 6″, W. 6³⁄₁₆″. Reproduced from Bernard de Montfaucon, *L'Antiquité expliquée et représentée en figures* (Paris: F. Delaulne *et al.*, 1722), V, Pl. LXXV. (Photo, Winterthur.)

shaped object placed on a pedestal (Fig. 61).[70]

In the toile "Diane chasseresse," exotic animals and classical figures and motifs serve as a lively framework for the gentle pastoral scenes of grazing farm animals amid ancient decaying ruins (see Fig. 38). In his book for the young artist Huet included several sketches of grazing cattle and sheep (Figs. 62 and 63), and the mood and arrangement of these animals are quite similar to those in his later textile design.[71] Moreover, Huet incorporated specific architectural forms in these landscape scenes, such as the ruined archway from one of his sketches (see Fig. 63) of the large castle with a circular tower (see Fig. 38). Perhaps Piranesi provided Huet with the inspiration for these scenes (Figs. 64 and 65).[72]

Of the three toiles discussed, "Diane chasseresse" seems the most aesthetically pleasing because of the opposition between the actual remains of antiquity and the idealized re-creation of classical designs and motifs. Here the real and the imaginary are adroitly balanced, with space for each unit to be examined and enjoyed. Huet's true artistic skill comes to the fore with the representation of these pastoral scenes. The contrived academic stiffness of "Scènes antiques" and "Emblems of Harvest" is entirely lacking.

The print entitled "Medallions and Cartouches," dated *circa* 1804, has a dense, diaper-patterned background that brings into sharp relief motifs of scattered cupids, still lifes, medallions, acanthus leaves, and swags (Fig. 66).[73] Strangely, the cartoon illustrated by Guérinet shows a background of fine vertical lines instead of a scalloped diaper pattern.[74] Similar scalloped patterns can be found in the minor decorative arts of antiquity, such as the vessel illustrated by Caylus in *Recueil d'antiquités* (Fig. 67).[75]

The identity and source for the figure of the

(Fig. 60).[69] The drapery forms are somewhat related in both designs. Earlier examples can be found in classical ceiling decorations: pairs of winged female figures are used in different rooms of Hadrian's Villa. In one room they are shown decorating a candelabrum with a long garland of flowers (see Fig. 51), while in another they tie a ribbon or fine chain around an urn-

---

[69] Raffaele, *Loggie di Rafaele nel Vaticano* (Rome: Marc Pagliarini, 1772), Pl. X.

[70] Ponce, *Arabesques antiques*, Pl. 12. See also Durand, *Recueil et parallèle*, Pl. 81.

[71] Huet, *Premier cahier de fragmens*, Pt. 2, p. 2, and Pt. 3, p. 2 and No. 426. See also Pt. 14, p. 3.

[72] Jean-Baptiste Piranesi, *Différentes vues de quelques restes de trois grands édifices quis subsistent encore* ([Rome, 1778]), Pl. VIII; see also Pl. VII and *Campus Martius Antiquae Urbis* (Rome, 1762), Pl. XIV, detail B.

[73] *Catalogue of a Retrospective Exhibition of Painted and Printed Fabrics* (New York: The Metropolitan Museum of Art, 1927), p. 34, No. 104.

[74] Guérinet, *Nouvelles collections*, Pl. 3.

[75] Anne-Claude-Philippe, comte de Caylus, *Recueil d'antiquités supplément* (Paris: N. M. Tilliard, 1767), VII, Pl. LXIX, Nos. 2 and 3.

FIG. 58. "Heads of Medusa." Engraving; H. 7¼" W. 6½". Reproduced from Bernard de Montfaucon, *L'Antiquité expliquée et représentée en figures* (Paris: F. Delaulne *et al.*, 1722), I, Pt. 1, Pl. LXXXV (detail). (Photo, Winterthur.)

FIG. 60. Raphael, Detail from wall decoration of Loggia in the Vatican. Engraving reproduced from Raffaele Sanzio, *Loggie di Rafaele nel Vaticano* (Rome: Marc Pagliarini, 1772), Pl. X. (Photo, Winterthur.)

FIG. 59. Huet, Detail of Fig. 38. Area shown, H. 8", W. 10".

FIG. 61. Detail of ceiling decoration from Hadrian's Villa. Engraving after drawing by Raphael. Reproduced from Nicolas Ponce, *Arabesques antiques des bains de Livie, et de la ville Adrienne, avec les plafonds de la ville-Madame* (Paris: The author, 1789), Pl. 12. (Photo, Winterthur.)

FIG. 62. Huet, Study from Jean-Baptiste Huet, *Premier [–18ᵉ] cahier de fragmens et de principes de desseins de tous les genres, dessinés d'une manière nouvelle et facile pour les éleves* (Paris: L. Bonnet, 1778), Pt. 2, Pl. 2. (Free Library, Philadelphia: photo, Winterthur.)

FIG. 63. Huet, Study from Jean-Baptiste Huet, *Premier [–18ᵉ] cahier de fragmens et de principes de desseins de tous les genres, dessinés d'une manière nouvelle et facile pour les éleves* (Paris: L. Bonnet, 1778), Pt. 15, No. 426. (Free Library, Philadelphia: photo, Winterthur.)

FIG. 64. Piranesi, Detail of interior view of a Doric temple of Neptune. Reproduced from Piranesi, *Différentes vues de quelques restes de trois grands édifices quis subsistent encore* [Rome, 1778], Pl. VIII. (Free Library, Philadelphia: photo, Winterthur.)

FIG. 65. Piranesi, Detail of ruins. Reproduced from Piranesi, *Campus Martius Antiquae Urbis* (Rome, 1762), Pl. XIV, detail B. (Free Library, Philadelphia: photo, Winterthur.)

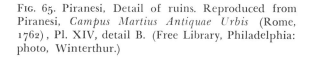

FIG. 66. Huet, "Medallions and Cartouches." Jouy, France, *ca.* 1804. Copperplate print on cotton; dimensions of repeat, H. 10¼″, W. 38½″ (Winterthur, 57.4.)

FIG. 67. Comte de Caylus, Roman vessel. Engraving; H. 1⅜″, W. 3⅝″. Reproduced from Anne-Claude-Philippe, comte de Caylus, *Recueil d'antiquités supplément* (Paris: N. M. Tilliard, 1767), VII, Pl. LXIX, No. III. (Photo, Winterthur.)

seated woman in the pointed elliptical medallion are difficult to determine (Fig. 68). Examples on painted Greek vases are reminiscent of this figure; Huet may have drawn his inspiration from specific pieces of Roman sculpture, however, such as Agrippina di Campidoglio (Fig. 69).[76] His combination of the owl, draped spear, the head of a woman, and lilies in the border of the medallion makes the identification more confusing.

Figures and motifs throughout the rest of the textile repeat are more easily recognizable. The head of Diana appears in profile in the other large medallion, with her attributes of the arrow and the crescent moon clearly shown. Lively balancing figures of cupids are placed on brackets decorated with stylized acanthus leaves and are accompanied by various symbols of Venus: the rose, the golden apple, and the dove. The still

[76] Conte Leopoldo Cicognara, *Storia della scultura dal suo risorgimento in Italia* (Venice: Nella Tipografia Picotti, 1818), III, Pl. XLIII.

FIG. 68. Huet, Detail of Fig. 66. Area shown, H. 10½″, W. 7⅜″.

FIG. 70. Huet, Detail of Fig. 66 showing Cupid, the head of Minerva, and the tripod of Apollo. Area shown, H. 10¾″, W. 6¹³⁄₁₆″.

FIG. 69. "Agrippina di Campidoglio." Engraving; H. 4⁵⁄₁₆″, W. 5⁹⁄₁₆″. Reproduced from Conte Leopoldo Cicognara, *Storia della scultura dal suo risorgimento in Italia* (Venice: Nella Tipografia Picotti, 1818), III, Pl. XLIII. (Photo, Winterthur.)

lifes atop the arrangements of flowers framed by a Greek palmette border refer to Bacchus, the god of wine, Minerva, and Apollo (Fig. 70). For this example, Huet may have used the Greek coin showing the head of Minerva illustrated in Montfaucon (Fig. 71), since he had copied this coin in the roundel seen in the overlapping print discussed earlier (see Fig. 2).[77] In this bust of Minerva, however, he simplified the design, giving it only a basic outline, omitting elaborate details, and providing it with a sculptural base. The tripod of Apollo with a coiled snake can be found illustrated in various contemporary sources.[78]

[77] Montfaucon, *L'Antiquité expliquée*, I, Pt. 1, Pl. LXXXIII, No. 6.

[78] Durand, *Recueil et parallèle*, Pl. 78; Le Noir, *Nouvelle collection*, Pt. 9, Pl. 1; Normand, *Nouveau recueil*, Pt. 2, Pl. 2b; Jules-François Boucher, fils, *VIᵉ cahier d'arabesques composés et gravés par François Boucher* (Paris: Fr. Chereau, 17–?), Pl. A, No. 1.

FIG. 71. "Minerva." Engravings; No. 5, H. 3″, W. 3⁷⁄₁₆″; No. 6, H. 1½″, W. 1½″. Reproduced from Bernard de Montfaucon, *L'Antiquité expliquée et représentée en figures* (Paris: F. Delaulne *et al.,* 1722), I, Pt. 1, Pl. LXXXIII, Nos. 5 and 6. (Photo, Winterthur.)

In addition to the above printed cottons designed by Huet, Winterthur's collection includes a small fragment that belongs to this group (Fig. 72). The design for the copperplate for this fragment is illustrated in Guérinet.[79] The Cooper-Hewitt Museum has examples of this print in its collection (Fig. 73). In the 1927 catalogue of the Metropolitan Museum of Art it is entitled "Classic Motives and Medallions" and dated *circa* 1805.[80]

The two figures in Winterthur's fragment can be identified by their attributes. Minerva, the goddess of wisdom, stands resting on her spear and holding the shield inscribed with a Medusa head. She wears a helmet, and her owl appears below in examples of the complete textile repeat. Venus holds in one hand the torch of love and in the other the golden fruit that she received from Paris.[81] The direct source for this grouping can be found in Montfaucon.[82]

In his design for the copperplate, Huet placed the two figures facing in the same direction as those illustrated in Montfaucon. He added the Medusa head to Minerva's shield, however, and transformed the circular column with the helmet seen in profile to a more monumental square pillar with a very ornate plumed helmet above it. A second owl is seen amid the plumed feathers of the helmet. Huet also portrayed Venus with a more elaborate costume and changed the size and position of the flaming torch. The artist may have had in mind another female figure with billowing drapery who occupies a prominent position in the frontispiece of Montfaucon's first volume (Fig. 74).[83] Both figures face directly outward and have their hair bound up, as opposed to the Venus figure in the gem (see Fig. 71), who has long, flowing hair and gazes slightly upward.

Below this medallion in the design repeat (see Fig. 73), Huet placed an unusual adaptation of Mercury's caduceus in which the twisting snake bodies develop into grotesque birds drinking

[79] Guérinet, *Nouvelles collections,* Pl. 15.
[80] *A Retrospective Exhibition,* p. 30, No. 83.
[81] Ogle, *Antiquities Explained,* pp. 43 and 48. See also La Chau, *Dissertation,* p. 44.
[82] Montfaucon, *L'Antiquité expliquée,* I, Pt. 1, Pl. LXXXIII, No. 5. See also Maffei, *Gemme antiche,* II, 160–65 and Pl. 74.
[83] Montfaucon, *L'Antiquité expliquée,* I, Pt. 1, frontispiece.

Fig. 72. Huet, Fragment, showing Venus and Minerva, from the print "Classic Motives and Medallions." Jouy, France, *ca.* 1805. Copperplate print on cotton; area shown, H. 6", W. 7¹³⁄₁₆". (Winterthur, 69.515.)

out of a flat dish balanced atop the staff. Behind the caduceus is a pair of large, outstretched, feathery wings of a swan or a goose.

Enclosed within the other medallions are the familiar attributes of Diana, Venus, Ceres, and Bacchus. In fact, the head of the young god of wine appears with clusters of grapes in his hair. It is interesting to note Huet's continuing use of a masklike face seen frontally with some form of ornamental tie beneath the chin. He employed this motif previously in the representation of the heads of Medusa (see Figs. 4 and 53), Ceres (see Fig. 22), and Mercury (see Fig. 35). By changing the headdress or the surround, the

artist implied a different character, but in essence the character remains unchanged.

On either side of the medallion with Venus and Minerva (see Fig. 73) stand two frontal female figures with long, flowing garments and billowing sashes, each holding in outstretched hands an arrow and a bow or a wreath of roses. The figures appear to be frozen in flight while balanced atop an abstracted capital form mounted on the head of a sheep. There are numerous classical examples which may have served as prototypes for this decorative device.[84] Two

[84] Piranesi, *Coupes, vases, candélabres,* Pl. 6. See also Durand, *Recueil et parallèle,* Pls. 65 and 81 B.

FIG. 73. Huet, "Classic Motives and Medallions." Jouy, France, *ca.* 1805. Copperplate print on cotton; H. 20″, W. 37¼″ (Cooper-Hewitt Museum of Decorative Arts and Design, Smithsonian Institution.)

examples are very similar and are possible sources for Huet's design. One is the spandrel decoration of a vault in the Baths of Augustus in Rome (Fig. 75), the other a figure illustrated by Comte de Caylus (Fig. 76).[85] In the detail of the vault decoration the figure stands on a form similar to those in Huet's design, she wears a similar costume, and she holds an object in each hand. For the addition of the long, swirling sash Huet may have been inspired by the figure in Caylus.

A round offering dish illustrated in Caylus (Fig. 77) possibly influenced Huet in the choice of a network of rosettes for the background of this textile.[86] Although the finished objects are unrelated, the similarities are evident.

From this discussion of neoclassic toiles designed by Huet, it is evident that the material transcends mere yardage of printed cloth. Because the designs were produced by a copperplate printing technique, they rival book illustra-

[85] Montfaucon, *Supplement,* III, Pl. LVIII. See also Caylus, *Recueil d'antiquités supplément,* VII, 184, Pl. XL.

[86] Caylus, *Recueil d'antiquités supplément,* VII, 248, Pl. LXVIII, No. 1. The figure in the center medallion also resembles one of the priestess in the "Emblems of Harvest" (Fig. 22).

Fig. 74. Detail of Allegory. Engraving; H. 13½″, W. 8¾″. Reproduced from Bernard de Montfaucon, *L'Antiquité expliquée et représentée en figures* (Paris: F. Delaulne *et al.*, 1722), I, Pt. 1, Frontispiece. (Photo, Winterthur.)

Fig. 76. Comte de Caylus, Detail of figure from Roman wall painting. Engraving; H. 3⅞″, W. 3¼″. Reproduced from Anne-Claude-Philippe, comte de Caylus, *Recueil d'antiquités supplément* (Paris: N. M. Tilliard, 1767), VII, Pl. XL. (Photo, Winterthur.)

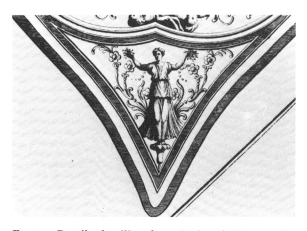

Fig. 75. Detail of ceiling from Baths of Augustus in Rome. Reproduced from Bernard de Montfaucon, *Supplement au livre de l'antiquité expliquée et représentée en figures* (Paris: La veuve Delaulne *et al.*, 1724), III, Pl. LVIII. (Photo, Winterthur.)

tions in clarity of print. The individual scenes, figures, and motifs are not confined to separate pages in a weighty volume to be meticulously studied in the library or private collection. They are present immediately in design repeats that can be comprehended at a glance and later studied for individual detail. Huet mastered the technique of incorporating myriads of small units into pleasing over-all designs that are further enhanced by repetition.

It is the affinity to book illustration, however, that makes this set of textiles so interesting. Huet, like his contemporaries, freely borrowed from books on classical art and archaeology for the inspiration of his figures and motifs. The final copperplate design was a blending of illustrations taken from frescoes, vase decoration, sculpture, coins, and gems. The size and scale were adjusted to accommodate the textile design. These textiles are, in essence, an encyclopedia of classical figures and motifs enjoyed and understood by the educated classes in both Europe and America at the end of the eighteenth and the beginning of the nineteenth centuries. Moreover, because of the dependence of contemporary artists on available books depicting antiquities, Huet's sources for his textile designs surely were the inspiration for classical designs in the other decorative arts, whether they were in the field of silver, glass, ceramics, wallpaper, or architectural ornament.

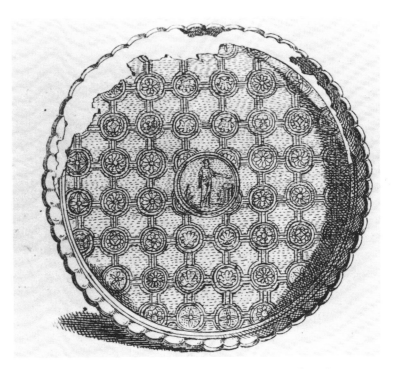

FIG. 77. Comte de Caylus, Roman dish. Engraving; H. 3½″, W. 3⁹⁄₁₆″. Reproduced from Anne-Claude-Philippe, comte de Caylus, *Recueil d'antiquités supplément* (Paris: N. M. Tilliard, 1767), VII, Pl. LXVIII, No. I. (Photo, Winterthur.)

The Sans Souci, a Fashionable Resort Hotel in Ballston Spa

Nancy Goyne Evans

EACH summer throughout the early nineteenth century, the small village of Ballston Spa, New York, sparkled with the gaiety and excitement created by hundreds of visitors. Great numbers of pleasure-seeking and health-conscious Americans journeyed there to sample the waters from the mineral springs so abundant in the area and to relax amid the convivial comforts of one of the numerous guesthouses in the community. The efficacy of the cool, sparkling waters in refreshing the body and exhilarating the spirits was known far and wide. Ballston enjoyed a position of prominence among American spas for several decades preceding the development of springs in other regions and the ascendancy of its old rival and neighbor, Saratoga. The easy, carefree life of the resort attracted travelers from every part of the Northeast, the South, and from as far away as the West Indies.[1]

The springs and their medicinal qualities were well known to the Indians long before the area was settled. Sir William Johnson, Superintendent of Indian Affairs under the British Crown, is reputed to have bathed in the mineral waters to relieve his gout. It was for the Rev. Eliphalet Ball, who with his family became an early permanent resident in the valley of the Kayaderosseras Creek, that the region was named Ballston. Soon after the Revolution settlers began moving into the valley, but until the late 1780's only

they and occasional Indians and travelers visited the springs.[2]

About 1787 Benajah Douglas, grandfather of Stephen A. Douglas, constructed a rude tavern and house to accommodate guests on a site near the public spring in the embryo community later to be incorporated as Ballston Spa.[3] Within three years the well-traveled entrepreneur Elkanah Watson passed through the village and reported that the accommodations were meager and poor, with a spring "in the midst of a quagmire" and a shower bath protected only by some bushes.[4] In 1792 Douglas improved his facilities with a new building, later known as the Aldridge House. During the same year Nicholas Low, a wealthy New York merchant who owned considerable land east of the spring, erected another lodging for guests and completed a new bathhouse. A Mr. Merrill managed Low's house during the first year; business was slow, but it began to improve the following season. Low, meanwhile, advised by his business agents of the vast potentiality of his lands adjoining the spring, had a survey made in which streets and lots were laid out for a village in a modified gridiron plan (Fig. 1). He and his representatives then initiated a vigorous promotional scheme to encourage settlement, especially by individuals with specialized craft training, whereby lots

[1] [George Baker Anderson], *Our Country and Its People: A Descriptive and Biographical Record of Saratoga County, New York* (Boston: The Boston History Company, 1899), p. 405; and Edward F. Grose, *Centennial History of the Village of Ballston Spa* (Ballston, N.Y.: The Ballston Journal, 1907), p. 56.

[2] John H. Steel, *An Analysis of the Mineral Waters of Saratoga and Ballston* (Albany: D. Steele, 1819), pp. 36–37; and *Things As They Are: or, Notes of a Traveller* (New York: Harper & Brothers, 1834), pp. 212–13.

[3] "The Records of Ballston Spa, Saratoga County," *New York State Local History Village Records* (Albany: The University of the State of New York, 1921), p. 7.

[4] William L. Stone, *Reminiscences of Saratoga and Ballston* (New York: Virtue & Yarston, 1875), pp. 405–6.

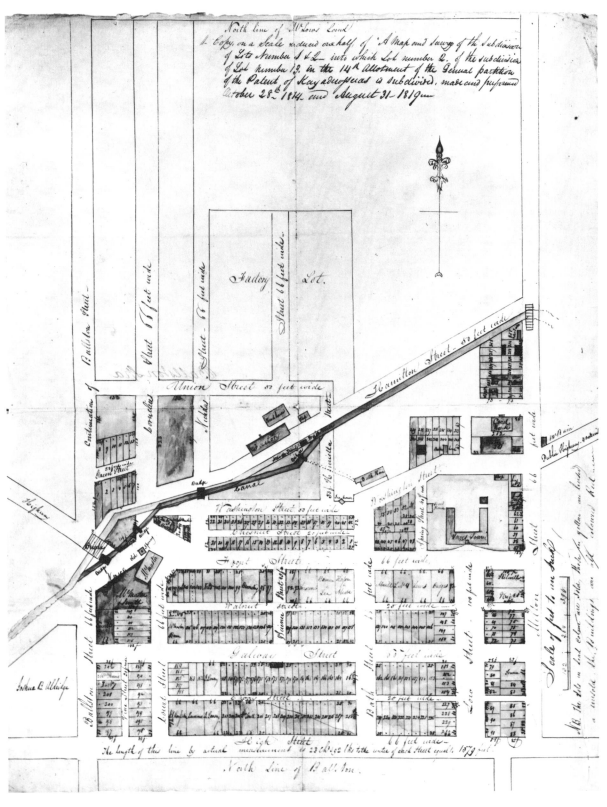

Fig. 1. Map of Ballston Spa, New York, after 1819. H. 20⅝″, W. 16⅜″. Sans Souci Hotel can be seen to right of
center. (N. Low Land Book No. 2, Manuscript Division, The New York Public Library.)

FIG. 2. Baroness Hyde de Neuville, *Ballston Spring, July, 1807*. Water color on paper; H. 7″, W. 9¾″. (New-York Historical Society.)

could be purchased outright or leased for term or life.[5]

In the ensuing years others in the village opened lodging places.[6] By 1800 the community was firmly established and bustled with activity almost the year around (Fig. 2). During the spring and autumn craftsmen erected new facilities or made improvements to older structures in preparation for the summer guests who thronged the boardinghouses and enjoyed the therapeutic and invigorative benefits of the celebrated waters. Business was brisk enough at Low's bathing house to encourage several permanent residents in the area to seek the managership of the facility. An agreement made between Low and Adonijah Rice on April 1, 1801, authorized Rice to take possession of the bathing house for a period of one year and stipulated that he both keep the place in complete repair and sink a cistern to provide a more ample supply of water. Rice also was directed to provide an attendant to collect admission fees and was expected to render to Low a just account of all receipts and expenditures. In return Rice received half the income in excess of the costs of maintenance and improvements.[7]

Two years later structural alterations were made to the bathing house by raising it on a new frame and adding a porch at the rear. Commenting on the new addition in a letter to his

[5] Land Book No. 2 of Nicholas Low, 1794–1862 (New York Public Library; hereafter N.Y.P.L.).

[6] Nathaniel Bartlett Sylvester, *History of Saratoga County* (Philadelphia: Everts & Ensign, 1878), p. 229.

[7] Agreement between Nicholas Low and Adonijah Rice, [1801], Accounts and Bills, Uncatalogued (Nicholas Low Collection [hereafter Low Collection] Library of Congress, Washington [hereafter L.C.]).

employer in New York City, George White, Low's agent in Ballston Spa, noted that with the "ruff floor & sitting benches round" the building promised to "be cooler & more convenient than any place round here." At the same time he spoke of getting ready to begin the "New House."[8]

The "New House" was destined to become the first large resort hotel in America[9]; and its name, the Sans Souci, was a fitting title for an establishment devoted to the encouragement of the carefree life. Erected on a square block site on the north side of Front Street, the three-story building was "pleasantly situated on the E[astern] margin of the Village" (Fig. 3).[10] When completed it boasted a frontage of approximately 160 feet, with wings, or pavilions, of almost equal length extending to the rear. The reputed cost varied from $30,000 to $60,000.[11]

Construction began in the autumn of 1803 under the general supervision of Martin Bromeling, whose contract with Low specified payment of $500 for his services during the first year and $1,000 during the second year.[12] As early as November 17, White reported that "the Stone work is done under the Back Piazza and the whole of the Stone Work of the House [has been] secured, and leveled off."[13] Above this foundation rose a frame structure with a long piazza across the front and a balustrade at the roof line, the work skillfully executed under the direction of the car-

penter James Hawkins.[14] The carpenters completed the framed shell very quickly because the exterior was ready for painting by the end of January the following year. Low chose white paint, a color found on many buildings in the community; and at George White's suggestion, "Venetian blinds" (shutters) were painted with a "Verdigrise" pigment.[15]

Finishing of the interior moved more slowly. On the ground floor were several lobbies, connected by stairways with rooms on the second and third floors, where there were accommodations for about one hundred and fifty guests. As

FIG. 3. O. H. Throop, *Ballston*. New York, 1826–1828. Engraving; H. 2¾", W. 4⅜". Reproduced from Theodore Dwight, Jr., *The Northern Traveller* (6th ed., New York: John P. Haven, 1841). Front Street with Sans Souci in right foreground. (Photo, Winterthur.)

work progressed during the summer of 1804, White kept close account of developments and, in relating his observations to his employer in July, noted, "The Hotel is cool and will be pleasant when finished."[16] By the close of the year he reported that the masons had finished "the Arches of the Hearths on the lower part of the Hotel," which, with other fireplaces in the

---

[8] Letter from George White, June 15, 1803, to Nicholas Low (Low Collection, Box 35, L.C.).

[9] Published sources suggest that the hotel was the first of its size anywhere in the United States. See Leslie Dorsey and Janice Devine, *Fare Thee Well* (New York: Crown Publishers, Inc., 1964); George Waller, *Saratoga: Saga of an Impious Era* (Englewood Cliffs, N.J.: Prentice-Hall, Inc., 1966); William Alexander MacCorkle, *The White Sulphur Springs* (New York: Neale Publishing Co., 1916); and Perceval Reniers, *The Springs of Virginia* (3rd ed.; Chapel Hill, N.C.: University of North Carolina Press, 1955).

[10] The hotel also was bounded by Milton, Washington, and Spring streets. See also Horatio Gates Spafford, *A Gazetteer of the State of New-York* (Albany: B. D. Packard, 1824), p. 39.

[11] [Henry Dilworth Gilpin], *A Northern Tour* (Philadelphia: H. C. Carey & I. Lea, 1825), p. 61; and John Melish, *Travels Through the United States of America in the Years 1806 & 1807, and 1809, 1810 & 1811* (Philadelphia: The author, 1815), II, 414.

[12] Bill from Martin Bromeling, Nov. 1, 1805, to Nicholas Low (Low Collection, Box 35, L.C.).

[13] Letter from George White, Nov. 17, 1803, to Nicholas Low (Low Collection, Box 35, L.C.).

[14] Letter from George White, Feb. 10, 1804, to Nicholas Low (Low Collection, Box 35, L.C.).

[15] Letter from George White, Jan. 13, 1804, to Nicholas Low (Low Collection, Box 35, L.C.). According to MS transcription, "The Contence of this Book Paints and Receipts for Wooden Work," *Bulletin of the Connecticut Historical Society*, IX (Jan., 1943), 12, the procedure "to coler green" was to "Mix verdigrees with white led untill the coler suits."

[16] Letter from George White, July 9, 1804, to Nicholas Low (Low Collection, Box 35, L.C.).

building, connected with four chimneys.[17] Work on the structure was nearing completion early in the following year when Hawkins, the carpenter, wrote to Low in New York City to inform him that he had just "partition'd and lath'd the 15 servants rooms."[18]

During the early stages of construction, Low had decided to add a small two-story structure, referred to as a "temple," to the end of the east wing of the hotel. On January 28, 1804, White reported that the cost of constructing "the Temple, with all materials for covered ways &c, workmanship &c [was] about $250." Within two weeks he wrote again to Low elaborating further on Hawkins's work on the temple and proposing a similar addition to the second wing:

His [Hawkins's] estimate for the Temple was also to have equal Seats on the N°. & S°. side, below & Above, & executed agreeable to what you mention in your last of the 30th which will make it convenient. If you choose at a future day you may have a House similar to it from the West Wing to contain 2 Billiard Tables 1. on the 1st. & 1. on the 2d. floor, with a Bar room below, which the decent of ground will admit off without digging; this would be very productive to the occupyer of the Hotel, as McMasters [proprietor of another boarding house] gets about $10 p Day in the Season for his 2. & I think they all will be occupied.[19]

Low quickly saw the advantages of this proposal and within a short time went ahead with plans for the gaming rooms and a tavern.[20]

Numerous outbuildings completed the facilities of the hotel. On the same lot carpenters erected a small workshop and a "woodhouse of clapboards" for storing firewood, and on land across Washington Street, behind the west wing of the hotel, workmen built a bakehouse and a washhouse. Whether or not the latter was equipped with any of Milton Alvord's patented "Washing Machines @ $10. each," which White reported were "Sayd to answer very well," is not certain. Located on Washington Street nearer the public spring was the icehouse; in the opposite direction, to the east of the bakehouse, a moder-

ate-sized corner lot bordering Milton Street was almost entirely taken up by a small shed, a coach house, and the stables. The waterworks Low built to convey an adequate supply of water to the hotel for use in cooking, bathing, and household chores was a necessity for an establishment the size of the Sans Souci.[21]

With the start of construction, White began considering furnishings for the new facility. His first contact was with William Stillwell, a craftsman negotiating to purchase a sizable building lot at the corner of Front and Milton streets just opposite the site of the Sans Souci. An unexpected turn of events delayed arrangements, however, and pointed up the need to employ additional craftsmen. In a letter to Low on November 6, 1803, White stated:

Mr. Stillwell is still confined with the fever & is supposed to be very unfavorable, so that nothing is done about his lott at the Corner, nor his prices obtained for furniture for [the] New House—Thier is a reputed good Cabinet maker at Milton, Elihu Alvord, who applyed to you when her[e] for work, & has since to me, I Have obtained his lowest prices & affixed them below, you can determine what is best, to be done. It will be well to bespeak some to be ready by June to have the Wood seasoned.[22]

Appended to the bottom of the letter are prices for the furnishings Alvord proposed to make for the hotel. The list includes, in part, the range of forms that would be needed to make both the private rooms and the public areas comfortable. The prices, quoted in shillings, can be considered typical for the period.

Best round back Chairs [Windsors] neatly painted	@ 7/6 ea.
d°. Square backed [Windsors] neatly compleated	11/ ea.
Single bedsteads 6.8 long 3½ Wide of Cherry [or] beech, lathing bottom with Screws	14/ ea.
Double Bedsteads 6.8 long 5 feet Wide, Compleated as above	15/ ea.

17 Letters from George White, Nov. 6, 1803, and Dec. 8, 1804, to Nicholas Low (Low Collection, Box 35, L.C.).

18 Letter from James Hawkins, [1805], to Nicholas Low (Low Collection, Box 35, L.C.).

19 Letters from George White, Jan. 28 and Feb. 10, 1804, to Nicholas Low (Low Collection, Box 35, L.C.).

20 Letter from James Hawkins, [1805], to Nicholas Low (Low Collection, Box 35, L.C.).

21 Letters from George White, Nov. 6, 1803, Jan. 28 and July 9, 1804, and March 30, 1805, to Nicholas Low (Low Collection, Box 35, L.C.). See also a map of Ballston Spa, New York ("A Copy, on a Scale reduced one half, of 'A Map and Survey of the Subdivision of Lots Number 1 & 2 . . . of the General partition of the Patent of Kayaderosseras . . . , made and performed October 28*th* 1814, and August 31, 1819' "), made for Nicholas Low (N.Y.P.L.).

22 Letter from George White, Nov. 6, 1803, to Nicholas Low (Low Collection, Box 35, L.C.).

Tables 3½ long 2.10 Wide of best
   Seasoned Cherry   16/ ea.
Bed Room Tables of Pine, painted, 2.4 long
   18 Inches Wide   10/ ea.[23]

Alvord's prices proved agreeable to Low, and by November 24 White had drawn up an agreement to be signed by the craftsman stipulating that the furniture be constructed in a substantial manner of seasoned materials at the prices quoted by Alvord. At the direction of Low, White altered the stated dimensions of the bedsteads by increasing the length two inches, and the width of the double bedsteads four inches, while the single ones were made two inches narrower. The bill for the entire order amounted to $187.19. The delivery date of 40 single bedsteads, 12 double bedsteads, and 101 round-back Windsor chairs was to be June 1, 1804.[24]

Because more bedsteads eventually would be needed, White proposed to his employer that Stillwell be asked to include bedsteads in the order he was working on, commenting that his materials probably would be better seasoned than those of Alvord. Low assented, and White contacted Stillwell, who replied directly to Low in New York City that "The Tables we engage⁴ to make is under way   The Bedsteads I understand you can get the Double for fifteen shillings and the single for fourteen that is much less that I can afford them for I am shure the price he has set on them is not far from what the materials will cost."[25]

During the months that followed, White reported considerable progress with the furnishings. Stillwell and his partner, a man named Miner, worked diligently on their order for 50 tables of cherry at $1.25 each.[26] Because the price per table was relatively modest, it seems reasonable to assume that they were of a small size suitable for

FIG. 4. Detail of the photograph of the piazza at the front of the Sans Souci, showing eighteenth-century Windsor chairs in use *ca.* 1870. (Photo owned by Mrs. Ralph B. Post: photocopy, Winterthur.)

use in the bedrooms. From Miles Beach, another craftsman who eventually purchased a building lot near the hotel,[27] White ordered 200 Windsor chairs to supplement those being made by Alvord.[28] Beach's craftsmanship fell short of expectations, however, and 44 pine-bottom chairs had to be returned. Some difficulty ensued in inducing Beach to make the necessary improvements within a reasonable time. By midsummer of 1804 a rather exasperated White wrote to Low, "I have requested Mʳ Broomley [Bromeling] again to apply to Mʳ Beach for the Chairs,   if he cannot get them to Suit, It will be well to engage 50 or 100 more from Alvord as his, & the Bedsteads are good."[29] It was not until the end of the following summer that the 44 chairs were finally altered, or replaced.[30] In the meantime, the two parties evidently were able to work out a satisfactory agreement, because Beach was favored with a second order for chairs. By June, 1805, he had supplied the hotel with 425 Windsors—350 fan-back side chairs, 50 square-back side chairs, and 25 armchairs.[31] The large number of Windsors ordered suggests that these chairs were in general use throughout the hotel—in the bedrooms, in the dining room, on the piazzas (Fig. 4), and prob-

[23] *Ibid.*
[24] Bill from Elihu Alvord, July 30, 1804, to Nicholas Low (Low Collection, Accounts and Bills, Uncatalogued, L.C.). See also Agreement between Elihu Alvord and George White, Agent for Nicholas Low, Nov. 24, 1803 (Low Collection, Box 125, L.C.).
[25] Letter from George White, Nov. 25, 1803, to Nicholas Low and letter from William Stillwell, Nov. 30, 1803, to Nicholas Low (Low Collection, Box 35, L.C.).
[26] Bill from Stillwell and Miner, Aug. 13, 1804, to Nicholas Low (Low Collection, Accounts and Bills, Uncatalogued, L.C.).

[27] The property was located on Front Street, a block below and opposite the Sans Souci; see Land Book No. 2 (N.Y.P.L.) and Map of Ballston Spa (N.Y.P.L.).
[28] Letter from George White, Jan. 13, 1804, to Nicholas Low (Low Collection, Box 35, L.C.).
[29] Letter from George White, July 9, 1804, to Nicholas Low (Low Collection, Box 35, L.C.).
[30] Shipping Ledger of Nicholas Low with section at back entitled, "Estate at Ballston Spa," 1803–1822, p. 496 (Low Collection, L.C.).
[31] Bill from Miles Beach, June 7, 1805, to Nicholas Low (Low Collection, Box 132, L.C.).

ably even in the lobbies and other public rooms.

White was pleased with Alvord's work and commented about it in a letter to his employer in February, 1804, "I have a sample of Alvords chair making, by an easey Chamber Chair he has made for me, the Chair & price does credit to the maker. I have desired him to make a Doz: for the accomodation of the Sick in the different houses here, they are much wanted."[32] During the next six months, Alvord also completed a number of small miscellaneous items that would be needed in the hotel: a trundle bedstead and "a small high Chair"; five knife boxes and two large tables for use in the dining room; "a small wheel for the spit" to be installed in the kitchen hearth; and "Sevan easy stools" priced at £1 each.[33]

The additional bedsteads that Stillwell had declined to make at Alvord's prices were finally made in Alvord's shop. Curiously enough, there was an advance in price to £0.18.0 and £0.19.0. Evidently, Alvord realized after completing the first lot that the profit had been too short for the time and labor involved in making the furniture. He delivered his second order of 57 single and 30 double bedsteads to the hotel before the start of the season in 1805. It required a day and a half of Alvord's time and three days' time of his "Boy" to set up the new furniture, to add slats to the 52 bedsteads delivered the previous year, and to reinforce 9 of the frames with screws. In addition, Alvord's bill itemizes 30 tables at £0.11.0 each and a table for Mrs. Low's use at £0.32.0. In its entirety the bill amounted to $270.32.[34]

The main hotel structure was nearly finished and some of its furnishings were ready for use by the end of 1804. As White observed in a letter to Low, "The Rooms, Beds, &c in the Hotel are very decent, clean, & look well."[35] By June of the following year, construction had been completed and the rest of the furnishings were in place. The Sans Souci opened its doors to guests in the sum-

mer of 1805 and enjoyed a successful first season. Elkanah Watson, who had found the area underdeveloped and the facilities crude in 1790, now had nothing but praise for the new establishment:

We left Albany on the 19th of August [1805], and the ensuing day reached the "Sans Souci", in Ballston, amid scenes of elegance and gayety. We seated ourselves at a sumptuous table, with about one hundred guests of all classes, but generally, from their appearance and deportment, of the first respectability, assembled here from every part of the Union and from Europe, in the pursuit of health or pleasure, of matrimony or of vice. This is the most splendid wateringplace in America, and scarcely surpassed in Europe in its dimensions and the taste and elegance of its arrangement. The building contains almost one hundred apartments, all respectably furnished. The plan upon which it is constructed, the architecture, the style of the out buildings, and the gravel walks girded with shrubbery—are all on a magnificent scale.[36]

In a further elaboration on the appearance of the landscaped grounds adjacent to the hotel, one author recorded that young elms were planted around the new building,[37] and by the time Sophia Quincy of Cambridge, Massachusetts, viewed the hotel in 1829, it was "very tastefully shaded with plantations of young trees."[38] These small groves formed a background for the "capacious courts, gardens, rural walks, and fine green lawns" that surrounded the building.[39] Within this delightful setting, the piazzas became popular gathering places.

The little village of Ballston Spa that had "grown up about the springs" could in 1805 boast "accommodations for near one thousand guests."[40] Besides the Sans Souci Hotel there were several large, comfortable boardinghouses. Joshua B. Aldridge was the proprietor of a spacious and attractive two-story frame house, with a

[32] Letter from George White, Feb. 10, 1804, to Nicholas Low (Low Collection, Box 35, L.C.).

[33] Bill from Elihu Alvord, Aug. 15, 1804, to Nicholas Low (Low Collection, Box 131, L.C.).

[34] Bill from Elihu Alvord, June 3, 1805, to Nicholas Low (Low Collection, Box 126, L.C.).

[35] Letter from George White, July 9, 1804, to Nicholas Low (Low Collection, Box 35, L.C.).

[36] Stone, *Reminiscences*, pp. 406–7. Gilpin, *Northern Tour*, p. 60, describes the Sans Souci as larger than any hotel at either of the English spas of Buxton or Harrogate.

[37] [J. S. Bulkeley], *Leading Men and Leading Pursuits of Ballston and Vicinity* (Ballston Spa, N.Y.: W. S. Waterbury, 1874), p. 47.

[38] *The Articulate Sisters: Passages from Journals and Letters of the Daughters of President Josiah Quincy of Harvard University*, ed. M. A. DeWolfe Howe (Cambridge, Mass.: Harvard University Press, 1946), p. 168.

[39] Spafford, *Gazetteer*, p. 39.

[40] Timothy Bigelow, *Journal of a Tour to Niagara Falls* (Boston: John Wilson and Son, 1876), p. 14.

Fig. 5. The Aldridge House, Front Street, Ballston Spa, built in 1792 by Benajah Douglas. Photographed in 1941. (Photo, The New York State Library.)

high-columned piazza at the front, located on the west side of the village a few rods from the Public Spring (Fig. 5). The south façade of the house eventually overlooked a lovely garden, which at least one observer considered to be "of unrivaled excellence in this quarter," and behind the house rose a high sand hill, upon which stood a pavilion approached by a long flight of steps (see Figs. 2 and 3).[41] Although it was not as large as Aldridge's, the McMaster family guesthouse on the flat land adjacent to the spring pleased those who desired a "retired situation."[42] A sizable boardinghouse, built by Stephen H. White in 1801 and later owned by the Cory family, rose on an elevated site at the south-

west corner of the village.[43] Several decades later the Mansion House and the Village Hotel were erected near the center of the village on Front Street, the Village Hotel only a few doors from the Sans Souci (Fig. 6).[44]

In addition to the large boardinghouses, there were many small ones. Lodgings at the principal places cost $8 a week, while the price at the lesser houses, where the accommodations were more modest, was $4 per week. Aside from these establishments, lodging could "be had in almost every family, and in the farmhouses adjacent, on terms to suit all descriptions of visitants."[45]

By 1800, Ballston Spa was established as a fashionable resort. Writing to her mother in the

[41] Spafford, *Gazetteer*, p. 39; see also Grose, *Centennial History*, p. 72.

[42] *The Tourist, or Pocket Manual for Travellers* (4th ed.; New York: Harper & Brothers, 1835), p. 92.

[43] Spafford, *Gazetteer*, p. 39.
[44] *The Tourist*, p. 92.
[45] Spafford, *Gazetteer*, p. 39.

summer of 1802, Eliza Southgate of Scarborough, Maine, commented on life in the village and at the boardinghouse where she had accommodations:

You meet here the most genteel people from every part of our country, —ceremony is thrown off and you are acquainted very soon. . . . For a week we sat down at the table every day with 60 or 70 persons, to-day we were all speaking of the latter being very thin because we had only 40. There are as many more at the other boarding house, continually going and coming, and now there is scarcely 10 persons here that were here when we came.[46]

The village grew and expanded its facilities as the summer visitors increased in number. Commenting on its rapid development, Timothy Bigelow noted in 1805 that there were already four meetinghouses and a courthouse in the community besides the dwelling houses, places of business, and boarding facilities.[47] Only six years later, John Melish, an Englishman, "took a view of the town as [he] passed through it." Typically, he was rather critical of its provincial appearance, stating that "it is soon seen, as it contains 70 dwelling-houses only," which he described as "mostly built of wood, and some of the boarding-houses are very handsome." He found the Sans Souci "uncommonly superb," and listed other facilities including an academy, a library, several taverns, five dry-goods and grocery stores, and two weekly newspapers, which boasted circulations of 700 and 400.[48]

Horatio Spafford, a chronicler of Ballston in the mid-1820's, was more objective in his descriptions. He reported that the courthouse, "dig-

[46] *A Girl's Life Eighty Years Ago: Selections from the Letters of Eliza Southgate Bowne* (New York: Charles Scribner's Sons, 1887), pp. 128–29.

[47] Bigelow, *Journal of a Tour*, p. 14.
[48] Melish, *Travels*, II, 414 and 416.

FIG. 6. J. Sands, *Ballston Springs*. 1836–1837. Engraving after painting by William H. Bartlett; H. 4¾", W. 7". Reproduced from George Virtue, *American Scenery* (London, 1838). The Village Hotel in left foreground; beyond it, behind the trees, the Sans Souci. (Photo, Winterthur.)

nified with the name of the 'academy,' " rose to a height of two stories. Church buildings had been erected by both the Baptist (see Fig. 6) and the Episcopal congregations. In all, there were then about one hundred houses and stores —wooden structures "huddled together, in imitation of city style." At least one printing office still functioned, the town had built a structure to shelter the fire engine, and the number of taverns had more than doubled. At the edge of town stood the empty brick buildings of the Ballston Spa Company, a defunct steam-powered cotton and woolen factory financed largely by Nicholas Low.[49] Within another decade the town had increased in size to 180 dwellings.[50]

The earliest mineral spring in Ballston was the Public Spring, located at the west end of the village. After the discovery and development of other earth fissures emitting mineral waters, this site often was referred to as the Old Spring (see Fig. 1). Early in the nineteenth century, however, the name Iron Spring became fixed in the local vocabulary when the town enclosed the spring within an iron railing and paved the interior area with stone (Figs. 7 and 8). Metal tubing was used to draw off the clear, sparkling water impregnated with gaseous carbonates that constantly bubbled as the gases escaped into the air.[51] Some visitors found the water disagreeable to the palate at first acquaintance; others remarked on its lively, full taste, comparing it to "brisk porter or champagne wine" when being drunk.[52] Generally, most patrons found that use of the waters produced a "purgative, diuretic, tonic, and exhilarating" effect. Many considered them a cure-all to be recommended as beneficial in the treatment of nearly every kind of ailment.[53]

The stream that flowed close by the Public Spring eventually was confined within a canal in order to divert it from the source of the mineral waters (see Fig. 1). Situated at a lower site about 200 yards west along the creek was Low's Spring,

used principally for bathing.[54] About 1817, other strong springs were discovered on Low's land; one of the most important of these, located immediately behind the hotel property, was named the Sans Souci Spring. In the northwest corner of the hotel property the New Spring occupied a site not far from the hotel bathing house, while adjacent to it stood a washhouse.[55] Over the years numerous smaller springs emerged and disappeared, including the Lafayette in 1825, the Washington in 1827, and the United States, or Saline, Spring.[56]

During construction of the hotel White purchased equipment for a new bathing house. A printed tourist's manual notes its location near the Sans Souci Spring.[57] Evidently this structure was nearing completion late in August, 1804,

FIG. 7. J. Hill, *A View of Ballston Springs taken from Aldridges Hotel.* 1815. Engraving after drawing by C. A. Le Sueur; H. 4", W. 7". Reproduced from William Meade, M.D., *An Experimental Inquiry . . . of the Mineral Waters of Ballston and Saratoga* (Philadelphia: Harrison Hall, 1817). (Photo, The New York State Library.)

when Martin Bromeling received a credit of $9.25 in the accounts for "sundry furniture [equipment] for bath house."[58] During the same month, Stillwell & Miner provided "two pine ta-

[49] Spafford, *Gazetteer,* p. 39.

[50] John W. Barber and Henry Howe, *Historical Collections of the State of New York* (New York: S. Tuttle, 1841), p. 492.

[51] Melish, *Travels,* II, 414.

[52] Bigelow, *Journal of a Tour,* p. 12.

[53] Melish, *Travels,* II, 414–15.

[54] Gilpin, *Northern Tour,* pp. 61–62.

[55] Map of Ballston Spa (N.Y.P.L.).

[56] Theodore Dwight, Jr., *The Northern Traveller* (6th ed.; New York: John P. Haven, 1841), pp. 82–83.

[57] *The Tourist,* p. 91.

[58] Shipping Ledger, p. 496 (Low Collection, L.C.).

FIG. 8. Photograph of Iron Springs. Ballston Spa, New York, 1920. (Photo, The New York State Library.)

since the ledger shows no entries for equipment until the autumn of 1805. On October 2 the bookkeeper recorded the purchase of five billiard tables, hauled from Albany by Richard and Samuel Barton[63] for a fee of £2.8.0.[64] A backgammon table, purchased a week later at a cost of $6.00, completed the furnishings.[65] The gaming rooms proved so popular with the guests that it became necessary periodically to purchase new sets of billiard balls and to repair the tables.[66] Randel and Knower of Albany received $16.00 for minor work to one of the tables in 1809.[67] In 1813 Abraham Randel spent thirteen days in Ballston replacing tacks and screws, glueing down cloth and trim, repairing the "beds," installing new pockets, and replacing worn leather; his bill for labor and materials amounted to $62.11.[68] The billiard accounts were kept separately from other accounts in the hotel. Between July 18, and September 5, 1812, the total receipts from billiards amounted to $171.60. Among the expenses charged against the account were the purchase of new billiard balls and the payment of board and wages to J. C. Ferris "for tending table." Low's share of the proceeds was $77.36.[69]

A tavern in the west wing of the hotel below the gaming rooms apparently opened its doors to patrons during the first season. As early as February 7, 1805, Joel Lee wrote to Nicholas Low for clarification of several points in a pending contract: "I am in expectation of agreeing with Mr Bain & Ritchie—for the use of your Tavern House adjoining your Hotel—for the year following—and should wish to know your mind with regard to a longer continuance—and also what encouragement you would be willing to give,—as to the rent &c."[70]

bles for shower hous" at a total cost of $5.00.[59] An earlier order for equipment included a number of bathing tubs and a "showering bath."[60] There are various entries in the ledger recording the purchase in the following years of both muslin and tow cloth for use in the house; and in 1812, the proprietor added an elegant touch when he installed carpeting. Waters from all the springs in the vicinity were available at the facility.[61] When Sophia Quincy visited the spa in 1829, she noted that the bathing rooms were "very convenient."[62]

Perhaps the gaming rooms at the Sans Souci were not ready for use until the second season,

59 Bill from Stillwell and Miner, Aug. 13, 1804, to Nicholas Low (Low Collection, Accounts and Bills, Uncatalogued, L.C.).

60 Shipping Ledger, pp. 495–97 (Low Collection, L.C.).

61 *The Tourist*, p. 91.

62 *Articulate Sisters*, p. 168.

63 It is possible that the name is spelled "Bartis."

64 Bill from Richard and Samuel Barton, Sept. 23, 1805, to Nicholas Low (Low Collection, Box 128, L.C.).

65 Shipping Ledger, p. 497 (Low Collection, L.C.).

66 *Ibid.*

67 Bill from Randel and Knower, July 11, 1809, to Andrew Delamano with reimbursement to Delamano by Nicholas Low, Sept. 15, 1809 (Nicholas Low Papers, Box II, Folder—Business Papers, June–December, 1809, Rutgers University Library, New Brunswick, N.J. [hereafter Rutgers]).

68 Bill from Abraham Randel, 1813, to Andrew Berger, hotel manager for Nicholas Low (Low Collection, Box 151, L.C.).

69 Account of Billiard Tables from Andrew Berger, Oct. 1, 1812, to Nicholas Low (Low Collection, Box 149, L.C.).

70 Box I, Folder—Letters Received 1804–1810 Relating to Real Estate (Nicholas Low Papers, Rutgers).

Fig. 9. Photograph of the front piazza of the Sans Souci. 1870. (Photo owned by Mrs. Ralph B. Post: photocopy, Winterthur.)

Generally, visitors enjoyed being out of doors in Ballston during the summer (Fig. 9), for the situation of the valley with its outlet to the north encouraged a circulation of temperate air.[71] Eliza Southgate discovered that her outdoor walks provided an excellent opportunity for studying "the different characters and dispositions" of the other guests.[72] During the 1820's, late afternoon tea sometimes attracted as many as three hundred people at the Sans Souci for "an amusing half hour" of refreshment "after which all adjourned to walk in one of the saloons—a fine place for the belles and beaux to display."[73]

The most popular of the evening entertainments was the ball. Three years before the Sans Souci opened, a visitor to the spa reported that it was an established custom to hold a ball every other night in the resort's guesthouses.[74] When Elkanah Watson visited the Sans Souci during its first season, he enthusiastically described the social fare for an evening and at the same time

provided another glimpse at the interior appointments of the hotel:

In the evening we attended a ball in a spacious hall, brilliantly illuminated with chandeliers, and adorned with various other appliances of elegance and luxury. Here was congregated a fine exhibition of the *beau monde.* A large proportion of the assembly was from the Southern States, and distinguished by their elegant and polished manners. In the place of the old-fashioned country dances and four-hand reels of the Revolutionary days, I was pleased to notice the advance of refined customs, and the introduction of the graces of Paris in elegant cotillion and quadrille. At table I was delighted in observing the style and appearance of the company, males and females intermixing in the true French usage of *sans souci.* The board was supplied with the luxuries of more sunny climes. There was a large display of servants, handsomely attired, while the music of a choice band enlivened the festivities.[75]

For those who were venturesome there were drives or excursions into the countryside surrounding the springs. Each morning vehicles of

[71] Spafford, *Gazetteer,* p. 40.
[72] *Girl's Life,* p. 128.
[73] *Articulate Sisters,* p. 172.
[74] *Girl's Life,* p. 128.

[75] Stone, *Reminiscences,* p. 408.

various kinds arrived at the front door of the hotel and were quickly filled with eager guests anticipating a pleasant social interlude in the country before the dinner hour.[76] The farms and farm houses, fields and forests, plains and hills gave "a lively interest to the perspective."[77] For a longer outing, a pleasant trip might be planned to Ballston Lake, located six miles south of the village. Somewhat farther northeast, along the route to the battleground at Bemis Heights on the Hudson River where General Burgoyne surrendered, lay Saratoga Lake, which was over twice the size of Ballston Lake. The lake country was especially popular with fishermen, and sportsmen delighted in the abundance of fowl and game to be found in the area.[78] Frequently, a small party organized an excursion of several days' duration; Eliza Southgate and her traveling companions joined such a group in the summer of 1802 and journeyed to Glens Falls and Lake George.[79]

The number of visitors to the spa steadily increased as the summers passed. During the season business was brisk at the Sans Souci, and at other times of the year the sight of workmen making repairs or additions to the facilities and furnishings was not unusual. Andrew Berger, said to be a French émigré, managed the hotel in 1811, when "Seventy Six Wash hand stands" were added to the bedrooms for the convenience of the guests before the season began.[80] In 1815 carpenters put up a new fence in front of the hotel; at the back, workmen erected a new icehouse and added paving stones to the stables.[81]

In true European fashion, a series of regulations had been established for the "convenience" of the guests and the house. On arrival, a gentleman was expected to register, listing the names of the members of his party and indicating the number of servants accompanying the group. By the terms of board each adult paid $10.00 per week for food and lodging, while accommodations for servants and children under twelve

were half price. Except for the servants, who took their meals earlier, dining hours were the same for all—breakfast at eight o'clock, dinner at two, and supper at seven. The hotel offered an extensive wine and liquor list; in deference to the ladies, however, neither drinking nor smoking was permitted in the drawing rooms. Guests were permitted to drink only in the dining room, or, in the case of gentlemen, at the bar, and to prevent mistakes from arising over liquor requests at the dinner table, each gentleman wrote his order on a small card provided by the waiters and signed his name at the bottom. When a gentleman and his party planned to leave, the management requested due notice of their departure so the bill could be prepared carefully in advance to avoid errors.[82]

Andrew Berger still managed the hotel in 1822 when Low reimbursed him for repairs and additions to the household equipment and furnishings such as tinning and repairing kitchen utensils and mending the smoke jack. A breadbasket was purchased for the dining room, and coffee urns and coolers there received a new coat of paint. A considerable quantity of new "crockery" ware replaced pieces that had been broken or damaged. These items alone cost $545.19. Sixty new chairs were purchased for the ballroom. The modest cost of $1.50 each suggests that they were either Windsors or fancy painted chairs.[83] Only a year earlier the other chairs in the hotel had been carefully inspected; 150 needed repairs, and 469 required a fresh coat of paint.[84]

Nicholas Low was eighty-three years old in 1822 and undoubtedly felt the care of owning and maintaining a prosperous resort hotel more a burden with each passing year. Between seasons in 1822–1823 he sold the property to Harvey Loomis, an Albany businessman.[85] By 1818 one observer had reported there were already 2,500 visitors to the spa during the "season," of which over 1,200 reputedly came from states south of

[76] *Articulate Sisters,* p. 168.

[77] Gilpin, *Northern Tour,* pp. 59–60.

[78] Steel, *Analysis,* p. 40.

[79] *Girl's Life,* pp. 129–30.

[80] Bill from Avery Swan, May 11, 1811, to Nicholas Low (Low Collection, Accounts and Bills, Uncatalogued, L.C.).

[81] Letter from Samuel Hicks, Jr., Dec. 27, 1815, to Nicholas Low (Low Collection, Accounts and Bills, Uncatalogued, L.C.).

[82] Sylvester, *History of Saratoga County,* p. 240. Copy of a circular entitled "Regulations Established at the Sans Souci Hotel," 1811.

[83] Bill from Andrew Berger, Sept. 1, 1822, to Nicholas Low (Low Collection, Box 153, L.C.).

[84] Bill from William L. White, April 20, 1821, to Samuel Hicks, Jr., for Nicholas Low (Low Collection, Accounts and Bills, Uncatalogued, L.C.).

[85] Mimeograph copy, "The Sans Souci Hotel" (rev. ed.; Ballston Spa, N.Y.: The Kayaderosseras Yorkers, 1967), p. 2.

New York.[86] That Southerners patronized the resort is corroborated in an observation made by Eliza Southgate as early as 1802. Dismayed by the dissipation and idleness of resort life, she commented in a letter to her mother that she had heard "the Southern ladies seem more at home here than the Northern ladies and do not appear to think industry necessary to happiness."[87]

By the 1820's many notable figures of state had visited the spa, as confirmed by a report in the *Ballston Spa Gazette* for August 12, 1822: "There are at present in the village, the Spanish minister, Chevalier de Anduaga and suite; the British minister, Mr. Canning and suite; and the ex-king of Spain, Joseph Bonaparte and suite. His excellency, Governor Clinton and the other Canal Commissioners had a meeting in this village last week."[88] Bonaparte and his party returned again three years later for a brief visit. They had lodgings at the Sans Souci, which *Harper's Tourist Guide* still described in 1830 as "the principle house . . . and . . . at least equal in plan and arrangement to any similar establishment in the country."[89] In a manuscript account book of the hotel, an entry for July 20, 1825, reveals the nature of some of Bonaparte's expenditures during his stay:

1 Bottle Madeira	$ 2	"
2 Bottles Claret	2	"
½ pint Brandy	"	37½
Horse & Chair to Saratoga	2	"
8 Dinners 6/	6	"
8 Dinners 4/	4	"
3 do 3/	1	12½
8 Suppers 4/	4	"
8 do 4/	4	"
3 do 4/	"	75
16 Lodgings 2/	4	"
3 do 1/	"	37½
	$30	62½

A small notation at the left of the entry indicates that "3 doz 1 p^c Washing" was also charged against Bonaparte's account that day.[90]

Other distinguished people who enjoyed the

pleasures of resort life in Ballston during this period include the literary men J. Fenimore Cooper and Washington Irving; the military heroes Andrew Jackson and Commodores Hull, Decatur, and MacDonough; and the political figures Daniel Webster, Henry Clay, John Calhoun, and Martin Van Buren.

From the early days of the resort, stagecoach transportation constituted the principal mode of travel to the springs. The route from New England and upper New York State was completely overland, while for residents of New York City and visitors from farther south, the water route up the Hudson to Albany was easiest. From Albany there were two roads—one by way of Schenectady, the other through Waterford. As one traveler suggested, "It makes a very agreeable jaunt to go the one way, and return the other."[91] As early as 1805, a turnpike "with a pavement covered with hard gravel" was under construction from Albany to Schenectady.[92]

After development of the railroad in the early 1830's, this method of transportation proved more convenient, with a choice of two routes. Cars of the Mohawk and Hudson Railroad left the depot on the north side of State Street in Albany several times a day and traveled fifteen miles to Schenectady. From there the Saratoga and Schenectady Railroad carried passengers northward, making a stop at Ballston Spa. An alternate route commenced at Troy, where the Rensselaer & Saratoga Railroad transported travelers from the River Street terminal across the Hudson to Waterford, Mechanicsville, and Ballston Spa, a distance of twenty-four miles.[93] Of the two routes, the one by way of Schenectady was the more favored.

By the mid-1820's Ballston had begun to feel the effects of the rising popularity of its neighbor and competitor, Saratoga. Because of the greater variety of its springs, and the exceptional quality and strength of the Congress Spring in particular, Saratoga began to enjoy a decided advantage in attracting both permanent residents and summer visitors. Places of lodging increased in number and facilities expanded accordingly. Near the Congress Spring guests could be accommodated at Congress Hall, a large hotel with galleries at the front, but

[86] Grose, *Centennial History*, p. 60.

[87] *Girl's Life*, p. 131.

[88] Hugh Bradley, *Such Was Saratoga* (New York: Doubleday, Doran and Company, Inc., 1940), p. 66.

[89] Grose, *Centennial History*, p. 67.

[90] Account Book of the Sans Souci Hotel, 1823–1826 (Ballston Spa Area Historical Society Museum, Ballston Spa, N.Y.).

[91] Melish, *Travels*, II, 416.

[92] Bigelow, *Journal of a Tour*, p. 12.

p. 42.

[93] *The Traveller's Guide* (New York: J. Disturnell, 1836),

Fig. 10. Photograph of the Sans Souci, showing new front piazza. 1870. (Photo owned by Mrs. Ralph B. Post: photocopy, Winterthur.)

still, as Elkanah Watson observed, "far inferior to the 'Sans Souci' in dimensions and appearance."[94] Saratoga really forged ahead when Dr. John Clarke settled in the area and introduced commercial bottling of the mineral waters with distribution over a large portion of the East.[95] As the jour-

nalist Theodore Dwight observed, "Saratoga was *the fashion* . . . and . . . nothing can withstand the influence of fashion among its votaries."[96]

After 1849 when the springs failed, the Sans Souci was used for a time as a law school. The building was again used as a hotel from 1853 until 1862, when it was converted to a ladies' seminary. With the discovery of new mineral springs in the late 1860's, the hotel flourished once more to the extent that the proprietor replaced the old piazza on the front with a new one (Fig. 10).[97] Decline

[94] Stone, *Reminiscences*, p. 408.

[95] Waller, *Saratoga*, pp. 66–67. A manuscript account suggests the popularity of the bottled waters:

Judge Tucker	Richmond 8th July 1822
Bo[t] of D Nesbit	
3 Doz.[n] Saratoga Water @ $3	6.00
Box	0.25
1 Bottle D°	–.25
Rec payment	$6.50

If the above Bill is any
thing overcharge from the former I am ready to
correct it

       D. Nesbet

See St. George Tucker—Accounts and Receipts, Box 65, Folder 1822 (Tucker-Coleman Collection, Swem Library, College of William and Mary, Williamsburg, Va.).

[96] Letter from Theodore Dwight, Sept. 4, 1821, to Benjamin Silliman (Yale, New Haven) (MS Division, Ch A 6.15, Boston Public Library).

[97] Bulkeley, *Leading Men*, p. 46.

Fig. 11. Photograph of the Sans Souci during demolition. 1887. (Photo owned by Mrs. Ralph B. Post: photocopy, Winterthur.)

set in again in the 1880's, and finally, in 1887, the Sans Souci was demolished in order to permit an expansion of the business district of the village (Fig. 11).[98]

Although destruction of the Sans Souci sizably reduced physical evidence of Ballston Spa's former glory, the story of its founding and growth and its far-reaching fame in the early nineteenth century still exists in the records of its founder and the printed journals of its early visitors. A short verse

[98] Grose, *Centennial History*, p. 58.

from the title page of a book of poetry written by one who had benefited in health from the use of the mineral waters perhaps best summarizes the fascination and allure of the resort in the days of its greatest popularity:

> At Ballston to the fountain I repair,
> Or hold sweet converse with the charming fair,
>   Or read a newspaper, or scribble rhyme,
>   Or sauntering stroll, and muse away my time.[99]

[99] [Thomas Law], *Ballston Springs* (New York: S. Gould, 1806), title page.

Benjamin West on William Williams
A Previously Unpublished Letter

David H. Dickason

ON APRIL 27, 1791, after living in America for three decades, an obscure artist named William Williams died in the Merchants' and Sailors' Almshouse on King Street in Bristol, in the West Country of England.[1] This sixty-three-year-old mariner-painter-storyteller bequeathed his few possessions to Thomas Eagles of Bristol, a wealthy merchant and classical scholar who had befriended him in his later impoverished years. His bequests included books and papers; artist's paraphernalia; his *Self-Portrait;* the portraits of his two wives; an unfinished picture "on the theme of Penrose"; and a neatly bound holograph clean copy of a long, unsigned, but presumably autobiographical narrative, "Mr. Penrose: The Journal of Penrose, Seaman."[2]

Among his several documents was a manuscript collection entitled "Lives of the Painters," which Williams had spent some years collecting. At the conclusion of this work, he had inserted a unique checklist of his own paintings (now apparently lost) representing three decades of active life as an artist; these pictures included 187 canvases completed in Philadelphia and New York and 54 additional works produced in the West Indies.[3]

This versatile but unrenowned individual was born in Bristol and baptized there on June 14, 1727.[4] From the routine of the local grammar school he soon escaped to sea, made two trips to Virginia, was shipwrecked on the Moskito Coast of Nicaragua, and spent about two years there with the Rama Indians. Thence he made his way to Philadelphia in 1747, where, at the age of twenty, he established himself as an artist and became the first painting teacher of the precocious Benjamin West. Twice married, Williams lost both wives,[5] and his two sons were killed as Revolutionary soldiers. In 1776, alone and depressed, he accepted the invitation of a country gentleman from Bedfordshire to sail to England with him and, henceforth, to paint for pleasure on his large estate. But Williams's benefactor died after eighteen months, so the artist moved to London where he re-established contact with his only friend, Benjamin West, then one of England's eminent painters. While in London, Williams served as a model in *The Battle of La Hogue,* one of West's historical works. About 1781, Williams drifted back to Bristol, opened a studio at No. 29 Clare Street, and produced a number of additional works including a landscape and several religious paintings. Subsequently, he yielded to economic pressures and entered the Almshouse as a pen-

---

[1] Manuscript entry, "Paybook" (Merchants' and Sailors' Almshouse, Bristol, Eng.), courtesy of the Society of Merchant Venturers, Edmund P. King, Esq., Treasurer. See also Burial Register (St. Augustine's Church, Bristol City Archives, Bristol, Eng.), courtesy of Rev. Canon P. Gay, MBE.

[2] Williams's two wills, by permission of Maj. Philip Graham-Clarke of Parc Llettis, Abergavenny, Wales. Williams had given the MS to Eagles some time before his death.

[3] See Thomas Eagles's summary of Williams's checklist in his transcription of West's letter.

[4] St. Augustine's Parish Register (Bristol City Archives, Bristol, Eng.).

[5] For discussion of Williams's marriages, including possibly a third in England, see the forthcoming monograph, David Howard Dickason, *William Williams, Novelist and Painter of Colonial America* (Humanities Monograph Series; Bloomington, Ind.: Indiana University Press, 1970). Col. John F. Williams of San Diego, genealogist of the Williams line in his *Fifty-Six Generations* (San Diego: [Privately printed], 1965), does not believe West's evidence here is completely reliable.

FIG. 1. William Williams, *Self-Portrait.* Bristol, Eng., after 1781. Oil on canvas; H. 30⅛″, W. 25⅛″. (Winterthur, 64.2202.)

sioner, where he painted his final, strong *Self-Portrait* (Fig. 1).[6]

After the old man's death, Williams's friend and patron Thomas Eagles belatedly read the manuscript entitled "Mr. Penrose." He was so impressed by the interest and uniqueness of the narrative that, as a memorial gesture, he decided to restyle its "rough sailor language" completely, to censor certain indelicate phrases and dubious episodes, and to offer it to London printers for commercial publication. He also employed two artists, Edward Bird, R.A., and the Bristol sailor-painter Nicholas Pocock, to make suitable illustrations.[7]

In 1805, fourteen years after Williams's death, Thomas Eagles invited Benjamin West, president of the Royal Academy, to call on him in his London quarters at No. 4 Pall Mall. Awaiting the arrival of his host, West glanced through Eagles's revision of the anonymous Penrose tale and at once recognized the author as his old mentor from his Philadelphia days, who at that time had regaled the youthful West with vivid anecdotes of his castaway days. Eagles, of course, was astounded at this singular coincidence and made memoranda of West's voluble responses to his eager questioning. Eagles was unable to place the manuscript for publication at suitable terms; therefore, in 1810, as a basis for authenticating the tale, he asked West to record the essential details of Williams's career as he could recall them. On Eagles's death two years later, this lengthy letter was passed on to his son, Rev. John Eagles, who, in 1815 (some twenty-four years after the author's death), arranged to have his father's revision of the manuscript published by John Murray. It duly appeared in four volumes under the revised title, *The Journal of Llewellin Penrose, a Seaman.*

Meanwhile, Williams's original manuscript, "Mr. Penrose," had been preserved by its first editor. Passed down through the family line, it has only now become available for publication. In its authentic form for the first time it is a much more vigorous, direct, and earthy tale than the well-meant but bowdlerized paraphrase by Thomas Eagles.[8] Williams's position in American literary history has thus been suddenly signalized, for in point of time of its composition (but not of its posthumous publication) *Mr. Penrose* has every claim to being America's hitherto unrecognized first novel. Aside from its historical significance, it is an intrinsically absorbing account of a Caribbean Crusoe's struggle to survive in an alien environment—a highly readable tale which is superior in many ways to Defoe's familiar narrative.

Similarly, in the annals of American art, Williams was until 1935 only a shadowy background figure with no known canvases to his credit. In that year a *Conversation-Piece* was identified as his work; between that time and the present, approximately a dozen portraits, "emblematical pieces," and landscapes have been established as his.[9] With the new information offered below, it seems possible that other discoveries and identifications will soon be made among the more than two hundred and fifty works now known to have been painted by Williams.

The following unpublished letter from West to Thomas Eagles is one of the prime sources of my biographical and critical study: *William Williams, Novelist and Painter of Colonial America,*

---

[6] Williams's *Self-Portrait,* which had come down through the Eagles family, is now owned by The Henry Francis du Pont Winterthur Museum, which also owns his *William Hall, David Hall,* and *Portrait of a Gentleman and His Wife.*

[7] Thomas Eagles had his MS revision of "Penrose" bound with some blank pages for illustrations, but the edition of 1815 included no art work, and a one-volume edition of 1825 included only two illustrations (both woodcuts), a frontispiece and a vignette on the title page. Eagles's MS, with thirty-nine original water colors by Bird, Pocock, and John Eagles, tipped in, is owned by Mr. Boies Penrose of Barbados Hill, Devon, Pennsylvania.

[8] William Williams, *Mr. Penrose: The Journal of Penrose, Seaman,* ed. David Howard Dickason (Bloomington, Ind., and London: Indiana University Press, 1969). Williams's manuscript is in the Lilly Library of Indiana University.

[9] For data in addition to the material in Dickason, *William Williams,* see William Sawitzky, "William Williams, First Instructor of Benjamin West," *Antiques,* XXXI (May, 1937), 240–42; and "Further Light on the Work of William Williams," *The New-York Historical Society Quarterly Bulletin,* XXV (July, 1941), 101–12. See also James T. Flexner, "The Amazing William Williams: Painter, Author, Teacher, Musician, Stage Designer, Castaway," *Magazine of Art,* XXXVII (Nov., 1944), 242–45, 276–78; and "Benjamin West's American Neo-Classicism, with Documents on West and William Williams," *The New-York Historical Society Quarterly,* XXXVI (Jan., 1952), 5–41. For discussion of Williams's *Imaginary Landscape,* see William H. Gerdts. "Four Significant Paintings: Acquisitions and Attributions," *The Museum* [Newark], X (Winter, 1958), 1–20. Gerdts's "William Williams: New American Discoveries," *Winterthur Portfolio 4* (Charlottesville: University Press of Virginia, 1968), pp. 159–67, is a recent informative summary and analysis. The Metropolitan Museum of New York has just identified and acquired a "new" painting by Williams, *Master Stephen Crossfield.*

which is now in press.[10] In that monograph certain portions of West's epistle are quoted but are rearranged in chronological sequence with reference to Williams's activities, and other portions are omitted. West's letter as printed here thus appears for the first time in its entirety and in its original form.[11] It is a document of major significance in the careers of both West and Williams.

London, Newman St.
Oct.[r] 10— 1810—

Dear Sir,

The voluminous manuscript under the signature of Penrose which I saw in your possession (through the introduction of our respected friend M.[r] Annesley of Reading), appears to me on the investigation of it to have been written by a W.[m] Williams of Philadelphia & founded on his adventures amongst the uncivilized aborigines in the West India Islands—and not by Penrose.

The following will shew you by what circumstances Williams and myself became acquainted, as well as that he was the writer of the above mentioned manuscript. Mr. Edward Pennington a gentleman of high respectability, & of the Society of Friends in the City of Philadelphia was in the habit of annually visiting my Father and family in

[10] See n. 5 above.

[11] This document is Thomas Eagles's copy of West's letter, in Eagles's own handwriting, used by permission of Mr. David Randall, Director, Lilly Library, Indiana University. Brief excerpts from Eagles's memoranda of 1805 and West's letter of 1810 were used by Rev. John Eagles in an "Advertisement" or preface that he composed for the 1815 edition of the restyled manuscript. He also paraphrased or quoted certain passages in his memoir on Williams, "The Beggar's Legacy," *Blackwood's Edinburgh Magazine,* LXXVII (March, 1855), 251–72, reprinted in his *Essays Contributed to Blackwood's Magazine* (Edinburgh and London: W. Blackwood, 1857), 457–502. The modern scholars listed (see n. 9 above) have, in turn, used certain passages from the "Advertisement" and the *Blackwood's* article. In the complete letter printed here, I have made some paragraph divisions for greater readability, but have retained the original text with its variable use of capitals and quotation marks and occasionally irregular punctuation and syntax.

It should be noted that West's original letter is owned by Mr. Boies Penrose, who has generously given permission for the use of the basic document. Eagles, in making his transcription, did a little surreptitious editing (correcting such errors as "dificulties," "dileniation," "discription," "happnd," "leasure," "likness," "naritive," "occured," "ornimenting," "perticuler," "pleasent," and "veriety") and occasionally altered the syntax. He did not, however, regularize the use of quotation marks.

Chester County Pennsylvania as a relative.—Observing some of my childish attempts at the delineation of domestick objects in colours extracted from roots, herbs & bark of trees; he prevailed upon my Parents to take with him to the City his little cousin for some weeks, as he had never seen that place. This happened in the year 1747 in my ninth year—and was a circumstance most grateful to my feelings—indulging the hope of seeing some [paintings: marked out] pictures in the city.

A few days after I was with M.[r] Pennington in the city, he bought me colours, & all the other materials for making pictures in oil. My first attempt was then a Landscape—in which were ships, cattle, & other things which I had been accustomed to see; but before I had finished the picture Samuel Shoemaker* a neighbour of M.[r] Pennington & a gentleman also of the Society of Friends, came to see the picture I was painting; & in the conversation which took place between those two gentlemen on the subject of the Fine Arts, M.[r] Shoemaker informed his friend Pennington that a few days before he had met a person in the street with a picture; & that he requested the person to favour him with a sight of it, which he found to be a Landscape of considerable merit, & painted by the person in whose hands the picture was.—

I learnt from him, said M.[r] Shoemaker, that his name was W. Williams that he had been recently married to a respectable townswoman of our City, & settled here, & that he followed the business of painting in general; he appeared to me to possess a powerful mind, and a great love for painting; and tomorrow I find he will have finished the landscape I commissioned him to paint for me: when it is sufficiently dry to be moved with safety, I will with thy permission friend Pennington bring both the Painter & the picture to thee, & thy little cousin West to see it.

The palpitation of joy which this conversation produced in my mind when I became certain of seeing it was what I can never forget, nor did hours ever pass slower away than those which intervened until I saw the picture, which in a few days was brought to M.[r] Pennington's. I believe the blush of joy which overspread my face on the picture being first exposed to view attracted the attention of those present even more than the

* quer[y] *Shummacher* [Eagle's note].

picture itself altho' a work of considerable merit: it being the first picture I had seen except the small essays I made in the country, and the one I was then attempting to paint in oil.

The attention of Mr Williams still rested on me—while the other persons were beginning to look at his Landscape and to commend it. Soon after Mr Williams addressed himself to Mr Pennington "I am of opinion, Sir, that this youth has the sensibility proper for the studying of painting":—he then turned to me, and wished to know if I had ever read the lives of any of the great Masters of painting—I replied it was the first time I had ever heard of such lives for I had never read any account of great men, but those in the Bible and New Testament, which my Parents directed me to read and remember.

"Well, then," said Mr Williams, "if Mr Pennington will give permission, I will lend you Richardson & du Fresnoy on Painting[12] to read at your leisure." He did so, and those two books were my companions by day, & under my pillow by night. Thus commenced my acquaintance with Wm Williams, which continued without interruption until I embarked for Italy in 1760.

From the year 47 to 60 my attention was directed to every point necessary to accomplish me for the profession of painting; this often brought me to the house of Williams and as he was an excellent actor in taking off Character—he often to amuse me, repeated his adventures amongst the Carribs & Negro tribes in the West Indies—Many of which adventures were strictly the same as related in your manuscript of Penrose as also his description of the scenery of those coasts—the birds on them, in particular the Flamingo birds, which he described when seen at a distance as appearing like companies of Soldiers dressed in red Uniforms. He spoke both the Negro and Carrib tongue, and appeared to me to have lived amongst them for some years.

I often asked him how he came to be with them —he replied that he had been put to the sea when young; that he never was satisfied with that pursuit, & that he took the first opportunity which

offered to desert it, by making his way for the West Indies, where he was shipwrecked, & thrown into great difficulties, but Providence had preserved him through a variety of dangers. He likewise informed me that he was a Welshman by birth; but brought up at a Grammar School in Bristol—where his greatest delight was to go & see an elderly artist who painted heads in oil, as well as small landscapes & his greatest wish was to be a Painter; but in that he was disappointed, & bound when young to a Virginia Capt who sometimes sailed out of London as well as from Bristol in the Virginia trade.—

"After going the second voyage with him, when in Norfolk, in Virginia—to tell you the truth he said, I left the ship & sailed for the West Indies, where I hoped to be unknown, that I might work my way to some place—& accomplish my wishes as a Painter:—and after some years had elapsed, I was able to come to this city [Philadelphia]— and ever since my arrival, I have studied the science of painting, by collecting the lives of the eminent painters* as well as the prints from their works." This I knew to be the truth, as it was to his books and prints I was indebted for all the knowledge I possessed of the progress which the fine Arts had made in the world, & which prompted me to view them in Italy.

The following circumstance came to my knowledge respecting Williams; not long after I arrived in London in the year 62. Becoming acquainted with a Col. Hunter who had then settled with his family in London from Virginia; one day dining with him, he asked me how I came at the knowledge of painting in the City of Philadelphia. I told him it was by the acquaintance of a Wm Williams—who had more enthusiasm for the Art than any person I had ever met with. "What a singular event is this replied the Col. I will tell you Mr West, what will surprise you as it did me. —When I went with the Governor of Virginia (Dinwiddie) as one of the Deputies to attend the Governor of Philadelphia in the year 55, to join the Governors from the other Provinces to hold the great Treaty at East Town in Pensylvania with the friendly Indian Chiefs: Mr Williams

---

[12] Jonathan Richardson, *Two Discourses* (London: W. Churchill, 1719); perhaps also *An Essay on the Theory of Painting* (2nd ed.; London: A. Bettesworth, 1725). Charles-Alphonse du Fresnoy, *De Arte Graphica: The Art of Painting, with Remarks*, trans. [John] Dryden (London: Printed by J. Hepinstall for W. Rogers, 1695). These treatises generally expounded neoclassic values in art.

* [Marked with an X by Eagles, with an extra page inserted in his transcription of West's letter to present his summary of Williams's checklist, to be found here at the conclusion.]

waited on me while I was at Philadelphia & informed me that when he was a Boy he had been bound to me when I was in the Virginia Trade; but not willing to continue in that Service had absented himself from my ship while lying in Norfolk in Virginia, & went to the West Indies from whence he came to this city some years after — that he was married and settled here — & that he had taken the business of painting in general.

"I have waited on you Sir" said he, "to declare who I am, & if I can make you any recompense for leaving your service, I shall do it to the utmost of my power."

I told him that I had forgot both him, and the circumstance untill his narrative brought both to my memory — that I was much pleased to see him as well as with the principles of his visit. I frequently called to see him in his family while I stopped at Philadelphia, and introduced him to several of my friends in that city. When he was on board my ship I often remarked him engaged in drawing, & soon distinguished him to be a Boy of no common capacity, and it was my intention had he remained with me to place him in my Counting house at Norfolk, to better his situation in life — But I was never more pleased than to find his respectable situation in Philadelphia, except this, which you have told me of his being the person who kindled the latent sparks of painting which he then discovered in you, into that blaze with which it now appears in this country."

"I am obliged to you Col." I replied "for the compliment; but it proves how little we are awake to those events which till their development have been the cause of even producing revolutions: for most undoubtedly had not Williams been settled in Philadelphia I sh^d not have embraced painting as a profession."

Mr Williams was a man of quick penetration, but his love of the Fine Arts became his most devout pursuit. Painting he cultivated as a Profession — Music as an amusement, & Poetry he often indulged himself in with considerable power: There was a piece of his Poetry addressed to me in my twelfth year — it was published in one of the daily papers in Philadelphia, & much admired, tho' no one knew who was the Author. On my preparing to embark for Italy he wrote me an acrostick on my name, which he sent to me after I had taken my leave of him — in which he predicted my future elevation in painting.[13]

Soon after my departure from Philadelphia for Italy Williams had the misfortune to lose his Wife, by whom he had two sons: he was most devoutly attached to the Mother Country (Great Britain) but his sons being born in Philadelphia they became attached to America & took up arms with thousands of other youths to join her Armies, & were killed in some of the battles. Mr Williams finding himself advancing in years — & much dejected at the loss of his sons, & the revolution of families & things in that Country; availed himself of a friendly proposition made to him by an English gentleman returning from America, to embark with him for England — to reside under his roof in Bedfordshire, & to paint there for his amusement the remainder of his life. On their arrival in London, Williams came to me & introduced his friend — They stopped in town about ten days; after which they went into Bedfordshire. In about eighteen months after his friend died — & Williams once more returned to London. — He was frequently at my house, & remained in London more than two years in the daily pursuit of collecting portrait prints of eminent painters — This brought him much into the society of those who collected such prints — in that number was Mr Nathl Smith the print seller. His son the present Thos. Smith saw, & knew more of Williams during his stay in London — & has favoured me with a paper which he has written to oblige me respecting what he knew of Williams while here.

At this time [1778] I was painting my picture of the Battle of La Hogue in which I introduced a likeness of Williams in one of the Boats, next in the rear of Sir George Rook[e]; & soon after this period I lost sight of him, & becoming apprehensive that he was dead, on my making enquiry of Mr Smith, what had become of him — he informed me that he was gone to Bristol, but for what purpose he did not know.

Thus good Sir agreeable to your and Mr Annesley's request I have given you what knowledge I possess of Wm Williams from the year 1747, to his departure from London to Bristol about the year 1781. —

---

[13] In Eagles's copy of West's letter the last four lines are repeated by error.

If you can compile from this account of Williams which I have arranged of him for three & thirty years—one that will be satisfactory to yourself and the World, that he was the Author of the Manuscript in y^r possession under the signature of Penrose—it is at your service for this purpose.

I have the honour to be with respect

Dear Sir—

Y^r most obed^t hum^l Servt

Benjn West

P.S. It has often occurred to me that Williams must have given the name of Penrose to his manuscript in compliment to a very great friend of his in Philadelphia of that name. Mr Penrose was one of the most elegant ship builders in all America, or I believe, to be found in Europe—And it was the painting, & ornamenting of his ships, that was Williams' best employment, as well as that the name of Penrose was pleasant to the poetical ear of such a man as Williams.

Thomas Eagles Esq.
Bristol

X in the Vol of his copying of the Lives of the Painters—at the end is a list of his Paintings—

A.D. 1750—Pictures painted at Philadelphia amongst 100—the owner of each is specified—is "Small Portrait of Benjamin Lay for Dr. Benjamin Franklin"[14]

1760—Pictures painted in Jamaica 54—

1769—Pictures painted in New York 87—amongst these is a "small whole length of William Williams Junr Painter" among innumerable portraits are

An Emblematical piece for ye Corsican Club

A small Moonlight for Lord Rosehill

A small whole length of Lady Rosehill

A Conversation of Mr. Denning & family

A large History of the Good Samaritan for Mr. C. Bush [Buck?]

A History piece of the Repose in Egypt for do. [ditto]

A small Landskip for Mr. J. Minshull

A large Tempest for Cap^n A. Rutgers

[14] For discussion of this work and its subject, see Wilford P. Cole, "Henry Dawkins and The Quaker Comet," *Winterthur Portfolio 4*, pp. 34–46.

Heads of States

Milton Kaplan

THROUGH the years, curators of American prints have generally accepted as basic one fact—that portraits are the most accurate pictorial documents. It is known that topographical prints are often imaginary views and that depictions of historic events were frequently invented by artists who were not actually present. Portraits, however, have always been regarded as deriving at least from an authentic image, if not from a direct confrontation with the sitter. It comes as something of a shock, therefore, to discover that during the nineteenth century, unexpected liberties frequently were taken with portraits of prominent Americans.[1]

Any student of American history should know that Martin Van Buren and Abraham Lincoln had little more in common than the fact that both were Presidents of the United States and that John Charles Frémont and Lincoln shared the honor of being Republican candidates for the Presidency in 1856 and 1860. Evidence has been gathered, however, which overwhelmingly supports the fact that these men were publicly presented as sharing something even more personal —each pair had the same body.

Lincoln's popularity and the tragic circumstances of his death created a tremendous public demand for his likeness; to satisfy this, portraits by the hundreds, in various media including engravings, lithographs, woodcuts, and *carte-de-vis-*

ite photographic copies of prints, were rushed to the market.[2] During the past several years evidence has been uncovered that at least five of these Lincoln prints, and possibly a sixth, are not totally genuine portraits of the nation's sixteenth President, but, instead, are second states or altered plates (and in one case, a third state) of previously published portraits of other well-known Americans.

Between 1837 and 1841, John Sartain, a Philadelphia engraver, produced a mezzotint of President Martin Van Buren, which was based on a painting by Henry Inman (Fig. 1); and between 1864 and 1865 he issued a "new" portrait of Abraham Lincoln (Fig. 2).[3] An examination of the two prints clearly reveals that the Lincoln portrait is an alteration of the Van Buren mezzotint: in addition to substituting Lincoln's face (based on a photograph taken at the White House in 1864 by Wenderoth & Taylor of Philadelphia), Sartain changed St. John's Church to the Capitol and Van Buren's cutaway coat to Lincoln's full-length frock coat, making in addition some minor changes in the collar.

The Frémont-Lincoln odyssey began in 1859 when a John Chester Buttre engraving of John

---

[1] This article is not intended to include all altered American portraits; there probably are many other examples, and the author would be greatly interested in knowing of them. All the prints reproduced here are in the collections of the Library of Congress, with the exception of the privately owned Blair portrait. Photographic copies of it, however, can be obtained from the Library of Congress.

[2] Winifred Poter Truesdell, *Engraved and Lithographed Portraits* (Champlain, N.Y.: The Troutsdale Press, 1933), lists more than 550 separately published prints.

[3] John Sartain (1808–1897) was a London-born painter and engraver who became prominent in Philadelphia after 1850; Henry Inman (1801–1846), although active in genre, miniature, and landscape painting, was known primarily for his portrait work. See George C. Groce and David H. Wallace, *The New-York Historical Society's Dictionary of Artists in America* (New Haven, Conn.: Yale University Press, 1957). The Van Buren mezzotint was published by William H. Morgan & Son, the Lincoln portrait by William Smith.

FIG. 1. John Sartain, *Martin Van Buren*. Philadelphia, 1837–1841. Mezzotint engraving, after painting by Henry Inman; H. 20³⁄₁₆″, W. 13³⁄₁₆″. (Library of Congress.)

FIG. 2. *Abraham Lincoln*. Second state of Fig. 1, 1864–65. (Library of Congress.)

Charles Frémont was published (Fig. 3) .[4] The following year Buttre issued a portrait of a beardless Lincoln using the same plate (Fig. 4) . It was published sometime between February 27 (when Mathew B. Brady made the photograph that Buttre used) and November 26 (when Lincoln was photographed for the first time with a beard) and may have been used as a campaign portrait during the presidential contest of 1860. Aside from the head, the only other changes in the engraving are the tie and the transformation of the globe of the

world into a lamp. Buttre later published a third state of the print in which he slightly modified Lincoln's features and gave him a beard (Fig. 5) . It is particularly interesting that the impression of this state clearly shows the outside circumference of the original globe, which resulted from over-inking of the plate causing all the lines that had not been properly burnished out to print.[5]

In 1859, Alexander Hay Ritchie copyrighted and published an engraving of Andrew Jackson

---

[4] Groce and Wallace, *Dictionary of Artists*, list Buttre (1821–1893) as a wood engraver, portrait painter, and publisher.

[5] Sometime during the 1860's (probably in 1864) , the Philadelphia lithographing firm of Herline & Hensel published an exact lithographic copy of the bearded Lincoln by Buttre.

FIG. 3. John C. Buttre, *John Charles Frémont*. New York, 1859. Engraving; H. 25$^{11}/_{16}$″, W. 18$^{11}/_{16}$″. (Library of Congress.)

FIG. 4. *Abraham Lincoln*. Second state of Fig. 3, 1860. (Library of Congress.)

FIG. 5. *Abraham Lincoln*. Third state of Fig. 3, 1860–61. (Library of Congress.)

FIG. 6. Alexander Hay Ritchie, *Andrew Jackson*. New York, 1859. Engraving, after painting by Dennis Malone Carter; H. 26″, W. 19½″. (Library of Congress.)

FIG. 7. Buttre, *Abraham Lincoln*. Second state of Fig. 6, after Feb. 9, 1864. (Library of Congress.)

(Fig. 6), which was based on a painting by Dennis Malone Carter.[6] Five years later Buttre published a portrait of *Abraham Lincoln. President of the United States* (Fig. 7) in which the following alterations were made: Jackson's cutaway coat became a full-length frock coat (examination of the original prints clearly reveals some of the lines of the cutaway coat); a watch fob was added to Lincoln's vest; the view of the Capitol Building was covered by the Houdon bust of Washington placed on a table near the window (and here again, because of inadequate burnishing out of the lines, part of the Capitol is still visible in the Lincoln portrait); and the paper on the desk in the Jackson portrait, which clearly reads "The

Union must and shall be preserved," had had several vertical lines added to it. The face of Lincoln was based on a photograph taken by Anthony Berger in Brady's Washington gallery on February 9, 1864. One question about this Lincoln print, however, remains unanswered: how did Buttre acquire the plate from Ritchie?

The story of the fourth Lincoln portrait began in 1862 when Henry Sartain[7] copyrighted and published a John Sartain mezzotint of *Frank P. Blair, Jr., Col. of the 1st Mo. Light Artillery* (Fig. 8), which was based on a painting by Ferdinand Thomas Lee Boyle of St. Louis. Two years later, Richard R. Landon of Chicago published a Sartain mezzotint of Lincoln that is clearly an altera-

[6] Ritchie (1822–1895) is listed as engraver and genre, portrait, and figure painter, and Carter (1818 or 1820–1881) as a portrait and figure painter, in Groce and Wallace, *Dictionary of Artists*.

[7] Henry Sartain was the son of John Sartain and trained as an engraver and painter. See Groce and Wallace, *Dictionary of Artists*.

Fig. 8. Sartain, *Frank P. Blair, Jr.* Philadelphia, 1862. Engraving, after painting by Ferdinand Thomas Lee Boyle; H. 21½″, W. 15¼″. (Photo, Library of Congress.)

Fig. 9. Sartain, *Abraham Lincoln.* Second state of Fig. 8, 1864. (Library of Congress.)

tion of the Blair portrait (Fig. 9) .[8] Other than the face of Lincoln, based on a photograph taken by Brady on January 8, 1864, there were very few changes made. The name of Benton was eliminated from the book to the right of the bust, "Campaign of 1864–5" was added to the map on the floor, the globe of the world was turned to show a different land mass, and the newspaper on the desk was changed from "Democratic" to "Daily M." Printed below the portrait to the left is the phrase, "The head after a photograph from life, the picture by Boyle." It is interesting to speculate why Sartain gave credit to Boyle. Had the artist found out that Sartain planned to publish a "new" portrait of Lincoln using the altered Blair plate and insisted that he be given credit? Or did

Sartain have some qualms about re-using the plate and, by giving credit to Boyle, ease his conscience?

Probably the most interesting hybrid Lincoln portrait in the group is an engraving that was published by William Pate in 1864 (Fig. 10) .[9] Although we have been unable to locate an impression of an engraving that would prove conclusively that this Lincoln portrait had come from an altered plate, there is circumstantial evidence that prior to its transformation, it had been a portrait of John C. Calhoun. Included in Evert A. Duyckinck's *National Portrait Gallery of Eminent Americans* is an engraving of Calhoun (Fig. 11) .[10] A comparison of it with the Pate engraving, based on a photograph taken by Berger in Brady's Washington Gallery on February 9, 1864,[11] reveals

[8] The 1863 city directories of Chicago list Landon as "agent, pocket books, maps, engravings, notions, etc."

[9] William Pate was listed as both engraver and printer in the New York City directories of 1860.

[10] New York: Johnson, Fry & Co., 1864, II, opp. p. 162.

[11] This is generally known as the "$5.00 bill portrait."

FIG. 10. William Pate, *Abraham Lincoln*. New York, 1864. Engraving; H. 26½″, W. 19⁹⁄₁₆″. (Library of Congress.)

FIG. 11. *J. C. Calhoun*. Engraving; H. 7⅜″, W. 5⅜″. Published in Evert A. Duyckinck, *National Portrait Gallery of Eminent Americans* (New York: Johnson, Fry & Co., 1864), II, opp. p. 162. (Library of Congress.)

only one change other than Lincoln's face. The titles of the papers on the desk in the Calhoun portrait, "Strict Construction," "Free Trade," and "The Sovereignty of the States," were changed to "Constitution," "Union," and "Proclamation of Freedom." The Calhoun portrait is, we are quite certain, a reduced version of a larger plate that was altered to produce this portrait of Lincoln. If such a plate did not exist, why would any engraver have presented the Great Emancipator in a pose so totally un-Lincolnesque?

The practice of altering previously published engravings to create new images of Lincoln was not limited to single figures. In 1852, Augustus W. Sexton of New York copyrighted the mezzotint *Union,* engraved by Henry S. Sadd and based on a painting by Tompkins Harrison Matteson, whose central figure was John C. Calhoun (Fig. 12). Eight years later the engraving was reissued by

Pate, and in it the face of Calhoun was changed to that of Lincoln (Fig. 13). Clearly visible in the Lincoln print are several of the lines which had made up Calhoun's hair. According to Winifred Poter Truesdell, another state of the print was later published with the head of Lincoln changed to Gen. Benjamin F. Butler.[12]

Abraham Lincoln was not the only celebrity given the same body–new head treatment. In 1848 William Smith of Philadelphia published a John Sartain mezzotint of Zachary Taylor (Fig. 14); and in 1864, after a number of changes, the plate was republished as a portrait of U. S. Grant (Fig. 15). On July 3, 1852, Waterman Lilly Ormsby copyrighted his engraved portrait of Gen. Frank-

[12] Truesdell, *Portraits*, p. 69.

FIG. 12. Henry S. Sadd, *Union*. New York, 1852. Engraving, after painting by Tompkins Harrison Matteson; H. 19⅜″, W. 26⁷⁄₁₆″. (Library of Congress.)

FIG. 13. *Union*. Second state of Fig. 12, 1860. (Library of Congress.)

FIG. 14. Sartain, *Major-General Zachary Taylor.* Philadelphia, 1848. Engraving after a daguerreotype; H. 20⅞″, W. 15¾″. (Library of Congress.)

FIG. 15. *Lieut. General U. S. Grant.* Second state of Fig. 14, 1864. (Library of Congress.)

lin Pierce, which was published in connection with Pierce's campaign as the Democratic nominee for President that year (Fig. 16) .[13] About ten years later, Pierce returned as *Maj. Gen. Geo. B. M'Clellan, Commanding United States Army* (Fig. 17). Ormsby made alterations in the uniform and the spyglass and converted the castlelike building into the United States Capitol. The change of the military headgear worn during the war with Mexico in the Pierce portrait to that of the Civil War in the McClellan portrait was not executed very well, and this is clearly visible in an examination of the original engravings.

The altering of engraved plates to create new portraits was not an original American contribu-

[13] Ormsby (1809–1883) is listed in Groce and Wallace, *Dictionary of Artists,* as a banknote and general engraver.

FIG. 16. Waterman Lilly Ormsby, *Gen. Franklin Pierce.* New York City, 1852. Engraving; H. 21¹⁵⁄₁₆″, W. 15⅝″. (Library of Congress.)

FIG. 17. *Maj. Gen. Geo. B. M'Clellan.* Second state of Fig. 16, *ca.* 1862. (Library of Congress.)

tion to the arts. In fact, it is quite possible that the New World had borrowed from the Old. In 1927, George S. Layard recorded 118 European plates that were changed into more than 130 new portraits, several plates being altered more than once.[14] Of special interest is the listing of at least two plates in which a man was transformed into a woman. Two of the portraits listed by Layard are of Charles I and Oliver Cromwell, engraved by Pierre Lombart (1613–1682), for which an Anthony Van Dyck painting of Charles I served as the model. In both the catalog and in Layard's book *The Headless Horseman,* the portrait of Charles I (Fig. 18) is listed as the sixth and the Cromwell portrait (Fig. 19) as the seventh of

[14] George Somes Layard, *Catalogue Raisonné of Engraved British Portraits from Altered Plates* (London: Philip Allan & Co., 1927), pp. 37–38.

FIG. 18. Pierre Lombart, *Carolus I*. London, after 1648. Engraving, after painting by Anthony Van Dyck; H. 21 11/16″, W. 13 15/16″. (Library of Congress.)

FIG. 19. Lombart, *Oliverius*. Altered state of Fig. 18, *ca.* 1653. (Library of Congress.)

seven different states of the Lombart plate.[15] However, H. M. Cundall lists them as the fifth and sixth of six states.[16]

Engravers were not the only printmakers who used the same body–different head technique. During the Civil War, the Cincinnati lithographing firm of Ehrgott, Forbriger & Company published at least twenty-eight portraits of military and political figures but used only nine stones. Minor changes were made in a number of the groups, but in several of them, particularly group A, the only changes were the faces. This group is especially interesting and somewhat amusing be-

cause none of the heads properly fit the bodies. The lithographs range in size from 9 15/16 inches by 9 7/16 inches to 13 5/8 inches by 10 9/16 inches:

Group A	Salmon P. Chase, Sec. of the Treasury
	O. P. Morton, Gov. of Indiana
	Andrew Johnson, Military Gov. of Tennessee (Fig. 20)
	David Tod, Gov. of Ohio
	Abraham Lincoln, President (Fig. 21)
Group B	George G. Meade, Maj. Gen., U.S.A. (Fig. 22)
	U. S. Grant, Maj. Gen., U.S.A. (Fig. 23)
	Ambrose E. Burnside, Maj. Gen., U.S.A.
	Robert C. Schenck, Maj. Gen., U.S.A.
Group C	George Stoneman, Maj. Gen., U.S.A. (Fig. 24)
	George H. Thomas, Maj. Gen., U.S.A.
	Daniel E. Sickles, Maj. Gen., U.S.A. (Fig. 25)

[15] George Somes Layard, *The Headless Horseman: Pierre Lombart's Engraving; Charles or Cromwell?* (London: Philip Allan & Co., 1922).

[16] H. M. Cundall, "A Much-Altered Engraved Copper Plate," *The Art Journal* (Oct., 1903), pp. 305–7.

FIG. 20. Ehrgott, Forbriger & Co., *Andy Johnson.* Cincinnati, 1861–65. Lithograph; H. 13⅜″, W. 9⅜″. (Library of Congress.)

FIG. 21. *A. Lincoln.* Another state of Fig. 20. (Library of Congress.)

FIG. 22. Ehrgott, Forbriger & Co., *Geo. G. Meade.* Cincinnati, 1861–65. Lithograph; H. 11⅝″, W. 9¹¹⁄₁₆″. (Library of Congress.)

FIG. 23. *U. S. Grant.* Another state of Fig. 22. (Library of Congress.)

FIG. 24. Ehrgott, Forbriger & Co., *Geo. Stoneman*. Cincinnati, 1861–65. Lithograph; H. 13⅝″, W. 10⅝″. (Library of Congress.)

FIG. 25. *Dan E. Sickles*. Another state of Fig. 24. (Library of Congress.)

	Quincy A. Gillmore, Maj. Gen., U.S.A.
Group D	Andrew H. Foote, Com., U.S.N. (Fig. 26)
	John A. Dahlgren, Comdr., U.S.N. (Fig. 27)
Group E	S. R. Curtis, Maj. Gen., U.S.A. (Fig. 28)
	John C. Frémont, Maj. Gen., U.S.A. (Fig. 29)
	William B. Franklin, Maj. Gen., U.S.A.
	E. E. Ellsworth, Col., U.S.A.
Group F	Joseph Hooker, Maj. Gen., U.S.A. (Fig. 30)
	Jefferson C. Davis, Brig. Gen., U.S.A. (Fig. 31)
	William S. Rosecrans, Maj. Gen., U.S.A.
Group G	William T. Sherman, Maj. Gen., U.S.A. (Fig. 32)
	John A. Dix, Maj. Gen., U.S.A. (Fig. 33)
Group H	Jonathan A. McClernand, Brig. Gen., U.S.A. (Fig. 34)
	Nathaniel Lyon, Brig. Gen., U.S.A. (Fig. 35)
Group I	Henry W. Halleck, Maj. Gen., U.S.A.
	Benjamin F. Butler, Maj. Gen., U.S.A.

Why were plates and lithographic stones altered and the resulting prints issued as new portraits? It

FIG. 26. Ehrgott, Forbriger & Co., *Commodore Foote*. Cincinnati, 1861–65. Lithograph; H. 9^{15}⁄$_{16}$″, W. 9^{5}⁄$_{16}$″. (Library of Congress.)

FIG. 27. *Com. Dahlgreen*. Another state of Fig. 26. (Library of Congress.)

FIG. 28. Ehrgott, Forbriger & Co., *S. R. Curtis*. Cincinnati, 1861–65. Lithograph; H. 11½″, W. 9⅜″. (Library of Congress.)

FIG. 29. *John C. Fremont*. Another state of Fig. 28. (Library of Congress.)

FIG. 30. Ehrgott, Forbriger & Co., *Joe. Hooker*. Cincinnati, 1861–65. Lithograph; H. 10¾″, W. 9¾″. (Library of Congress.)

FIG. 31. *Jefferson C. Davis*. Another state of Fig. 30. (Library of Congress.)

FIG. 32. Ehrgott, Forbriger & Co., *W. T. Sherman*. Cincinnati, 1861–65. Lithograph; H. 9½″, W. 9⁷⁄₁₆″. (Library of Congress.)

FIG. 33. *John A. Dix*. Another state of Fig. 32. (Library of Congress.)

Fig. 34. Ehrgott, Forbriger & Co., *Jno. A. Mᶜ Clernand.*
Cincinnati, 1861–65. Lithograph; H. 13¼″, W. 9⁷⁄₁₆″.
(Library of Congress.)

Fig. 35. *Nathˡ Lyon.* Another state of Fig. 34. (Library
of Congress.)

was a matter of economics, as Layard suggested;
and, although intaglio prints were his major concern, his answer is also applicable to lithography.

Copperplates were very expensive; the demand for a
topical plate would sometimes last only for a few
weeks. Between them, the engraver and the publisher
evolved the expedient of altering and adapting plates
to their immediate need. Obviously it took much less
time to burnish out the head . . . than to engrave an
entirely new plate. It cannot always have been easy to
find a suitable plate, and in some cases the engravers
shewed extraordinary ingenuity in their adaptations.[17]

Apparently documentary prints are not always
what they claim to be. These depictions of people,
places, events, and things have commonly been accepted at face value. For the most part, it seems
that too little time has been spent by both the
print curator and the user of the pictorial record
in evaluating American historical prints. The result is that they have been used too often without

---

[17] Layard, *Catalogue Raisonné*, p. vii.

qualification as accurate presentations of whatever they portray.

During the observance of the centennial of the Civil War, there was a great demand for pictures of battle action, and quite often Currier & Ives lithographs were used to answer the need. An examination of them reveals a certain sameness— troops charging in from the right or from the left, dead soldiers, dead horses, all in very similar positions. They are not illustrations of actual battle actions based on eyewitness sketches made on the battlefields; they are the work of artists who drew what they imagined the battle actions to have been. Their only relevance to the war is that they were published between 1861 and 1865.

This same aspect occurs in the pictorial material used in today's American history textbooks, particularly in those sections dealing with the early years of the American experience. Throughout the nineteenth century, surveys of American history were being published, and publishers and authors enhanced their books with illustrations. Artists were hired to create the desired pictures; but their illustrations, like the Currier & Ives prints, were not based on sketches or drawings that had been made during the years of settlement, the colonial period, or the Revolutionary War. They generally were the artists' imaginings of how those events might have appeared. Today these illustrations reappear in American history textbooks, unaccompanied by explanations or statements about them.

With the increasing use of visual records, it is incumbent upon both the print curator and the historian, in an attempt to separate truth from fiction, to examine closely the great body of pictorial material. American historical prints should be as carefully analyzed as are such primary source material as diaries, letters, and journals. Otherwise, the perpetration of fiction will continue.

Daniel Trotter: Eighteenth-Century Philadelphia Cabinetmaker

Anne Castrodale Golovin

THE following notice appeared in *Claypoole's American Daily Advertiser* of Philadelphia on May 6, 1800: "Died a few days since, of a lingering illness, Mr. Daniel Trotter, a well-known and much respected inhabitant of this city. 'Mark the perfect man, and behold the upright, for the end of that man is peace.' "[1] Although this brief statement speaks eloquently of the character of the cabinetmaker Daniel Trotter, much more can be said about the life and work of this craftsman.

One of six children of the Quaker shoemaker William Trotter and his wife, Elizabeth, Daniel Trotter was born in Philadelphia in 1747. He was twelve when his father died, and four years later, death claimed his mother.[2] By the time he was orphaned, Trotter had received the major part of his formal education. Undoubtedly he had the benefit of schooling provided by the Society of Friends in Philadelphia, since, in 1701, a charter had been granted by William Penn for a Quaker school to teach "the rich at reasonable rates and the poor to be maintained for nothing." The anti-

slavery leader and educator Anthony Benezet and the historian Robert Proud were masters at this school during the years when Trotter was no doubt learning the fundamentals of reading, writing, and arithmetic in combination with religious precepts.[3]

Pursuing the accepted course toward becoming a master craftsman, Daniel Trotter was apprenticed, probably at age fourteen, to the Quaker cabinetmaker William Wayne.[4] His choice of trade was not unique in the family for the Trotter name in Philadelphia was linked with the production of furniture prior to Daniel's time. Benjamin Trotter, his great-uncle born in 1699, was a chairmaker whose recognition as a "zealous Preacher amongst the Quakers" outlived his reputation as a craftsman, and his uncle Joseph Trotter was a joiner.[5] Of Daniel's own generation were his cousins Jeremiah and Josiah Elfreth, who trained in the cabinetmaking craft.[6] His elder brother, Joseph, became a chairmaker, and Jo-

[1] Trotter's death was noted in the *Mirror of the Times, & General Advertiser* (Wilmington, Del.) on May 10, 1800: "Also at Philadelphia, of a lingering illness, Daniel Trotter, a well-known and much-respected inhabitant of that city."

[2] Arithmetic Book of Nathan Trotter (Thompson Collection, Historical Society of Pennsylvania, Philadelphia [hereafter HSP]); George Morgan, *The City of Firsts, Being a Complete History of the City of Philadelphia from Its Founding in 1682 until the Present Time* (Philadelphia: Historical Publication Society, 1926), p. 532; 1756 Tax List of the City of Philadelphia, p. 9 (HSP); and Chart of the Trotter Family Genealogy, designed and executed by Newbold H. Trotter, 1868 (HSP). For a brief but thorough study of the Trotter family background, see Elva Tooker, *Nathan Trotter, Philadelphia Merchant, 1787–1853* (Cambridge, Mass.: Harvard University Press, 1955), pp. 24–33.

[3] Howard Brinton, *Quaker Education in Theory and Practice* (Wallingford, Pa.: Pendle Hill, 1940), pp. 37–38.

[4] Nancy Ann Goyne, "Furniture Craftsmen in Philadelphia, 1760–1790: Their Role in a Mercantile Society" (unpublished Master's thesis, University of Delaware, 1963), p. 20.

[5] Pemberton Papers, XX, 4 (HSP); Harold E. Gillingham, "The Philadelphia Windsor Chair and Its Journeyings," *The Pennsylvania Magazine of History and Biography* (hereafter *PMHB*), LV, No. 3 (1931), 306; and Philadelphia Monthly Meeting Minutes, E-4, pp. 258–59 (Department of Records, Philadelphia Yearly Meeting of Friends). Joseph Trotter died in 1770; see Will Book P, p. 21 (Office of the Registrar of Wills, Philadelphia Municipal Archives [hereafter PMA]).

[6] Deed Book EF-22, pp. 80–82 (Office of the Recorder of Deeds, PMA). Daniel Trotter's aunt Hannah Trotter married Jeremiah Elfreth, a goldsmith; Jeremiah, Jr., and Josiah were their offspring; see Will Book P-340, p. 231 (Office of the Registrar of Wills, PMA).

seph's son, William I. Trotter (with whom the tradition ended), entered the cabinetmaking business.[7]

In 1768, at age twenty-one, Daniel Trotter received a "freedom sute" from Wayne signifying the successful completion of his apprenticeship.[8] The following year Trotter was living in South Ward with the master cabinetmaker George Claypoole, presumably working for him as a journeyman.[9] In August, 1769, Jonathan Zane paid Trotter £1.15.0 for a coffin;[10] however, the independence implied by this transaction may be misleading since a journeyman sometimes made and sold items on his own while still employed by a master.

A bill to Samuel Wallis, dated September 7, 1771, for a walnut cradle, a pine table, a "crib bedstead," and "1 safe" indicates that by this date Trotter had entered a partnership with John Webb.[11] Like Trotter, Webb was a devout Quaker who was described by an acquaintance as "a very excellent member of the Society of Friends. He was a cabinetmaker by trade. . . . Mr. Webb was a practically pious man, keeping his own end in view by the *memento mori* of his own measured coffin under his bed. He was a preacher of the Society of Friends."[12]

Partnerships among Quaker craftsmen and mer-

chants in the eighteenth century were quite common. The parties involved usually agreed on a specific number of years for the duration of the partnership, after which they were at liberty to withdraw.[13] An announcement of the termination of this alliance was published in the *Pennsylvania Gazette* of April 27, 1774:

All persons that have any demands against the partnership of WEBB and TROTTER, cabinetmakers, are desired to bring in their accounts on or before the 13th of May next, as the partnership will then expire. Webb moves to front-street, nearly opposite the bank Meeting-house; and those indebted, are requested to make payment. N.B. Said partners have for sale, a few pieces of furniture; also a neat two sail boat, which they will sell cheap for cash.

By 1773, Daniel and his brother Joseph resided with their father's widowed sister, Hannah Elfreth.[14] At this time, Daniel was successfully courting nineteen-year-old Rebecca Conarroe who, with her family, lived in the Northern Liberties, a suburb of Philadelphia. Following Quaker requirements, Trotter and his prospective wife declared their intention to marry at the Society of Friends Monthly Meeting of the Northern District of Philadelphia in September and October of 1773.[15] The wedding took place at the meeting-house on November 9, with fifty-three friends and relatives present, among whom were four of Trotter's fellow cabinetmakers: Josiah Elfreth, David Evans, John Webb, and Stephen Maxfield.[16] Trotter and his bride rented a house (still standing) owned by Mary Saunderson on the south side of Elfreth's Alley, a narrow street one block in length, close to the Delaware River (Fig. 1).[17]

With a population of approximately forty thousand people, Philadelphia was the largest city in

---

[7] *The Philadelphia Directory* (Philadelphia: Francis White, 1785), entry for "Joseph Trotter"; Bond to Refund and Indemnify Matthew West and Wife and William I. Trotter to William Trotter and Ephraim Haines Administrators of Daniel Trotter Deceased, MS 67x90.20 (Trotter Papers, Downs Manuscript and Microfilm Collection, The Henry Francis du Pont Winterthur Museum [hereafter DMMC]).

[8] See entry dated June 16, 1768, in account of William Wayne with Joseph Graisbury, Joseph Graisbury Ledger (1759-1774) (Reed and Forde Papers, HSP).

[9] Provincial Tax List for 1769, p. 191 (Division of Public Records, Pennsylvania History and Museum Commission, Harrisburg); photocopy owned by Mrs. Hannah Roach, Philadelphia.

[10] Jonathan Zane paid "One Pound one Shilling & Six Pence in Cash & Thirteen Shillings & Six Pence by Discount in All One Pound fifteen Shillings in full for a coffin." See entry for Daniel Trotter, Aug. 1, 1769, Receipt Book of Jonathan Zane (1761-1773), AM-949 (HSP).

[11] Microfilm copy of Wallis Papers, Vol. 3, XX-2-3 (HSP). Although no references to this partnership include Christian names, tax records for 1773 confirm the fact that John Webb and Daniel Trotter were working together in Upper Delaware Ward. See Philadelphia County Tax Assessment Ledger, 1773, p. 126 (Department of Records, PMA).

[12] Abraham Ritter, *Philadelphia and Her Merchants as Constituted Fifty to Seventy Years Ago* (Philadelphia: The author, 1860), pp. 122-23.

[13] Frederick B. Tolles, *Meeting House and Counting House* (Chapel Hill: University of North Carolina Press, 1948), p. 92.

[14] Philadelphia County Tax Assessment Ledger, 1773, p. 66 (Department of Records, PMA).

[15] Northern District Monthly Meeting Minutes, RS-268, pp. 53, 56-57 (Department of Records, Philadelphia Yearly Meeting of Friends [hereafter NDMMM]).

[16] Arithmetic Book of Nathan Trotter (Thompson Collection, HSP); marriage certificate of Rebekah Conarroe and Daniel Trotter, Nov. 9, 1773, in the possession of Col. and Mrs. C. Raynor-Smith, Old Lyme, Conn.

[17] Provincial Tax List, 1774, pp. 12 and 137 (Division of Public Records, Pennsylvania History and Museum Commission, Harrisburg); photocopy owned by Mrs. Hannah Roach, Philadelphia.

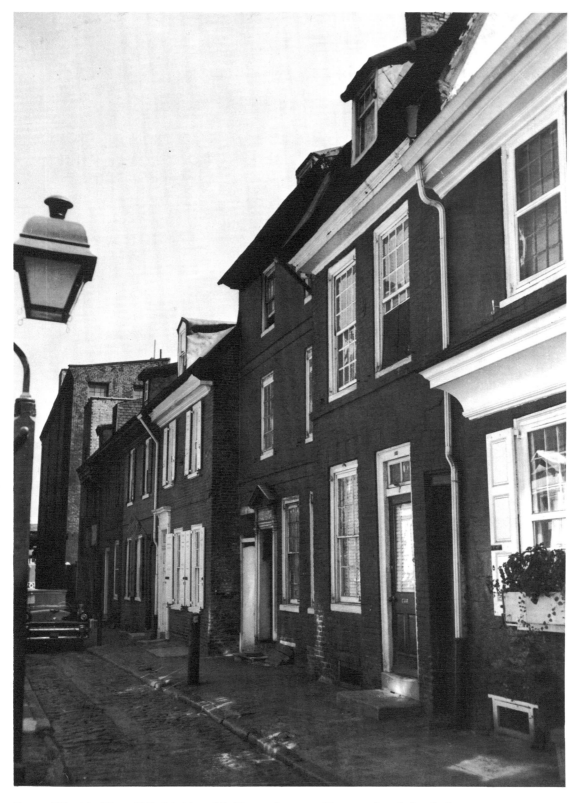

FIG. 1. Elfreth's Alley, Philadelphia, with Trotter house at No. 114, fourth façade from right. (Photo, courtesy of the Philadelphia Historical Commission.)

the colonies in the mid-1770's, and its prospering society formed an ideal setting for a skilled craftsman.[18] In 1775, Trotter and an apprentice were at work in the shop on Water Street which he leased from Leonard Shallcross until 1797 (Fig. 2).[19] After the signing of the Declaration of Independence, several difficult years ensued in which incomes were sapped by taxes to finance the Continental Army. The demand for luxury items—including fine furniture—decreased, undoubtedly affecting Trotter's trade. The war years were especially difficult for Trotter because of his religious persuasion. According to the discipline of the Society of Friends he was not permitted to "unite with any in warlike measures, either offensive or defensive."[20] Refusal to participate in the Revolution was a costly matter. The Militia Act of 1777 required all males between the ages of eighteen and fifty-three capable of serving in the militia to be drafted.[21] As a penalty for nonperformance, Trotter was required to pay a heavy fine, and for not attending exercise days, designed to drill those who were not actually fighting, he paid additional sums.[22]

Quakers were prohibited from taking an oath of allegiance to the Commonwealth of Pennsylvania, thereby renouncing fidelity to King George III, because of the Biblical command to "swear not, neither by heaven, neither by the earth, neither by any other oath."[23] Thus, Trotter was forced to pay double taxes in fulfillment of the Act for the Further Security of Government passed on April

FIG. 2. John M. Gries, *View of the Old Building*. Philadelphia, 1848. Water color and ink; H. 13″, W. 12½″. (Courtesy of Theodore T. Newbold.)

1, 1778.[24] To pay these penalties was also against the Society's regulations, and although Trotter is noted in the records as having paid the fines, there is no indication that he did it voluntarily. Elizabeth Drinker, the wife of the Quaker merchant Henry Drinker who was a friend of Trotter, described in her diary a technique used to obtain the sums from those who would not pay in cash. She wrote in 1779:

This Morng. in meeting time (myself at home) Jacob Franks and a Son of Cling ye Vendue master, came to seize for ye Continental Tax; They took from us, one walnut Dining Table, one mahogany Tea-Table, 6 hansom walnut Chairs, open backs Crow feet and a Shell on ye back and on each knee—a mahogany fram'd, Sconce Looking-Glass, and two large pewter

---

[18] Carl and Jessica Bridenbaugh, *Rebels and Gentlemen* (New York: Reynal and Hitchcock, 1942), p. 3.

[19] RS-268, pp. 140–41 (NDMMM). The inscription under the Gries water color (Fig. 2) indicates that Trotter used the North Water Street shop from 1774 to 1797; municipal records, however, note his presence there from 1775 through 1795. The latter source mentions that from 1791 to 1795 Trotter rented Leonard Shallcross's shop and wharf. In the 1795 city directory, Trotter's addresses are given as 100 North Front Street and 11 Elfreth's Alley. See Constables Return for the City of Philadelphia, Upper Delaware Ward, 1775, p. 11 (Department of Records, PMA); Philadelphia County Tax Assessment Ledger, Upper Delaware Ward, 1795, p. 18 (Department of Records, PMA); and Edmund Hogan, *The Prospect of Philadelphia* (Philadelphia: The author, 1795).

[20] *Rules of Discipline of the Yearly Meeting of Friends Held in Philadelphia* (Philadelphia, 1843), p. 19.

[21] Arthur J. Alexander, "Pennsylvania's Revolutionary Militia," *PMHB*, LXIX (Jan., 1935), 18.

[22] *Pennsylvania Archives*, ed. William H. Engle (3rd ser., Harrisburg, Pa.: [The state], 1896), V, 435, 466, 478, 493, 517, 524, and 537.

[23] James 5:12; see also *Rules of Discipline*, pp. 67–68.

[24] John Bach McMaster, *The Life and Times of Stephen Girard* (Philadelphia: J. B. Lippincott Co., 1918), I, 14–15.

Dishes, carrid them of from ye Door in a Cart to Clings.[25]

Agents seized household property from the Drinker home on other occasions during this period for sale at auction to cover unpaid taxes. Despite these ill-favored conditions, Trotter maintained his rented shop, and his business increased.

The occupational tax records, calculated from yearly income, indicate that during the 1770's and 1780's, the majority of joiners in Philadelphia were in the lower income stratum of society.[26] Rarely did one attain or even approach the wealth enjoyed by the great merchants and "gentlemen" of the city. The basis for taxation' during these years differs, making comparisons of the amounts paid invalid; however, it is Trotter's relative position within each scale that is significant to this study.

Trotter first departed from the minimum tax level in 1773, and by the time peace was attained a decade later, he appears to have had an income slightly above average for his craft. Trotter emerged as one of the most successful furniture makers in the city in 1786. His occupational tax of £100 for that year was exceeded only by Josiah Elfreth, who was assessed an additional £10; the cabinet and looking-glass maker John Elliott, whose assessment was £300; Richard Palmer, of whom £200 was required; and Samuel Williams, who had combined his joiner's business with a lumberyard and also paid £200. George Claypoole, David Evans, John Gillingham, and William Savery were taxed no more than half the amount paid by Trotter, and those equal with him were Jonathan Gostelowe, Parnell Gibbs, Jeremiah Snowden, Samuel Claphamson, John Linnington, and Jacob Wayne. These names represent a minor fraction of the total number of furniture makers active in Philadelphia, most of whom worked independently on a small scale or hired out for wages.

It is evident from tax records that during the 1780's business was brisk in Trotter's shop, while at the same time, he became more active in the Society of Friends. On many occasions, Trotter was appointed one of four members of the Northern District Monthly Meeting of Friends to attend the quarterly gathering of representatives from all meetings in the Philadelphia area. He was repeatedly designated to distribute literature to the homes of Friends, to keep order among the young people during services, and to collect monthly subscriptions from members. Trotter often served on several committees simultaneously, and as he grew older, he was among those who dealt with matters of greatest concern to the meeting. From the nature of the duties assigned to him it is obvious that he was considered by other Quakers to be righteous, reliable, and a man of good judgment. Ultimately, he was requested to serve as an overseer of the meeting, a position of honor and responsibility, which he accepted.[27] Since a Quaker meeting has no official leader or minister, overseers, "faithful and judicious men and women," perform the pastoral duties "exercis[ing] a vigilant and tender care over their fellow members."[28]

An individual who speaks often and well in the Quaker meetings is officially recognized as a "preacher." Trotter never received such recognition. This fact and other information regarding his activities as a Friend reveal Daniel Trotter as a quiet man who sat silently in the weekly worship services, but who, outside the meeting house, worked conscientiously in the interest of the Society of Friends.

As a staunch Quaker, it is not surprising that, in 1789, Trotter became a member of the Pennsylvania Society for Promoting the Abolition of Slavery and for the Relief of Free Negroes Unlawfully Held in Bondage and for Improving the Condition of the African Race, the first organization founded in the United States with this aim.[29] Knowledge of Trotter's capabilities was apparently widespread, and he was immediately given

[25] Entry for Sept. 14, 1779, Elizabeth Drinker Diary (Henry Drinker Papers, HSP).

[26] This is based on a survey made of Philadelphia Tax Assessment Ledgers, 1773-1775, 1780-1781 (Department of Records, PMA); subsequent reference to occupational taxes of 1783 and 1786 are based on William Macpherson Hornor, Jr., *Blue Book, Philadelphia Furniture, William Penn to George Washington* (Philadelphia: The author, 1935), pp. 317-26.

[27] RS-269, pp. 191-92 (NDMMM). The repeated references to Daniel Trotter in the Northern District Monthly Meeting Minutes serve as the basis for the preceding statements regarding his religious activities during the last two decades of the eighteenth century.

[28] *Rules of Discipline*, pp. 69-70.

[29] Pennsylvania Abolition Society (hereafter PAS) Minutes, 1789-1800, AMS-01, p. 85 (HSP); Morgan, *City of Firsts*, p. 23.

responsibility. At the meeting on January 4, 1790, in which Benjamin Franklin was chosen president of the society, Trotter was appointed to the Acting Committee whose function was to consider and take action in specific instances in which slaves had not been released on the completion of their periods of indenture.[30] Service on this committee required weekly attendance at meetings; from his appointment until the expiration of his term on October 4, 1790, he was absent only three times. In addition to these stated meetings, Trotter met with Mayor Samuel Powel and with judges regarding these cases, as well as with wealthy citizens, mostly merchants, who were illegally holding slaves.[31] There is no indication in Society minutes of his working on a committee or of his accepting an office after 1790, although he remained a member of the organization until his death.[32]

In 1789, Trotter exhibited interest in another direction by purchasing for ten pounds a share of stock in The Library Company of Philadelphia.[33] This, the earliest of subscription libraries in this country, was founded in 1732 under the direction of Benjamin Franklin for the benefit of the young tradesmen and mechanics in the city, but by Trotter's time it claimed many members from the top stratum of Philadelphia society.[34]

Quakers of the eighteenth century read both for delight and for education, and Trotter's library is illustrative of this. As William Penn had recommended, his library was built around a group of religious books including, of course, a Bible (a large folio edition with prints) and "Friend's Books."[35] Of these latter publications, he owned the writings of John Carver, John Howard, John Woolman, Thomas Chalkey, Sarah Grubb, and

Job Scott and a collection of Quaker memorials. Trotter's rather pedestrian taste is reflected in the other books in his possession. There were eight volumes of the first-century historian Flavius Josephus's *Jewish Antiquities* and four by the English antiquary Richard Gough. Alexander Pope, the popular eighteenth-century poet, was represented in Trotter's collection, which also contained eight volumes of the English literary magazine *Spectator*. He had an incomplete set of John Payne's *New and Complete System of Geography*, published in New York in the 1790's. No doubt for the benefit of his children, Trotter purchased the book *Elegant Extracts, or Useful and Entertaining Pieces of Poetry*. Of practical value was William Buchan's *Domestic Medicine; or, The Family Physician*. Also among his volumes was an unidentified "Book Designs Cabinetwork" for use in his shop.[36] During the last decade of the century, at least, the *Philadelphia Gazette and Universal Daily Advertiser* was read in the Trotter home, making it possible for the family to keep abreast of developments in the city and abroad.[37]

Although it is apparent that Trotter did not restrict all of his energies or interests entirely to the shop, much time was necessarily devoted to his trade. Trotter's continued success in business is evident from his real estate dealings. In 1781, he bought approximately twelve acres of land in Springfield Township, Burlington County, New Jersey, the area where his wife had lived before coming to Philadelphia in 1772.[38] He invested in 411¼ acres in Northampton County, Pennsylvania, in 1792, which were bordered by the holdings of fellow Philadelphians Jacob Downing,

[30] PAS Minutes, p. 106 (HSP).

[31] Acting Committee Minutes of PAS, AMS-056 (HSP).

[32] List of Members of PAS, 1784–1819, AMS-03 (HSP).

[33] Minute Book, III, 156 (Library Company of Philadelphia). At the time of Trotter's death, this share was valued at £40; see, Proceeds of the Inventory of Daniel Trotter's Estates, 67x90.12 (Trotter Papers, DMMC).

[34] George M. Abbot, *A Short History of the Library Company of Philadelphia* (Philadelphia: By Order of the Board of Directors, 1913), p. 16; and Austin K. Gray, *Benjamin Franklin's Library* (New York: Macmillan Co., 1937), p. 7. Daniel Trotter was requested in 1797 to "make a Case for the time piece" for the Library Company; unfortunately, the clock is not known to have survived. See Minute Book, IV, 64 (Library Company of Philadelphia).

[35] Tolles, *Meeting House*, pp. 163 and 193.

[36] Scattered references to these books are found in records of the estate of Daniel Trotter in the Trotter Papers (DMMC). Charles Evans, *American Bibliography* (reprinted, New York: Peter Smith, 1941–1942), was used to further identify some of the volumes whose titles were abbreviated.

[37] Original subscription forms in a private collection were viewed by this writer in July, 1961.

[38] Trotter bought twelve acres, three roods, and fourteen perches of land in Springfield Township. In 1796, he sold the property to Thomas Conarroe, who probably was the brother of Daniel's wife. Two years later, Trotter repurchased six acres, three roods, and three perches of this land. See Deed Book V 2–228, p. 231 (Office of the Recorder of Deeds, Burlington County Court House, Mount Holly, N.J.). See also William Wade Hinshaw, *Encyclopedia of American Quaker Genealogy* (Ann Arbor, Mich.: Edwards Brothers, Inc., 1938), II, 493.

Henry Drinker, William Drinker, Cadwalader Evans, and William Smith.[39]

In Philadelphia, Trotter purchased two houses and several lots during the 1780's and 1790's. In September, 1783, he paid Mary Saunderson £400 for the two-story brick house and lot on Elfreth's Alley where he and his wife had lived since their marriage.[40] Ten years later Trotter purchased from Thomas Coats, for £230 specie, a messuage and lot 64 feet by 68 feet "more or less" on the north side of the alley; in 1795, he divided the lot and sold two small portions of it each with a tenement for a total of £550, a substantial profit.[41] On the remaining land Trotter constructed two frame shops. The first, finished in 1795, was used for his business, except for the cellar, which he rented at the rate of £12 per year. The second shop was erected by 1799.[42] The Trotter home on Elfreth's Alley was sold in May, 1795, for £825, and during the same month transactions were completed for the purchase of a messuage and lot on the west side of Front Street, north of Elfreth's Alley, for £1,875.[43]

Although the Trotters did not live elegantly, they doubtless enjoyed a high degree of comfort in their new home. According to contemporary descriptions, the house—built over twenty-two years before Trotter acquired it—was three stories high with two rooms on each floor. It had "an old fashioned Chimney" with a winding staircase between the front and back rooms reaching from the cellar to the garret.[44] At the back of the house was a paved yard, a garden, and a smaller two-story building containing the kitchen and three other rooms.

That they did not adhere in their manner of living to the degree of plainness advocated by the eighteenth-century Quaker leader John Woolman, who wept at the sight of a silver vessel in the home of a Friend,[45] is indicated by the presence of approximately 110 ounces of silver in the Trotter household in 1800. Among the silver objects owned by Daniel Trotter at the time of his death were a sugar dish and tongs, a "small old cream pot," a "new cream jug," two cans, a teapot, numerous spoons, and a pair of plated candlesticks. He also had "1 Sett Tea China" ciphered "R T," another set simply designated as "China," and two china bowls bearing the cipher "D T" on them, as well as some queen's ware. For serving, Rebecca had three japanned "Waiters" decorated with her initials.[46]

Absolute plainness did not dominate the dress of the family. Trotter and his sons had jackets and coats with velvet collars, vests of the same fabric, and fancy pantaloons; silver buckles and gold sleeve buttons ornamented their apparel.[47] Trotter apparently allowed his family some degree of conformity to the fashion of the day, as did many Philadelphia Quakers in the latter part of the

[39] Trotter probably was influenced to make this investment by Henry Drinker, who was particularly interested in developing Northampton County. In a letter to Samuel Meredith, Drinker recommended the "strait & remarkably lofty" timber, the crop potential of the land, and the abundance of fish in the brooks and lakes. See Letter of Nov. 11, 1791 (Henry Drinker Papers, HSP); and Survey Book C-227, p. 231 (Land Office, Department of Internal Affairs of Pennsylvania, Harrisburg).

[40] Deed Book D-7, p. 502 (Office of the Recorder of Deeds, PMA).

[41] Deed Books D-47, p. 336, and D-53, pp. 266 and 273 (Office of the Recorder of Deeds, PMA). Perhaps Trotter borrowed the £1,100 in 1792 and 1793 to assist in these ventures. In 1792 he borrowed £600 from his unmarried sister Hannah, and in 1793 he obtained loans of £200 from the spinning-wheel maker Davenport Marot and £300 from the hatter Thomas Trotter. Although the interest was paid on each loan, full reimbursement was not made until after his death. See Bonds Executed by Daniel Trotter, 67x90.16–18 (Trotter Papers, DMMC).

[42] Philadelphia County Tax Assessment Ledger, South Mulberry Ward, 1795, 1798, and 1799 (Department of Records, PMA). In 1794 Trotter's records indicate building activity; in 1795 he paid tax on "A Lott and Unfinished Work Shop," but the Philadelphia directory for that year lists this new address as one of his locations, indicating that the shop must have been completed during 1795. See Hogan, *Prospect of Philadelphia*, "Daniel Trotter."

[43] Deed Books D-7, p. 502, and D-53, p. 266 (incorrectly indexed under John Trotter) (Office of the Recorder of Deeds, PMA).

[44] John Harper advertised the house for sale in the *Pennsylvania Gazette* (Philadelphia), on July 28, 1773. See Survey Book 3, p. 110 (Philadelphia, Contributionship Insurance Company, microfilm copy in DMMC). Bills and receipts in the Trotter Papers (DMMC) from 1798 and 1799 referring to construction suggest that, in addition to building a shop on Elfreth's Alley, Trotter had his Front Street house renovated.

[45] Janet Whitney, *John Woolman, American Quaker* (Boston: Little, Brown and Co., 1942), p. 362.

[46] This information is derived from references to household effects in the accounts of Trotter's estate (Trotter Papers, DMMC).

[47] Bills to Daniel Trotter, for tailor work, from Hilyard and Pippitt, 67x90.38; William Ashby, 67x90.22; Benjamin Thaw, 67x90.50 (Trotter Papers, DMMC). For references to buckles and buttons, see accounts from Trotter's estate, 67x90.8–9 (Trotter Papers, DMMC).

eighteenth century. In 1795, after reading John Woolman's "A Word of Remembrance and Caution to the Rich," which warned against accommodation to the surrounding society, Elizabeth Drinker commented, "I believe there are few, if any, who live up to J.W.'s plan or rule, yet I think there are [some] who go a great way towards it."[48]

Rebecca Trotter died at the age of forty-two, about two weeks after the delivery of her last child, Mary, on February 12, 1797.[49] On February 25, the Trotter's neighbor, Elizabeth Drinker, carefully recorded the circumstances in her diary:

A boy came here in a hurry to enquire for Danl. Trotter said his wife was dead—Sister went there, found it likely to be the case—she had been much better for some days past since her lyeing-in, and today was setting up discorseing with her family &c.—she was suddenly taken sick at stomach, fainted and appeared gone, the Docr. was sent for, who thought, when he saw her, it was to no purpose.—he however advised friction &c.—poor Daniel came home while sister was there, she left him in a very great distress, several women were there continueing their efforts to recover Becky—but it proved without effect![50]

At the time of their mother's death, the ages of the seven Trotter children—four sons and three daughters—ranged from two weeks to twenty-two years. Ten children had been born to Rebecca and Daniel; three, however, had preceded their mother in death. One son died of consumption, another was a victim of the yellow fever epidemic of 1793, and a daughter expired after a long period of poor health.[51] Eighteen-year-old Elizabeth, the eldest daughter, no doubt assumed much of the responsibility of caring for the motherless children and of maintaining the home, with the aid of the housekeepers, Elizabeth Johnson and Lydia Davis.[52]

Trotter's health failed during the latter part of the 1790's. His son Nathan explained his father's condition as follows:

The death of his dear wife was a close trial to him but being fully confirmed that it was her great and everlasting gain, he became resigned to the will of Providence, whose ways are unsearchable—about this time his health began to decline, and left him in much weakness of body a considerable time previous to his death.[53]

No doubt this accounts for his establishing a partnership in April, 1798, with Ephraim Haines, a young man who had just completed his apprenticeship in Trotter's shop.[54] Since William, the only son old enough to be of assistance to his father, had undertaken mercantile pursuits rather than training to become a cabinetmaker, Daniel had no one in the family with whom to share the burden of his business.[55]

The Philadelphia tax records for 1798 leave no doubt that Ephraim Haines was indeed fortunate to have been taken into Trotter's business. Of approximately sixty cabinetmakers and joiners listed in the Philadelphia County Tax Assessment Ledgers in that year, apparently only eleven owned their dwellings.[56] For tax purposes Trotter's house was valued at $1,600 and his shop at an additional $350, while the next highest evaluation of $1,334 was made on the home and shop of Thomas Bryan. The worth of David Evans's house was listed as $1,200, John Alexander's as $1,075, Thomas Williams's as $1,100, and John Webb's as $1,000; the remaining five ranged from $200 to

---

48 Entry for April 9, 1795, Elizabeth Drinker Diary (Henry Drinker Papers, HSP).

49 Arithmetic Book of Nathan Trotter (Thompson Collection, HSP).

50 Elizabeth Drinker Diary (Henry Drinker Papers, HSP).

51 Arithmetic Book of Nathan Trotter (Thompson Collection, HSP) lists birth and death dates of Trotter children as follows: William (Oct. 2, 1774–March 2, 1815); Mary (Aug. 4, 1776–Oct. 13, 1796); Elizabeth (July 22, 1778–July 2, 1803); Thomas (July 1, 1780–March 13, 1788); Joseph (Jan. 9, 1783–[1853]); Daniel (Jan. 24, 1785–Sept. 11, 1793); Nathan (Aug. 1, 1787–[Jan. 11, 1853]); Thomas Conarroe (Sept. 9, 1789–Oct. 10, 1821); Rebecca (Oct. 16, 1791–Nov. 28, 1815); and Mary (Feb. 12, 1797–Feb. 7, 1827).

52 Daniel Trotter Receipt Book (Dec. 9, 1797, and Aug.

26, 1799) mentions Elizabeth Johnson, 67x89.1 (Trotter Papers, DMMC). A reference to Lydia Davis in a document in a private collection, seen by the author in July, 1961, indicates that she was a housekeeper for Trotter.

53 Arithmetic Book of Nathan Trotter (Thompson Collection, HSP).

54 Haines began paying shop rent to Trotter on April 1, 1798, leading to the conclusion that the partnership commenced on this date. The entry reads, "To 2 Years Shop Rent from 1 Apl. 98 to 1 Apl. 1800 a 100 Dr pr an . . . one half is . . . 37.10.10." See Ephraim Haines Account with Daniel Trotter, 67x90.64 (Trotter Papers, DMMC).

55 Tooker, *Nathan Trotter*, p. 8. RS-271, p. 222 (NDMMM), shows that Ephraim Haines married Elizabeth Trotter in Jan., 1799.

56 This is the year closest to the death of Trotter in which tax records exist for all wards in Philadelphia. It must be noted, however, that only those artisans whose occupations accompany their names have been included in this survey; undoubtedly some have been omitted from consideration because their occupations were not mentioned. See Philadelphia County Tax Assessment Ledgers, 1798 (Department of Records, PMA).

$800. A survey of the chairmakers, joiners, carvers, upholsterers, and turners included in the same source indicates that only the carver William Rush's dwelling was valued at the same amount as Trotter's, and none was higher. This is an indication of Trotter's success at a time when most Philadelphia furniture craftsmen lived in rented rooms or houses and worked in rented shops.

The relief which must have accompanied his having a partner in the shop did not affect Trotter's recovery. After a life full of activity and industry, Daniel Trotter died on April 30, 1800, at age fifty-two.[57]

A short time before his departure he desir'd several of his family to come to his bedside and then separately bid them affectionately farewell. He then lay in a calm & resign'd frame of mind, until he breath'd his spirit into the hands of his Maker & we now trust he has enter'd into those mansions of peace prepared for the righteous.[58]

In the May 8, 1800, issue of the *Federal Gazette,* Ephraim Haines requested the settlement of outstanding accounts with the dissolved firm of Trotter and Haines and announced that "The Cabinet Making business in its different branches, will be continued as usual by Ephraim Haines, at the old stand, Nos. 100 north Front street, and 11, Elfreth's alley."[59]

Daniel Trotter's business probably began on a small scale. By the end of his life, however, he maintained an enterprise more resembling a factory and warehouse than the modest-sized shop often envisioned for the eighteenth-century cabinetmaker. In 1800, he had available for clients almost the full range of furniture forms "ready made."[60] An auction, announced in *Claypoole's American Daily Advertiser,* May 17, 1800, was held at Trotter's shop soon after his death, and the amount of furniture "being part of the stock on hand" is of considerable interest:

On Wednesday morning the 21st inst precisely at 9 o'clock at No 100 north Front Street
Will be sold by auction
A Variety of Excellent New Mahogany Furniture
Being part of the stock on hand belonging to the estate of Daniel Trotter, deceased
Among which are
Bureaus, circular and square
Chairs of different patterns, hair cloth and brass nail seats, etc.
Arm and easy do
Dining tables, card, sideboard and breakfast do. different patterns
Wardrobe and desks
Cradles, bason stands and candle do
Field, high and low post, and trundle Bedsteads mahogany and painted
A number of well finished mahogany portable writing desks, with sundry other article in the cabinet making line
ALSO
Household and Kitchen Furniture
consisting of—
Mahogany bureaus, tables, &c. bedstead chairs, sofa, looking glasses, and irons
China ware, iron utensiles do
The furniture may be viewed the day previous to the sale.

John Conelly, auct.

The proceeds of this auction were $582.45.[61] Additional pieces were disposed of at a private sale, yielding a total of $863.45 (see Appendix A).[62] There is no way to determine how long Trotter had maintained a stock of these proportions or if, indeed, it can be considered an indication of a healthy business; but had there been no anticipated demand, it is unlikely that production would have continued and reached this level. To accumulate such an inventory, Trotter required

[57] Trotter left no will, and although there was once an inventory, it can no longer be located. See Administration Book K, 40 (Office of the Registrar of Wills, PMA), and Orphans Court Docket, Vol. 23, 325–26 and 343 (Office of the Orphans Court, PMA).

[58] Arithmetic Book of Nathan Trotter (Thompson Collection, HSP).

[59] According to Philadelphia city directories, Ephraim Haines continued as a cabinetmaker until 1804, when he is noted as having a "mahogany yard." In 1805, he had a "warehouse" in addition to his lumber business, and from 1806 through 1811 he operated only a "cabinet warehouse" at 100 North Front Street, after which he discontinued the sale of furniture.

[60] Clients sometimes left orders for furniture; twelve such cases are recorded in the Daniel Trotter General Account Book, 67x89.2 (Trotter Papers, DMMC).

[61] Furniture Belonging to Trotter and Haines Sold at Vendue, 67x90.5 (Trotter Papers, DMMC), includes appraised values of each item as well as the amount for which it sold. In this context there is some question as to how to interpret the following entry in another account of the estate: "1800 9 mo 9 day sum repaid to J. Conelly for sundries sold & for which no purchasers were found included in the amount sales paid to the Adm. $618.92." Daniel Trotter Estate, Case YE-1 (Trotter Family Collection, Baker Library, Graduate School of Business Administration, Harvard University, Cambridge, Mass.).

[62] Things Sold at Private Sale Belonging to Trotter and Haines, 67x90.14 (Trotter Papers, DMMC).

assistance; that he had it is evident from the presence of nine "Joiners Work benches" in the shop.[63] Apprentices and journeymen constitute the most obvious source of help.

Trotter's first known apprentice, Solomon Atkinson, a Quaker from Third Haven on Choptank, Maryland, arrived in Philadelphia in 1775 and remained there until 1786, when he returned to Maryland.[64] In 1784, 1785, and 1788, Daniel Trotter had suits made "for Boy," as a bill from the tailor Benjamin Thaw designates. Presumably the nameless boy was an apprentice for whom Trotter had accepted the customary responsibility of providing clothing.[65]

The 1790 census of Philadelphia indicates that in the Trotter household there were four males sixteen years of age or over and six males under sixteen.[66] The size of the Trotter family is reflected in these figures since five of the younger males were sons of Daniel.[67] Although the three older males in addition to Trotter probably were apprentices or journeymen involved in his business, their identities remain a mystery.

It is certain that he had an understudy the following year. On May 2, 1791, a certificate was issued by the Burlington Monthly Meeting of Friends in New Jersey commending Ephraim Haines, "a Youth apprenticed with Daniel Trotter," to the care of members of the Northern District Meeting. The certificate probably was issued at least eight months after Haines entered Trotter's shop, since in September, 1790, he signed a receipt "for Daniel Trotter," as apprentices sometimes did for their masters.[68] According to his father's will, proved in 1789, Ephraim was to be

sent to school until he was old enough to be "put to a trade, then [bound] to the trade he choses."[69] After deciding to become a cabinetmaker, he went to Philadelphia for training.

Ephraim Haines and Solomon Atkinson are exemplary of numerous ambitious youths from rural areas of the middle states who came to this city to learn a craft. Probably a majority of these young men returned to their homes, as did Atkinson, taking with them the styles and techniques of Philadelphia cabinetmaking. Haines chose to remain in the city and to become his master's partner and son-in-law.

Elizabeth Drinker, commenting in her diary about the marriage of Trotter's daughter Elizabeth to Haines, described the bridegroom as "one of her fathers prentices's."[70] The phraseology implies that there were others in the Trotter workshop. One such youth is mentioned in a bill to Trotter from Nathan Mathias dated June, 1794, for "Making a Suit of Clothes for aprentice Robert"; on the reverse side is inscribed, "Robert parhams Bill Taylor Work."[71] The fact that Haines was indebted £30 to the estate of Daniel Trotter for the "Time of 2 Apprentice Lads" leads to the conclusion that there had been only two present in the shop for the duration of the Trotter-Haines partnership.[72] Robert Parham is doubtless one of the two, and Abraham Lower is a likely candidate for the second.[73] In October, 1796, Trotter purchased a hat for "Abm," and Elizabeth Drinker noted "Abraham an apprentice to Daniel Trotter," in her diaries of May, 1797, and May, 1798.[74] A probable surname is found in a bill of June,

---

[63] Bill from Estate of Daniel Trotter to Ephraim Haines, 67x90.6 (Trotter Papers, DMMC).

[64] RS-268, pp. 140–141, and RS-269, p. 222 (NDMMM).

[65] Bill from Benjamin Thaw to Daniel Trotter, 67x90.50 (Trotter Papers, DMMC). During this decade, Trotter had two joiners living in his home: his cousin Josiah Elfreth in 1781 and 1782 and Henry Ingle in 1795. See Provincial Tax List for Mulberry Ward, 1785 (Pennsylvania History & Museum Commission, Harrisburg, Pa.), photocopy owned by Mrs. Hannah Roach, Philadelphia; and *Pennsylvania Archives*, 3rd ser., XV, 620–21, and XVI, 469.

[66] *Heads of Families at the First Census of the United States Taken in the Year 1790* (Washington: Government Printing Office, 1908), p. 231.

[67] Arithmetic Book of Nathan Trotter (Thompson Collection, HSP).

[68] RS-270, p. 115 (NDMMM). See entry for Sept. 6, 1790, Receipt Book of Thomas Williams, 1787–1804 (Friends Historical Library, Swarthmore College).

[69] George Haines, *Ancestry of the Haines, Sharp, Collins, Wills, Gardiner, Prickitt, Eves, Evans, Moore, Troth, Borton, and Engle Families* (Camden, N.J.: S. Chew & Sons, Co., 1902), p. 103. Haines was born on Oct. 23, 1775, according to the Evesham Monthly Meeting Birth and Burial Records (1693–1809), p. 23 (Friends Historical Library, Swarthmore College).

[70] Entry for Jan. 8, 1799, Elizabeth Drinker Diary (Henry Drinker Papers, HSP).

[71] 67x90.41 (Trotter Papers, DMMC).

[72] Bill from Estate of Daniel Trotter to Ephraim Haines, 67x90.6 (Trotter Papers, DMMC).

[73] Parham maintained contact with Haines and was, in fact, a resident in the Haines home in 1806. See Philadelphia County Tax Assessment Ledger, Lower Delaware Ward, 1806, p. 21 (Department of Records, PMA).

[74] Bill from Joseph Bispham to Daniel Trotter, 67x90.23 (Trotter Papers, DMMC); and entries for May 21, 1797, and May 14, 1798, Elizabeth Drinker Diary (Henry Drinker Papers, HSP).

1799, from Isaac Norris to Trotter in which he was charged for a hat for Abraham Lower.[75] The next year Lower was included in the city directory as a cabinet- and chairmaker at 55 North Third Street. Also mentioned in the Norris bill to Trotter is the purchase of a hat for Edward Durborow. Although Durborow appears nowhere else in the Trotter accounts, he may have been an apprentice or a journeyman in Trotter's shop. Beginning in 1800, "Edward Derborough" was noted in the Philadelphia County Tax Assessment Ledgers; he is first identified as a joiner two years later, and by 1813, he had his own business.[76]

Trotter's use of journeymen cabinetmakers was no doubt more commonplace than the sparse records indicate. Journeymen, not being bound to a single master as were apprentices, moved from shop to shop as work was available. In some instances, however, they long remained with a single master. William Faries, hired by David Evans to work in his cabinetmaking shop from September, 1780, to November, 1791, is noted in Evans's daybook as "working for self at D. Trotter's Bed," on June 3, 1791.[77] That this was an isolated occurrence is improbable.

Thomas Janvier, another journeyman (and a notably productive one), was working with Trotter during 1795 and 1796. Seldom is the relationship between a master and a journeyman of this period as well documented as that of Trotter and Janvier, who, prior to his arrival in Philadelphia, had worked for John Janvier in Cantwell's Bridge, Delaware.[78] An account book provides a record of Janvier's activities during a major part

of the years 1795 and 1796.[79] By July 4, 1795, he had left Delaware and was in Philadelphia, where he assisted Trotter at least until September 11, 1796. During this period Janvier made 57 slat-back chairs, 44 heart-back chairs, 20 square-back chairs, 3 close-stool chairs, 2 arm chairs of an unspecified type, 15 coffins, 2 clockcases, 13 stands, 8 tables, and 2 high-post bedsteads. In addition, he worked on walnut chairs and stove patterns, sawed commode fronts, and did other miscellaneous tasks including "running and sawing chair backs."[80] His productivity in a single month is noteworthy; in March, 1796, for example, he made for Trotter a pair of oval dining tables, 12 heart-back chairs, and 2 walnut coffins. Although Janvier usually paid on a piecework basis, he received £0.15.0 on the few occasions he was compensated for a single day's labor, which was twice the prescribed wage for the expected eleven hours of

[75] Trotter Papers (DMMC).

[76] Philadelphia County Tax Assessment Ledger, South Mulberry Ward, 1800, p. 5, and Lower Delaware Ward, 1802, p. 11 (Department of Records, PMA); and *The Philadelphia Directory and Register for 1813* (Philadelphia: John A. Paxton, 1813), "Edward Durborow."

[77] David Evans Day Book (1782–1795), AM-9115, Vol. 2, facing p. 56 (HSP).

[78] Charles G. Dorman, *Delaware Cabinetmakers and Allied Artisans, 1655–1855* (Wilmington: Historical Society of Delaware, 1960), pp. 44–45. Accounts of the relationships between master and journeyman cabinetmakers in Philadelphia during this period may be studied in more detail in the David Evans Day Books (HSP), discussed in Dard Hunter, Jr., "David Evans, Cabinetmaker" (unpublished thesis, University of Delaware, 1954); and in Samuel Ashton's Papers (DMMC), discussed in Morrison H. Heckscher, "The Organization and Practice of Philadelphia Cabinetmaking Establishments, 1790 to 1820" (unpublished Master's thesis, University of Delaware, 1964).

[79] John Janvier Account Book (1795–1796) (Public Archives Commission, Delaware State Archives, Dover, Del., from microfilm in DMMC). Although the document bears no positive identification, this writer believes it to be the account book of Thomas Janvier for the following reasons. First, a comparison of the writing in the account book with the Thomas Janvier signature in Daniel Trotter's receipt book leaves little doubt that it was the same hand which wrote them both. Second, the last entry in the section of the Janvier manuscript itemizing the type of work done shows that on Sept. 11, 1796, Daniel Trotter owed the workman £28.8.2½ in addition to a balance of £25 left after a payment on the account made on June 24, 1796, which is noted on the adjacent page. The total of the two amounts is approximately £53. The Trotter Receipt Book notes that on Sept. 12, 1796, the day after the final entry in the Janvier accounts, Thomas Janvier was paid $132—the equivalent of £49.10.0. In a sum so large as this, the odd £3.18.2½ may have been dropped; or perhaps there was a small amount of money due to Trotter which was not mentioned in the records. The similarity of the two sums and the proximity of the dates would appear to be more than a coincidence. Third, Thomas Janvier definitely is known to have been in Philadelphia in 1796 working as a journeyman cabinetmaker (see p. 162). Fourth, John Janvier's name appears at the beginning of the account book, but it is followed by "Dr" (debtor), just as Trotter's name is written "Daniel Trotter Dr." This would indicate that both John Janvier and Daniel Trotter were in debt to the writer of the manuscript for the work noted under each of these headings. Another entry reads "Francis Janvier dr to Thomas Janvier to Cash Lent," which supports the attribution of this document to Thomas Janvier.

[80] For the probable meaning of "running," see *Oxford English Dictionary*, "run," sense 53c: "To cut (a mark), draw or trace (a line), on a surface." This could refer to the process of tracing the outline of a pattern or template on a piece of wood before sawing.

work.[81] Measured drawings of a desk, a chest of drawers, a clockcase, and "Chinese Doors" for a cupboard—none of which conform to known published design sources—appear in the back of the Janvier account book. These may have been provided by Trotter, since the master in a shop determined the design of furniture produced for him, but Janvier could have simply made the sketches for his own information. Doubtless, other journeymen were similarly active in Trotter's shop producing finished pieces of furniture for sale, which, if labeled or branded, would bear Trotter's name.

While Janvier was working for Trotter, the journeymen cabinetmakers of Philadelphia rebelled against the masters, creating a stormy situation.[82] Newspaper notices and published price books delineate the problems. *The Philadelphia Cabinet and Chair-Makers' Book of Prices,* published in 1794 by the journeymen, standardized wages to be paid by employers for piecework. This was based on *The Cabinet-Makers' London Book of Prices, and Designs of Cabinet Work* (1788). After the second edition of the Philadelphia price book appeared in 1795, the controversy mounted in intensity. Members of the Federal Society of Journeymen Cabinet and Chair–Makers of the City and Liberties of Philadelphia finally declared they would not work for master craftsmen who had taken a stand against their demands, nor would they work with journeymen employed by such masters. This statement was printed less than two weeks after Janvier is first known to have been working for Trotter. It is unlikely, as will later become apparent, that Trotter enticed Janvier to come to Philadelphia because he was unsuccessful in hiring local journeymen. In April, 1796, an announcement was made in the Philadelphia *Aurora* that, since their employers had not been sympathetic to the request for higher wages resulting from a rise in the cost of living, the journeymen had established a "Ware-Room" where they were marketing their own goods while on the strike against their employers. By September, 1796, the *Cabinet-Makers' Philadelphia and London Book of Prices* was printed, and its "Introduction" indicates that an agreement had been reached between employers and employees granting wages acceptable to the journeymen. This introductory statement was signed by three employers and three "Workmen." Thomas Janvier was one of the workmen. That he was chosen indicates a prominence among his peers and a major role in the negotations between the two groups. Trotter was undoubtedly sympathetic to the journeymen's cause; otherwise, according to the resolution of 1795, Janvier should have left his employ.

During the second half of the eighteenth century, turners, carvers, painters, and upholsterers were available to aid urban cabinetmakers in their production. Trotter's accounts disclose dealings with such craftsmen, as well as with chairmakers and other cabinetmakers. The role played by these individuals in Trotter's enterprise is frequently undefined in the shop records; therefore, Philadelphia directories, which include occupations, provide the only clue to the capacity in which some artisans worked for him. Occasionally, Trotter simultaneously hired two or three practitioners of crafts allied to furniture making. His choice of any one of the available craftsmen was probably based on nothing more complex than proficiency, proximity, or the prospect of prompt service.

Detailed records from Trotter's estate include "Sundry Cabinet Makers Tools" that were worth £27.12.10½, but no mention is made of a lathe.[83] Thus, it is not surprising that he employed turners who would have produced posts for bedsteads and perhaps legs for chairs and tables. In 1794 and 1795 Trotter paid a total of £3.6.7 for unspecified services to Nathaniel Bayne and John Gass (turners who had a shop at 85 North Front Street). Twice in 1796, John Stow was employed by Trotter, once receiving £4.14.9 for "turning work done" and the second time, £5.12.5 simply for "Work."[84] Robert Taylor made turnings for him in 1795 and 1796 and on one occasion provided him with pine boards; for his assistance, he received £15.6.11½.[85]

Several carvers were engaged by Trotter in the 1790's. In the period between August 17, 1795,

[81] Charles F. Montgomery, *American Furniture: The Federal Period, 1788–1825* (New York: Viking Press, 1966), pp. 23 and 25.

[82] *Ibid.,* pp. 21–23. Subsequent references to the dispute are based on information in this source.

[83] Bill to Ephraim Haines from the Estate of Daniel Trotter, 67x90.6 (Trotter Papers, DMMC).

[84] Trotter Receipt Book (Trotter Papers, DMMC).

[85] *Ibid.* This was probably the same Robert Taylor noted in the 1801 Philadelphia city directory as a Windsor chairmaker, living with the cabinetmaker Alexander Shaw at 99 South Front Street. He may have been a journeyman at the

and August 18, 1797, John Morris appears ten times in Trotter's receipt book, having been paid altogether £40.8.6.[86] One explicitly phrased entry states that John Morris "Receivd 4m. 30th-1796 of Daniel Trotter 36/ in full for Carveing 8 chair Backs." In the same year Morris fashioned scrolls on a clockcase made in the shop of Davis Evans.[87] Because the talents of a single carver were employed by numerous cabinetmakers, it is evident that furniture cannot be attributed on the basis of carved decoration alone, even when a well-documented item exists with which to compare others.

John Watson, who also' worked for David Evans, was involved in Trotter's business in an unusual capacity.[88] He was paid in February, 1792, for "Cutting Leafs" on eight "pott Handles,"[89] referring to the carved ornamentation on wooden handles used by silversmiths and pewterers for their coffeepots and teapots. The basic shape of the handle was fabricated by either Trotter or one of his workmen, and Watson provided the decorative details, charging £0.1.10½ per handle. When selling such items the following year, Trotter's price for plain teapot handles was £0.7.6 and for plain coffeepot handles £0.10.0; if the handles were carved, £0.2.6 was added to the cost. Trotter sold thirty-nine handles between January 1 and September 4, 1793.[90] Among those who purchased them were the silversmiths John David and Joseph Lownes. The wording of the entries in Trotter's records implies that some were made to order: "1 Coffee pott Handle Carved for R" and "1 [teapot handle] Carved for M."[91] To think that

a cabinetmaker produced only furniture is erroneous, as the study of Trotter's accounts indicates.

Trotter's name is connected with the carving required in the preparation of wood patterns for iron and castings. As early as 1786, Henry Drinker, who was part owner of the Atsion Furnace in New Jersey,[92] recorded the following entry in his journal:

3rd Month 4th 1786
Sundry Accounts Drs to Daniel Trotter

Atsion Castings for altering a stove pattern	2.10.0
making an end iron pattern	0.11.3
6 sash weight patterns	0.12.0
altering & repairing 2 stove patterns	2.10.0
repairing a stove pattern	3. 0.0
mending a ditto	1.10.0
making a cabbouse pattern	6.10.0
ditto a ten plate stove ditto	11. 5.0
4 new plate patterns for large openstove	5. 0.0
2 chimney back patterns	2.10.0
1 sett chimney back & jam patterns	3.15.0
	39.13.3[93]

Whether Trotter himself made any of the patterns is questionable. Perhaps then, just as in the next decade, he employed other artisans to do this work and served only in the capacity of a middleman. According to his receipt book, Henry and James Reynolds carved stove-plate patterns for him in 1796, 1798, and 1800. They were sons of James Reynolds, who advertised in 1766 that he had recently arrived from London where he had been trained as a carver and gilder.[94] When working on patterns for Trotter, the brothers were doing carving for other individuals. For example, they "Recd May 25th 1798 of Daniel Trotter twelve dollars in full for Carving a front plate for Charles Jolley," a Philadelphia iron merchant.[95] Orders for patterns obviously were

time Trotter employed him, since there is no listing in the city directories in the 1790's for a turner or Windsor chairmaker bearing this name. See *The Philadelphia Directory* (Philadelphia: C. W. Stafford, 1801).

[86] The John R. Morris who carved the ebony furniture ordered by Stephen Girard from Ephraim Haines was with little doubt the "John Morris Junier" who accepted these payments. John Morris, Sr., died in 1798, according to an advertisement of his estate in the *Pennsylvania Packet* (Philadelphia), Nov. 22, 1798. See Microfilm Copy, Ser. 2, Reel 210 (Stephen Girard Papers, American Philosophical Society, Philadelphia [hereafter Stephen Girard Papers, APS, unless the source is another microfilm series and reel in which case it will be noted]).

[87] Hunter, "David Evans," p. 38.

[88] Hornor, *Blue Book*, p. 101.

[89] Trotter General Account Book (Trotter Papers, DMMC).

[90] *Ibid.*

[91] David and Lownes are the only surnames included in the account. "R" and "M" could refer to Joseph Richardson

and John Mills, the silversmiths with these initials listed in *The Philadelphia Directory and Register* (Philadelphia: James Hardie, 1793).

[92] Arthur D. Pierce, *Iron in the Pines: The Story of New Jersey's Ghost Towns and Bog Iron* (New Brunswick, N.J.: Rutgers University Press, 1957), p. 33.

[93] Journal of Henry Drinker, 1776–1791, Vol. 9, 105 (Henry Drinker Papers, HSP).

[94] *Pa. Gaz.*, Sept. 4, 1766. The elder Reynolds no doubt also worked for Trotter since, in 1798, Trotter paid "eleven dollars in full for the Estate of James Reynolds decd being a ballance of account." See Trotter Receipt Book (Trotter Papers, DMMC).

[95] Trotter Receipt Book (Trotter Papers, DMMC). See also entry for Charles Jolly in *The Philadelphia Directory* (Philadelphia: C. W. Stafford, 1798).

Form	Color	Dec. 1791	Jan. 1792	Feb.	Mar.	Apr.	May	June	July	Aug.	Sept.	Oct.	Nov.	Dec.	Jan. 1793	Feb.	Mar.	Total
Bedstead, field	Moho								1		2		2					5
high post	Green Moho	1	1		2			2	2		7	1	1	1	1			1 17
low post	Green Moho						1	2	3			1			1			4 4
trundle	Green Moho						1								1			1 1
(No description)	Moho												1			1		2
Chair, arm	Moho											1						1
Chest	Brown Lead		1		1			1	2									3 2
Cornice, window & bedstead							6											6
Crib	Moho			1					1									2
Dough trough	Lead								1									1
Table	Green Moho										6 1							6 1
Total		1	2	0	3	1	8	5	9	1	16	3	2	2	3	0	1	57

TABLE 1. Furniture painted by George Flake for Daniel Trotter between December, 1791, and March, 1793

left with Trotter, who engaged the Reynoldses to execute them. The presence of an unfinished ten-plate stove pattern in Trotter's inventory in 1800 suggests either that the rough form was made by the cabinetmaker and given to the carver for ornamentation, or that entire patterns—possibly those requiring little or no decoration—were produced in Trotter's shop.[96]

In his later years Trotter received bills from painters that not only indicate the extent of services but also afford an insight into his production.[97] John Gardner's account with Trotter began in 1787 and continued to 1800.[98] During this period, he gilded twenty-four frames, lettered sixteen coffin plates, painted a bucket and sixteen high- and low-post bedsteads, and ornamented or gilded seven cornices. Probably for Trotter's personal use was a floor carpet that Gardner painted on both sides in 1787.

George Flake painted furniture from Trotter's shop early in the 1790's (Table 1).[99] While green was the only color, aside from gold, mentioned in the Gardner bill, Flake employed green, brown, lead color, and "Moho Couler," sometimes simply indicated as "Mo." The latter presumably refers to a simulation of mahogany by the use of a painted or stained reddish-brown ground color over which darker graining may have been applied. When billing Trotter, John Gardner differentiated between the two types of bed frames and, in the 1780's, charged £0.10.0 for painting a low-post bedstead and, as late as 1791, £0.12.6 for a high-post bedstead. The price that Trotter paid Flake from 1791 to 1793 for painting a high- or a low-post bedstead was £0.7.6. In January, 1793, George Markley was billed £3 for a painted high-post bedstead of which £0.7.6 would probably have been for the painting process.[100] The variety of forms to which George Flake added a painted finish in approximately sixteen months, as well as the over-all quantity of furniture, is notable. Flake's wages during this period were £17.9.11.[101]

96 Inventory of the Property of Trotter and Haines, 1800, 67x90.1 (Trotter Papers, DMMC).

97 An account with the merchant Samuel Wetherill in 1785 and 1786 mentions Trotter's purchase of oil, putty, varnish, rosin, and whiting as well as white lead and "virdigrease" or green pigment. The last two items may be an indication that furniture was painted in Trotter's shop. Ledger of Samuel Wetherill and Sons, 1778–1788 (Wetherill Papers, Industrial Research Unit, Wharton School, University of Pennsylvania, Philadelphia, microfilm copy in DMMC).

98 Bill from John Gardner to Daniel Trotter, 67x90.37 (Trotter Papers, DMMC).

99 Bill from George Flake to Daniel Trotter, 67x90.36 (Trotter Papers, DMMC).

100 Bill from Daniel Trotter to George Markley, 67x90.66 (Trotter Papers, DMMC).

101 On Dec. 20, 1791, when the Flake account begins, Trotter owed him £41.12.6 for which no itemized record exists. In addition to painting furniture for Trotter, Flake "glazed lights" on several occasions. Trotter may have supplied carpenters with carved mullions of a decorative

Another painter, William Fling, was paid £3.1.3 in 1798 and £36.2.1 after Trotter's death, presumably for the same type of work.[102] Trotter's bills to clients and painter's bills to Trotter indicate that he produced an abundance of common furniture which today might mistakenly be called country pieces.

Trotter's earliest remaining account with an upholsterer dates from February, 1786, when John Davis stuffed two settees using canvas covers for £13.10.0; during that year, he also padded six chair seats and covered them with haircloth for £2.8.0.[103] A comparison of this sum with the price of six mahogany chairs sold to Stephen Girard in 1786 reveals that the upholsterer may have received 8 shillings of the £3.3.4 that Trotter charged for each chair.[104] Davis worked for Trotter in 1788 as well and sold haircloth to him in 1789. During the last decade of Trotter's life, he patronized the upholsterers Andrew Henry, Thomas Jaquett, John Joad, and John Page.[105] Extensive records exist for the middle of this period—principally receipts for payments—which show that in the last four months of 1796, Trotter expended £88.17.6 for the stuffing and upholstering of furniture.

Hepplewhite's *The Cabinet-Maker and Upholsterer's Guide,* as published in 1789 and 1794, advised that "mahogany chairs should have seats of horse hair, plain, striped, chequered, &c. at pleasure."[106] This fabric, combining an actual horsehair weft with a cotton, linen, or wool warp, was the covering for seat furniture most often noted in Trotter's accounts. In addition to striped and plain haircloth, he had furniture upholstered in linen, moreen, and satin.[107] Trotter kept in stock quantities of haircloth and "curled hair"[108] for the stuffing of chairs and sofas, and occasionally chairs were brought directly to Trotter rather than to an upholsterer for restuffing and re-covering. An undated entry in his general account book indicates that Trotter retailed haircloth; he sold approximately 114 yards to merchants, hatters, tailors, cabinetmakers, upholsterers, and "strangers," charging in most instances 10 shillings per yard. The 1800 inventory of the Trotter-Haines shop includes 85¼ yards of haircloth from which they apparently planned to supply their own needs as well as those of other craftsmen.

Trotter had numerous affiliations with fellow cabinetmakers of the city. During the 1780's and early 1790's, William Savery, John Elliott, Benjamin Randolph, George Claypoole, Thomas Tufft, John Gillingham, Jonathan Gostelowe, and Thomas Affleck, craftsmen who helped to bring furniture making in Philadelphia to its peak of excellence, either retired from business or died.[109] Trotter was one of the few individuals trained early in the Chippendale period to continue working through the end of the eighteenth century. With the exception of John Aitken and David Evans, the joiners with whom he had business transactions are, today, unrecognized figures.

Venetian blinds known to have been procured from Trotter were made in David Evan's shop.[110] In addition to making the blinds, Evans or his workmen sometimes painted and installed them. But it was Trotter who received the payment and was then indebted to Evans, whose price for a single blind ranged from £2 to £3. Of the ten entries on Evans's bill to Trotter, covering the period from 1792 to 1796, all but one mentions the individual for whom the blinds were made; thus they

---

type for door or window frames which Flake fitted with glass, or the painter may have installed glass into the doors of a secretary, bookcase, or cupboard for Trotter.

[102] Trotter Receipt Book (Trotter Papers, DMMC).

[103] Bill from John Davis to Daniel Trotter, 67x90.35 (Trotter Papers, DMMC).

[104] Stephen Girard Papers (APS).

[105] For references to Henry, Jaquett, and Joad, see Trotter Receipt Book and Trotter General Account Book (Trotter Papers, DMMC). Bill from John Page to Daniel Trotter, 67x90.44 (Trotter Papers, DMMC).

[106] *The Cabinet-Maker and Upholsterer's Guide . . . from Drawings by A. Hepplewhite and Co., Cabinet-Makers* (2nd ed.; London, 1789), p. 2.

[107] A reference to moreen is in a bill dated July 16, 1792, from Daniel Trotter to Samuel Coates, Reynell and Coates Collection, Vol. III (Baker Library, Harvard University,

---

Cambridge, Mass.). Trotter paid £15.2.1 for a piece of "sateen seating" on May 2, 1795 (Trotter Receipt Book, DMMC). Mordecai Lewis ordered, among other furniture, a "Sopha in Linnen" and "14 Mahogany Chairs Loos Seates in Linnen" (Trotter General Account Book, DMMC).

[108] Curled hair, actually matted horsehair, was also used for filling mattresses. Trotter's bill to George Ashton in 1797 mentions "to 35 lb of Curled Hair & Making a Matrass 8.1.13," Stephen Collins Accounts, Box 33 (Stephen Collins Collection, Library of Congress, Washington). The Trotter-Haines Inventory lists 83 pounds of curled hair valued at £11.1.4 (Trotter Papers, DMMC).

[109] Hornor, *Blue Book,* pp. 236–37.

[110] Bill from David Evans to Daniel Trotter, 67x90.34 (Trotter Papers, DMMC).

were most likely custom-made. Why his clients would not have gone directly to Evans is a mystery. Perhaps once a cabinetmaker established a relationship with a client, he would arrange to provide items requested of him that were not produced in his own shop.

Trotter's earliest account with David Evans illustrates a practice not uncommon among members of his craft. On March 4, 1779, Trotter owed Evans for "44 ft walnit got at Sundrie Times for Coffins," and in partial payment for this, he gave him a "Tea Table Top Mahogany, & Bedsted Stuff."[111] Furniture makers at times supplied each other with wood in lieu of cash remuneration, which was willingly accepted in either rough or a more finished form. Other instances of such exchanges occur in Trotter's records; for example, Thomas Woodsend recorded in Trotter's receipt book in 1797 a payment of $32 on his account "in Cash & Mahogany," and Lewis G. Affleck provided Trotter with mahogany worth $92 in 1796.[112]

Possibly the practice of providing wood to fellow cabinetmakers explains a number of transactions Trotter had with other practitioners of his craft. One receipt signed by John Aitken, probably the joiner from whom George Washington ordered furniture during the 1790's, indicates that Trotter was in debt to him in 1796 to the extent of $149.24 without a hint as to how this debt was incurred.[113] Samuel Williams accepted a note from Trotter for $249.67 in 1797.[114] He had advertised in *Dunlap's American Daily Advertiser* several years earlier, on March 14, 1793, from his "board yard" and joinery shop at the corner of Petty's Alley on Fourth Street where, in addition to mak-

ing a wide range of furniture forms, he sold Jamaica, Bay, and Providence mahogany, walnut, and other woods suitable for the furniture maker. In both of these instances it is conceivable that Trotter was paying for a quantity of wood.

The majority of Trotter's accounts related to the purchase of wood bear the names of merchants, over half of whom dealt solely in lumber. In addition to walnut and mahogany, Trotter bought quantities of cedar, hemlock, poplar, oak, the "best white pine," and heart pine.[115] The shop inventory taken after his death includes these and an even more diverse range of woods: gum, apple, cherry, satinwood, and a small amount of "purple Wood." Mahogany veneer and "A Lott of Stringing Shades &c," the narrow strips of wood used for inlay on furniture, were also on hand.

In this inventory, about half of the entries for mahogany were designated specifically as "Bay" or "St. Domingo." Trotter and Haines had approximately £276 worth of the Bay, £107 of Santo Domingo, and £135 of unspecified mahogany, or, calculated in feet, approximately 3,665 of Bay, 1,290 of Santo Domingo, and 1,810 of the unspecified mahogany plus some small odd lots. These quantities make the supply of walnut—a less fashionable wood in Trotter's period—valued at slightly more than £5 (about 600 feet) almost negligible.

At the end of the eighteenth century, "Bay" mahogany, imported from the Bay of Honduras in Central America, rather than the dark mahogany from Santo Domingo in the West Indies, was recommended by Thomas Sheraton, the popular English furniture maker and designer of Daniel Trotter's period, in the following terms:

Hispaniola or Santo Domingo produces mahogany not much in such use with us . . . . From [Honduras] is imported the principal kind of mahogany in use amongst cabinet makers, which generally bears the name of Honduras mahogany, and sometimes Baywood, from the bay or arm of the sea which runs up to it.[116]

In 1791 Trotter purchased two "pieces" of Bay of Honduras mahogany, totaling 1,127 feet, from the merchant Henry Drinker. The cabinetmakers

[111] David Evans Day Book, 1774–1781, AM-9115, I, 70 (HSP).

[112] The cabinetmaker Thomas Woodsend first appears in the Philadelphia city directory in 1811. He may have been working in Trotter's shop as a journeyman in 1797. See *The Philadelphia Directory* (Philadelphia: James Robinson, 1811). Trotter Receipt Book (Trotter Papers, DMMC). Lewis was the son of Thomas Affleck who continued his father's furniture-making business for a short time after the latter's death (Hornor, *Blue Book*, p. 237).

[113] Trotter Receipt Book (Trotter Papers, DMMC). See also entries for Feb. 21 and March 13, 1797, George Washington Household Account Book, 1793–1797 (HSP). It must be acknowledged that there was another John Aitken in Philadelphia during this period who was a silversmith. See *The Philadelphia Directory* (Philadelphia: C. W. Stafford, 1797).

[114] Trotter Receipt Book (Trotter Papers, DMMC).

[115] This information is based on numerous references to the purchase of wood in the Trotter Papers.

[116] Thomas Sheraton, *The Cabinet Dictionary* (London: printed by W. Smith, 1803), p. 120.

Jacob Wayne, John Webb, George Claypoole, and Thomas Burling and Son also bought mahogany from the same shipment.[117] In 1795, Stephen Girard, in joint account with Captain John Cochran, who had recently returned from a voyage to the West Indies, sold Trotter two mahogany logs measuring 126 feet 4 inches at nine pence per foot.[118] Furniture attributed to Trotter's shop exhibits the use of both Honduras and the Santo Domingo woods.

The mahogany Trotter procured from Drinker and Girard was purchased in the form of logs that had to be prepared for his use by sawyers. Jacob Mitchell and John Supplee were mahogany sawyers and both worked for Trotter in that capacity.[119] William Rigby, a cabinetmaker on North Front Street, shared the expense of cutting wood with Trotter at least once; Supplee's receipt states: "Receivd 6 m 26th 1795 of Daniel Trotter four pounds 5/7½ in full of his part for Sawing a quantity of Mahogany in Company with Wm Rigby."[120] It may have been more usual for cabinetmakers jointly to have large amounts of wood sawed, dividing the end product and the charges involved, than is indicated by the single entry in Trotter's records.

One of the most intriguing of Trotter's transactions with members of his craft occurred in the midst of the dispute between journeymen and master cabinetmakers. He paid Richard Folwell £11.5.0 on May 21, 1796, "in full for printing Lists of the Prices of Cabinet Work."[121] Probably related to his publication is an entry in Trotter's general record book:

Account of Book sold in Company with Thomas Williams

To Conrad Gilbert	5/7½
Jacob Martin	5/7½
Lewis Affleck	5/7½
Widdow Rigby	5/7½
1 d Thomas Roberts	7/6
1 d Ts Janvier	7/6

1 John Webb	7/6
Ely Eldridge	7/6
Samuel Walton	5/7½
David Evans	5/7½
Wm Bleakey	7/6
1 d Countryman	7/6
Joseph Woolen	7/6
Joseph Bromley	7/6
John Janvier	7/6

Included in this list are ten Philadelphia cabinetmakers, eight of whom had their shops in Trotter's neighborhood during the latter part of the 1790's.[122] William Bleakey and Joseph Bromley have not been identified but may have lived outside of the city, as did the cabinetmakers John Janvier of Cantwell's Bridge, Delaware, and Joseph Woolen of Lower Dublin, Pennsylvania.[123] Since the book was sold in alliance with another cabinetmaker and seemingly exclusively to cabinetmakers, it almost necessarily pertained to their trade. The entry is undated, but the period during which it could have been made is limited by the presence among the buyers of "Widdow Rigby," who managed her husband's business after he died in 1796.[124] The payment for publishing the price list and the account of book sales probably relate to *The Philadelphia Cabinet and Chair-Makers Book of Prices*, printed by Richard Folwell in 1796, which includes no indication of authorship. Although Trotter may have been completely responsible for the contents, it is possible that it was done in conjunction with Thomas Williams or other cabinetmakers. Two prices are quoted for the book Trotter marketed; the difference—only £0.1.10½—can perhaps be accounted for by the presence or absence of illustrations. Unlike the books of prices mentioned previously, this one includes only retail prices for finished products. It lists approximately seventy furniture forms available in walnut and mahogany. Montgomery, in *American Furniture, The Federal Period, 1788–1825*, has suggested that this publication may have been intended to alert the public of

[117] Henry Drinker Journal, 1791–1798, XV, 58, 59, and 63 (Henry Drinker Papers, HSP).

[118] Ledger Book C, 1794–1796, p. 82 (Papers of Stephen Girard, Girard College, Philadelphia).

[119] John Supplee is not listed in the Philadelphia directories of the 1790's; however, from the nature of his accounts with Trotter, it is obvious that he was a sawyer. See Hogan, *Prospect of Philadelphia*, entry under "Jacob Mitchell."

[120] *Ibid.*, see entry under "William Rigby"; also, Trotter Receipt Book (Trotter Papers, DMMC).

[121] Trotter Receipt Book (Trotter Papers, DMMC).

[122] Philadelphia directories reveal the presence of these cabinetmakers in the city.

[123] Dorman, *Delaware Cabinetmakers*, pp. 42–43; Hornor, *Blue Book*, p. 326.

[124] William Rigby appears in the Philadelphia directories for the last time in 1795. Although his will is inaccessible in the Philadelphia Municipal Archives because of its poor condition, it was filed in 1796.

standard prices at a time when the rebellious journeymen were operating a business independent of the master craftsmen.[125]

Chairmaking as referred to in the published price books did not encompass the production of Windsor chairs. This was a separate art within the woodworking crafts of this period. At least two Windsor chairmakers found Daniel Trotter's shop an outlet for their merchandise. An entry in Trotter's receipt book is self-explanatory: "Received 6 mo 24—1798 of Daniel Trotter Thirty four Dollars in full for Windsor Chairs sold by him for my account. D[avid] Moon." William Moon was paid £10.10.10 probably for the same commodity.[126] The other known reference to Trotter's selling of Windsor chairs appears in his bill to Jean Girard, who purchased six of this type in 1787 for £2.5.0.[127]

Attention thus far has been focused on the craftsmen and merchants who contributed services or goods to Trotter's business. Of equal importance are his customers. Surviving shop records indicate that Trotter's customers spanned the social and economic scale from laborers to "gentlemen."[128] Approximately half of them could have been members of the Society of Friends, according to information in Hinshaw's *Encyclopedia of American Quaker Genealogy*.[129] Patrons were not confined to Trotter's section of the city north of High Street; in fact, about 50 per cent of those recorded lived south of that boundary, where another center of cabinetmaking activity existed. This provides a surprisingly well-balanced profile

which, of course, might be altered if complete records existed.

It has been noted that, in addition to providing these customers with furniture, Trotter sold upholstery fabric, patterns for objects cast in iron, handles for teapots and coffeepots, window cornices, and Venetian blinds. His shop was also the source for such utilitarian articles as ironing boards, stocking boards, window screens and hooks, yardsticks, bread trays, mahogany rulers, curtain rails with pulleys, hatters' bows and baskets, sailmakers' benches, and an oven peal and stopper. Coffins, often purchased from Trotter, were available in a variety of woods.[130]

Repair work comprised an important facet of Trotter's business. There are repeated references to this in his accounts, sometimes precisely noted as "mending two chairs new slatt in each chair," "planning and polishing a Card Table," "putting new Claw foot to a Stand," "a new frame for a chair seat," and "new top for dining table." Of particular interest is an alteration made in 1786 mentioned in a bill from Trotter to the hatter James Carmen for "putting Rockers on a Chair."[131]

Trotter's early records show him doing such ordinary chores as "handling an ax," whetting a saw, putting up shelves and a rack, raising a stool, adding a lock to a closet door, and even "mending a hen Coop." Bedsteads were frequently set up or disassembled for clients. Although he probably executed even the most menial tasks when he was first in business, these jobs most likely would have been delegated to apprentices or journeymen as the personnel in the shop increased. During his later years, an increasing amount of Trotter's time probably was devoted to ordering supplies, keeping accounts, and dealing with customers, diminishing his involvement in the actual production of furniture and provision of services to his customers.

For a man of Trotter's apparent stature in the cabinetmaking craft, remarkably little is known of his furniture. In the absence of a body of exam-

[125] Montgomery, *American Furniture*, p. 22.

[126] Trotter Receipt Book, entry for Dec. 6, 1793 (Trotter Papers, DMMC). A notation "Received the 6 of [Novem] 1798 tenn Pound tenn and tenn pence for Chairs" was crossed out, and beneath it Trotter wrote "Receivd 12 m. 6th-1798 of Daniel Trotter ten pounds 10/10 on account" followed by William Moon's signature. William Moon was noted as a Windsor chairmaker in *The Philadelphia Directory* (Philadelphia: James Robinson, 1808).

[127] Stephen Girard Papers (APS).

[128] Trotter's customers have been located and identified through Philadelphia directories; among them were druggists, hatters, insurance brokers, ironmongers, mariners, merchants, painters, shoemakers, shopkeepers, silversmiths, upholsterers, and tailors.

[129] Although a name corresponds to that of a person who dealt in Trotter's shop, it is possible that it may refer to a different individual than that included in Hinshaw's *Encyclopedia*, and perhaps some of these clients were Quakers but not listed in the Hinshaw compilation. Therefore, it is recognized that this evidence is not inclusive.

[130] This information is taken from scattered references in bills issued by Daniel Trotter, 67x90.55–78 (Trotter Papers, DMMC); Stephen Girard Papers (APS); Trotter's bill to George Ashton (Collins Collection, L.C.); and Trotter's bill to Samuel Coates (Reynell and Coates Collection, Baker Library, Harvard University).

[131] 67x90.57 (Trotter Papers, DMMC).

ples bearing his label, brand, or signature, documents are the best source of information about the nature of his output (see Appendix B).[132] From these it is certain that Trotter made both common and high-style furniture. Mahogany was the primary wood favored in Trotter's shop, and he produced forms in walnut on only rare occasions, the last known instance being in 1796. It is surprising that a sufficient amount of walnut furniture was still fabricated in Philadelphia in that year to warrant separate listings of retail prices for pieces made of walnut and of mahogany in *The Philadelphia Cabinet and Chair-Makers Book of Prices*. Trotter and Haines owned 2,006 feet of cherry boards in 1800, implying a rather high degree of usage, but only a table produced from this wood is mentioned in the accounts. The common native woods in his shop (already enumerated) were employed principally for concealed constructional elements of mahogany furniture and sometimes for the less sophisticated pieces, both painted and unpainted. Pine and poplar were favored for the latter purpose. From his ownership at the end of the century of "A Lott of Stringing Shades &c.," purplewood, satinwood, and mahogany veneer, it is evident that Trotter was willing to adopt the new styles of the 1790's that prescribed the use of inlays, woods of contrasting colors, and veneers. The accounts give clear indication that he made the full range of furniture forms. Bedsteads, bureaus, chairs, and tables appear most often in his accounts, with numerous variations specified for each of these forms except for bureaus. Enough data can be gleaned from extant bills and orders for furniture to show the broad capabilities of Trotter and his assistants.[133]

No pieces as yet have been allied with the bills and orders for furniture from Trotter's business, except in the case of Stephen Girard, the renowned Philadelphia merchant and financier whose furnishings are now owned by Girard College. It is interesting that Girard, a French immigrant, chose to patronize Trotter. If he was familiar with the excellence of French cabinetmaking, Girard was perhaps better qualified than most natives of Philadelphia to evaluate the many joiners active in the city when he arrived in the 1770's. The fact that during his first years in Philadelphia, Girard was a close neighbor of Trotter may have been an important factor in his initial decision to go to Trotter's shop.[134] Girard continued as a client of Trotter for approximately two decades, indicating satisfaction with his skill and craftsmanship. Because of the importance of this patronage to a study of Daniel Trotter, a brief consideration of Girard himself in this period is pertinent.

In June, 1776, at age twenty-six, Stephen Girard arrived in Philadelphia to set up trade with the West Indies.[135] His early efforts were hindered, however, by the Revolution. Despite uncertain business conditions, Girard married Mary Lum, the daughter of a shipbuilder, in 1777. The couple bought a modest house and a few acres of land in Mount Holly, New Jersey, where Girard bottled and sold clarets and brandies imported from Bordeaux, the town of his birth.[136]

Soon after the British Army left Philadelphia in the summer of 1778 (having been there since the previous September), Girard and his wife returned to the city and subsequently rented a house and a store on North Water Street where he established a wholesale business.[137] In a letter to his father in France early in 1779, he described his situation in the New World:

As regards my business, the English seized a new brig belonging to me that was in the river, when they left, all I possessed was a small estate in the country valued at ten thousand in paper money of Santo Domingo, But, by hard work, I have since then finished furnishing my house, bought a small Negro, increased my

[132] Reference has been made to Trotter's use of a brand to identify his products, but no evidence of such a practice is known to this writer. See Carl M. Williams, "Adam Haines of Philadelphia, Master Cabinetmaker of the Marlborough School," *Antiques*, LI (May, 1947), 317. A chest of drawers said to bear the label of Daniel Trotter was advertised on the back cover of *Antiques*, XXXII (Oct., 1937), but the location of this piece is not known.

[133] The same sources noted in n. 132 and MS 67x90.57 (Trotter Papers, DMMC) form the basis for these statements.

[134] Constable's Return for Philadelphia, 1780, pp. 11–12 (Department of Records, PMA). Mrs. Hannah Roach, who has done extensive research into Philadelphia land records, has determined that Girard's rented residence in 1780, as noted in the Constable's Return, was on Elfreth's Alley (author's interview with Mrs. Hannah Roach, Philadelphia, May 9, 1968).

[135] McMaster, *Girard*, p. 7.

[136] *Ibid.*, pp. 10 and 12. See also Cheesman A. Herrick, *Stephen Girard, Founder* (Philadelphia: Girard College, 1923), p. 19.

[137] McMaster, *Girard*, p. 14.

capital to thirty-five thousand and hope soon to make good my past losses.[138]

This letter was written months before the first extant bill from Daniel Trotter was issued in August, 1779, for six mahogany chairs; Girard obviously continued to add to his household possessions.[139]

The Chippendale-style chairs in the Girard College Collection have been ascribed in the past to the shop of Daniel Trotter on the basis of this bill in the amount of £12 for six mahogany chairs issued by him to Girard in 1779. The configuration of the splats on these chairs is derived from a design depicted in Plate XVI of Chippendale's *The Gentleman and Cabinet-Maker's Director* (London, 1762) —a pattern frequently occurring with slight variations in Philadelphia-made chairs of this period. Whereas nine chairs have square front legs, box stretchers, and pierced Gothic splats with carved detailing (Fig. 3), there are three other chairs that have splats of essentially the same design but with flat frontal surfaces, cabriole front legs, and claw-and-ball feet (Fig. 4).[140] There is some question, in fact, as to whether the nine straight-legged chairs were made at the same time; all bear the quarter-round blocks to brace the corners of the seat rails, and the side rails are mortised through the back legs as would be expected of Philadelphia chairs, but the back rails of four of these are composed of pine with an exterior facing of mahogany, while the other five have back rails of solid mahogany. This constructional fea-

FIG. 3. Daniel Trotter (att.), Side Chair (one of nine). Philadelphia, possibly 1779. Mahogany; H. 39¼″, W. 21½″, D. 16⅞″. (Girard College Collection: photo, courtesy of the Board of Directors of City Trusts, The Estate of Stephen Girard, Deceased.)

---

[138] *Ibid.*, p. 19.

[139] Girard kept meticulous accounts of his financial transactions, many of which survive; in addition to these, he saved letters received and letter books containing his responses, as well as bills rendered to him (Stephen Girard Papers, APS). A study of references to the purchase of furniture in the Girard Papers and of the Girard furnishings permits the attribution of most pieces to specific craftsmen. Although this writer has examined a majority of the Girard accounts predating 1800, only when this vast collection has been indexed can it be stated with absolute certainty that all references to Girard's dealings with cabinetmakers have been located.

Objects of a style postdating the death of Trotter, as well as those forms, with one exception, of an appropriate style but not mentioned in his bills to Girard, have been eliminated from consideration. That the strength of the attributions varies has been noted in the comments about the individual pieces.

[140] Chairs of the type having ball-and-claw feet were made for Edward Garrigues of Philadelphia and have been attributed to David Evans; Hunter, "David Evans," pp. 28–29, Pl. 5.

ture may be indicative of two separate sets within the group of straight-legged chairs. It is not possible to determine to which set of chairs the 1779 bill would pertain.

Girard's requests of Trotter were not consistently for fine furniture. From Trotter he ordered pine kitchen tables, a pine "Cabbin table," painted bedsteads, a dough trough, and such common items as an ironing board, a pair of stocking boards over which woolen stockings were stretched to dry, a board for a parrot stand, and packing boxes to protect goods during voyages on

FIG. 4. Trotter (att.), Side Chair (one of three). Philadelphia, possibly 1779. Mahogany, H. 38½", W. 23½", D. 16". (Girard College Collection: photo, courtesy of the Board of Directors of City Trusts, The Estate of Stephen Girard, Deceased.)

his ships. Trotter also was responsible for repair work in the Girard household.[141]

For "putting up a Counting House & Sundry other Jobs" in April, 1780, Trotter was reimbursed £75 in the abnormally inflated currency of the time. Rather than actually building it, as the terminology might imply, he was undoubtedly responsible for furnishing the area where business was to be conducted and possibly for installing

shelves and counters, to which he later added a drawer.[142]

In 1787, Girard and his brother Jean joined in a partnership that lasted for two years.[143] Although Jean spent a majority of the time in El Cap, Santo Domingo, he came to Philadelphia at least once during that period. While in the city in late 1787, Jean acquired from Trotter a desk, a cradle, a mahogany ruler, and six Windsor chairs, presumably on the advice of Stephen, in whose home he would have seen examples of this craftsman's work.[144]

A bill for six mahogany chairs purchased by Girard from Trotter for £19.0.0 in 1786 has been associated with a group in the collection that, according to style, could have been made by Trotter (Fig. 5). No prototype has been found for this distinctive chair-back design. The unusual feature of cabling at the top of the channels on the front legs, however, can be traced to England, where furniture in the style of Adam and Hepplewhite was occasionally decorated in this manner.[145] Cabling at the bottom of the flutes—more common in American usage—occurs on the legs of pieces produced in Newport, Philadelphia, New York City, and Massachusetts.[146]

Ladder-back chairs of this type often have been attributed to Trotter on the basis of the Girard set. An examination of samples from other collections reveals numerous differences among them, and the workmanship of a variety of artisans is easily discernible. Constructional details are not consistent. In fact, the practice of extending the tenon from the side rails completely through the back legs, usually considered typical of Philadelphia chairs, is not always followed. Obvious variations exist in the external features of these ladder-back chairs—in proportions, carving, and leg ornamentation. One of the most conspicuous departures from the Girard chairs is the use of the honeysuckle motif at the center of each slat in place of the plumlike motif.[147] *The Cabinet-*

[141] Stephen Girard Papers (APS).

[142] *Ibid.*

[143] Herrick, *Stephen Girard*, p. 25.

[144] McMaster, *Girard*, pp. 80–81.

[145] Ralph Edwards, *English Chairs* (London: Her Majesty's Stationery Office, 1951), No. 98.

[146] Joseph Downs, *American Furniture: Queen Anne and Chippendale Periods* (New York: Macmillan Co., 1952), Nos. 311, 125, 147, and 55.

[147] For illustrations and a study of variations of the basic style, see Milo M. Naeve, "Daniel Trotter and His Ladder-back Chairs," *Antiques*, LXXVI (Nov., 1959), 442–45.

FIG. 5. Trotter (att.), Side Chair (one of six). Philadelphia, possibly 1786. Mahogany; H. 38¾″, W. 21″, D. 18½″. (Girard College Collection: photo, courtesy of the Board of Directors of City Trusts, The Estate of Stephen Girard, Deceased.)

Makers Philadelphia and London Book of Prices of 1796 refers to "A Splatt Back Chair, Honeysuckle pattern, with mahogany rails." The term "Splatt Back" was used in this source to designate a chair with horizontal slats in the back, and the "Honeysuckle pattern" would refer to the decorative motif at the center of the slats. Slat- or ladderback chairs were undoubtedly produced by a variety of master and journeyman furniture makers in Philadelphia during the last decades of the eighteenth century.

In May, 1790, Girard purchased from Trotter a set of "6 Mahogany Chairs Covered & Brass

nailed." Of the furniture from Girard's household exhibited at Girard College, a set presently consisting of five chairs best suits the description (Fig. 6). The mention of brass nails implies that the fabric seat covering extended over the seat rails, a feature peculiar to this set of chairs. It was then the custom when a chair was upholstered in this fashion to apply one or two rows of brass-headed nails along the lower edge of the seat rails. Because of the brief description included in the 1790 bill, the attribution of these chairs to the workshop of Daniel Trotter is more certain than that for the other chairs in the collection.

Judging from the large number of similar chairs extant, this type of "pretzel-back" chair was popular during the latter part of the eighteenth century in Philadelphia. Although there were others belonging to the Philadelphia school of cabinetmaking at this time who employed the design, in only one case is the name of the craftsman revealed; a chair closely resembling this example bears the label of Jonathan Gostelowe.[148] Although no published sources are known for the chair back now termed the "pretzel-back," English prototypes exist for this design. Variations of the pretzel-back pattern may be found in the work of New England cabinetmakers as well as those in Philadelphia.[149] That this type of chair was acceptable in fashionable homes during the latter part of the eighteenth century is illustrated by surviving examples believed to have been owned by George Washington.[150]

Mahogany bedsteads were purchased from Trotter by Girard in 1786, 1787, 1790, and 1796 for £7, £5.12.6, £6, and £9.10.0, respectively.[151] Only two bills mention the term "field bedstead," but the prices cited denote high posts. Four mahogany bedsteads with tall corner pillars and testers, which, according to style, most likely were made prior to 1800, are in the Girard College Collection (Fig. 7). The example second from the left

[148] Raymond B. Clark, Jr., "Jonathan Gostelowe, Philadelphia Cabinetmaker" (unpublished Master's thesis, University of Delaware, 1956), p. 162, Pl. 5.

[149] Albert Sack, *Fine Points of Furniture* (New York: Crown Publishers, Inc., 1950), p. 47. For a similar English example, see Luke Vincent Lockwood, *A Collection of English Furniture of the XVII & XVIII Centuries* (New York: Tiffany Studios, 1907), p. 233, Pl. CCXV.

[150] Montgomery, *American Furniture*, Pl. 81.

[151] Stephen Girard Papers (APS). All subsequent references to bills from Trotter to Girard are from this source.

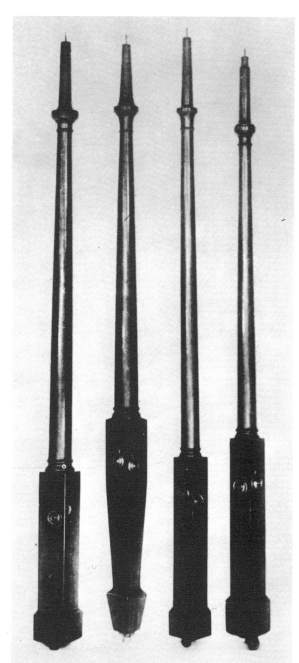

FIG. 6. Trotter (att.), Side Chair (one of five). Philadelphia, probably 1790. Mahogany; H. 38⅝", W. 21¼", D. 18½". (Girard College Collection: photo, courtesy of the Board of Directors of City Trusts, The Estate of Stephen Girard, Deceased.)

is similar to a design in Hepplewhite's *Cabinet-Maker and Upholsterer's Guide,* Plate 106. The other three exhibit features found in the published works of both Chippendale and Hepplewhite. The style of these posts is probably sufficient cause to exclude from consideration the bill to Girard from Ephraim Haines in 1804 and one from Henry Connelly in 1812, each for a bedstead. Because of the manner in which these bedsteads are stored, it has not been possible to determine for which posts the headboards were intended (Fig. 8).

Furniture was among the commodities exported

FIG. 7. Trotter (att.), Bedstead Posts. Philadelphia, possibly 1785–1796. Mahogany; H. (left to right) 65¼", 64½", 65½", 63½". (Girard College Collection: photo, courtesy of the Board of Directors of City Trusts, The Estate of Stephen Girard, Deceased.)

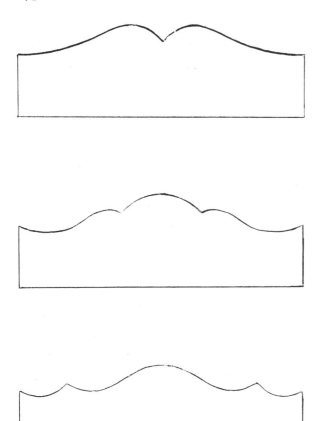

Fig. 8. Types of Headboards for the High-Post Bedsteads in the Girard College Collection. (Drawings by Anne Castrodale Golovin, 1962.)

from Philadelphia by Girard. On at least one occasion, a mahogany desk made by Trotter was purchased by Girard to be sent out of the city. This in itself is not unusual at a time when Philadelphia-made furnishings were being shipped to New England, the southern states, the West Indies, South America, and even to the islands near Africa. The desk, however, was bound for France, a most unusual destination for a piece of American furniture. On February 3, 1791, Girard worte to Messrs. Martin of Cette, France, stating that Captain Dot had brought him the elder Martin's request for an "American desk," and that Girard was having one made.[152] The next communication from him was on March 26:

I have loaded the desk for the account of your Mr. Martin, the oldest son, on board the brig "La Virginia;" by returning to the memorandum and invoice you will see that it amounts to £12–2s–6, making 32⅓ piastres fortes. If this piece of furniture meets with your approval, kindly remit to me by the return of the said vessel in verdigris in small tablets, well dried. In one of the drawers of the said desk I placed a large map of this continent which you will kindly hold at the disposal of Mr. Samatan.[153]

The bill was then itemized, indicating that £11.5.0 was for the desk and £0.17.6 for "Box, Nails hauling." Five days later Trotter received £11.17.6 from Girard for a mahogany desk and packing case.[154] On the back of a statement dated April 24, 1791, beginning "Stephen Girard Bought of Daniel Trotter," is the inscription, "Daniel Trotters Bill of a Mahogany Desk Sent to Marseille."[155]

Having heard from Messrs. Martin, Girard wrote to them on October 22, 1791, "I am very sorry, gentlemen, that you find the price of this piece of furniture high; I can assure you that I had it made by the best workman with every intention of pleasing you."[156] Girard's unqualified statement that the desk was made by "the best workman" possibly reflects a popular opinion of Trotter's capabilities as a craftsman; in any case, it shows Girard's own respect for Trotter's talents.

Girard purchased mahogany writing desks from Trotter in 1782, 1791, and 1793. The 1791 bill specifically states that Girard bought a packing case for the desk and that it was sent to France. Thus, the mahogany writing desk still in the Girard College Collection (Fig. 9) could have been acquired in either 1782 or 1793. The price in both instances was £11.5.0.

The compartmented interior behind the slant-top section of this desk contains eight arched pigeonholes set above eight small drawers, with a central closed locker in which are additional divisions. The dovetailing is heavy, and there are no dust boards between the drawers. A close similarity exists between this desk and the lower section of the desk and bookcase mentioned below (Fig.

[152] Translation of Letters Sent Out, Microfilm Copy, Ser. 2, Reel 121 (Stephen Girard Papers, APS).

[153] *Ibid.*

[154] Receipt Book, 1790–1793, Ser. 3, Reel 130 (Stephen Girard Papers, APS).

[155] Stephen Girard Papers (APS).

[156] Translation of Letters Sent Out, Microfilm Copy, Ser. 2, Reel 121 (Stephen Girard Papers, APS).

FIG. 9. Trotter (att.), Desk. Philadelphia, probably 1782 or 1793. Mahogany; H. 41⅛″, W. 41¼″, D. 22⅝″. (Girard College Collection: photo, courtesy of the Board of Directors of City Trusts, The Estate of Stephen Girard, Deceased.)

10). The constructional details of the latter, however, are considerably finer than those of the writing desk and show the work of a painstaking craftsman.

There is no known bill in the Girard manuscript material that includes an obvious reference to a desk and bookcase in the Girard College Collection (see Fig. 10). The basis for the attribution to Trotter is found in the top left-hand drawer of the writing section of the desk; printed in pencil on the bottom surface of the drawer interior are the letters "DT" (Fig. 11). This style of lettering is appropriate for the late eighteenth century and could have been placed there by Trotter. A fainter penciled inscription, "John" and "W," is also discernible. Trotter's partnership

with John Webb terminated in 1774, two years prior to Girard's arrival in Philadelphia. There is no evidence that the two joiners worked together after that date; however, it is possible, since they lived in close proximity, that they combined efforts on some of their furniture.[157] The abbreviated name also could refer to the carver John Watson, who, early in the 1790's, decorated tea- and coffeepot handles for Trotter; it may have been he who was responsible for the detailed ornamentation on the pediment of the desk and bookcase.

The bookcase interior has one permanent and two movable shelves, as well as three small drawers at the base. The writing section of the desk contains seven small drawers and seven pigeonholes. This piece is well constructed with fine dovetailing and dust boards separating the drawers.

Girard's business prospered, and in 1795, he built a home at 23 North Water Street; the following year, when the house was ready for occupancy, he placed a large order for furniture.[158] A portion of the furnishings was of French origin, which Girard requested a friend and business associate, Monsieur Hourquebie, to procure for him in Bordeaux.[159] In 1796 Girard supplemented his foreign acquisitions with items from Trotter's shop, including a large painted bookcase, two painted low-post bedsteads, a mahogany field bedstead, a mahogany circular bureau, a breakfast table, and a large dining table.[160]

Two low-post painted bedsteads (Figs. 12 and 13) that remain in the Girard College Collection are possibly those procured from Trotter by Girard in August and October, 1796, for £2.7.0 each. In Trotter's account with the painter George Flake, it is recorded that the latter painted bedsteads "Moho Couller," suggesting that he simulated a mahogany grain. These pieces are, perhaps, examples of painted graining by Flake. Girard also bought two low-post beds from Ephraim Haines in 1801 and 1802. Only the first of these is noted to have been painted, and its price was twice as much as the £2.6 paid for the

[157] According to Philadelphia tax records and the city directories, John Webb lived beside Trotter at least in 1774 and from 1787 to 1792.

[158] McMaster, *Girard,* p. 279.

[159] *Ibid.,* pp. 360–61.

[160] Stephen Girard Papers (APS).

Fig. 10. Trotter (att.), Desk and Bookcase. Philadelphia, *ca.* 1780–1790. Mahogany; H. 98″, W. 44″, D. 23½″. (Girard College Collection: photo, courtesy of the Board of Directors of City Trusts, The Estate of Stephen Girard, Deceased)

FIG. 11. Initials "DT" on drawer bottom of Desk and Bookcase in Figure 10. (Girard College Collection: photo, courtesy of the Board of Directors of City Trusts, The Estate of Stephen Girard, Deceased.)

FIG. 12. Trotter (att.), Low-Post Bedstead. Philadelphia, possibly 1796. Pine (painted); H. (head) 32½", (foot) 22¾", W. 42". (Girard College Collection: photo, courtesy of the Board of Directors of City Trusts, The Estate of Stephen Girard, Deceased.)

FIG. 13. Trotter (att.), Low-Post Bedstead. Philadelphia, possibly 1796. Pine (painted); H. (head) 31¼″, (foot) 21⅜″, W. 40½″. (Girard College Collection: photo, courtesy of the Board of Directors of City Trusts, The Estate of Stephen Girard, Deceased.)

Fig. 14. Trotter (att.), Bureau. Philadelphia, probably 1796. Mahogany; H. 37½", W. 41½", D. 23⅜". (Girard College Collection: photo, courtesy of the Board of Directors of City Trusts, The Estate of Stephen Girard, Deceased.)

Fig. 15. Trotter (att.), Bureau. Philadelphia, probably 1787. Mahogany; H. 37¼", W. 43½", D. 20¼". (Girard College Collection: photo, courtesy of the Board of Directors of City Trusts, The Estate of Stephen Girard, Deceased.)

unpainted one. One would expect a more similar cost for bedsteads so alike as two that survive. Again in 1804, Girard purchased a painted low-post bedstead from Haines for $5.00; it is unlikely, although possible, that it was made to correspond to the one Girard obtained two years earlier for a higher price. No known design source exists for this type of bedstead, which was widely produced in America over a long period beginning in the eighteenth and continuing into the nineteenth century.

A bill from Trotter to Girard mentions the purchase of "a Mahogany Circular Beauroe," in October, 1796, for £11.5.0. Although not circular in the strict sense, the convex curve of the front of a bureau in the Girard College Collection (Fig. 14) could warrant the use of this terminology. Another bureau, with a straight front (Fig. 15), in the collection—similar in most obvious respects but with slight differences in proportion—may be the one procured from Trotter in July, 1787, for £6. No other references to the purchase of bu-

reaus have been found in Girard's accounts. Variations of this basic bureau design were commonly produced in this country during the late eighteenth and early nineteenth centuries.

In 1796, Girard paid Trotter £11 for a "Large Dining Table & 2 Circular do" presumably for his new Water Street dwelling. Only the ends of what must have been the dining table mentioned in the bill remain (Fig. 16). The "Large Dining Table" was likely a rectangular extension of the ends with drop leaves. The design of the ends is not particularly distinctive or elaborate, but it is a simple expression common during the early Federal Period in the United States. Girard purchased a dining table from Henry Connelly in 1812 and another in 1817; the latter is noted to have had six legs and to have cost $20.00, while the former sold for only $16.00. The descriptions, prices, and dates of the Connelly tables are inappropriate for the two table ends in the collection.

After Trotter's death, Girard continued to accumulate household furnishings. Among the cabi-

FIG. 16. Trotter (att.), Dining Table End (one of two). Philadelphia, probably 1796. Mahogany; H. 28½″, W. 48″, D. 23½″. (Girard College Collection: photo, courtesy of the Board of Directors of City Trusts, The Estate of Stephen Girard, Deceased.)

netmakers who then enjoyed his patronage was Trotter's son-in-law and partner, Ephraim Haines.[161]

The principal part of the great fortune of this merchant-prince was designated for the establishment of a school in Philadelphia for the education of poor, white, male orphans. The Girard will stipulated that his "furniture of every sort" be placed in the school buildings where "they may be most useful."[162] When Girard College opened in

1848, many of his possessions, which had been carefully guarded in the interim, were transferred to the monumental Founders' Hall, where they remain today. In this group of furniture, one has a sample of the total range in which Trotter worked.[163]

Daniel Trotter learned cabinetmaking during the Chippendale period; he was, however, flexible to changes in fashion, and by the last decade of his life, he had adopted the simple, classic designs of the Federal style. Among the objects attributed to him in the Girard College Collection, the Chippendale and the Federal styles, as well as a transitional style incorporating elements of both, can be observed.

During the latter decades of the eighteenth century, Philadelphia was enjoying an economic vitality unmatched by any American city. Daniel Trotter was an enterprising individual in this setting, and although his financial success never rivaled that of his friend Henry Drinker or his patron Stephen Girard, he achieved a degree of prosperity unusual for his occupation. The surviving accounts pertaining to Trotter provide a rare and clearly defined body of material in which to explore the activities of a single artisan responsible for the "manufacture" of both fine and unsophisticated furniture.

---

[161] *Ibid.*

[162] Office of the Registrar of Wills, Will Book 10, p. 206 (PMA).

[163] For their assistance in the preparation of this study, I wish to thank Milo M. Naeve, who most generously shared his discovery of the main body of manuscripts relating to Daniel Trotter and assisted in the analysis of them; Theodore T. Newbold, who allowed access to the Trotter Papers while they were in his possession; Mrs. Hannah Roach, who made available the products of her extensive research on the vicinity in which Trotter lived; Mrs. Nancy Goyne Evans, who provided important references to Trotter from manuscript collections I have not examined; and Dr. Karl Friedman, past president of Girard College, who permitted me to study the furniture in the Girard College Collection and the Stephen Girard Papers before they were microfilmed.

Appendix A

Index of Furniture Available in the Trotter and Haines Shop in 1800

This index of furniture forms known to have been in the Trotter and Haines shop at the time of Daniel Trotter's death in 1800 was compiled from three sources in the Trotter Papers (DMMC): A Record of Things Sold at Private Sale Belonging to Trotter and Haines (67x90.14), A List of Furniture Belonging to Trotter and Haines Sold at Vendue (67x90.5), and The Goods Divided Before the Vendue and Taken by Ephraim Haines (67x90.4). The forms are listed alphabetically with variations within a single form specified; the quantity of each item is noted as well as the minimum and maximum prices obtained for it.

Bedstead—10

High post carved—1	$30.00
High post, foot mahogany—1	12.25
No description (hereafter ND)—8	4.50–13.00

Bureau—9

Circular—4	29.50
Column corner—1	18.50
ND—4	20.00

Chair—38

Easy—2	18.00–18.50
Heart back—6	7.30
Mahogany—12	3.00– 7.25
Square arm mahogany—6	7.25
Square back mahogany—12	7.25

Cradle—8

Mahogany—5	$30.00 (total)
ND—3	6.00

Desk—13

Mahogany large—1	27.50
Portable—12	85.00 (total)

Secretary—1

ND—1	29.00

Stand—13

Candle—6	4.00– 4.50
Candle—cherry—1	3.00
Corner basin—1	7.25
Corner wash—2	6.00– 6.75
Square basin—2	3.50– 3.75
ND—1	5.00

Stool—6

ND—6	6.10

Tables—23

Breakfast—sash corner—1		9.50
—oval—1		8.50
—square—2		7.00– 7.25
—ND—3		9.00–10.00
Card	—circular	9.00–10.50
	—square—1	8.00
Corner	—sash—2	12.00
	—ND—2	10.00
Dining	—5	11.00–16.00
• End	—circular	7.70

Appendix B

Index of Forms Produced in the Shop of Daniel Trotter

The information included in the following index of forms marketed by Daniel Trotter has been abstracted from all known accounts pertaining to his business. The form headings are arranged alphabetically; under each of these, the occurrences of the specific type of object in the Trotter records are listed according to date (year, month, and day) with the prices, if they are known. In all cases, the original terminology and spelling have been maintained.

Bedsteads

1782	2	2	field Bedstead painted a Sacking Bottom & Line	£ 7. 0. 0
1786	8	14	low post Bedstead Sacking & line	2.13. 9
	9	29	Mahogany Bedstead	7. 0. 0
1787	2	9	Mahogany field Bedstead	5.12. 6
1788	2	7	Bedstead painted Sacking & line	2.15. 0
1790	5	3	Mahogany Bedstead	6. 0. 0
1791	10	17	field Bedstead painted	2.15. 0
	10	24	high post Bedstead	2. 5. 0
1793	1	2	high Post Bedstead painted	3. 0. 0
	11	29	low post Bedstead	1. 5. 0
	12	26	low post Bedstead	1. 5. 0
1794	4	16	high post bedstead painted sacking & line	4. 8. 9
	6	2	field Bedstead	3. 7. 6
1796	1	23	low post Bedstead	2. 5. 0
	8	13	Low Post Bedstead painted	2. 7. 6
	9	23	Mahogany field Bedstead Caps & Castors	9.10. 0
	10	27	Low post Bedstead painted	2. 7. 6
	11	26	high post Bedstead posts & head Board Mahogany [Sacking & line]	
	11	26	high post Bedstead poplar painted [Sacking & line]	
1797	3	29	Bedstead painted Sacking line & Castors	3.11. 3
Undated			High post Bedstead	
			High post Bedstead posts & head Board Mahogany	
			Mahogany high post Bedstead & Cornice	
			Poplar Do Do	
			high post Bedstead poplar painted	
			2 Low posts 1 Trundle all to be painted	
			high post Bedstead painted Sacking & line	
			High post Bedstead	
			High post Bedstead painted	

Benches

| 1787 | 11 | 15 | 3 new benches [for sailmaker] | £ 2. 5. 0 |
| 1789 | 3 | 31 | 3 benches to set on | 11. 3 |

Bookcases

| 1787 | 2 | 16 | Walnut Bookcase | 6. 0. 0 |
| 1796 | 7 | 29 | Large Bookcase painted | 20.15. 0 |

Boxes

1782	4	27	furr Box	12. 0
	5	1	furr Box	10. 0
1783	6	1	Box	4. 6
	7	14	Box	6. 0
1785	4	28	4 Boxes	16. 0
	4	30	1 Box	5. 0
1796	8	5	Box	11. 3
1798	1	15	Box for papers	12. 6

Bureaus

1785	1	7	Mahogany Beauroe	10. 0. 0
1786	6	7	Mahogany Bureau	8. 0. 0
	10	26	Mahogany Bureau	7.10. 0
1787	5	17	Mahogany Beauroe	8. 0. 0
	6	22	Mahogany Beauroe	6. 0. 0
1790	7	29	Mahogany Bureau	6. 0. 0
1790	4	9	walnut Beaurow	3.10. 0
	5	26	Beauroe	6. 0. 0
1794	10	21	Large Mahogany Beauroe	9. 0. 0
			Beauroe	5. 0. 0
1795	9	10	Mahogany Bureau & Castors	8.17. 6
1796	6	9	Mahogany Bureau	8. 0. 0
	10	13	Mahogany Circular Beauroe	11. 5. 0
	11	26	2 Circular Beauroes	
1798	5	3	Mahogany Circular Beauroe	11. 5. 0
Undated			6 Circular Beauroes	
			2 plain Beauroes	15. 0. 0
			1 Beauroe fluted	

Canopy Rails

| 1792 | 9 | 7 | Sett of Canopy Rails | 10. 0 |

Case of Drawers

| 1788 | 5 | 5 | Case of Mahogany Drawers | 21. 0. 0 |

Chairs

1779	8	3	6 Mahogany Chairs	12. 0. 0
1786	9	29	6 Mahogany Chairs	19. 0. 0
1787	12	13	6 Windsor Chairs	2. 5. 0
1788	2	25	2 Chairs	11. 3
	2	26	Easy Chair	9. 0. 0
1790	5	3	6 Mahogany Chairs Covered & Brass Nailed	14. 0. 0
	7	29	6 Mahogany Chairs	12. 0. 0

1794	10 18	6 Mahogany Chairs	£15. 0. 0
1796	11 26	6 Chairs Brass nailed	
	11 26	2 Arm Chairs Brass nailed	
	11 26	6 Chairs Loos seates Covered with hair	
	11 26	6 Chairs Canvas Bottoms	
Undated		8 Chairs 2 of them Armd	
		6 Chairs Loos Seates Covered	
		8 Loos Seats hair Covers	
		8 Chairs Covered with hair Seating & Brass nailed	
		2 Armd Chairs Covered with hair Seating & Brass nailed	
		14 Mahogany Chairs Loos Seates in Linnen	
		6 Chairs Brass nailed	
		Easy Chair & 1 Arm do of Mahogany with a Close Stool	14. 0. 0

Chests

| 1788 | 7 15 | Large close Chest | 1.17. 6 |
| 1790 | 2 12 | pine chest | 15. 0 |

Coffins

1788	7 15	Large close Chest	1.17. 6
1771	12 13	Coffin	
1772	6 8	Coffin [Webb & Trotter]	3. 0. 0
1773	4 12	Mahogany Coffin [Webb & Trotter]	7. 0. 0
1784	5 13	Walnut Coffin	2.15. 0
1789	8 3	small red Cedar Coffin	1. 7. 6
1791	1 3	Mahogany Coffin	3. 5. 0
	6 3	Gum Coffin	2. 5. 0
1792	2 1	Gum Coffin for an Apprentice	2. 0. 0
1793	6 7	Mahogany Coffin 3 ft 6 in long	3.10. 0
	9 9	Coffin	2. 5. 0
	9 20	Coffin	2.15. 0
	9 26	Coffin of Mahogany	5. 5. 0
	10 16	Stained Coffin	2.12. 6
	10 25	Ridge top Coloured Coffin	2.12. 6
1794	9 30	Walnut Coffin for a young man	3.10. 0
1795	7 18	Walnut Coffin	3.15. 0
	9 16	Mahogany Coffin 2 ft 9 in long	3. 7. 6
1796	8 13	Mahogany Coffin 2 feet long	2.10. 0
1796		Coffin $24.00	
1797		Coffin	1.17. 0
1798	5 19	Mahogany Coffin with a folding top	9. 0. 0
1799		Coffin	5. 0. 0
Undated		Coffin $24.00	

Corner Shelf

| 1794 | 10 31 | Mahogany Corner Shelf | 7. 6 |

Cornices

1790	2 20	3 Window Cornices with pullies	12. 6
1796	6 9	Bed Cornice	1. 0. 0
	7 21	2 Window Cornices swelled fronts and pullies hung for double drapery	1. 5. 0
	11 26	8 Window Cornices	

Undated		6 Window Cornices 2 Swelled 4 Scallop & painted	
		6 Window Cornices	
		Bed Cornice Sacking & line	

Cot Frames

| 1789 | 12 2 | 5 Cot Frames | £ 1.17. 6 |
| | 12 4 | 1 Cot Frame | 7. 6 |

Cradles

| 1771 | 9 7 | Walnut Cradle [Webb & Trotter] | |
| 1787 | 11 30 | Walnut Cradle | 1.10. 0 |

Desks

1780	11 17	Mahogany Desk	15. 0. 0
1782	9 28	Large Writing Desk & Stools	11. 5. 0
1787	11 10	Desk	6. 0. 0
1791	4 24	Mahogany Desk	11. 5. 0
1793	12 2	Mahogany writing Desk	11. 5. 0

Dough Trough

| 1797 | 3 20 | Dough Trough slideing Covers | 2.12. 6 |

Frames

1773	10 6	2 Family Picture frames gilt with a case [Webb & Trotter]	3.15. 0
1787	11 24	Small frame & Glass	3. 6
1789	1 26	Slate frame	1. 6
1790	2 16	picture Frame	4. 0
1791	5 14	Small frame	2. 6
1792	12 14	Mahogany frame & Glass	12. 0

Hatter's Baskets

| 1783 | 2 16 | 2 Hatters Baskets | 10. 0 |
| 1795 | 1 3 | Hatters Baskets | 10. 0 |

Hatter's Bows

1782	12 27	2 Hatters bows	1.15. 0
1783	1 17	2 Hatters bows	1.15. 0
	12 3	2 Hatters Bows	1.10. 0
1791	11 8	Hatters bow	
1792	12 6	3 Hatters bows	1.10. 0

Ironing Board

| 1786 | 1 19 | Ironing Board | 1. 2. 6 |
| 1797 | 11 7 | Ironing Board | |

Packing Boxes

1782	8 15	5 packing Boxes	2. 1. 8
	8 21	4 packing Boxes and 1 Small one	1.19. 4
1784	3 27	packing Case	7. 6
1787	5 30	packing Box	4. 2
1787	8 27	packing Box	5. 0
1791	4 24	packing Case	12. 6
1793	2 2	packing Box	1.10½

Rockers

1786	2	8	putting Rockers on a Chair	£	4. 0
1791	5	26	pr of Cradle rockers		4. 0
	10	17	pair of Mahogany rockers		5. 0
1793	5	31	pair of Rockers		

Rulers

1787	12	13	Mahogany Ruler	1. 6
1793	1	26	Mahogany ruler [and 2 yard sticks]	2. 3
1797	4	10	6 Mahogany Rulers	7. 6

Shelf

1794	7	31	mahogany Corner Shelf	7. 6

Side Boards

1796	11	26	Bolection Side Board	
1797	11	7	Mahogany Side Board	22.10. 0
Undated			Side Board	

Sign Boards

1790	5	17	sign Board	5. 0

Sofas

1796	4	25	Cabriole Sofa in hair Cloth	24. 0. 0
	11	26	Cabriole Sofa	
1797	7	1	Sofa Covered with hair Cloth & Brass nailed	24. 0. 0
Undated			Sofa Covered & Brassnailed	
			Sopha in Linnen	

Stands

1786	9	7	Walnut Stand	1.15. 0
1787	4	14	Walnut Stand	1.17. 6
1797	11	7	Mahogany Stand	2.12. 6
1798	1	18	Stand	
Undated			Wash Stand	
			Common wash Stand	
			Stand	
			Stand	2.12. 6

Stocking Boards

1789	11	19	pair of Stocking Boards	3. 9

Stool

1793	12	11	Mahogany Counting house Stool	£	15. 0

Tables

1771	9	7	pine Table [Webb & Trotter]	
1781	12	8	Mahogany Card Table	6. 0. 0
1785	9	6	pine Table	1. 2. 6
	12	8	Mahogany Breakfast table	5. 0. 0
1786	1	19	pine Kitchen Table	1. 5. 0
	8	28	pine Cabbin Table	12. 6
1787	6	22	pine Table	15. 0
1790	6	26	pine card Table painted	1.17. 6
	10	23	Card Table	3.10. 0
1791	1	10	Walnut Breakfast Table	2. 5. 0
	5	26	Mahogany Dining Table 4 feet	5. 0. 0
1794	2	22	writing table covered with green cloth	8. 0. 0
	5	24	Mahogany dining table	5.10. 0
	7	31	Mahogany Breakfast Table	3.10. 0
1796	8	31	2 Walnut Card Tables	11. 5. 0
	8	31	1 Walnut Breakfast plain	
	10	13	Breakfast Table	3. 0. 0
	10	13	Large Dining Table & 2 Circular do	16. 0. 0
	11	26	2 Circular Card Tables	
	11	26	four feet Dining Table, 2 circular ends	
1797	6	24	Mahogany Dining Table	6. 0. 0
	6	24	Mahogany Dining Table Smaller	5. 0. 0
	6	24	Oval Breakfast Table mahogany	4.15. 0
	11	7	1 pine Table	
1798	9	12	Mahogany table	4. 5. 0
Undated			3 Dining Tables	
			1 Small Dining Table	
			1 large Dining Table	
			2 Breakfast Tables	
			6 Circular Card Tables	
			2 Circular Card Tables	9. 0. 0
			2 Hollow Corner Card Tables	
			2 pine Tables 1 four feet & 1 three feet 6 drawers in each	

Trays

1790	3	9	bread tray	6. 6
Undated			Butter Tray	
			Knife and fork tray	

A Reconstruction of Charles Bulfinch's First Federal Street Theatre, Boston

Richard Stoddard

IN 1902 the Boston Public Library acquired from the estate of Gardner Brewer two small trunks containing the papers of the proprietors and trustees of the Federal Street Theatre in Boston. Apparently the papers had come into the Brewer family in 1852 when the firm of Merriam, Brewer & Company purchased the real estate belonging to the proprietors of the theater. Comprising more than 3,600 items, the papers cover the years 1793 to 1852 and include correspondence, inventories of scenery and other properties, leases, receipted bills from the craftsmen who built the theater, minute books of the proprietors' and trustees' meetings, and other manuscripts. These documents lay virtually unnoticed and unused by historians until 1955, when John Alden, Keeper of Rare Books at the Boston Public Library, published "A Season in Federal Street: J. B. Williamson and the Boston Theatre, 1796–1797," in the *Proceedings of the American Antiquarian Society*.[1]

In 1966 an indexed, descriptive catalogue of the manuscripts was compiled.[2] It shows that the papers of the Federal Street Theatre are a valuable collection, providing new data not only to theater historians but also to art historians and architectural historians. Since they are the records of the proprietors and trustees, and not of the managers, the papers pertain primarily to such matters as the construction of the theater (and its reconstruction after it burned in 1798), administrative affairs, sales and purchases of theater stock, and repairs and alterations to the theater. Occasionally they add something to our knowledge of actors,

---

[1] LXV, Pt. 1 (1955), 9–74. Appended are an inventory of scenery and other properties, drawn up by John Brown Williamson in 1796–1797, and an indexed list of plays performed during that season. The only previous use of the Boston Public Library manuscripts (hereafter BPLM) —and then only of the minutes of the proprietors' and trustees' meetings—had been by Ruth Michael, "A History of the Professional Theater in Boston from the Beginning to 1816" (2 vols.; unpublished Ph.D. dissertation, Radcliffe College, 1941). This is an admirably thorough treatment of mainly literary and biographical material including a list of performances at the Federal Street Theatre from 1794 to 1816. Some of the manuscripts were recently discussed in my "Aqueduct and Iron Curtain at the Federal Street Theatre, Boston," *Theatre Survey*, VIII (1967), 106–11. To

date, the most detailed treatment of the theater from an architectural point of view was Frank Chouteau Brown's brief and sometimes erroneous "The First Boston Theatre, on Federal Street: Built 1793, finally discontinued 1852. Charles Bulfinch, Architect," *Old-Time New England*, XXXVI (1945), 1–7. Some of Brown's errors have been repeated in Brooks McNamara's rather cursory treatment of the Federal Street Theatre in his recent *The American Playhouse in the Eighteenth Century* (Cambridge, Mass.: Harvard University Press, 1969), pp. 121–27.

[2] The form of citations to the manuscripts in the Boston Public Library must be explained. All the Federal Street Theatre documents, except the minutes of the proprietors' and trustees' meetings, have call numbers consisting of the general locator Ms.Th.1 plus a specific folder and/or item number. The folder number has a letter-prefix designating such categories as treasurer's accounts, contracts, letters, etc. For example, Ms.Th.1.C 5 is item 5 among the contracts, and Ms.Th.1.T 3 (10) is item 10 in folder 3 of the treasurer's accounts. The paginated minutes of the proprietors' and trustees' meetings are in two bound volumes that have the call numbers T.71.6. Vol. 2, which will be cited as "Minutes, II, 10," and T.71.6. Vol. 3, which will be cited as "Minutes, III, 10." Often receipted bills contain both a date of submission and a date of payment: where a choice had to be made, I chose the earlier date. When costs of construction, salaries, etc., are cited in pounds sterling, the exchange rate was 6s. to the dollar (pounds must be increased by a factor of $3\frac{1}{3}$ to obtain the 1790 dollar value).

the repertoire, and similar managerial concerns, but it is to the study of architecture, scenery, and lighting that they offer the most useful new information. In this article, the papers and other sources will be utilized to develop an architectural reconstruction of the first Federal Street Theatre, designed by Charles Bulfinch, built in 1793–1794, and destroyed by fire in 1798. The second (rebuilt) theater, which opened in 1798 and stood until 1852, will be treated in a separate paper. Two discussions are appropriate because in each case the problems are different, and because the reconstruction of the first theater is a task of considerable scope.

Some essential facts and dates must be set forth as a basis for the reconstruction of the first theater. Under the management of Charles Stuart Powell, it opened on February 3, 1794, and the first season ran until July 4 of that year. Powell also managed the second season, from December 15, 1794, to June 19, 1795. From November 2, 1795, until April, 1796, John Steel Tyler (brother of the playwright Royall Tyler) was the manager, assisted by John Hodgkinson from November to January. John Brown Williamson succeeded Tyler, carried the third season to its end on May

16, 1796, and managed the following season, from September 19, 1796, to June 7, 1797. In December, 1797, John Sollee, who had agreed to manage the theater in its fifth season, canceled his agreement after only a few performances; thus, on January 22, 1798, Giles Leonard Barrett and Joseph Harper became tenants-at-will. On February 2, 1798, a fire destroyed all but the brick walls of the structure.[3]

The theater was built at a cost of about $40,000, which was raised by a subscription of sixty shares held first by fifty-six proprietors and at the time of the fire by as few, perhaps, as thirty-six. The proprietors elected a board of five trustees to carry on the daily business. Charles Bulfinch was a trustee from April 10, 1793, to April 5, 1796.

The best illustration of the first Federal Street Theatre is an anonymous and undated water color now in the collection of the Bostonian Society (Fig. 1). That part of the water color depicting the theater is, more precisely, a line drawing

[3] See William W. Clapp, Jr., *A Record of the Boston Stage* (Boston and Cambridge, Mass.: James Monroe and Co., 1853), pp. 1–60; Michael, "History of the Professional Theater in Boston," I, 42–231; and Minutes, II and III *passim* (BPLM).

FIG. 1. Anonymous, "Burning of the Federal Street Theatre." Boston, n.d. Water color; H. 6⅞", W. 12¾". (The Bostonian Society.)

in brown ink. The walls of the building are colored with a light-red wash, and the architectural details are left uncolored. In the allegorical scene the theater is afire in the background, and Athena, Thalia, and Dionysus, with the help of several *putti,* are preparing or celebrating its reconstruction. Athena holds a sketch of the façade of the second (rebuilt) theater, and one of the *putti* holds a scroll marked "Ground Plan of Theatre." In the sketch held by Athena, a phoenix rises from a cloud of smoke and fire above the theater. The phoenix is notable because the phrase, "A *Phoenix* Stage, which *propagates* by FIRE" was used by Robert Treat Paine, Jr., in the prologue written for the reopening of the theater in 1798.[4] This bit of evidence and the correspondence of Athena's sketch to the actual second theater indicate that the artist drew the first theater either from memory or from another drawing or painting that has been lost. In any case, we can regard the water color as generally reliable, because it agrees not only with contemporary description of the building but also with the only other known illustrations of the theater: the Bulfinch medal and an engraving on a Paul Revere urn.

The large gold medal awarded by the proprietors to Bulfinch for his design of the theater and supervision of the construction entitled him to a seat for life. The medal—still owned by the Bulfinch family—was made by Joseph Callender, a Boston engraver and a diesinker for the Massachusetts Mint.[5] His bill to the proprietors, dated March 31, 1795, was for £27, a considerable amount at the time.[6] The engraving on the obverse of the medal (Fig. 2),[7] representing the façade of the theater, is almost identical to that on a silver urn by Paul Revere (Fig. 3), now in the collection of the Museum of Fine Arts in Boston.[8]

FIG. 2. Joseph Callender, Medal presented to Charles Bulfinch by the proprietors of the Federal Street Theatre. Boston, 1795. Gold; Dia. 2½". (Courtesy of Commander Charles Bulfinch: photo, Harvard Theatre Collection.)

[4] *Russell's Gazette,* Nov. 5, 1798. An engraving based on the water color is printed in Justin Winsor, *The Memorial History of Boston* (Boston: J. R. Osgood and Co., 1882–1883), IV, 363.

[5] George C. Groce and David H. Wallace, *The New-York Historical Society's Dictionary of Artists in America, 1564–1860* (New Haven: Yale University Press, 1957), p. 103.

[6] Callender's bill is Ms. Th.1.T 8 (319) (BPLM).

[7] I am grateful to Miss Helen D. Willard of the Harvard Theatre Collection and to Commander Charles Bulfinch for permission to reproduce Harvard's photograph of the medal.

[8] Charles Place, *Charles Bulfinch, Architect and Citizen* (Boston: Houghton Mifflin Co., 1925), pp. 60–61, published a photograph of the medal and a transcription of the in-

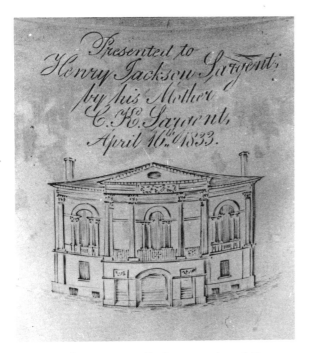

FIG. 3. Paul Revere, Detail of trumpet-footed Urn presented to Henry Jackson by the proprietors of the Federal Street Treatre. Boston, 1796. Inscription added, 1833. Silver; H. 11½″. (The Museum of Fine Arts, Boston.)

A discussion of illustrations of the Federal Street Theatre must include mention of a series of four water colors, by an unknown artist, in the Harvard Theatre Collection. These water colors, part of the Shaw Collection, represent the first theater, the first theater afire, the second theater in 1798, and the second theater in 1835. They are amateurish in execution, with little of the detail found in the Bostonian Society water color. Architectural details (such as cornices and capitals) are mere blurs, and close examination indicates that all are copies of published engravings. The first is a copy of an engraving in Justin Winsor's *Memorial History of Boston;* the second is a similar copy with the addition of flames and smoke and a crowd of shadowy spectators and fire fighters; and the third and fourth (representing the second theater) are copies of engravings by Abel Bowen.[9]

Unless new illustrations come to light, it must be concluded that the iconography of the first Federal Street Theatre is complete with the Bostonian Society water color, the Bulfinch medal, and the Revere urn. No drawing of the interior of either theater has been found, but the Brewer manuscripts allow us to clarify and supplement these illustrations.

The land on which the Federal Street Theatre was built was acquired in July and August, 1793, by the purchase of lots from William Tudor, Thomas Brattle, and Edward H. Robbins, for a total cost of £1,215.[10] An engineer's drawing of the theater property, prepared in 1852 when the second theater was to be sold at auction, shows that the theater was built primarily on the Brattle-Tudor lots, which are superimposed on the plan in dotted lines (Fig. 4).[11] The boundaries of the Robbins land are difficult to establish, but it is clear that it included the lot marked "Distill House," "Lot Nº 2," the path that became Theatre Alley, and a good portion of land to the west of the alley.

Before 1798, two other land transactions were made by the proprietors. One was the purchase of a house lot on the south side of Franklin Street (part of which, in 1803, became the site of the Church of the Holy Cross, another Bulfinch design), which evidently was not used for structures

scription. His photograph clearly showed the reverse inscription to read: ". . . To Charles Bulfinch, Esqʳ For his unremitted and liberal Attention in the Plan and Execution of that Buildings [*sic*]." Place's transcription has been repeated again and again. It is puzzling to find that, as Fig. 2 shows, and as another photograph in the Harvard Theatre Collection shows even more clearly, the inscription now reads "Building" followed by a semicolon.

The urn, not presently on exhibit at the Museum of Fine Arts, is identified by the number 25.597. A full-length photograph of it appears in Marjorie Drake Ross, *The Book of Boston: The Federal Period, 1775 to 1837* (New York: Hastings House, 1961), p. 86. In a letter to the editor of the *Journal of the Society of Architectural Historians,* XXIV (1965), 108, John Alden discussed the urn and the medal, suggesting that the urn might have been the work of Revere's sons, and correcting certain statements about the medal in Harold and James Kirker's *Bulfinch's Boston, 1787–1817* (New York: Oxford University Press, 1964).

[9] IV, 363. The Bowen engravings appeared, respectively, in Caleb A. Snow, *A History of Boston* (Boston: The author, 1825), p. 333, and Abel Bowen, *Bowen's Picture of Boston* (3rd ed.; Boston: Otis, Broaders, and Co., 1838), p. 188. The two Bowen engravings will be discussed in my conjectural reconstruction of the second theater.

[10] Suffolk County Deeds, Liber 176, fols. 205, 206, and 258 (Registry of Deeds, Suffolk County Courthouse, Boston, Mass.).

[11] The plan is bound with Suffolk County Deeds, Liber 632, folio 1 (Registry of Deeds, Suffolk County Courthouse, Boston, Mass.).

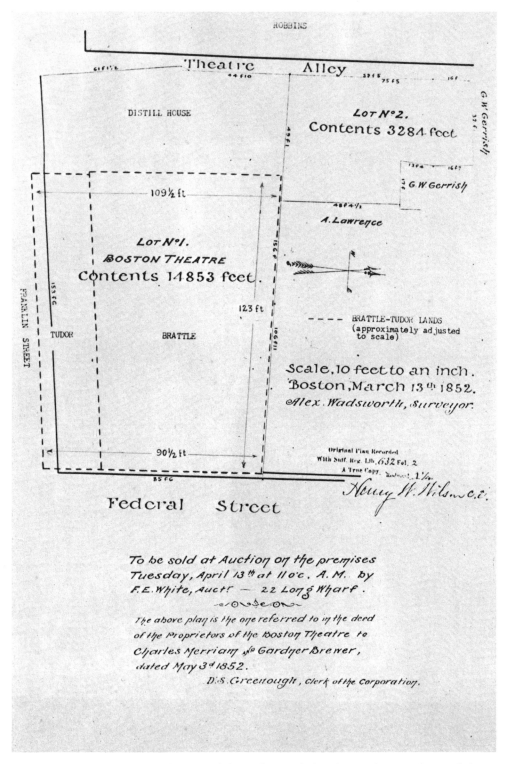

ROBBINS

Theatre Alley

DISTILL HOUSE

LOT Nº 2.
Contents 3284 feet

G. W. Gerrish

G. W. Gerrish

A. Lawrence

109½ ft

LOT Nº 1.
BOSTON THEATRE
Contents 14853 feet.

123 ft

FRANKLIN STREET

TUDOR   BRATTLE

90½ ft

Federal Street

- - - - BRATTLE-TUDOR LANDS
(approximately adjusted to scale)

Scale, 10 feet to an inch.
Boston, March 13th 1852.
Alex. Wadsworth, Surveyor.

Original Plan Recorded
With Suff. Reg. Lib. 632 Fol. 2
A True Copy. Reduced 1½.

Henry W. Wilson, C.E.

To be sold at Auction on the premises
Tuesday, April 13th at 11 o'c. A.M. by
F.E. White, Auctr. — 22 Long Wharf.

The above plan is the one referred to in the deed
of the Proprietors of the Boston Theatre to
Charles Merriam and Gardner Brewer,
dated May 3d 1852.
D.S. Greenough, Clerk of the Corporation.

FIG. 4. Alexander Wadsworth, Plan of the real estate belonging to the proprietors of the Boston Theatre (Federal Street). Boston, 1852. Lithograph; H. 14½″, W. 9½″. (Suffolk County Deeds, Liber 632, Folio 1.)

connected with the theater.[12] The second transaction was the purchase in November, 1797, of a small lot adjoining the Robbins land to the north. This purchase included a building that was definitely used as a scene shop in 1797 and probably had been similarly used, on a rented basis, since 1795.[13]

A block of stores called "the old Red Shops" stood on the Brattle-Tudor land when it was purchased by the proprietors; and in April, 1793 (although the deeds were not received in the Registry of Deeds until July), the proprietors compensated nine people for being dislocated from these shops. On April 20 the buildings were sold and removed shortly thereafter.[14] On part of the Robbins land, perhaps at the point indicated on the overlay of the plan, stood a "Distill House," which was dismantled in April or early May.[15] By May 20 excavation for the foundation of the theater was completed, and the contractor billed the proprietors for digging a foundation "110 feet long & 61 feet wide," to which he added "digging 6 feet longer."[16]

Construction of the building was begun by June 1, but it was not until July 18 that the trustees signed a contract with the local firm of Bell, Simpson & Hearsey to execute the masonwork.[17] Although little is known about William Bell and Henry Simpson, William Hearsey was a master mason (probably one of a line of housewrights and masons from Hingham) who was later one of the principal contractors for Bulfinch's Massachusetts State House.[18] The total cost of the mason-

work done by these men, not considering later repairs and alterations, was at least £1,000.[19]

The housewrights who completed the interior carpentry and roofing of the theater—at a total cost of £1,950.14.6—were Thomas Hearsey and Oliver Wiswall, Jr.[20] Other carpentry work was done by the local housewrights Thomas Clement, Thomas Bolter, and the partners Hunt & Burrell. Hemlock and some oak were used for joists; planks were probably pine.[21]

Receipted bills for the masons and housewrights show that by the end of October, 1793, the exterior masonwork was completed and the roof begun. One of the bills, from a laborer requesting payment for "Extra work done in Wheeling & Removing Dirt occasioned by the Carpenters having the roof of the Theatre on the ground where the Dirt was to be levelled,"[22] sheds some light on a method of construction. The framework of the roof probably was constructed on the ground in sections and then hoisted into place.

The minutes of the proprietors' meetings show that they met at the Concert Hall in Boston from their first meeting on April 9, 1793, when the subscription for shares was undertaken, until October 7. Beginning on December 1, they met at what they called either their "hall in Federal Street" or "the Theatre."[23] By that date, then, the theater was in some way habitable: in December the roof was slated and fitted with rainspouts and gutters;[24] glazing had at least begun; and probably the rooms on the street floor were crudely finished, if not plastered and painted. The glaziers were Norton Brailsford and Isaac Green of Boston, who later glazed the Massachusetts State House.[25] Plastering and painting were completed in January,

---

12 Ms.Th.1.D 34 and T 10 (2) (BPLM).

13 *Ibid.,* D 32 and P 21. See also, Suffolk County Deeds, Liber 189, folio 192. The scene shop is visible as a black rectangle on the Hales Map of Boston (1814), partly reproduced in Walter Muir Whitehill, *Boston: A Topographical History* (Cambridge, Mass.: Harvard University Press, 1963), pp. 56–57. The map shows the second theater as well, but distorted in outline.

14 Ms.Th.1.T 3 (3), T 2 (BPLM).

15 Ms.Th.1.T 3 (27) (BPLM).

16 *Ibid.* (13).

17 *Ibid., passim,* and Minutes, II, 11 (BPLM).

18 Archives, Vol. 266, p. 273, and Vol. 267, p. 69 (Massachusetts State House; hereafter MSH). Place, *Bulfinch,* p. 232, discussed the "Herseys" of Hingham. See also, Samuel Brown Papers, Nov. 23, 1802 (work on *Constitution* by Hearsey), and June 5, 1801, and Aug. 30, 1803 (work on ships *Berceau* and *Argus* by William Bell) (Massachusetts Historical Society; hereafter MHS). Among the Henry Knox Papers (MHS) is a contract, dated April 17, 1794, by which Henry Simpson, Jr., and *James* Hearsey agreed to build a house for Knox in Thomaston, Maine. The bricks

were specifically to be "of the size in the Boston Theatre" and rates of payment the same as were paid the masons who worked on the theater.

19 Ms.Th.1.T 3 (39), T 7 (210), and T 8 (315) (BPLM).

20 Ms.Th.1.C 1, C 12, and T 8 (316) (BPLM). Hearsey, a master carpenter and one of the Hingham Hearseys, built Bulfinch's Church of Christ in Lancaster, Mass., in 1816. He was born in Hingham in 1763 and died in Harvard, Mass., in 1839; see Place, *Bulfinch,* p. 232. Wiswall remains unidentified.

21 Ms.Th.1.T 7 (176), T 6 (170), and T 5 (32–36): lumber: T 3 (24, 49, and 64), and T 8 (187) (BPLM).

22 *Ibid.,* T 3 (71).

23 Minutes, II, *passim* (BPLM).

24 Ms.Th.1.T 2 (101), and T 4 (101) (BPLM).

25 *Ibid.,* T 8 (284), and Archives, Vol. 267, pp. 56 and 208 (MSH).

1794. Most of the nonornamental painting was the work of the local firm of Edwards & Hinkley.[26] Much of the ornamental work, including stucco-work on the interior ceilings, painting and gilding of cornices and capitals inside the theater, and upholstering, was completed in January and early February, 1794.[27] In January, too, the stage machinery was finished.[28]

The manuscripts indicate, however, that the exterior ornamental woodwork (capitals, columns, pilasters) was not finished when the theater opened on February 3. The woodcarvers were John and Simeon Skillin of Boston, who later undertook the carving for the Massachusetts State House.[29] The total cost of the Skillins' carving for the theater was £610.5.4, which was paid in installments from February 27, 1794, to January 15, 1796.[30] Several receipts, including payments to a housewright for "putin up Carved Woork out Side" and to a caterer for punch to celebrate the completion of major phases of the construction, indicate that the façade columns were not erected until near the begining of the second season, probably in October, 1794.[31] This suggestion is difficult to reconcile with descriptions written soon after the opening that praise the theater for its beauty, but it is, nevertheless, well founded.

Although many of the furnishings for the theater were bought or completed in the last month before the opening, it is likely that on opening night only the lobbies, auditorium, and stage were completely finished. The mirrors for the actors' dressing rooms were not delivered until opening day (and paid for later),[32] and one might imagine that, although the appointments for the audience had been hastily completed, the actors had to be satisfied with half-finished accommodations.

A description and reconstruction of the Federal

Street Theatre must depend primarily on the only known extensive contemporary account of the theater that has come down to us—that written by Bulfinch himself. With Thomas Pemberton's introductory remarks, it is quoted here in full:

THE PLAY-HOUSE Or Theatre, the first building erected purposely for theatrical entertainments in the town of Boston, was opened the 3d of February, 1794, with the tragedy of Gustavus Vasa Erickson, the deliverer of Sweden.

We are obliged to Charles Bulfinch, esq. the architect, a gentleman of taste and ingenuity, for the following accurate description of this building.

"The Theatre in Federal street, is a lofty and spacious edifice, substantially built of brick, with stone fascias, imposts, &c. It is one hundred and forty feet long, sixty-one feet wide, and forty feet high. As it stands in a conspicious situation, it has been thought necessary to observe a strict symmetry on the outside. It has the appearance of two stories in height; the lower a basement, with three arches in the front and five on each side, the windows square. The second story is more lofty, with large arched windows. The front and rear are decorated with Corinthian columns and pilasters; and in front a projecting arcade gives the convenience of carriages landing their company under cover.

"In the construction of this house, every attention has been paid to keep the entrances to the different parts distinct, and to afford numerous outlets. The doors to the pit and gallery are on each side; that to the boxes is in the front. This entrance is large and commodious. After landing under cover, the company pass through an open waiting room to two staircases, which lead to the corridors at the back of the boxes.

"The form of the audience part of the theatre is circular, one quarter of the circle being cut off for the stage opening. Four Corinthian columns support the ceiling, which is formed of four large eliptick arches. One of these is the opening of the front gallery; two others, those of the side galleries or slips; and the fourth the proscenium, or opening of the stage.

"The columns which support the ceiling, give the leading divisions of the boxes, &c. The pedestal continued forms the front of the lower boxes. The cornice of the entablature and balustrade give the front and side galleries. The second row of boxes is suspended between, without visible support. All the boxes are three seats deep; and it may be affirmed, that there are fewer inconvenient seats than any other form is subject to.

"The back walls are painted of a light blue, and the front of the boxes, the columns, &c. are of straw

[26] Ms.Th.1.T 8 (281) (BPLM).

[27] *Ibid.*, T 4 (134), T 6 (146A and 164), and T 7 (196).

[28] *Ibid.*, T 4 (124), and T 6 (148 and 166–67).

[29] Archives, Vol. 267, p. 43 (MSH). The Skillins were well-known ship carvers, and the sons of the ship carver Simeon Skillin, Sr. John Skillin carved the first figurehead for the *Constitution*; see Groce and Wallace, *Dictionary of Artists in America*, p. 583.

[30] Frequent references will be made to the Skillins' bill, Ms.Th.1.T 10 (6), and further references will not be footnoted. See also, Ms.Th.1.T 7 (231 and 231A), T 8 (312), and T 9 (2 and 9) (BPLM).

[31] *Ibid.*, T 1, T 8 (283), T 2B, T 7 (222 and 247), and T 8 (287).

[32] *Ibid.*, T 6 (165).

and lilach colour: the mouldings, balustrades, and fret work are gilded: a crimson silk drapery suspended from the second boxes, and twelve elegant brass chandeliers of five lights each, complete the decoration.

"The stage opening is thirty-one feet wide. It is ornamented on each side with two columns; and between them, a stage door and projecting iron balcony. Over the columns, a cornice and balustrade is carried across the opening; and above is painted a flow of crimson drapery, and the arms of the Union and of the state of Massachusetts, blended with tragick and comick attributes. A riband depending from the arms bears the motto, 'All the World's a Stage.'

"Under the stage are a number of rooms, for the convenience and accommodation of the players.

"At the east end of the building, a noble and elegant dancing room is contrived. This is fifty-eight feet long, thirty-six wide, and twenty-six high, richly ornamented with Corinthian columns and pilasters, and a ceiling *en berceau,* elegantly finished with stucco in compartments. The furniture of glasses, chandeliers, and girandoles are very handsome, and promise much satisfaction to the lovers of innocent and cheerful amusement.

"There are also spacious card and tea rooms, and kitchens with the proper conveniences."[33]

The theater was a freestanding building on the northeast corner of Federal Street and what became Franklin Street, although in the deeds to the land the latter is called only a passageway. The proprietors of the theater helped to make Franklin Street into the principal thoroughfare that it is today by giving up five feet of Tudor's land to widen the passageway. This was the land that the overlay shows overlapping the 1852 boundary lines. At the rear of the theater (to the west) was another lane that became Theatre Alley. During the life of the first theater, it remained a rude, unplanked path.[34] In 1793–1795 the Tontine Crescent, a block of residences designed by Bulfinch, was built behind the theater to the southwest. The Massachusetts Historical Society (founded 1791), of which some of the pro-

prietors of the theater were members, met for a time in the central part of the Crescent, over the archway. Indeed, William Tudor, a proprietor and trustee of the theater, was one of the society's founders. The "coziness" of the city at this time (population in 1794 was about 20,000) is evident in this architectural and social harmony. In 1803, the Church of the Holy Cross joined the Bulfinch ensemble.

The theater was built on a stone foundation, a few feet of which was evidently visible above the ground. The street floor, or basement floor, as it was called, contained three separate entrances for playgoers: in the front of the building, under the portico, was the entrance to the boxes; at the sides of the building were the entrances to the pit and galleries, each framed by five narrow arches. The entrances not only made the theater safer by affording numerous outlets but also served to keep classes distinct.

Elbridge Gerry, in a letter to Samuel Adams, dated July 17, 1789, commented on these class distinctions. Gerry sent the letter to Adams by way of John Henry, a manager of the John Street Theatre in New York. Henry wished to establish a theater in Boston, and Gerry, who was in favor of it, wrote that among the arguments for repeal of the Massachusetts law prohibiting theatrical exhibitions was the fact that all classes could attend the theater without destroying the "necessary distinction of ranks." Therefore, a theater would "sweeten society" by decorously allowing the poor man to enjoy the same entertainment as the gentleman.[35]

The architectural detail on the street floor of the theater was simple. The string course, or fascia, and imposts were made of stones "Smooth-hewde & Polished"; the foundation stones were simply smooth-hewn.[36] The rectangular street-floor windows are shown without lintels in all illustrations of the theater. At the corners of the façade, shallow masonry piers repeated the line of the pilasters above them. The only ornaments on the ground floor were the panels flanking the front arch under the portico. Green and Brails-

---

[33] The account was published by Thomas Pemberton as part of "A Topographical and Historical Description of Boston, 1794," *Collections of the Massachusetts Historical Society,* 1st ser., III (1794, reprinted 1810), 255–56; and, without attribution to Bulfinch, in *The Federal Orrery* (Boston), Nov. 10, 1794, whose editor, Robert Treat Paine, Jr. (master of ceremonies at the theater from 1795 to 1799), made one change: "tragick and comick attributes" became "emblems tragic and comic."

[34] The alley was not planked until 1807; see Minutes, III, 41 (BPLM).

[35] Samuel Eliot Morison, "Two 'Signers' on Salaries and the Stage," *Proceedings of the Massachusetts Historical Society,* LXII (1928–1929), 59. The Massachusetts law was passed in 1750 and renewed periodically until it was modified in 1793 to permit a theater in Boston only.

[36] Ms.Th.1.T 3 (33–34) (BPLM).

ford's glazing bill indicates that the box-entrance doorway, and probably the other doorways as well, were fitted with fanlights.[37]

As mentioned earlier, the foundation for the theater was dug 110 feet by 61 feet, and then 6 feet longer. In other words, the ground dimensions of the building proper were 116 feet by 61 feet. Since Bulfinch said that the theater measured 140 feet by 61 feet, the extra length of 24 feet must be attributed to a portico, porticoes, or portico and wing. Although none of our illustrations shows the rear (west) end of the theater, it seems that, rather than another portico, a pedimented and colonnaded wing, enclosed and of proportions similar to the portico in front (both projections being about twelve feet long), stood at that end of the building.

Evidence of this scheme is considerable. Bulfinch mentioned columns and pilasters at front and rear but described only a "projecting arcade," or porte-cochere, at the front. An arcade twenty-four feet wide would not have been necessary to accommodate carriages, and the Bostonian Society water color, which is reasonably well-scaled, suggests an arcade considerably shallower. The Skillins' bill provides further proof: it includes capitals for eight Corinthian columns twenty inches wide, for six Corinthian pilasters twenty inches wide, and for two Corinthian return (right angle) pilasters of the same width. Twenty inches was the greatest width of any column or pilaster for which the Skillins carved capitals, and it seems reasonable to assign the largest columns and pilasters to the exterior. The next largest columns were twelve-and-one-half inches wide and can be attributed to the proscenium and other parts of the interior. The Bostonian Society water color and the medal show two flat pilasters at the rear of the portico and a similar pilaster at each side of the façade.

Since it would be unreasonable to contradict these illustrations, it must be concluded that the return pilasters were placed at the rear of the theater. Two schemes are possible: the return pilasters were at the sides of the rear wall and flat pilasters at the rear of a west portico, or the returns were at the inside corners of an enclosed rear wing and the flat pilasters at the sides of the main rear wall. The first alternative seems unlikely: if return pilasters were to be used at all at the corners of the building, they would have been more appropriate on the conspicuous façade corners than on the rear wall corners. The second alternative, in which both the front and rear walls have flat, side pilasters, appears reasonable. In this suggested scheme, the theater has an enclosed rear wing with return pilasters at the inside corners (where the wing joins the main building) and engaged columns in the rearmost wall. If it is difficult to imagine that Bulfinch would have placed engaged twenty-inch-wide columns in the wall of a rear wing, it might be suggested that they were placed free, or only slightly engaged, in a very shallow portico. The west end was the stage end of the theater, and an enclosed wing would have provided greater depth for the stage and stage machinery. If we accept the implications of Bulfinch's description, then the ground floor of this wing was not arcaded as was the projection in front. His Hartford State House (1793–1796), however, was designed with front and rear porticoes, and both were arcaded on the ground floor. Perhaps the Hartford design had a precedent, in this respect, in the theater.[38]

The details of the second-floor fenestration can be inferred from both the masons' bill for window construction and the Skillins' bill for woodcarving. Bell, Simpson & Hearsey's first itemized bill asks payment for "Setting 30 Common Window & door . . . Dito 13 Large With Dubb [double] Arches."[39] The thirteen double-arched (arched and set in an arched recess) elements were the principal windows in the second story. Their disposition is clearly shown in the water color: three in the façade and five on each side. The Skillins' bill includes sixteen Corinthian capitals for pilasters 10½ inches wide, apparently for the exterior window ornament. According to the water color and the medal, four of these pilasters can be assigned to each window in the façade, leaving only two pilasters for each of the central side windows.

This proposed pattern of fenestration and ornamentation is supported by other evidence. The only illustration of the windows in the side walls is the water color, which, although it does not

[37] *Ibid.*, T 8 (281 and 284). Cf. T 4 (83), a mason's bill for "Vernishan" (Venetian) windows over doors.

[38] If other schemes for the west end seem more likely, first see the later discussion of alterations. See also, Minutes, II, 20 (BPLM).

[39] Ms.Th.1.T 5 (2) (BPLM).

clearly indicate pilasters in the central side window, does indicate a balustrade on that window such as we see on the front (pilastered) windows. Comparison with Bulfinch's Massachusetts State House (1795–1798) provides further confirmation. The principal windows in the façade of the theater were very similar, if not identical, to the central second-floor windows (double pilastered on each side) in the wings of the State House. The proposed central side windows in the second floor of the theater would have resembled the flanking windows at the State House, with single pilasters on each side (Fig. 5).

Although the medal and water color only suggest the treatment of the principal windows, it is likely that they were balustraded like those at the State House. The bill of Edwards & Hinkley requesting payment for painting "Bannesters under windows" offers some further evidence. Other details in the second story included at least the following: four hundred modillions for the cornices; an oval ornamental panel (perhaps a window) in the pediment; and on the portico, a swag on the entablature and an iron railing.[40]

In the absence of illustrations of the interior, Bulfinch's description must supply the bulk of information. Many additional details, however, can be found among the craftsmen's bills and other manuscripts. A bill for painting and a note in the treasurer's accounts show that the cellar had at least three wallpapered rooms, and that by April, 1795, one or more of these rooms was rented to Moses Hays, an insurance broker.[41] In addition, there were two kitchens and a room used for the storage of oil for lighting equipment. The kitchens, located at the northeast corner of the cellar, had two large hearths for cooking. On November 12, 1794, they and other rooms in the cellar, along with two "Parlours" on the street floor above them, were leased to Michael Mahoney, a restaurateur, for an annual rent of £60.[42] He was given sole use of a stairway leading from the kitchens to these parlors. An inventory of scenery, machinery, and furnishings in the theater, drawn up by John Brown Williamson in 1796–1797, is an important source of data.[43] It shows that by that time, and

FIG. 5. Charles Bulfinch, Massachusetts State House (detail of West Wing). Boston, 1795–1798. Photograph (1964) used as illustration in Sinclair H. Hitchings and Catherine H. Farlow, *A New Guide to the Massachusetts State House* (Boston: John Hancock Mutual Life Insurance Co., 1964), p. 32. (Courtesy of John Hancock Mutual Life Insurance Co., Boston.)

probably before, the "back cellar" under the stage was being used for the storage of lighting equipment, platforms, and the like.

When a spectator passed through the box entrance, he found himself in a waiting room, which the proprietors called the "Great Entry." In this room was a ticket office. To the right of the entrance were the doorways to the parlors, variously called "tearooms," "card rooms," or "coffee rooms." For the first three seasons Mahoney operated these rooms as a restaurant. In the fourth and fifth seasons he was replaced by another restaurateur, J. B. Lerebour.[44]

---

[40] *Ibid.*, T 10 (6) and T 8 (281).

[41] *Ibid.*, T 8 (315) and D 19.

[42] *Ibid.*, C 6.

[43] The Williamson inventory (Inv. 2) is printed in John Alden, "A Season in Federal Street: J. B. Williamson and

the Boston Theatre, 1796–1797," *Proceedings of the American Antiquarian Society*, LXV, Pt. 1 (1955), 37–53. Further references to the inventory will not be footnoted.

[44] Ms.Th.1.T 11A (2), and T 11B (88) (BPLM).

To the left of the entering spectator was the doorway to the long room that occupied the southeast corner of the street floor. The proprietors called it the "Hall," and the "70 Green fan Backed Chairs" in the Williamson inventory indicate that they held their semiannual meetings there. The hall saw more frequent use as well: on November 12, 1794, it was leased to Peter (Pierre) Landrin Duport, a dancing master, for £60 annual rent.[45] He also was allowed fortnightly use of the assembly room on the second floor of the theater "for the practice of his schollars."

The Skillins' bill supplies some information about the decorations of the hall: "2 Ancient Ionick Capitals for the Hall . . . 16 Ionick Capitals for the Windows . . . 250 Modilions for the Hall . . . 190 feet of Scrowl work for the Hall."[46] Consecutive with the last item, but unascribed, are "46 feet 6 inches of Ogee moulding" and "2 Tablets," which perhaps also formed part of the decorations. The prices for the capitals, thirty shillings each, may be compared to the Skillins' price of £5 for a 10½ inch Corinthian pilaster cap, which suggests that the hall capitals were all for small pilasters. The two "Ancient Ionick" capitals perhaps were for pilasters framing the doorway. If there was a window inside the arcade of the pit entrance, the window capitals could have been distributed four to a window; however, the nature of their arrangement is not clear.

According to Bulfinch, after passing through the "Great Entry" the spectator reached two staircases leading to the corridor at the back of the boxes. Probably both staircases led to the corridor at the back of the first tier of boxes and then continued to the corridor behind the second tier. Bell, Simpson & Hearsey's whitewashing of "circle back of upper & lower boxes"[47] indicates that there definitely were two curved box corridors, or lobbies. The lobbies, and perhaps the parlors, were illuminated with oil-burning girandoles purchased in London: "4 Girandoles Carv'd and gilt in bur.^hd [burnished] gold with 4 branches to each cut glass pans and brass nossills compleat . . . 10 Small Girandoles Carv'd & gilt in bur.^hd gold with

Carv'd Boxes cut glass pans and brass Nossills compleat."[48]

The pit occupied the middle section of the street floor and had entrances at either side of the building, as did the galleries. A note in the *American Apollo*, February 6, 1794, about the opening night, confirms that both pit and galleries had two entrances each and, incidentally, shows another aspect of the unfinished condition of the theater. The *Apollo* correspondent wrote that, "Admission into the pit and gallery by *one* avenue to each, when two to each are provided, crowds one side of pit and gallery, while the opposite side is quite at ease."

On either side of the street floor were an arcaded entranceway, a doorway into a foyer with a ticket office, a stairway ascending to the galleries, and a door leading straight into the pit, perhaps up a few steps. The dimensions of the pit, the number of pit benches, and, for that matter, the size of the auditorium itself, are unspecified. The seating capacity, however, might suggest the size, and tabulations of capacity are available: on November 23, 1793, Charles Powell agreed with the proprietors to sell no more than 179 tickets for the boxes in the first tier, 171 tickets for the second tier, 450 for the galleries ("calculating 15 Inches to each Person"), and 305 for the pit (again, 15 inches per person)[49]—total capacity was therefore 1,105. On February 18, two weeks after the opening, the proprietors voted to confer with Powell about seating because the house was "too much crouded."[50] The only other tabulations of capacity appear in Williamson's and Sollee's leases: 350 in the boxes, 280 in the pit, 280 in the gallery, and 150 in the slips or side galleries.[51] Thus, it may be assumed that, after a period of adjustment, the capacity was set at 1,060.

Recalling that "the form of the audience part is circular, one quarter of the circle being cut off for the stage opening," and that "the stage opening is thirty-one feet wide," it is possible by geometric calculation to fix the diameter of the circular auditorium at about forty-four feet.[52] This repre-

[45] Minutes, II, 37 (BPLM). See also Lillian Moore, "The Duport Mystery," *Dance Perspectives* 7 (New York: Dance Perspectives, Inc., 1960).

[46] Ms.Th.1.T 10 (6) (BPLM).

[47] *Ibid.*, T 8 (315).

[48] *Ibid.*, D 14 and D 15.

[49] Minutes, II, 15 (BPLM).

[50] *Ibid.*, pp. 20–21.

[51] *Ibid.*, pp. 59 and 90–91.

[52] The proscenium line, 31 feet, forms the hypotenuse of a right triangle both of whose legs are radii of the circle of the auditorium. The radius is thus calculated to be 21.9

Vue perspective de l'intérieur de la Salle qui fait voir la partie du Théâtre

FIG. 6. P. G. Berthault, View of the interior of the auditorium of the Grand Théâtre, Bordeaux. Engraving from Victor Louis, *Salle de spectacle de Bordeaux* (Paris: The author, 1782), Pl. XX. (Reproduced by permission of the Harvard College Library.)

sents the distance between the back walls of the boxes, which, as Bulfinch noted, were three benches, or about seven to eight feet, deep. Therefore, the width of the pit (the distance between the first-tier box fronts) was at most about thirty feet. The distance from the back of the pit to the proscenium line was also about thirty feet. Allowing fifteen inches per person, a pit of this size could accommodate 280 on eleven or twelve rows

of benches, leaving space for access, for the orchestra pit, and for a shallow stage apron.

British and American theaters at this time, however, generally had deep aprons. A good example is the Chestnut (spelled "Chesnut" until 1840) Street Theatre in Philadelphia, designed by the Royal Academician John Richards in collaboration with Charles Catton and Robert Smirke, which opened for dramatic performances two weeks after the Federal Street Theatre.[53] The

feet. It may be argued that by "one quarter of the circle being cut off" Bulfinch meant one-quarter of the diameter and not one-quarter of the circumference (as I have assumed). But calculations based on this alternative produce a pit too small to accommodate 280. See also n. 61 below.

[53] For descriptions and views of the interior and exterior of the Chestnut Street Theatre, see Harold Kirker, "The New Theatre, Philadelphia, 1791–92," *Journal of the Society of Architectural Historians,* XXII (1963), 36–37;

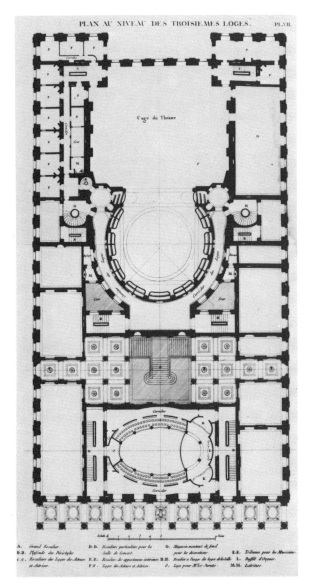
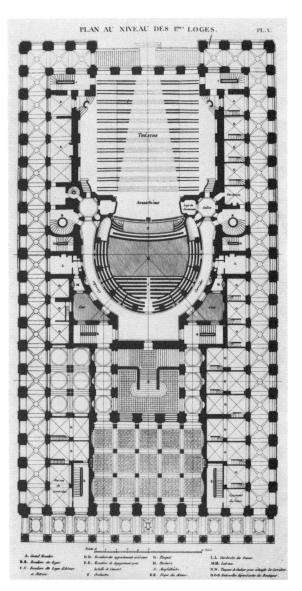

FIG. 7. Plans of the first and third tiers, Grand Théâtre, Bordeaux. Engraving from Victor Louis, *Salle de spectacle de Bordeaux* (Paris: The author, 1782), Pls. V and VII. (Reproduced by permission of the Harvard College Library.)

Chestnut Street Theatre serves as an interesting gauge by which to judge the Federal Street Theatre: for instance, the apron of the former was twelve to fifteen feet deep, a depth that would have intolerably crowded the pit of the latter. Did

McNamara, *American Playhouse*, pp. 104–18; and Thomas Clark Pollock, *The Philadelphia Theatre in the Eighteenth Century* (Philadelphia: University of Pennsylvania Press, 1933), pp. 52–54. The estimate of apron depth (which, to judge from illustrations, is reasonable) comes from Barnard Hewitt, *Theatre U.S.A., 1665–1957* (New York: McGraw-Hill, 1959), p. 40, who also prints a contemporary description.

Bulfinch's design, then, follow the British pattern? The question raises the matter of sources, which must be discussed before proceeding to describe the boxes, ceiling, and proscenium.

Bulfinch made a "Grand Tour" in 1785–1787. In his letters written from Europe, printed in his biography by Ellen S. Bulfinch, the only theater mentioned (aside from the remains of a Roman amphitheatre at Nîmes) is the Grand Théâtre in Bordeaux, designed by Victor Louis and built in 1773–1780 (Figs. 6 and 7). Of the Bordeaux theater, Bulfinch wrote, "The theatre is the most superb in France—it is a noble structure of yᵉ Corinthian order, and cost only £130,000 Sterling."[54] In London, Bulfinch probably saw Drury Lane as altered by the Adam brothers in 1775 and Covent Garden as altered by Richards in 1784.[55] By 1794 Bulfinch had seen plays in Philadelphia and New York, at the Southwark and John Street theaters, respectively. In addition, he surely must have known the Board Alley Theatre in Boston, a temporary structure fitted up in 1792 by an Englishman, Joseph Harper, and demolished in 1793.[56] It has been suggested that Bulfinch knew the Chestnut Street Theatre as well and, indeed, that he "relied almost entirely" on it for his interior design.[57]

Of these theaters that Bulfinch definitely or probably knew, Louis's neoclassical design differs significantly from the others. This theater was one of the first modern European theaters to include a domed ceiling and an auditorium in the shape of a three-quarter circle. It was an influential design on the Continent and in England; for example, Benjamin Wyatt's scheme for the interior of Drury Lane (1812) owed a great deal to the Grand Théâtre.[58] Of the theaters familiar to Bulfinch, all but the Bordeaux and the Chestnut

Street examples were built on the Georgian English pattern, with auditoriums in the shape of rectangles rounded off at the end opposite the stage and with flat ceilings. The Chestnut Street auditorium was horseshoe-shaped, "a portion of a circle terminating in right lines on each side of the stage," and it, too, had a flat ceiling.[59]

Comparison of Figure 5 with Bulfinch's description of the Federal Street Theatre suggests that the source of its design was the Bordeaux theater, not the Chestnut Street Theatre.[60] The illustration of the Bordeaux theater may be supplemented with the following descriptions. A Bulfinch contemporary, the English architect George Saunders, stated that:

All persons acquainted with the theatre at Bourdeaux [*sic*], are unanimous in their decision in it's favour. They all agree that the voice of the actor spreads more equally in this than in any other theatre. . . . It is decorated with 12 columns of the whole height from the amphitheatre to the arches under the ceiling, between which the upper ranges of boxes are managed. It's great diameter is 64 feet, and between the boxes it is 53 feet wide; from the stage-front to the opposite boxes, 47 feet. The stage-opening is about 40 feet. Great care has been had to use none but the most [acoustically] beneficial materials for the inside: the ceiling is painted in fresco, and the whole most elegantly adorned. . . . The form is regulated thus.

[54] Ellen Susan Bulfinch, *The Life and Letters of Charles Bulfinch, Architect* (Boston: Houghton, Mifflin, and Co., 1896), pp. 52–53.

[55] On Georgian London theaters, see Richard Southern, *The Georgian Playhouse* (London: Pleiades Books, 1948).

[56] On the John Street, Southwark, and Board Alley theaters, see McNamara, *American Playhouse*, pp. 52–69 and 72.

[57] Harold and James Kirker, *Bulfinch's Boston, 1787–1817* (New York: Oxford University Press, 1964), p. 61. The Messrs. Kirker follow Place, *Bulfinch*, p. 60, in suggesting that the exterior design was derived from John Crunden's *Convenient and Ornamental Architecture* (London: I. and J. Taylor, 1788). They cite Crunden's Plate 35 and further suggest that Bulfinch modified this design with elements from the theater at Birmingham and from the Chestnut Street Theatre. Two of these designs have lateral wings, and only one is of the Corinthian order, but it is true that some elements from them—notably arched windows and Crunden's portico—are also found in the exterior of the Federal Street Theatre. In regard to the Kirkers' remarks on the interior design, see n. 60 below.

[58] Wyatt's use of Louis's design has recently been discussed by Rand Carter, "The Drury Lane Theatres of Henry Holland and Benjamin Dean Wyatt," *Journal of the Society of Architectural Historians*, XXVI (1967), 200–216. The earliest example I have found of the dome and three-quarter plan is Luigi Vanvitelli's theater in the palace at Caserta, Italy, begun in 1752. See Martin Hammitzsch, *Der moderne Theaterbau* (Berlin: Ernst Wasmuth, 1906), pp. 94–95.

[59] Kirker, *Journal of the Society of Architectural Historians*, XXII (1963), 36–37.

[60] Harold and James Kirker's contention that the Chestnut Street Theatre interior was Bulfinch's source (see n. 57) encounters several difficulties. Aside from the shape of the auditorium, some features of the designs were substantially different. The Chestnut Street Theatre ceiling was flat and its boxes supported by narrow columns (features of Holland's 1794 Drury Lane Theatre as noted by Carter, *Journal of the Society of Architectural Historians*, XXVI [1967], 204–6), and the Federal Street Theatre ceiling was domed and its second tier "suspended." The treatment of the proscenium of the former was closer to the tradition of provincial Georgian theaters in England, while Bulfinch's proscenium—regardless of its proscenium doors—was conspicuously Continental. Messrs. Kirker were led by their inferences to speculate that Bulfinch made a trip to Philadelphia during which he saw the Chestnut Street Theatre; they should have taken into account, however, that in Feb., 1793, the Philadelphia theater was only "nearly completed," and that during much of 1793 a yellow fever epidemic kept the Chestnut Street Theatre from opening and would have discouraged travel into the city (see Pollock, *Philadelphia Theatre*, pp. 52–54 and 61). In addition, one must remember that in the spring of 1793 Bulfinch was busy in Boston with his scheme for the Tontine Crescent, and later with both the Crescent and the Federal Street Theatre (see Place, *Bulfinch*, p. 56).

Within the greater circle a square is inscribed, three sides of which are given to the theatre, and the fourth is left open for the stage.[61]

And, in 1911, William Henry Ward noted:

The auditorium . . . was the first so designed as to permit of a symmetrically planned ceiling. The "parterre" is three-quarters of a quasi-circle in plan, and the surrounding podium which forms the first gallery carries an order of composite columns embracing two tiers of balconies. From the two columns which frame the opening towards the proscenium and the two diagonally opposite them, spring four depressed arches, which, with the pendentives between them, carry a circular saucer dome. On the three sides of the auditorium the pair of columns intervening between these angle ones carry flattened semi-domes. On the fourth side the straight cheeks of the proscenium converge towards the stage, which is framed in between another pair of columns.[62]

The Federal Street Theatre was, of course, much less grand than the theater at Bordeaux. The latter was huge—almost three hundred feet long—and it contained an oval concert hall as well as a theater. Along its sides and rear wall were closely placed, two-story-high pilasters, and the façade boasted a dodecastyle portico of the same height. The exteriors, therefore, had little in common, but Bulfinch's designs for the auditorium, proscenium, and ceiling seem to have been directly influenced by Louis's. An auditorium in the shape of a three-quarter circle, twin columns at each side of the proscenium, "framed" galleries, and "suspended" boxes are features common to both theaters. Bulfinch's description of the ceiling is incomplete, but Bell, Simpson & Hearsey, in their first itemized bill, asked payment for "Whitewashing the Dome Ceiling," indicating that this feature also resembled the Bordeaux theater.[63] It must be noted that Bulfinch was de-

signing for an English manager and English actors, and he did include some features of the Georgian theater, notably proscenium doors in place of Louis's stage boxes and a pit rather than a parterre. The apron of the Federal Street Theatre was probably shallow and curved like the one at Bordeaux.

Before the auditorium can be described more fully, it is necessary to return momentarily to the exterior of the theater. Bulfinch noted that strict symmetry was followed, that the theater was sixty-one feet wide, and that the assembly room measured fifty-eight feet by thirty-six feet. From this it seems immediately apparent that the assembly room stood lengthwise across the east end, and that masonry made up the difference between the length of the room and the width of the building. Given Bulfinch's description, no other location for the assembly room is conceivable. Further evidence is found in Bulfinch's bill for ornamentation of the assembly room: it shows payment for two sets of "Marble Chimney furniture" for fireplaces that communicated with the chimneys visible on the medal.[64]

Close examination of the Bostonian Society water color, especially of the cornice near the chimney, shows that the central side windows and their flanking rectangular windows were set in a shallow pavilion. This is corroborated by engravings of the second theater, which was built inside the old walls. Evidently the assembly room was illuminated by the two side windows at the southeast and northeast corners of the building and, of course, by the three windows in the façade. Therefore, the thirty-six-foot width of the assembly room was the distance from the façade to the point where the pavilion began. If the theater was strictly symmetrical, the west end had the same length from the rear wall to the pavilion, and the pavilion was forty-four feet wide. From these figures, it can be inferred that the proscenium line was at the west line of the pavilion; that the pavilion marked that part of the theater containing the auditorium, lobbies, and passageways to the galleries; and that the stage was about thirty-six feet deep from the proscenium line to the main rear wall, plus about ten feet in the wing. It is also possible to fix the length of the parlors (taken to-

[61] George Saunders, *A Treatise on Theatres* (London: Printed for the author, 1790), p. 75. His Fig. 4 is a floor plan of the auditorium. It appears that Bulfinch followed this method of inscribing a square in a circle, defining the proscenium line by one side of the square.

[62] William Henry Ward, *The Architecture of the Renaissance in France* (London: B. T. Batsford, 1911), II, 452. See also Henri Prudent and Paul Guadet, *Les Salles de spectacle construites par Victor Louis à Bordeaux, au Palais-Royal et à la place Louvois* (Paris: Librairie de la construction moderne, 1903), pp. 19–27.

[63] Ms. Th.1.T 8 (315) (BPLM), dated Feb. 10, 1794. The bill cannot refer to the assembly room ceiling, since the latter was not finished until Oct. 1794; Ms.Th.1.T 7 (264) (BPLM).

[64] *Ibid.*, T 8 (289).

gether) and the "Great Entry" and "Hall" at about thirty-six feet.

Bulfinch failed to indicate whether or not the pit was raked, although the pits in American and British theaters usually were treated in that manner. The only clue is a notation in the Williamson inventory indicating storage of articles "Under the Pitt," which may mean the cellar. Some inferences can be made, however: the assembly room was twenty-six feet high, and the "Great Entry," parlors, and "Hall" under it were about ten feet high (allowing for the height of the foundation and for the thickness of the ceilings). The assembly room probably was entered from one of the box-lobbies. If it were to be entered from the lobby of the second tier of boxes, ten feet of height would have to accommodate the pit and the first tier of boxes, surely an inadequate height to accommodate both; therefore, it must have been entered from the lobby of the first tier, with the floor of the first tier and the floor of the assembly room on the same level, or about fourteen feet above the street. This was also the approximate level of the stage. The fact that there was adequate height to accommodate a raked pit, coupled with the influence of Anglo-American tradition, suggests that the pit was indeed so designed. The height of the stage would have required the raising of the pit floor in order to bring the first row of pit benches to a practical level for good sight lines. The rake would have started at this built-up level, and the pit probably was entered by ascending a few steps and by walking through a passageway under the boxes.

In front of the stage was an orchestra pit, doubtless behind a low barrier. It had to be large enough to accommodate ten musicians, for beginning with the second season the managers were bound in their leases to keep at least that number of "suitable" musicians in the orchestra.[65] In the 1796–1797 season the orchestra included at least violins, a bassoon, a flute, an oboe, a clarinet, a pianoforte, and kettle drums.

The columns supporting the proscenium and the auditorium ceiling, itemized in the Skillins' bill, were capped by "Four Capitals for Columns of 12½ inches" and "2 three Quarter Capitals for Columns of 12½ inches," described by Bulfinch as of the Corinthian order. Bulfinch did not describe

the construction of the proscenium clearly, but in both the Georgian English tradition and in the Bordeaux theater, the proscenium columns (whether framing doors or stage boxes) were disposed one behind the other—one column upstage, one downstage. It appears that of the two columns framing each proscenium door at the Federal Street Theatre, the downstage column was, in fact, one of the four columns supporting the ceiling of the auditorium. This arrangement is also found in the Bordeaux theater. The Skillins' three-quarter capitals were probably for the two columns opposite the stage. If they were engaged slightly in the auditorium wall, then three-quarter capitals would have been appropriate to them. These columns opposite the stage rose from the rear of the first tier of boxes and separated the second tier into three large "divisions" (as Bulfinch called them) similar to the smaller divisions at Bordeaux (see Fig. 6). Like Louis's second and third tiers of boxes, the second tier at the Federal Street Theatre was cantilevered. The divisions resembled large, curved balconies.

If, indeed, the auditorium ceiling was a dome, it probably was a saucer dome like the one at Bordeaux, since there was little available height to accommodate a higher type. Bulfinch described the ceiling as "formed of four large eliptick arches. One of these is the opening of the front gallery; two others, those of the side galleries or slips; and the fourth is the proscenium, or opening of the stage." The arches did not actually form the ceiling; they supported it, or seemed to support it. The two downstage proscenium columns and the two columns opposite the stage formed a square base for the dome. Pendentives springing from the columns divided the galleries into three distinct parts. The stage was viewed from the galleries through the arches.

Christian Gullager, the chief scene painter at the Federal Street Theatre from 1793 to 1797, was paid for what he called simply "painting the Scealing."[66] Possibly he was referring to the ceiling of the assembly room, but the date of his bill can be inferred to be January 17, 1794, and at that time most effort was directed toward finishing the auditorium. If, indeed, Gullager painted the auditorium ceiling, then it may well have been elabo-

---

[65] Minutes, II, 17 and 91–92 (BPLM)

[66] Ms.Th.1.T 7 (236) (BPLM). On Gullager, see Groce and Wallace, *Dictionary of Artists*, p. 280.

rately finished like that at Bordeaux. The omission from Bulfinch's account of a description of such a ceiling, and the masons' whitewashing of it, however, cast considerable doubt on the prominence of its decoration.[67]

The second tier of boxes at the Federal Street Theatre was broken up into three cantilevered balconies ("divisions") by the two auditorium columns, just as Louis's second and third tiers in the Bordeaux auditorium were broken up into a greater number of balconies by the twelve columns. At the Federal Street Theatre, the boxes had three rows of benches and were separated by low partitions. There were ten side boxes and five front boxes in each tier—if such terms can be applied to a circular auditorium—and the usual capacity was thirteen per box. The fifth and eleventh boxes in the first tier (those located at the rear "corners" of the auditorium) accommodated twelve; the corresponding boxes in the second tier, only seven.[68]

These variations were caused by the intrusion of the columns supporting the ceiling. In the first tier, the columns stood against the rear wall in the corners of the fifth and eleventh boxes and reduced the capacity of each box by one. The complication in the second tier was, of course, more extensive, because the tier was actually divided into three parts by the two columns. If the four columns supporting the ceiling did indeed form a square—that is, if the ceiling was a circular dome—then the three divisions of the second tier would have been of equal length, and the reduction in capacities of all the boxes should have been more or less the same if the divisions were of the same shape. The side balconies, however, were evidently shaped differently from the front balcony: the corners of both were probably rounded off, but the rounding, or tapering, of the side balconies near the auditorium columns was apparently greater than that of the front balcony. A different shaping of the side balconies was necessary because Bulfinch's balconies were longer and deeper than Louis's, and he had to make adjustments so

that his side balconies caused no sight-line interference with the front balcony.

The first and fifteenth boxes in each tier had a capacity of only six each. They might appear to be stage boxes over the proscenium doors; however, Bulfinch described only an "iron balcony" at that location. If boxes 1 and 15 were stage boxes, then the proposed symmetrical design of an auditorium with a domed ceiling on a square base would be upset, because each side of the auditorium would have only four boxes, while there would be five similar front boxes, all having approximately the same capacity. If boxes 1 and 15 were, instead, the first boxes in each tier, then their small capacity might be explained by the same considerations suggested above. The first boxes were also "corner" boxes, and their size was reduced by the shape of the tier as it tapered toward the downstage columns of the proscenium. According to this suggested scheme, there were no stage boxes, or the capacity of boxes over the proscenium doors was not tabulated by the proprietors.

The first boxes in each tier presented a problem to the architect: unless the three-quarter-circle design of the auditorium were modified, the first-box spectators would find themselves sitting with their backs half-turned to the stage. Benjamin Wyatt explained that he coped with this problem in his 1812 Drury Lane "by springing the Proscenium from the *back,* instead of from the *front* of the Boxes . . . and by rounding off the fronts of the Boxes nearest the Stage, until they joined the wall which separates the Proscenium from the Spectatory."[69] Bulfinch, following Louis, arrived at the same design some years before Wyatt.

On the decoration and appointments of the auditorium, Bulfinch supplied some information about the color scheme (light blue, straw, lilac) and gilding. The Skillins' bill indicates that the cornices were ornamented with "108 feet of Reed & Ribbon for the Theatre" and with 190 modillions. Bills from Richard Collins, a Boston stuccoworker, and from Jeshua & Co. for "Stocko Work round the Cove" suggest that the coving of the ceiling was ornamented, as it was at Bordeaux.[70] The stuccowork and fretwork were gilded and

---

[67] A further argument against an elaborately painted ceiling is the fact that Gullager was apparently paid only £15 for the ceiling—one third of his fee for a set of wings and back shutters for the stage; see Minutes, II, 12 (BPLM).

[68] Minutes, II, 15 (BPLM).

[69] Benjamin Wyatt, *Observations of the Design of the Theatre Royal, Drury Lane* (London: Printed for J. Taylor, 1813), p. 30.

[70] Ms.Th.1T 4 (134–35) (BPLM).

painted by George Sugden, who noted in his bill, "103.ᶠᵗ Run Cove, prickt in Green to Stucco work."[71] If green detail seems to clash with the blue of the walls as Bulfinch described them, then so does an item in Sugden's bills showing payment for painting 240 yards of "Green Distemper Colour in Boxes."[72] Furthering the confusion is Bell, Simpson & Hearsey's bill for putting up "12 Roles of Plane Paper in Boxes."[73] If a resolution of these contradictions must be made, it might be suggested that the interiors of the first-tier boxes were papered, and the second-tier interiors painted either green or blue.

The crimson silk for the draperies mentioned by Bulfinch was purchased in London by his agent, Josiah Taylor.[74] The Williamson inventory indicates that it was made into "3 Long Silk Curtins hanging under the Uper Boxes" and "2 dᵒ dᵒ in Belconas" (either the upper side boxes or galleries). The draperies were embellished with tassels and fringes, and to them can be added "a Large Taboureen [tabaret?] Valance to ornament Lower Boxes," also crimson in color.[75]

The Williamson inventory reveals that ten of the twelve chandeliers mentioned by Bulfinch were hung on the box fronts (presumably the second tier) and the remaining two on the gallery fronts. They were purchased in London from Kendrick's, King Street, Covent Garden, the firm that furnished most of the stage lights. A description of the chandeliers is in Kendrick's bill, forwarded by Josiah Taylor:

Twelve Elegant Branches for five lights Each, highly finished With Wrought Threaded Arms Pillars on Each Side, Enriched Vase striped pans, & Emboss'd Eagle in the Centre (Emblematically fixed on A Globe[)] at 6 6 0 [six pounds six] . . . Twelve Superb Brackets w.ᵗʰ Brass Backs & chaced Eagle's Head With Rings to Suspend the Above Branches from. [@] 2 2 0 . . . Sixty Vases With Well Lamps ornamented With Quilled Basons for the above Branches [i.e., a vase for each of the five lights on each of the twelve chandeliers] . . . Twelve Yards of Hard Soldered Chain to hang the Branches to the Brackets.[76]

They were oil lamps (thus the "wells" and "basons"), and along with them Kendrick's sent wicks, wick trimmers, and other accessories. Elegant as they may seem, these lights were outdone by the girandoles purchased from the same supplier and hung in the assembly room.

Checks for the boxes were issued at the front entrance and collected by boxkeepers. The box doors were, of course, numbered, and they were furnished with "Rose Handles" and perhaps studded with ornamental nails.[77] Although at first they had only "catches," in 1795 they were fitted with bolts, probably in response to a demand for greater privacy.[78] The upholstery of the benches is not specified in the manuscripts.

The galleries of the theater were divided into a front gallery and the slips. Some rough measurements can be estimated from what is known of the size of the auditorium. If the gallery fronts followed the line of the boxes (as was true at Bordeaux), then the width of the slips and front gallery could have been little more than eight feet at their narrowest points. So little space might accommodate three rows of benches in the slips and account for the small capacity (150) there, but it surely does not account for the 280-seat capacity of the front gallery. Evidently the front gallery extended forward over the second-tier boxes, supported on a beam across the columns at the rear of the auditorium. Such an arrangement would have permitted seven or eight rows of benches and might, with crowding, have accommodated 280 people. It must be remembered that there was a distinct separation of the galleries into three parts by the pendentives resting on the auditorium columns. This "framing" would have limited the length and depth of the rows of benches, especially in the slips.

The standard stage curtain is described in an upholsterer's bill as "a Green Curtain of 113 Yds Morine Ringing Taping &c."[79] Another bill, from a painter named John Johnston, for "painting a Curtain, & arm of the States &c. with a Large Drop Curtain in front of the Stage . . . £45," was paid on April 5, 1794.[80] It refers to the emblem

---

71 *Ibid.,* T 6 (146A-47) and T 7 (196).
72 *Ibid.,* T 6 (147).
73 *Ibid.,* T 7 (210).
74 *Ibid.,* D 9.
75 *Ibid.,* T 7 (251A).
76 *Ibid.,* D 16.

77 *Ibid.,* T 6 (171) and T 7 (214).
78 *Ibid.,* T 10 (34) and T 9 (15).
79 *Ibid.,* T 7 (251A).
80 *Ibid.,* T 8 (307). Johnston was a Boston portrait and figure painter; see Groce and Wallace, *Dictionary of Artists,* p. 355. In addition to the emblem, he painted a drop

over the stage, described by Bulfinch. The emblem was not painted on the proscenium; it was painted separately, or perhaps carved, and hung at the top of the proscenium, as indicated in a caterer's bill showing payment for "Punch when raising the Eagle."[81] This was another of the many occasions (sometimes called "raising suppers") when workmen were rewarded with refreshments on completion of a phase of the work.

Beneath the stage (at approximately street level) were the dressing rooms, perhaps five since that many dressing glasses were delivered to the theater on opening day. In the winter of 1794–1795, Bell, Simpson & Hearsey installed two hearths in what they called "Col. Tylers rooms."[82] Tyler at that time was master of ceremonies at the theater, a post that required him to usher people to their boxes and to preserve "decorum."[83] He doubtless had an office or a private apartment (evidently two or more rooms) in the building, probably located at the stage end, west of the dressing rooms.

Other dressing rooms were added later. A report of the fire, in the *Federal Gazette and Daily Advertiser* for February 3, 1798, supplies data about the new dressing rooms and leads to the subject of the construction of the stage:

When Mr. [John] Hodgkinson was in Boston, with his company, in the autumn of 1794 [actually 1795], he had two dressing rooms erected back of the stage balconies. These were the only dressing rooms in the Theatre which were warmed by Stoves, and from this circumstance has ensued its demolition. One of the servants of the house had kindled a fire in the south room, left some wood under the stove to dry, and went to attend his duty in other parts of the Theatre, shutting the door after him.—After his departure, it is supposed the Stove became unusually heated, and kindled the wood that was near it. This however, is certain, the flames were first discovered in the South balcony, and from thence caught the flyers over the stage, when their progress became irresistible.

There was a dressing room on each side (north and south) of the stage, behind the "balconies" of

the proscenium (which, incidentally, are not called "stage boxes").

The rigging and machinery of the stage included many hundreds of feet of cordage plus rollers, sheaves, blocks, cleats, and weights for the counterweighting of scenery.[84] The construction of the machinery was probably supervised by Emanuel Jones, a scene painter and machinist who later was employed in the Charleston Theatre and at the time of his death in 1822 was the keeper of the Charleston Academy of Fine Arts.[85] Jones started working for the proprietors on August 29, 1793. On November 27, 1793, he signed a contract for £450 annual salary and agreed to the following:

to paint in Scene Painting . . . and to superintend And operate as a Machinist in the Theatre for one full and complete year commencing on the twenty-ninth day of August AD. 1793 . . . and will attend every Night the Theatre shall be opened for exhibition during said Term, to direct & conduct the Machinery and Scenes as shall be directed by the manager.[86]

Scenery was arranged according to the system, typical of the eighteenth century, of wings and back shutters that were held at top and bottom in grooved carriages. At the Federal Street Theatre there were six pairs of carriages. Sometimes simply called "grooves," the carriages were actually "nests" of grooves, each accommodating several wings or shutters, only one of which was extended onto the stage in a given scene. Back scenes might also be mounted on rollers. Since the Williamson inventory lists thirty-one rolling scenes and only eleven "Flatts" (back shutters), this appears to have been the most frequent arrangement at the Federal Street Theatre. The inventory also notes "7 Skey borders" and "4 Tormentors," used to border the stage at top and sides. Some of the entries for rolling scenes have the notation "hoist by hand," suggesting that special machinery lifted the others. The inventory shows that the most common setting consisted of only three pairs of wings and a back scene, the full depth of the stage being reserved for magnificent scenes such as palaces.[87]

---

curtain that must have been replaced, for on Oct. 13, 1795, the proprietors voted a committee to hire someone to paint a new drop curtain; see Minutes, II, 52 (BPLM).

[81] Ms.Th.1.T 7 (233) (BPLM).

[82] *Ibid.*, T 8 (315).

[83] The duties of the master of ceremonies are described in Minutes, II, 17 (BPLM).

[84] Ms.Th.1.T 4 (124) and T 6 (166–67, 173, 175) (BPLM).

[85] Groce and Wallace, *Dictionary of Artists*, p. 357.

[86] Minutes, II, 14–15 (BPLM).

[87] For a good discussion of wing-in-groove scenery, with illuminating photographs, see McNamara, *American Play-*

The areas to the sides of, and above, the stage can be only vaguely described. The Williamson inventory indicates that an area "over flyes" was used for the storage of machinery, props, furniture, and lumber "on bums." On one side of the stage was the green room, and perhaps the side opposite was used as storage space for wings and flats or costumes. As was previously noted, the paint and carpentry shop was located in a separate building in Theatre Alley.

The machinery included a thunder machine consisting of elm "rollers," or troughs, down which iron shot were rolled.[88] The soffit of the proscenium was either called or fitted with a "sounding board." When Williamson renovated the theater prior to the opening of his season, he noted that among his improvements was a "New Sounding Board."[89] The stage lights included hanging Argand lamps, Argand and candle wing lights, a sixty-lamp oil-burning footlight machine that could be raised and lowered, and economy lamps consisting of wicks floating in lard. The Argand lamps were imported from London; most of the candle lamps were made by a local tinsmith.[90] Heating of the theater was by fireplaces and cast-iron stoves. Sanitation was evidently limited to a "Necessary House" located in the north yard.[91]

One part of the theater remains to be described: the assembly room. It might be interpreted as an echo of the separate concert hall in the Bordeaux theater. Of all the rooms in the theater, it was the most elegantly appointed. Henry Jackson, one of the first trustees of the theater, described the cost of the room in a letter to Gen. Henry Knox, January 26, 1794:

Tomorrow week, we open our new Theatre. I assure you its one of the most Elegant & beautiful buildings on the Continent. the Theatre Room is a perfect picture, and I believed far surpass's the one in your City

[the John Street Theatre in New York]. . . . Our Bills for building the Theatre to this time amount to *thirty five thousand dollars,* in finishing the Assembly Room we expect it will make an addition of *5 thousand dollars* more.[92]

As Jackson's letter suggests, the assembly room was the last part of the theater to be completed, not being finished until December, 1794. The room was used for subscription balls and concerts. The dimensions were fifty-eight feet by thirty-six feet, and twenty-six feet high; the ceiling was vaulted and compartmented. Since the theater itself was only forty feet high, it seems likely that the curve of the vault extended up into the peak of the roof. A barrel vault would lend itself well to such a space. The Senate Reception Room, formerly the Senate Chamber, of the Massachusetts State House is a barrel-vaulted room of nearly the same proportions. On January 10, 1798, the *Columbian Centinel* described the chamber as "55 feet long, 33 wide, and 30 high; highly finished in the Ionic order; two screens of Columns, support with their entablature a rich and elegant arched ceiling" (Fig. 8).[93] The following descriptions of the decorations of the assembly room provide a comparison with the Senate Reception Room.

The Skillins' bill included: "4 Capitals for [Corinthian] Columns of 10½ inches . . . 4 Capitals for [Corinthian] Return pillasters of 10½ inches," plus, perhaps, the 46½ feet of ogee molding and tablets mentioned in the discussion of the hall.

Bulfinch himself submitted a bill in December, 1794, for composition work, for a total price of £30.3.0. The following are excerpts with elisions for prices of separate items:

Composition ornaments for Assembly room viz 60 feet Reed & Ribbon . . . 60 feet d° smaller . . . Oak and Acorn branches . . . Hop leaves . . . 20 feet Gulock [guilloche] . . . 24 festoons . . . 2 Tablets for Chimneys . . . 1 D° for Door . . . 40 feet large Ogee . . .

---

house, pp. 62–65. The number of grooves is inferred from two MSS: a whitesmith's bill for "6 Irons for sceen sliders" (Ms.Th.1.T 10 [14] [BPLM]) and the Williamson inventory, which lists "6 Wing Carrages."

[88] Ms.Th.1.T 9 (15) and T 7 (223) (BPLM).

[89] *Ibid.,* Inv. 1. Holland's alterations to Covent Garden in 1792 included fitting the proscenium with a sounding board; see Walley C. Oulton, *The History of the Theatres of London* (London: Martin and Bain, 1796), II, 118.

[90] Ms.Th.1.D 16, T 7 (209) (BPLM). The Williamson inventory, in a tabulation of weekly expenses, lists 15 pounds of hog's lard.

[91] Ms.Th.1.T 10 (7) (BPLM).

[92] Henry Knox Papers (MHS) includes another letter, dated April 13, 1794, showing that Bulfinch's original estimate of the cost was $20,000.

[93] The *Centinel* description is reprinted in Sinclair H. Hitchings and Catherine Farlow, *A New Guide to the Massachusetts State House* (Boston: John Hancock Mutual Life Insurance Co., 1964), pp. 99–102, which includes excellent photographs of the room.

Fɪɢ. 8. Charles Bulfinch, Massachusetts State House, Senate Reception Room (formerly the Senate Chamber). Boston, 1795–1798. Photograph (1964) used as illustration in Sinclair H. Hitchings and Catherine H. Farlow, *A New Guide to the Massachusetts State House* (Boston: John Hancock Mutual Life Insurance Co., 1964), p. 60. (Courtesy of John Hancock Mutual Life Insurance Co., Boston.)

150 ft. small d° . . . 60 ft. beeds . . . 2 Setts Marble Chimney furniture.[94]

Charles Clement, who remains unidentified, also submitted a bill for composition ornaments, which included 36 feet of large ogee, 45½ feet of "ribband and Stick," and festoons of flowers and leaves. Richard Collins supplied the compartmented ceiling, and perhaps other ornaments.[95]

It is possible to associate some of the components of the separate bills (the Skillins' ogee with Clement's ribbon-and-stick, for example) and to identify motifs used in both the assembly room and the Senate Reception Room (oak leaves and acorns), but such close reconstruction is not necessary. It is sufficient to show that, although the order was different, the form and general scheme of decoration of the assembly room were probably those used later by Bulfinch in the reception room, and that in this case (and for that matter, generally) his work at the theater was a preparation, both of himself and his artisans, for the State House.

The four Corinthian columns for which the Skillins carved capitals might well have formed a "screen" at each end of the assembly room (the four return pilasters being corner pilasters), similar to the two-columned screen in the reception room. Such a screen would have provided a con-

[94] Ms.Th.1.T 8 (289) (BPLM). A similar bill from Bulfinch for composition work at the State House is in Archives Vol. 266, p. 310 (MSH).

[95] For Clement, see Ms.Th.1.T 8 (273) (BPLM), and for Collins, T 7 (264).

venient "shelter" for nondancers during a ball.

Much of the approximately $5,000 expended on the assembly room was for architectural ornament, but the proprietors went to considerable expense in the furnishings as well. The Williamson inventory shows that the windows were hung with crimson curtains, that the floor was covered with a beige carpet, and that the furniture included twenty-four long wooden benches. Two large mirrors, purchased in New York for $700 and framed locally, were probably mounted on the wall opposite the façade windows.[96] The lighting equipment, including chandeliers and girandoles, was purchased in London through Bulfinch's agent, Josiah Taylor. In a letter to Bulfinch, Taylor described three girandoles, which will serve to suggest the richness of these furnishings:

Girandoles (7 feet long each) in which are introduced The American Eagle standing on a Tablet, on which is inscribed SPQA (Senatus Populus Que Americani) from the back of the Eagle are suspended chains, which connect with the branches for the lights, which terminate in an eagles head. The Frame for the looking glass is formed of 13 links interwoven, as on the Coin of the United States. Wheatears are introduced as emblems of plenty; the whole connected & enriched with foliage and ribbons . . . as handsome as ever made in London.[97]

In the spring of 1796 Powell, who had quarreled with the Federal Street proprietors, organized support for a new theater in Boston—the Haymarket—which opened on December 26, 1796, and was demolished in 1803. When the proprietors learned of Powell's plans, they resolved to improve their own theater by making an addition to the rear, for which Bulfinch supplied two alternative schemes. The written specifications, unsigned but in his hand, have been preserved. They show the care with which he approached even so small a job as the construction of an addition.

One manuscript is "an estimate of the expence of altering the Theatre, by making an addition to the Stage, removing the whole of the dressing rooms under the stage and building new ones above the scenes—which will give room for the machinery under the stage. NB. a passage for Carriages 15 ft wide will be left at the end under the stage." The other is an estimate "upon the plan of

suffering the dressing rooms under the stage to remain, as at present, and making the whole addition to rest on arches. This alteration will give room on the stage, but no advantages for the machinery under it."[98]

There are no diagrams, but each scheme is accompanied by an estimate of necessary materials: thousands of bricks, feet of lumber, "squares" (units of 100 square feet) of flooring, roofing, and plastering. The purpose of the improvements was evidently twofold: to "give room on the stage" and to accommodate more stage machinery. Increased stage depth and added machinery, notably traps, were required to allow the theater managers to produce more elaborate pantomimes and spectacles, which they had learned were essential parts of the repertoire of a successful theater. Such productions would be necessary to combat the threat of the Haymarket Theatre.[99]

Since no illustration of the rear of the theater is available, the exact nature of the addition cannot be determined. Evidently both schemes involved enlarging and deepening the rear wing while retaining (or adding) a ground-floor arcade. The less ambitious scheme simply required the extension of the stage into this newly enlarged, two-story-high space. The more ambitious scheme required that the wing be, in effect, three stories high. The stage would extend to the back wall of the addition, and above this extension ("above the scenes") dressing rooms would be built to replace the substage dressing rooms. The projected dressing rooms above the scenes would be on a level with those built by Hodgkinson.

John Brown Williamson, who had had considerable managerial experience in provincial theaters in England, offered the proprietors his advice for making the improvements.[100] There is no indication that Williamson's advice was taken; he probably would have encouraged the more ambitious scheme, since he was bidding for the managership in 1796–1797. The proprietors appear to have chosen the simpler scheme, however, and the alteration was completed in the early autumn of 1796.[101]

[96] *Ibid.,* T 8 (310A) and T 8 (266).
[97] *Ibid.,* D 11.
[98] *Ibid.,* Tru 39 and 43.
[99] Alden, *Proceedings of the American Antiquarian Society,* LXV, Pt. 1 (1955), 24–29, discusses the Federal Street–Haymarket rivalry and its effect on the Federal Street Theatre repertoire.
[100] Ms.Th.1.L 106 (2) (BPLM).
[101] The absence of any list of machinery "under the

Judge (later Governor) Increase Sumner, writing to his friend William Cushing on February 14, 1794, described the success of the newly opened Federal Street Theatre:

The public mind . . . has been almost entirely directed towards theatrical entertainments. Such has been the rage for this new species of exhibition, that the gallery tickets, on the first night, were sold by speculators for more than twelve times their prime cost. . . . The house is indeed superb, and, it is said, exceeds any thing of the kind in America.[102]

In many respects, the first Federal Street Theatre did indeed exceed anything of its kind in America, including John Richards's Chestnut Street Theatre in Philadelphia. The latter, with its horseshoe-shaped auditorium, was probably the first in America to improve on the basically rectangular auditorium derived from the Georgian English theater.[103] Richards prepared designs in London and may have been influenced by Michael Novosielski's design for the Opera House, or King's Theatre, in the Haymarket. In 1790–1791, Novosielski rebuilt the Opera House and included a horseshoe auditorium that was "at the time a novelty in British theatres."[104] Richards also may

have been inspired by recent French designs, such as Lenoir's Théâtre de la Porte St. Martin (1781), De Wailly and Peyre's Odéon (1782), and Heurtier's Théâtre des Italiens (1783) in Paris, or the Grand Théâtre in Bordeaux.[105]

It is clear that, in England, Henry Holland's design for Drury Lane (1794) was influenced by Novosielski's Opera House and possibly by Holland's own familiarity with recently built French theaters,[106] and that in America, James Hoban and Thomas West's Charleston Theatre (1793) drew on the Opera House as a model for proscenium, balconies, and proscenium doors.[107] Although John Richards may have been inspired by the Opera House or French designs, his Chestnut Street Theatre as built was a compromise with the old Georgian traditions, especially in the treatment of the proscenium and forestage. It was in the auditorium of the Federal Street Theatre that the new French influence were first fully expressed in America.

Bulfinch showed remarkable acuteness in going directly to the sources of English architectural fashions for his auditorium design. He chose one of the best examples of French neoclassical theater architecture and adapted it to the needs of an English acting company and an American public. In doing so, he independently completed the break from the Georgian auditorium design, and

---

stage" in the Williamson inventory is perhaps the strongest evidence of the adoption of the simpler scheme. The quoted description of the fire makes no mention of dressing rooms near those built by Hodgkinson. When Charles Whitlock applied for the management of the 1799–1800 season he suggested several improvements to the (now rebuilt) theater. Among them was the raising of the dressing room roof one story so as to raise the chimneys and cure smoking in the dressing rooms (Ms.Th.1.M 19 [BPLM]). If, as seems likely, the rear wing was simply overroofed after the fire, then here is proof that the addition was two stories high. Some items in the manuscript suggest the dimensions of the enlarged wing; for example, the purchase of a lot of lumber including many beams over 40 feet long (Ms.Th.1.C 9 [BPLM]) and what appears to be the digging of a foundation 43 feet square (*ibid.*, T 11A [25]). During the enlarging of the wing, Thomas Hearsey also made minor alterations to the façade of the theater, but the nature of these changes is unknown (*ibid.*, T 11A [9]).

[102] Gen. W. H. Summer, "Memoir of Governor Increase Sumner," *New England Historical Genealogical Register,* VIII (1854), 116–17.

[103] On this point, new research on earlier buildings, such as the Charleston Theatre (1793), is necessary.

[104] John Britton and Augustus Pugin, *Illustrations of the Public Buildings of London* (London: J. Taylor, 1825–1828), I, 73. For information on Novosielski, see H. M. Colvin, *A Biographical Dictionary of English Architects* (Cambridge, Mass.: Harvard University Press, 1954), pp. 420–21.

[105] Descriptions and views of these theaters are in Alexis Donnet, *Architectonographie des théâtres de Paris* (Paris: P. Didot, 1821), I, 22–29, 32–42, and 108–16, and II, Pls. 2, 3, and 8. Bulfinch might well have seen these buildings during his tour: he visited Paris in 1786 en route to Bordeaux, spoke soon after of being acquainted with plays, and implied previous knowledge of French theaters when he called the Bordeaux theater "the most superb in France" (see Bulfinch, *Bulfinch,* pp. 48–52). It is suggestive, at any rate, to note that the auditorium of the Théâtre de la Porte St. Martin was a truncated circle in plan, that the auditorium of the Théâtre des Italiens had a domed ceiling, and that both theaters had cantilevered box tiers. It was perhaps from recent French theaters that James Lewis borrowed ideas for his design of an unbuilt theater at Limerick, which McNamara compares with Benjamin Latrobe's design for a theater (also unbuilt) at Richmond; see *American Playhouse,* pp. 143–45; cf. pp. 125 and 135.

[106] See Carter, *Journal of the Society of Architectural Historians,* XXVI (1967), 204, who also discusses then-current French treatises dealing with theater architecture. Novosielski, too, might be expected to have been familiar with French developments, and it should be noted that Holland's alterations to Covent Garden in 1792 included cantilevered box tiers (Oulton, *History of the Theatres of London,* II, 119).

[107] McNamara, *American Playhouse,* p. 87.

he expressed the new French ideas more fully than had yet been done even in England, or would be done there until Wyatt's Drury Lane opened in 1812.[108]

When John Hodgkinson and his comanagers decided to build the Park Theatre in New York, they chose two Frenchmen, the Mangin brothers, as architects. The auditorium at the Park Theatre, which opened in 1798, was "a segment of a large circle," its upper tiers of boxes were cantilevered, and it seems to have a domed ceiling.[109] The resemblance of the Park Theatre to the Federal Street Theatre is, in these respects, unmistakable. If Hodgkinson, who had worked at the Federal Street Theatre, did not take Bulfinch's ideas to New York, then the Mangins must have been familiar with the Boston theater or were borrowing from the French sources that had inspired Bulfinch.[110]

Bulfinch's design was not merely fashionable: his circular auditorium provided, as he put it, "fewer inconvenient seats than any other form is subject to," and the cantilevered construction avoided columns that obstructed sight lines. A

spectator at the Park Theatre noted that this arrangement, "when the house is filled, presents an unbroken line of spectators, which forms no uninteresting part of the spectacle."[111] In addition, the circular form was in accordance with the latest acoustical theory as articulated in 1790 by George Saunders, who also was influenced by French neoclassicism. His own model design, including an auditorium in the shape of a three-quarter circle, exhibited, in his words, "a form the most analogous to the *antique* that it is possible for our arrangements to permit."[112]

An impressive building in its own right, the Federal Street Theatre also deserves attention as the first professionally designed American theater by a native architect. It deserves even further attention as an early example of the American Classical Revival. If the exterior reflected Adam-Chambers influences, which characterized Bulfinch's other work, then the interior placed the building definitely in the later tradition of the Classical Revival. If Bulfinch was eclectic, he was wisely eclectic. If he borrowed from Victor Louis, he skillfully adapted his borrowings, and he had the satisfaction of seeing so celebrated an architect as Benjamin Wyatt borrow from the same source nearly twenty years later. The interior design of the first Federal Street Theatre shows that Bulfinch was a perceptive and forward-looking professional.

108 Frank Jenkins, "John Foulston and His Public Buildings in Plymouth, Stonehouse, and Devonport, *"Journal of the Society of Architectural Historians,* XXVII (1968), 124–35, hints at the possibility that Foulston, in his Theatre Royal, Plymouth (1811–1813), rather than Wyatt, was the first English architect to adopt the Bordeaux auditorium plan.

109 McNamara, *American Playhouse,* pp. 133–37. McNamara, p. 137, quotes a humorous account referring to the domed ceiling, which perhaps by its very nature renders this reference suspect.

110 If my conclusions here are accepted, they pose a challenge to McNamara's contention that "throughout the whole of the eighteenth century there was no significant influence on the American theater building that did not have its origin somewhere in the English traditions of stagecraft and theater architecture"; see *American Playhouse,* p. 1.

111 McNamara, *American Playhouse,* p. 136.

112 Saunders, *Treatise on Theatres,* p. 87. He also discusses (pp. 46–47) a model design proposed by Pierre Patte in *Essai sur l'architecture théâtrale* (Paris: Moutard, 1782). Saunders's own model design is on pp. 85–90 and Pl. XI of his *Treatise,* and his discussion of acoustics is on pp. 25–29. I have found no evidence that Bulfinch knew Saunders's book.

Index

Notes on Contributors

Paula Sampson Preston is former curator of textiles and ceramics and registrar at Old Sturbridge Village.

Hannah D. French is research librarian in charge of special collections, Wellesley College.

Ernest J. Moyne is a professor, Department of English, University of Delaware.

Walter Klinefelter spent many years in the service of the Commonwealth of Pennsylvania and is now retired.

Margaret A. Fikioris is textile conservator, Winterthur Museum.

Nancy Goyne Evans is registrar, Winterthur Museum.

David H. Dickason is a professor of American literature, Department of English, Indiana University.

Milton Kaplan is curator of Historical Prints, Prints and Photographs Division, Library of Congress.

Anne Castrodale Golovin is associate curator, Department of Cultural History, Smithsonian Institution.

Richard Stoddard is a graduate student, Yale University.